THE AKYEM FACTOR IN GHANA'S HISTORY

THE AKYEM FACTOR IN GHANA'S HISTORY
1700–1875

Kofi Affrifah
Senior Lecturer, Department of History
University of Cape Coast, Cape Coast

GHANA UNIVERSITIES PRESS
ACCRA
2000

Published by
Ghana Universities Press
P. O. Box GP 4219
Accra, Ghana

© Kofi Affrifah, 2000
ISBN 9964-3-0261-4

Produced in Ghana
Typeset by Ghana Universities Press
Printed by Venus Printing Press, Accra

In Memory of My
Father, Kwaku Kruh & Mother, Afia Kesewa
as well as
Maternal Grandfather, Kwasi Krah, Uncles, Charles Ofori
and Yaw Donkor who financed my education

CONTENTS

Preface	xiii
Introduction	1

Chapter

1. **THE EMERGENCE OF ABUAKWA AND KOTOKU TO C.1699** — 6
   - 17th and 18th Centuries Akyem Abuakwa — 6
   - 17th and 18th Centuries Akyem Kotoku — 7
   - Abuakwa and Kotoku Migration From 16th Century Adanse — 7
   - Second Migrations from Adanse to Akyem: 17th Century — 9
   - Original Inhabitants of Akyem — 13
      - Subjugation of Akyem by the Adanse Migrants — 13
      - The 17th Century Migrants and Economic Revolution in Akyem — 14
      - Introduction of Firearms into the Gold Coast — 16
      - The Akyem Need for Firearms — 17
      - Summary — 18

2. **THE SEARCH FOR SUPREMACY AND SECURITY 1700–1727** — 23
   - The Founding of Akyem Bosome — 23
      - Foreign Policy Objectives of Abuakwa and Kotoku — 24
      - Abuakwa Attitude towards Akwamu — 26
      - Barriers to the Coast-bound Trade of the Akyem — 27
      - Abuakwa's Relations with Assin and Fante — 28
      - Abuakwa-Agona Relations — 30
      - Intra-Akyem Differences — 32
      - Attempted Abuakwa Invasion of Agona — 33
      - Kotoku-Asante Relations — 35
      - The Kotoku-Asante War of 1717–1718 — 37
      - Summary — 42

3. **AKYEM ASCENDANCY IN THE EAST 1728–1744** — 46
   - The Akyem Defeat of Akwamu 1729–1730 — 46
      - The War — 48
      - Effects of the Nyanoase War — 50
      - Division of the Empire — 52

Privileges/Profits of Hegemony	54
Tributes, Taxes and Gifts	54
The Afro-European Trade	54
The Gold Industry	55
Easy Access to the Coast Trade	57
Problems of Hegemony	58
Provincial Administration	58
Relations with the European Companies	59
Unhealthy European Competition	60
Troubles from Old Akwamu	63
Akyem Attitude Towards New Akwamu	64
Headaches from Agona and Fante	66
Relations with Asante	66
The 1742–1743 Akyem-Asante War	68
Summary	70
THE FORTY YEARS WAR 1744–1784	75
Reasons for the Kotoku Submission	75
Pobi's Resistance	76
Distraction of Asante Attention	77
Pobi Adopts Guerrilla Tactics	77
Pobi Incorporates Toprefu into Abuakwa	78
Beginnings of an Eastern Sector Alliance	78
Emergence of a Western Sector Alliance	79
Other Objectives of Pobi	80
Disintegration of the Western Alliance	81
Abuakwa Seeks Peace with Asante	81
Renewal of Abuakwa-Asante Tension	83
Pobi Organizes a Broader-Based Southern Alliance	84
Abuakwa and Asante at War 1764–1765	85
Disintegration of the Alliance	85
The Benna War	86
Collapse of the Asante-Fante Cooperation	88
Obirikoran's Temporary Submission to Asante	89
Obirikoran Renews the Resistance	90
The Abuakwa-Asante War of 1768	90
Abuakwa Rebels Again	92
Abuakwa Divided Over Asante	93
Death of Obirikoran, 1784	95

5.	FROM SERVITUDE TO SOVEREIGNTY 1784–1831	102
	Incorporation of Old Akwamu into Abuakwa	102
	Disabilities of Vassalage	103
	Atta Owusu's Rebellion against Asante	105
	The European Companies and the War	108
	The Untimely Death of Atta Owusu	110
	Kwadwo Kuma's Accession to Power in Kotoku	111
	The Kotoku Phase of the Akyem Liberation Movement	112
	Kwadwo Kuma's Fall	113
	Effect of Kuma's Death	114
	Post 1816 Akyem-Asante Relations	115
	Civil War in Abuakwa	115
	The Liberation Movement in Akyem: The Final Phase	117
	The Akantamasu War	121
	Summary	122
6	THE AKYEM, JUABEN, THE BRITISH AND THE DANES 1832–1850	128
	The Permanent Residence of the Kotoku and the Bosome Migrants	128
	Abuakwa-Kotoku Relations in the 1830s and 1840s	129
	The Juaben as Refugees in Akyem Abuakwa	131
	Anglo-Danish Reaction to Developments in Akyem	132
	The Delay in the Juaben Departure	135
	Effect of the Juaben Residence in Akyem	137
	The Anglo-Danish Scramble for Akyem	137
	The Economy of Akyem in the 1830s and 1840s	139
	Gold and Long-Distance Trade	140
	Continued Anglo-Danish Competition for Akyem	141
	Summary	142
7.	INTRA-AKYEM RELATIONS AND THE BRITISH 1850–1860	146
	The Introduction of the Poll Tax	146
	The Akyem as Good Tax-payers	147
	Abuakwa-Kotoku Quarrels in 1857	148
	Kotoku-Asante Relations	149
	Continued Abuakwa-Kotoku Quarrels	150
	The Freeman Mediation and Settlement	154
	Strained Kotoku-Akuapem Relations	155
	The Abuakwa-Kotoku War to 1860	157
	The War	160
	The Asante Role	161

	The Last Stages of the War	162
	The Akaanten Settlement	164
	Immediate Effect of the War on the Protective	165
	Administration	165
	Summary	166
8.	IMPACT OF THE KOTOKU EMIGRATION TO AND RESIDENCE IN WESTERN AKYEM 1860–1867	171
	Expansion of Christianity in Eastern Akyem	171
	Tension Between Agyeman and Dompre	172
	The Founding of Oda	173
	Problems Arising from the Kotoku Presence in Western Akyem	174
	The Asante Invasion of the Protectorate in 1863	176
	Remote Causes of the Asante Attack	179
	Immediate Causes of the Asante Attack	181
	The Invasion	182
	Reaction of the Administration up to April 1863	184
	Effect of the Battles on the Protectorate Administration	185
	Effect of the Battles on the Invaders	186
	Pine's Aggressive Plans against Asante	189
	Reaction in Britain to the War in the Gold Coast	190
	Peace Moves	192
	Post-Peace Tensions between Kotoku and Asante	192
9.	DOMPRE OF NSAWAM 1867–1871	199
	The Founding of Nsawam	199
	The Economy of the Lower Volta Basin	200
	The Kotoku of Nsawam and Volta Politics	201
	T. B. Freeman's Attempt to Solve the Volta Conflict	203
	The Situation as Simpson Found it	205
	Simpson's Military Approach	206
	Dompre Fights on without Official Support	208
	The Protectorate Rallies Behind Dompre	209
	The 1870 Volta Expedition	210
	Dompre's Death	214
	Kotoku-Ga Conflict	216
	Summary	217
10.	THE AKYEM, ASANTE AND THE BRITISH 1871–1875	223
	Strained Relations Between Western Akyem and the Asante	223
	Strained Abuakwa-Asante Relations	225
	Asante Objectives	226

	The Invasion	227
	The Sagrenti War: Akyem Role	228
	Impact of the Sagrenti War on the Akyem	230
	Abuakwa Subversion in Juaben	232
	The Founding of New Juaben	234
	Summary	234
11.	CONCLUSION	238
	Appendices	242
	Bibliography	246
	Index	258

ABBREVIATIONS

AAT	—	Akyem Abuakwa Traditions
ABT	—	Akyem Bosome Traditions
AKT	—	Akyem Kotoku Traditions
As-AkT	—	Asante-Akyem Traditions
BMA-PJA	—	Basel Mission Archives – Paul Jenkins's Abstracts
BGCA	—	Bulletin of Ghana Geographical Association
BPP	—	British Parliamentary Papers
CAM	—	Committee of African Merchants
CCC	—	Cape Coast Castle
CCO	—	Christiansborg Castle, Osu
CO	—	Colonial Office, London
CUP	—	Cambridge University Press
DAFG	—	Diverse Arkivalier fra Guinea
DFUA	—	Department fur Underigske Anliggender
EC	—	Elmina Castle
FO	—	Foreign Office, London
GJ	—	Guineiske journaler
GNQ	—	Ghana Notes and Queries
IAS	—	Institute of African Studies, Legon
IASRR	—	Institute of African Studies Research Review
JAH	—	Journal of African History
NBKG	—	Nederlansche Bezittengen ter Kust van Guinea
NUP	—	Northwestern University Press
OUP	—	Oxford University Press
RAC	—	The Royal African Company
SL	—	Sierra Leone
TGCTHS	—	Transactions of the Gold Coast and Togoland Historical Society
THSG	—	Transactions of the Historical Society of Ghana
THSN	—	Transactions of the Historical Society of Nigeria
VgK	—	Vest-India Kompanie
WIC	—	West Indische Compagnie

PREFACE

This study examines relations between the Akyem states of Abuakwa, Kotoku, and to a lesser extent Bosome, on the one hand and their neighbours on the other during the period between about 1700 and 1875. Also examined are intra-Akyem relations as well as the nature of contacts between the Akyem and the various European nationals who came to the Gold Coast primarily to trade. The aim is to determine the contribution of the Akyem peoples to the political evolution of the Gold Coast (Ghana today).

The choice of this period is not altogether arbitrary. During the first twenty-seven years of the eighteenth century, Abuakwa and Kotoku for example struggled to preserve their political independence and territorial integrity and if possible, achieve political ascendancy over their neighbours. A successful attack on Akwamu in 1729 enabled the Akyems to assume imperial domination over the states and people inhabiting the entire area between river Ayensu in the west and the lower Volta in the east. This ascendancy they enjoyed till 1742–1743 when a defeat at the hands of Asante shattered their empire. From then on, the desire to ward off Asante overlordship became the main preoccupation of the Akyem states. Kotoku submitted to Asante in 1744; Abuakwa was more successful in resisting Asante, but eventually had to succumb to them in 1783. Bosome, nestling in extreme Western Akyem, south of the Birem river, was virtually a political backwater.

Right from the first decade of the nineteenth century, Abuakwa and Kotoku started to struggle to regain their independence. But they could only achieve this goal in 1826 when they allied themselves with other European states namely, Britain and Denmark to defeat Asante in war. In 1831, a formal peace treaty with Asante endorsed Akyem independence. However, the elimination of Asante domination only led to a situation whereby the Akyem peoples, and several others became subjected to greater European political supervision. This culminated in British colonial rule in 1874 and also led to the founding of the New Juaben State in Akyem in 1875.

This work has grown out of a doctoral thesis presented to the University of London in 1976. The acknowledgement in the thesis remains as valid today as it was in 1976. I am indebted to a large number of people who, in diverse ways, helped in the course of my research. In England, the archivists, librarians, and attendants of the Public Record Office, the British Museum, and the Commonwealth Society, all in London; also the officials of the various libraries of the University of London; in Denmark, the archivists and other officials of the Royal Archives and the Royal Library in Copenhagen; in Holland, all the archivists and officials of the Rijks Archief, the Hague; and in Ghana the officials of the National Archives in Accra, and of the libraries of the Universities of Ghana and Cape Coast.

My stay in Copenhagen was made most enjoyable by Mr. and Mrs. Bendsten who offered me lodging and boarding; Miss Ingborg Stenmann through whom I came to know the Bendstens; Professor and Mrs. Jeppesen of the University of Copenhagen; and fellow researcher Ole Justesen, who all played host to me from time to time. Ole was specially helpful in translating some of the Danish sources for me.

In Holland, several Ghanaians there made my brief stay a happy one, particularly the late Professor Bamfo Kwakye who was then on sabbatical in Eindhoven. Dr. (now Professor) van Dantzig of the University of Ghana was most helpful in directing me to some of the Dutch sources; besides, he put at my disposal some of his own material collected from the Dutch documents. Mrs. Marion Johnson of the University of Birmingham was also helpful in directing me to some of the Danish documents.

I also want to thank my cousin, Mr. S. K. Boateng and his family as well as the late Nana Ofori Atta III, Okyenhene, who readily came to my aid whenever I was faced with accommodation problem in London. In this respect my townsman Mr. I. E. Offeh Brobey, and my brother-in-law, Mr. Amponsa Abedi were equally most supportive.

In many ways I owe a huge debt of gratitude to Professors A. A. Boahen of the University of Ghana, F. Agbodeka and Morton-Williams of the University of Cape Coast (UCC): they read the draft and offered useful advice. My special and most sincere thanks, however, go to the late Mr. D. H. Jones of the School of Oriental and African Studies, University of London, for his meticulous supervision.

Another special and great gratitude goes to my wife, Amma, who besides sharing with me the depressions and occasional joys of a research student, worked to supplement the financial support I received from the University of Cape Coast. But for that support and the study leave granted me by the University of Cape Coast, this study would have been impossible. My gratitude to UCC is beyond words.

A big thank you also goes to the several typists involved in the typing of both the draft and the final product. I say a special thank you to Mrs. V. Williams and her group of professional typists in London. I am much obliged to Mr. Paul Mensah and Mrs. Josephine Gifty Acquah, both of the Department of History, University of Cape Coast and to Mr. W. B. Peters of the Central Library, University of Cape Coast, for their invaluable contribution to the success of this work.

KOFI AFFRIFAH
Department of History
University of Cape Coast
1999

INTRODUCTION

By the beginning of the eighteenth century, Akyem Abuakwa and Akyem Kotoku had been established as knitly organized inland states for about two centuries. Bosome, the third Akyem state seems to have been founded in the first decade of the eighteenth century. By then the Akyem peoples were already well known to the European traders on the Gold Coast.

In 1702 William Bosman, who for several years had served as an official at Elmina Castle and was a shrewd observer of the political situation on the Gold Coast, described "the Akims" (the Akyem) as the only neighbouring people who did not fear "the haughty arrogant and warlike Quemboe" (Akwamu).[1] Akwamu then was a formidable imperial power in the eastern sector of the Gold Coast.[2] Bosman also noted that the Denkyira whom he described as a people with "a towering pride" in the western section of the Gold Coast were feared by all their neighbours except the Akyem and the Asante.[3]

At the time Bosman was writing, Asante had already defeated Denkyira, in 1701.[4] The post facto nature of his assertion therefore tends to invalidate his view on Denkyira-Asante relations. It is, however, significant to note that the Asante defeat of Denkyira in 1701 generated a series of Akyem-Asante conflicts which did not end till 1875. The hostile relations between these two inland peoples became a major factor in the inter-state politics on the Gold Coast throughout the period under consideration. Contemporary observers are unanimous on this point. During the eighteenth century the Europeans on the coast constantly regretted the prevalence of the conflicts which was a hindrance to the smooth flow of trade from the forest to the forts, castles, and lodges on the coast.[5] There was not much change in the situation during the nineteenth century.

George Maclean, who was the president of the British mercantile administration at Cape Coast Castle during the late 1820s and 1830s, underscored the importance of the Akyem-Asante relations in 1831 when he refused to conclude, on behalf of a British-led Afro-European alliance, peace negotiations with Asante unless Akyem leaders were present to assent to the peace terms.[6] Horton, a Sierra Leonean medical officer in the British establishment in the Gold Coast, commented on the hostile Akyem-Asante relations in 1868: he described the Akyem as the only people who could challenge with success Asante "power when it was at its greatest glory."[7] In 1871 Salmon, then the Administrator of the British possessions in the Gold Coast, made the perceptive remark that "of all the states Akyem are the most allied by kindred to the Ashantees and at the same time the most bitterly hostile to them."[8]

All these observations point to the Akyem states and peoples as an important factor in Ghana history, thereby indicating that the Akyem provide a perspective from which the history of Ghana in the eighteenth and nineteenth centuries can be examined profitably.

However, to date, this factor has not been explored to any great length. Perhaps Major W. F. Butler's *Akimfoo: The History of a Failure* (London 1875) is the first important work on the Akyem, although it is not history *per se*. In the work, Butler recalls his efforts to mobilize the Bosome and Kotoku in support of the British invasion of Asante in 1874. After Butler's, no other work on the Akyem appeared till the late 1920s when J. B. Danquah started his studies on Akyem Abuakwa: *Akim Abuakwa Handbook* (London 1928) *Akan Laws and Customs* (London 1928), *Cases in Akan Law* (London 1928) and *An Epistle to the Educated Youngmen in Akim Abuakwa* (Accra 1929); others are *Ancestors, Heroes, and God* (Kyebi 1938), and *Akan Doctrine of God* (London 1941). To this class can be added M. J. Field's *Akim-Kotoku: An Oman of the Gold Coast* (London 1948). But all these are not historical expositions. Field's study on Kotoku is more of anthropology than history.

Since the 1960s some attention has been paid to the Akyem, though in a peripheral manner, by scholars such as Wilks, Daaku, Fynn and Kwamena-Poh, in monographic studies on Akwamu, Asante and Akuapem.[9] There has been a considerable improvement on this pathetic situation since the 1970s. A few articles on the Akyem, especially Abuakwa, have been written by John K. Fynn, Albert Adu Boahen, Robert Addo-Fening, Paul Jenkins and Jarle Simenson; these are appropriately cited in the text. Two doctoral theses on Akyem Abuakwa, have also appeared. But these are not studies on the Akyem states as a unit or factor in the overall evolution of Ghana. This work is intended to fill that gap.

Information on the Akyem states in general is not terribly lacking; they constituted an important segment of the gold-digging industry of 18th century, Gold Coast. This fact, together with their political ambitions in relation to their neighbours, obliged the European traders on the coast to pay considerable attention to them. In reports to Europe the white traders made fairly detailed observations on the Akyem. European interest in them and their country received a new dimension in the second half of the nineteenth century when the Basel Evangelical Mission Society selected it as a new field, in addition to Ga-Adangbe and Akuapem, for evangelization. The reports of the missionaries constitute an invaluable mine of information on the religious as well as the political, social and economic life of the Akyem peoples.[10] Also quite informative are the reports of the officials who were occasionally sent on missions to Akyem by the embryonic colonial administration which began to function in the Gold Coast from the 1830s.

It must be pointed out, however, that in terms of state and chronology there is a substantial imbalance in the archival material and the secondary sources. For example documentary evidence on Bosome is virtually nil. Nor does oral tradition provide a satisfactorily detailed and useful alternative source of information on the state.[11] Consequently Bosome has not received as full a treatment as has been accorded Abuakwa and Kotoku. On the whole it has been treated as an appendage to Kotoku with which it was sometimes closely connected, on grounds of *abusua* (matriclan) ties.

Written evidence on Abuakwa and Kotoku is, on the whole, tolerably satisfactory, even though there is some regrettable deficiency. For instance information on Kotoku during the period between 1744 and 1812 leaves much to be desired. Nothing of note seems to have happened in that state during that long period to draw the attention of the European traders on the coast. In contrast, there is ample documentary material on Abuakwa. The reason is that the white traders on the coast were forced to follow with interest and anxiety Abuakwa's bitter conflicts with Asante, for the confrontations and clashes between the two adversely affected the forest-to forts trade. But in the 1860s and early 1870s documentation is more prolific on Kotoku than Abuakwa, owing to the former's conflict with Asante. On the whole, evidence from the written sources is sufficient to warrant a reliable reconstruction of the history of relations between the Akyem peoples and their neighbours as well as intra-Akyem relations.

Where the documents are not so helpful is in the matter of the origins and early history of the states. In this respect one has had to rely on oral tradition as the only alternative source of information. However, this type of evidence has been used sparingly in the current work. This is not due so much to one's distrust of oral tradition as lacking worthy evidence. For truth is sometimes deliberately and easily distorted to suit the interest of the narrator,[12] or inadvertently glossed over.

The traditions of the Akyem Abuakwa provide a good illustration. Under the patronage of Okyenhene (King) Ofori Atta I (1912–1943) the divisional and other sub-chiefs committed their stool[13] histories to writing during 1925–1926.[14] The existence of this corpus should place the researcher in Abuakwa in a better position than his counter-part elsewhere in Ghana or in other parts of West Africa. But, as is well known to specialists on oral history, traditions which crystalize under the patronage of progressive rulers, like Ofori Atta I, tend to be twisted in ways which are extremely difficult to detect.

The Abuakwa are not positively known to have buried the unsavoury aspects of their past, as the Asante for example are believed to have done.[15]

But certain assertions in their traditional history point to efforts to distort or to sheer ignorance. A case in point is their traditional view of Ofori Panin, one of their rulers. Many, if not most, of the stool histories (there are more than twenty of them) claim that Ofori Panin led the Abuakwa from Adanse to Akyem where he founded the Abuakwa state.

All the traditions speak of only one Ofori Panin in the Abuakwa list of rulers. Therefore, it stands to reason to identify him with the Ofori whose reign European documentary sources date to the period 1704–1727.[16] At least circumstantial evidence from the European sources would also suggest that the migration spoken of in the traditions probably occurred not later than the mid-seventeenth century or further back.[17]

Thus unless the European documentary evidence is assumed to be wrong, tradition would seem to be telescoped in the matter of the migration from Adanse. There is therefore the need for circumspection in the use of the traditional histories. Indeed the caution has been applied equally to the oral traditions of the other two Akyem states as well as those of non-Akyem peoples consulted, for they all may have their own biases.

I have relied more on documentary than traditional evidence. This is in no way to suggest that the written sources could not be wrong too. Concern is more about the degree of distortion. Though sometimes partisan in their local relations, the European traders were generally objective in their observations on events in the Gold Coast. Moreover, they provide the contemporary dating which facilitates the construction of a chronological frame that may be accepted with confidence.

NOTES AND REFERENCES

1. Bosman, W., (Ed.), 1967, *A New and Accurate Description of the Gold Coast of Guinea*, Frank Cass & Co. London 1705, p.65.
2. Wilks, I., 1958, "Akwamu 1650–1750: A Study of the Rise and Fall of a West African Empire". M.A. Thesis, University of Bangor (unpublished); also his article, "The Rise of the Akwamu Empire 1650–1710" in *Transactions of the Historical Society of Ghana (THSG)* Vol.III, Part 2 (1957) pp. 99–136; and his "The Mossi and Akan States 1500–1800" in Ajayi, J. F. A. & Crowder, M., (Eds), 1971, *History of West Africa*, London. Vol. I pp. 363–369.
3. Bosman, *A New and Accurate Description*, pp. 73 & 77.
4. Details are in Chapter 2
5. Cf. Chapters 2, 3 & 4.
6. This issue is discussed fully in Chapter 5.
7. Horton, J. A. B., 1868, *West African Countries and Peoples*, Frank Cass & Co. London, p.16.

Introduction

8. Salmon, C. S., Cape Coast Castle (CCC) to Kennedy, E. A., Freetown, Sierra Leone (SL.) 30 October, 1871. C096/89, Public Record Office (PRO), London.
9. Wilks, I., 1958, *Akwamu 1650–1750*: Fynn, J. K. 1971. *Asante and Its Neighbours 1700–1807*, Northwestern University Press (NUP), Longman Group Ltd., London. Daaku, K. Y., 1970, *Trade and Politics on the Gold Coast 1600–1720*, Oxford University Press, Oxford. Kwamena-Poh, M. A., 1973, *Government and Politics in the Akuapem State 1730–1850*, NUP, Longman Group Ltd., London.
10. The Basel Mission sources used in this study derive largely from Paul Jenkins' Abstracts from Basel Mission Gold Coast Correspondence. A copy of the Abstracts is available at the Balme Library, University of Ghana, Legon Accra. This source is referred to in this study as Basel Mission Archives – Paul Jenkins' Abstracts (BMA-PJA).
11. Ward, W. E. F., 1957, on the contrary says that Bosome has a full tradition. Cf *A History of Ghana*, George Allen & Unwin Ltd., London. p.111. There isn't much in that work to justify the claim.
12. Akinjogbin, I. A., 1967, *Dahomey and Its Neighbours 1708–1818*, Cambridge University Press (CUP), Cambridge, p.4.
13. To the Akan of Ghana the Stool is the equivalent of Throne. The people of northern Ghana have Skin instead of Stool.
14. The histories are available at the Palace, Kyebi. They are referred to in this work as Akyem Abuakwa Tradition: Kyebi, or as the case may be (AAT: Kyebi etc.), 1925–1926.
15. Ward, W. E. F., *op cit.*, pp.62 and 140–141.
16. Cf. Chapter 2.
17. This subject is fully discussed in Chapter 1.

Chapter 1

THE EMERGENCE OF ABUAKWA AND KOTOKU TO C. 1699

Hostility generally marked relations between the Abuakwa and the Kotoku on the one hand and their neighbours on the other during the eighteenth and nineteenth centuries. However, the phenomenon can be traced as far back as the period between mid-sixteenth century and the middle years of the seventeenth century when migrant lineages from Adanse continually arrived in the Akyem district to either found or fortify Abuakwa and Kotoku. From then on the political and economic ambitions of the Asona rulers of Abuakwa and the Agona chiefs of Kotoku[1] made it impossible for peaceful relations to exist between them and their neighbours.

Today the Akyem district consists roughly of the western half of the Eastern Region of Ghana. In area it is about 3,200 square miles or 8288 square kilometers.[2] It is mostly a low land, but has a few hilly portions. There is the Begoro section of the so-called Kwawu mountains in the eastern parts of the district. There is also the Atewa-Atwiredu hill range which stretches southeastwards from Asamankese in the north to the Kyebi-Apapam area in the south where a small gap separates it from the Begoro hills. Finally at the extreme south of the district, in the Nsawam-Adoagyri neighbourhood, is the Nyanoa or Akyem Peak.

17TH AND 18TH CENTURIES AKYEM ABUAKWA

Available evidence shows that the district today is just a fraction of what it used to be in the sixteenth and seventeenth centuries. In 1629 Dutch traders based at Mouree near Cape Coast drew a map of the Gold Coast on which "Akim" or "Great Acany" was shown as one of the few big inland states.[3] Among "Akim's" immediate neighbours were Agona and "Songuaij" to the south, Akwamu to the south-east, "Acany" (i.e. Assin) to the west, "Quahoe" (Kwawu) to the east, and to the north "Akan". In 1729 M. D. Anville defined "Akim" in almost similar terms.[4]

In between 1629 and 1729 there were several references to "Akim" or its inhabitants. In 1660 Villaut mentioned "Acanis le Grand"[5], and in the late 1670s Heerman Abramsz referred to the "Akims Akannists" who lived "behind Craa" (Accra).[6] Until 1730 when they migrated to trans-Volta, only the Akwamu lived between Akyem Abuakwa and Accra (or Ga) district. It is, therefore reasonable to identify Akim, Great Acanij, or Acanis le Grand, "Akim Akanny" (implied by Abramsz) of the European records with Akyem Abuakwa.[7]

Akyem Abuakwa of the seventeenth century, in broad terms, consisted of the territory between the Pra and its second largest tributary, the river Birem (see Map 4).

17TH AND 18TH CENTURIES AKYEM KOTOKU

Kotoku traditions recorded since the 1840s down to the present show in no uncertain terms that the Kotoku, at least the ruling lineage, inhabited and ruled over the district which is now called Asante-Akyem from the middle years of the seventeenth century to the early 1820s when they migrated to Akyem south of the Birem river.[8] This district was immediately to the north of "Akim" (i.e. Akyem Abuakwa). The 1629 Dutch map of the Gold Coast called it "Akan" while the 1729 Anville map designated it "Akam". It thus stands to reason to conclude that Akan or Akam was no other place than Akyem Kotoku (i.e. Asante-Akyem today).

That this district formed part of Akyem is substantiated by a recorded Asante oral tradition which says the name Asante-Akyem was given to the district by Asantehene Opoku Ware I (1717-1750) after conquering the Kotoku.[9] In 1679 Heerman Abramsz spoke of the "Cocoriteese Accanists" who traded with the people of "Adancee" (Adanse) to which place they "bring most gold".[10] As Adu Boahen rightly suggests, "Cocoriteese" is clearly a European corruption of Kotoku who, according to Daaku, were also known as "Kwadukros" during their Asante-Akyem days.[11] Boahen suggests further that "Kwadukros" sounds even much nearer to 'Cooriteese' than Kotoku. In view of all this Boahen concludes, quite convincingly, that "There cannot be a shred of doubt . . . that Akan shown north of Great Akani on the map of 1629 and referred to as Cocoriteese (in 1679) was Akyem Kotoku".[12]

Seventeenth century Akyem Kotoku consisted, broadly, of the territory between the Pra and its third largest tributary, river Anuru, often spelt Anum (see Map 4). On the basis of all the foregoing we conclude that seventeenth century Akyem was made up of both 'Akim' and 'Akan' or 'Akam' of the 1629 and 1729 European maps of the Gold Coast. By the same token the term Southern Akyem will refer to Akyem Abuakwa, while northern Akyem means Akyem Kotoku (Asante-Akyem today) up to about 1825.

ABUAKWA AND KOTOKU MIGRATION FROM 16TH CENTURY ADANSE

The paramount ruling lineages of both Abuakwa and Kotoku do not claim to be aboriginal to Akyem. They say that their ancestors migrated to Akyem from Adanse.[13] Akwamu, Akuapem, and, most important of all, Adanse traditions confirm the claim.[14]

Neither the Akyem nor the others remember exactly when the emigrations from Adanse occurred or when the migrants arrived in Akyem. Nor do we have direct and strong evidence to help us determine the issue with confidence. But there is sufficient circumstantial evidence to warrant educated guesses.

The migrations do not appear to have taken place in one swoop; they occurred over a long period between about the second half of the sixteenth century and the middle years of the seventeenth. This assertion is based largely on Akwamu history and seventeenth century European evidence in relation to events in Adanse.

Adanse today is located mainly on the Kwisa (or Kusa) hills, in southern Asante, on the Kumasi-Cape Coast road. Fomena, Dompoase, Akorokyere (Akrokerri) and the gold mining centre of Obuasi are its leading towns. In the seventeenth century, Adanse seems to have consisted of the territory between river Ofin and its Oda tributary. Adanse thus formed part of the Ofin basin which by AD. 1500 had been divided into what Fage describes as important centres of "Akan culture and statedoms".[15] Perhaps it is in this sense that one must understand Adanse to which place not only the ruling lineages of Abuakwa and Kotoku, but also those of Twifo, Wassa, Kwawu, sections of the Fante, Agona and Akwamu, all trace their origins.

The Abrade clan rulers of Akwamu trace their roots to Twifo, one of the Ofin basin states. They claim to have migrated from the place after losing out in a hegemonial rivalry.[16] Probably their departure from the Ofin basin occurred some time in the last decades of the sixteenth century, because by the 1620s they were firmly established behind the inland section of the Ga district and were already a terror to their neighbours through their predatory activities.[17]

The power struggle which forced the Abrade rulers to emigrate from the Ofin area may have compelled others also to leave. Among these may well have been the Asona clan leaders from Sebenso and the Agona *abusua* from Atoam in Twifo.[18] Probably it was the Sebenso migrants who founded "Akim" while those from Atoam created "Akan" (or "Akam") in southern and northern Akyem respectively, in view of the fact that by the 1620s, the two were firmly established states in Akyem.

When did the Sebenso and Atoam migrants from Adanse arrive in Akyem? The question cannot be answered directly because we do not have any reliable information now. The alternative is speculation. With regard to the Asona migrants from Sebenso they may have reached Akyem some time in the second half of the sixteenth century. In any case Stromberg, a Basel missionary in 1862 obtained from "Apietu, a grey-haired elder of Kibi" a tradition which listed twelve Abuakwa rulers, with reigns ranging between ten and forty years. On the basis of this oral history, Stromberg suggested that mid-sixteenth century as marking the beginnings of the Akyem Abuakwa state.[19] Perhaps the same goes for the Akyem Kotoku state.

The next question is, who led the Sebenso and Atoam migrations from the Ofin basin to Akyem? With respect to the Sebenso migrants the leader may have been one of the last three or four of the twelve kings who, according to Reindorf, reigned in "Adanse".[20] The twelve were Kutunkrunku, Apeanin Kwaframoa, Damram, Pobi Asomaning, Oduro, Boakye I, Boakye II, Agyekum Adu Oware I, Agyekum Adu Oware II, Agyekum Adu Oware III and Animkwatia. If indeed Adadientam, Pamen and Takyiman oral traditions are right in claiming Animkwatia as the first Abuakwa ruler to reign and die in Akyem,[21] then he might well have led the sixteenth century Asona migrants from Sebenso to Akyem. Leadership of the Agona clan migrants from Atoam cannot be resolved because their list of rulers does not seem to go as far back as the first half of the seventeenth century.

SECOND MIGRATIONS FROM ADANSE TO AKYEM: 17TH CENTURY

The late sixteenth century hegemonial struggles in the Ofin basin apparently continued into the seventeenth century, reaching a crescendo in the 1640s and 1650s and triggering off a series of fresh migrations from the area. During the first half of the century, Adanse wielded a dominant position among the "Akan statedoms". Adanse, Reindorf claims, achieved its supremacy through diplomacy and religion by means of its god Bona.[22] Militarism was undoubtedly another and the most effective factor. The rise of Denkyera in the middle decades of the century[23] suggests this. In 1659 the Dutch traders in the Gold Coast reported of wars in what they called "distant Adancee", adding the detail that Adanse had "disappeared" (i.e defeated).[24] The conqueror of Adanse was Denkyera.[25]

The rise of Denkyera had a destabilizing impact on the ethnographic pattern in the Ofin basin. The wars there and the consequential emergence of Denkyera as the dominant power in the basin had a centrifugal effect on several of the various clan communities in the district. Many of them were obliged to emigrate in order to seek peace and security elsewhere. Among such emigrants were some of the Adanse themselves who allegedly left for Akyem but later returned to settle permanently on the mountain of Kwisa (Kusa).[26] Others were the Asona clan lineage of Kokobiante[27] and groups of Agona *abusua* from Atoam, who later became known as the Akyem Kotoku.[28]

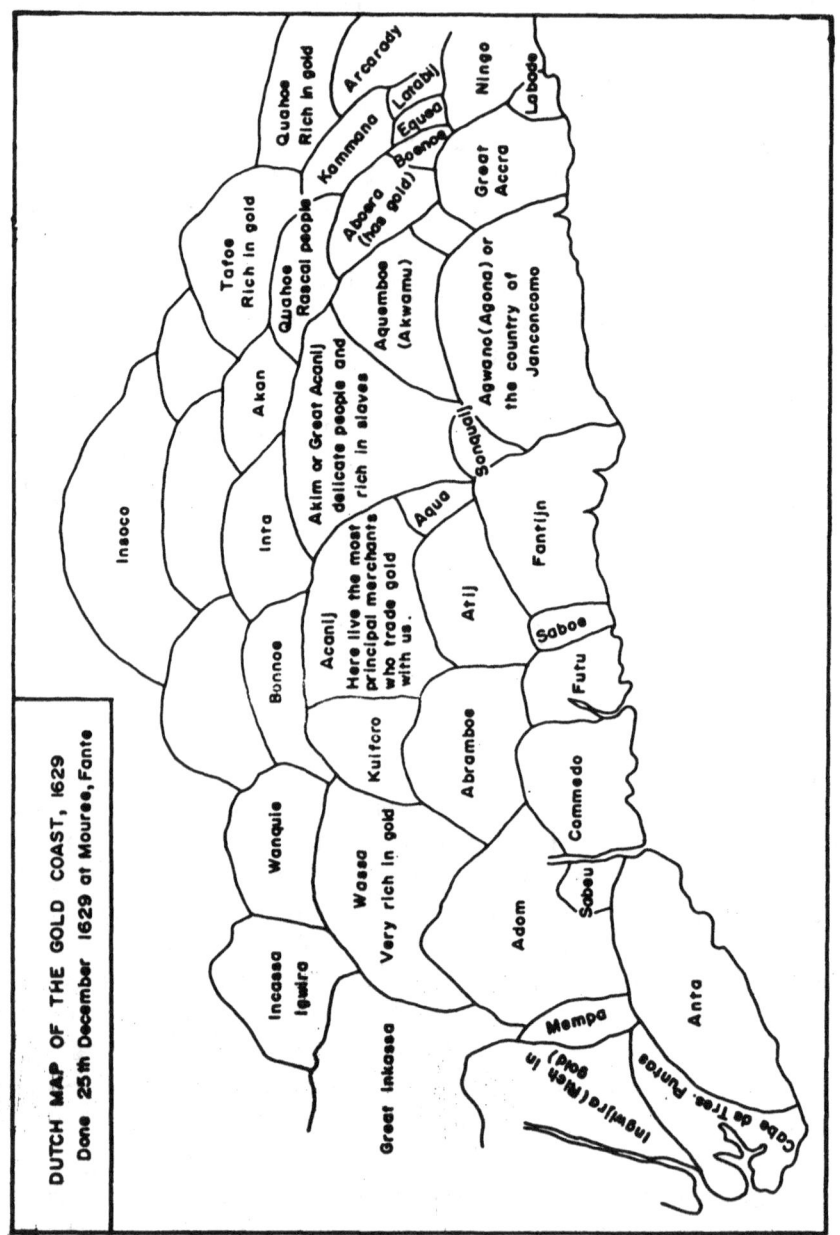

Fig. 1: A Dutch Map of the Gold Coast in 1629
Source: Fynn, J. K. 1971. *Asante and its Neighbours, 1700–1807*, NUP, Longman Group Ltd., London.

The Kotoku have no doubts in their minds as to the cause of their emigration from Adanse: they say Denkyera tyranny was the cause. Reindorf, presumably relying on tradition, asserts that on the death of Obrempon Akrofi, King of Atoam, the Denkyerahene, Owusu Bore, demanded from Akrofi's successor, Asiedu Apenten, part of deceased Akrofi's estate.[29] The request suggests a Denkyera suzerainty over Atoam because the Denkyera demand symbolized the application, by the Denkyerahene, of the Akan custom of *ayibuade* which entitled an overlord to claim a portion, or sometimes the whole of the estate of a deceased vassal or subject.[30] Asiedu Apenten refused to oblige, Denkyera went to war with him and he was killed in the war. Reindorf goes on to say that to avoid further conflict with Denkyera, Ofosuhene Apenten, Asiedu's successor, and a section of his subjects, migrated altogether from Atoam and first went to "Ahuren" (Ahwiren) near lake Bosomtwe, and later

> wandered to different places, owing to the incessant invasions of the Asante, till they finally settled in the Akyem country, with the name of Akyem Kotoku.

Since clan affinity always acted as a magnet among the Akan, it is reasonable to imagine that Ofosuhene Apenten and his followers decided to go to northern Akyem because they would be welcomed by their kinsmen who had gone to settle there in the sixteenth century. The arrival of Ofosuhene and his followers would increase the power of the already existing Kotoku state, the capital of which, it has been suggested, was Adukow, at a place in the neighbourhood of modern Juansa on the Konongo-Agogo road.[31] Later a section of the Kotoku reportedly moved further south, first to settle at Dampon, and finally at Da (Oda) near what is now Afosu.[32] A similar inability to tolerate the Denkyera hegemony apparently compelled the Asona ruling lineage of Kokobiante, in Adanse, to leave and go to Akyem (south).[33] Akwamu tradition, confirming Abuakwa's, relates:

> The chief of Kotobiante, a stool in Adanse serving Denchera, is said to have offended against the Dencherahene and to escape the penalty, fled with a handful of his followers to Nyanao where he threw himself on the protection of the King of Akwamu.[34]

The tradition goes on to say that the Akwamuhene advised the Kokobiante migrants to go to his hunters in "the Birrim district (the Atwea of Asamankese and Kyibi)" who had plenty of land to spare, an advice which the migrants heeded. It is more probable that the Kokobiante migrants on their own initiative went direct to southern Akyem to join their Asona kinsmen already settled there since the last decades of the sixteenth century.[35] Again clan affinity would be the pulling factor.

Other Asona lineages, also from Adanse, claim to have migrated to

Akyem. One was the group from Anyinabirem who in Akyem first founded Takyiman and later moved out to reside at Kukurantumi. This lineage claims that it joined the Abuakwa state system on grounds of clan relationship.[36] Who were the leaders of the Kokobiante and Atoam migrants from mid-seventeenth century Adanse? The traditions mention Ofori Panin[37] and Ofosuhene Apenten[38] respectively. These assertions are doubtful, especially in the case of Ofori Panin.

Virtually all Abuakwa stool traditions know of only one Ofori Panin who is claimed to have been both the leader of the Kokobiante migration from Adanse and the founder of the Abuakwa state in Akyem. Normally the term "Panin" in Akan monarchical culture means "The First" i.e. Ofori I, implying that other Oforis follow. On this occasion, however, "Panin" is used to distinguish our Ofori from an Abuakwa sub-chief who, as will be shown in Chapter 3, founded the paramount dynasty of the Akuapem state in the 1730s. Therefore, it is legitimate to conclude that the Ofori Panin of the traditions must be the Ofori whose reign, according to European records, spanned 1704–1727 (Cf. Chapter 2). We also argue that unless Ofori lived to a very old age, he could not have led the migration from Adanse.

But longevity is precisely what tradition claims for Ofori. He is alleged to have attained ninety-nine years. On this issue Addo-Fening writes that Ofori,

> the first Akyem (Abuakwa) chief ever to be mentioned by name in European records in 1704 was described as 'head chief' of the 'district of Akim', 'Affory' was certainly Ofori Panin who is known to have ruled at Banso as King of Akyem Abuakwa till his death in April 1727. Adanse tradition remembers him as a youngman and an Odikro [i.e. chief] at the time of the Adanse-Denkyira war [c.1659].[39]

Using oral traditional evidence, Addo-Fening has actually suggested 1630 as the "probable birth date" of Ofori and that "he died at the ripe age of ninety-nine years".[40] On this basis alone he could have led the Kokobiante migration from Adanse. As for his founding the Akyem Abuakwa state, it must be rejected. The state was already in existence before he came from Adanse.

It is equally not easy to accept Ofosuhene Apenten as the leader of the Atoam migrants, without feeling a bit uneasy in one's mind. European traders on the coast noted that an Apenten was the Kotokuhene in 1715.[41] and recorded his death in a war with Asante in 1717.[42] Reindorf says that the King of " Asante-Akyem" in 1792 was called Ofosuhene Apenten, adding that this king was taken prisoner in a war with Asante.[43] This must be a reference to the 1717 Akyem-Asante war of the European records. It is, therefore, quite reasonable to suggest that Apenten of Reindorf. If he led the Atoam migrants out of Adanse in the 1650s as Reindorf says, then he must have had a long reign of about fifty-five years. We contend that such long reigns – fifty-five for Apenten and sixty-seven for Ofori – were possible but highly improbable in the seventeenth century political milieu of the Gold Coast. The leader of the Atoam migration from Adanse to Akyem (north) must have been one of the predecessors of Ofosuhene, of whom there were at least four.

ORIGINAL INHABITANTS OF AKYEM

Akyem was not an empty territory when the migrants from Adanse arrived. The district was already inhabited. With respect to northern Akyem, Ward says that

> the tradition of Agogo in Ashanti-Akim relates that when the first [Kotoku] settlers established their home there, they had to fight against a powerful ruler called Otara Fuom or Otara Finam.[44]

Ward states further that this name has been identified as being Guan. The tradition thus suggests that northern Akyem was inhabited, most probably by Guan people. Regarding the southern sector of Akyem, certain Guan/Kyerepon groups of Akuapem recall that their ancestors once lived in what is now the heart of Akyem Abuakwa before they moved into Akuapem. On this issue Kwamena-Poh asserts that the "Okerekponkpo" (i.e. the Guan/Kyerepon of Akuapem) once

> sojourned in parts of modern Akyem Abuakwa district. The Abiriw and the Apirede people who were together until their arrival (in Akuapem) settled for some time at Ogyadam (Gyadam) and Agyempremso (where modern Akyem Tafo is) and Breku Akatawia (near modern Begoro) . . .[45]

Subjugation of Akyem by the Adanse Migrants

Lack of reliable evidence makes it difficult to show how the Abuakwa and Kotoku immigrants from Adanse managed to impose their dominant authorities on the existing societies in southern and northern Akyem. There is, however, enough circumstantial evidence to help us speculate as to why they were successful. Fragmentation of those communities appears to have been a vital enabling factor of success for the Adanse immigrants. In Akyem, the Guan/Kyerepon must have lived in small political groups, each independent of the other, much in the same way as they did in Akuapem until the 1730s when an Abuakwa warlord organized them into a unitary state (see Chapter 3). Certain Asante-Akyem traditions also recall that it was this fragmentation factor which helped the immigrant Kotoku to conquer the area.[46]

In contrast to the petty individualism of the existing communities, at least some of the immigrants from Adanse appear to have enjoyed a considerable degree of clan homogeneity and solidarity. This was particularly the case with the Abuakwa immigrants. Several of them were allegedly of the Asona clan. The Sebenso, Kotobiante, and many others were all of this clan, and they all claim to have come from Adanse.

There is no way of proving the validity of the claim of emigration from Adanse. But with regard to the clan solidarity, they surely could exploit it to achieve political domination over other peoples, especially if those others were as disunited as the pre-Abuakwa societies in Akyem seem to have been. It is interesting to note that besides Kyebi, four out of the five divisional stools of Akyem Abuakwa are all of the Asona abusua, namely Kukurantumi, Begoro, Kwaben and Wankyi. Asiakwa is the odd one: it is of the Oyoko clan. This clan solidarity had a parallel in seventeenth century Asante where Oyoko clan lineages came together in a concerted effort to subdue that country and impose their domination on it.[47]

The 17th Century Migrants and Economic Revolution in Akyem

The influx of Adanse migrants into Akyem in the mid-17th century led to an economic revolution in the area(i.e. 'Akim' of the 1629 Dutch map). The revolution transformed Akyem Abuakwa from a slave-exporting economy to one based on extractive industry. During the first three decades of the seventeenth century, Akyem Abuakwa, in terms of international trade, was, according to the Dutch, a prolific source of slaves.[48] It also had alluvial gold which its inhabitants may have exploited as far back as the sixteenth century, as Paul Ozanne suggests.[49] But production up to the first thirty years of the seventeenth century was not significant enough to draw the attention of the European traders, the Dutch in particular, who described several other districts, including Wassa, as very rich in gold.[50]

But from the 1660s onwards Akyem Abuakwa became better known as a leading gold exporter. In the 1670s Abuakwa was so rich in gold that she could give a loan to Akwamuhene Ansa Sasraku, to purchase materials for his war with the Ga (Accra).[51] In 1701–1702 William Bosman observed that "Akim" (i.e. Akyem Abuakwa) produced "as large quantities of gold as any that I know; and that also the most valuable and pure of any that is carried from [this] coast".[52] A veritable economic revolution had clearly taken place in Akyem Abuakwa. Considering that Akyem Kotoku was just to the north of Abuakwa, the economic revolution in the latter may well have affected the former also. For the area was equally rich in gold. In 1679, Heerman Abramsz noted that the "Cocoriteese Accanists" (the Kotoku) carried a lot of gold for sale in "Adancee".⁵³ The economic revolution was so total that in the eighteenth and nineteenth centuries the name Akyem to the European, was almost synonymous with gold.⁵⁴

The cause of the economic revolution was threefold. Firstly, the mid 17th century Adanse immigrants would naturally increase Abuakwa and Kotoku presence in Akyem, and ipso-facto the labour force in the district. Secondly, they would spread the technological know-how for mining for which Adanse was well known long before the seventeenth century.⁵⁵ Thirdly, the wealth of Akyem gave its inhabitants a strong purchasing power in the European trade on the coast; therefore. it was necessary to increase gold production.

The 'gold' revolution had a chain effect on the political outlook of the Akyem states. Their wealth had a considerable impact on their foreign policy. For instance it strengthened them in their relations with neighbours, especially those located between them and the coast trade, such as Agona and Akwamu. Akyem-Akwamu relations were not particularly cordial during the second half of the seventeenth century. In 1659, according to Addo-Fening, the Akyem (Abuakwa) fought an important war with Akwamu; in 1682 they did the same; and in that same year Barbot noted that for several years past immigrants from Adanse had been making serious incursions into Akwamu territory.⁵⁶ Occasionally, however, hugging replaced hatred and hostility, as happened in 1677 when the Akyem Abuakwa leadership was reported to have given a loan to Akwamuhene Ansa Sasraku, to assist him in his war against the Ga.

The financial aid was a sound diplomatic move by the Akyem. It was aimed, presumably, to achieve two objectives. First, the loan would influence Akwamu, a powerful immediate neighbour to the south-east, to give Abuakwa and Kotoku leaders a free hand to consolidate themselves in the Akyem country. Second, the loan would be expected to persuade the Akwamu to give the Akyem a free passage in the trade with the Europeans on the coast. The second goal must have been uppermost in the minds of the Akyem for, by the last quarter of the seventeenth century each state in the Gold Coast had become very anxious to share fully in the coast trade. Indeed, as others have rightly pointed out, from now onwards the European trade on the coast became the foremost factor in determining the nature of inter-state relations on the "gold" coast.⁵⁷

The main reason was that the trade, aside from providing them with exotic European goods, was the only source from which people could acquire firearms and other munitions of war. Demand for guns and other war materials grew in leaps and bounds⁵⁸ on account of their extraordinary military power. In May 1700, Akwamuhene Addo launched an economic sanction against Christiansborg Castle, Osu, because the Danes had allegedly sold guns to his enemies.⁵⁹ The enemies in question were probably the Akyem Abuakwa. For, in the 1699–1700 period, an Akyem army raided three Akwamu border towns.⁶⁰

The Akyem here could not have been the Kotoku because this was about the time they were in alliance with the Denkyera against Asante. In June – July 1700, the Dutch expected the Asante to attack Denkyera because the Asante had just purchased large quantities of arms and ammunition,[61] apparently from them (the Dutch). These were incontrovertible pieces of evidence of the peoples' recognition of the important role of firearms in war situations.

Introduction of Firearms into the Gold Coast

In all probability the Portuguese may have been the first Europeans to have introduced firearms into Africa, possibly from the 1480s. The use of the weapon here may have been shortlived because the Pope banned its sale in Africa. Presumably the Holy Father feared that the weapon might increase the military power of Muslims and heathens against Christian Europe.[62]

From the seventeenth century, however, papal enunciations no longer had a force on Europe. Protestant trading nations like England and Holland had no respect for the Bulls of the Vatican. They sold guns and ammunition to whoever cared to buy from them, muslim or heathen. As far as West Africa was concerned, the fact of the matter was that an intense competition had emerged among various European traders there – Portuguese, English, Dutch, French, Danish, Swedish and Brandenburger. Each of them was anxious to grab as much of the African trade as they possibly could. By the beginning of the seventeenth century the English and the Dutch had assumed dominant positions in the trade, having destroyed the Portuguese monopoly which had been so effective in the fifteenth and sixteenth centuries.

A very important effect of the European rivalry was the proliferation of firearms in West Africa generally and the Gold Coast in particular, because it was here that the various Europeans had built most of their castles, forts and lodges.[63] In 1601 it was known that the Dutch were very busy selling firearms to their supporters in the Gold Coast and were teaching them how to shoot accurately.[64] In the 1610s both the Portuguese and the Dutch armed their supporters with guns.[65] The last two decades of the century saw the peoples of the Gold Coast clamouring for firearms with insatiable fervour.[66] In 1680 the English traders based at Cape Coast reported that firearms had become, as they put it, "a mighty drug".[67] To meet the demand in West Africa the Royal African Company of England was even prepared to jettison patriotism briefly by importing Dutch manufactured guns for re-export to the Gold Coast and other parts of West Africa; the move drew strong protests from English manufacturers.[68] The Dutch appear to have exploited the firearms demand on the Gold Coast and elsewhere to full advantage. For at the turn of the century the English traders at Cape Coast Castle reckoned that every year the Dutch were selling as much as 20,000 tons of gun-powder and large quantities of carbines and blunderbusses (guns) in the Gold Coast.[69]

The proliferation of firearms led to the intensification of violent activities in the Gold Coast. During the second half of the seventeenth century the entire country was as it were, in a state of war. Inter-state and intra-state wars became very rampant and rife almost like an outbreak of cholera. There was surely a link between the demand for guns and the numerous wars. Richard Gray says that in the sixteenth and seventeenth centuries Zambezi basin, the use of firearms made very little difference in terms of military advantage.[70] Contemporary Gold Coast does not provide as clear cut evidence as Gray uses to support his case against the overall importance of guns in wars in the Zambezi basin. In eighteenth and nineteenth centuries Gold Coast, as will be shown in other chapters below, the evidence clearly points to the importance warring factions attached to firearms. The evidence shows that demand for firearms always preceded wars. Those making the demands often turned out to be the combatants or surrogates for the warring factions, an indication of their recognition of the power of guns in wars. At the beginning of the eighteenth century Van Sevenhuysen, the chief Dutch Official at Elmina Castle at the time, in a letter to his employers in Holland, said that there was a connection between demand for guns and wars in the Gold Coast.[71] Some states and peoples developed the practice of blocking trade routes to prevent arms and ammunition from getting through to both actual and potential enemies.[72] At any rate with respect to the seventeenth century, at least one powerful evidence leaves no room for doubt about the linkage. In 1679 Heerman Abramsz, Chief of the Dutch personnel at Elmina Castle, made the following revealing observation:

> Since rifles and gun-powder have been introduced, things have become much worse, the natives having become much more warlike . . . Consequently the whole [Gold] Coast has come into a kind of state of war.[73]

The Akyem Need for Firearms

To acquire firearms was imperative for Abuakwa and Kotoku. For besides misunderstandings with Akwamu, relations with Asante were no better. The mid-seventeenth century Denkyera hegemony which had forced the Asona and Agona clan lineages out of Adanse had equally sent Oyoko clan groups hurtling into the upper reaches of the Ofin river.[74] Here they pooled their resources and exploited their clan solidarity to conquer the country, and in the last years of the century formed the Asante Union or Confederation.

Reindorf recalls incessant Asante attacks on Kotoku,[75] the more immediate Akyem state. The conflict between the two was to be expected. Both were engaged in the pursuit of similar goals of territorial acquisition and expansion and were only separated by the Anuru (or Anum) river. Bickerings and battles between them were inevitable. That by the last years of the seventeenth century the Akyem and the Asante had become hostile to each other was underlined by developments in 1698-1701. Asante and Denkyera were at war, Akyem Kotoku went to assist the latter. Almost at the same time, Akyem Abuakwa was at loggerheads with Akwamu, who were friends of Asante. Indeed, the political conditions prevailing inland at the end of the seventeenth century, compelled the two Akyem states to forget about the mid-century Denkyera tyranny. Their thinking was that from then on the power to watch most was Asante.

Summary

By the end of the seventeenth century, Abuakwa and Kotoku had become strong centralized states in the Akyem country. Like several other Akan or Twi states, both were monarchical. Abuakwa was located between the Pra and its second largest tributary river Birem, while Kotoku nestled between the Pra and its third largest tributary, river Anuru. The ruling house of the former was of the Asona matriclan and the latter's was of the Agona *abusua*. Each had already adopted a foreign policy geared towards the acquisition of:

(i) political hegemony over neighbours where possible, and
(ii) wealth, through unimpeded participation in the European trade on the coast,

The trade had become particularly attractive to them because, aside from its offering them exotic European goods, it was the only source from which they could obtain firearms by the use of which they could achieve military and political superiority over neighbours. These objectives necessarily plunged them into continual, if not continuous conflict with neighbours engaged in the pursuit of similar goals. Thus by the end of the century all the factors which were to influence the relations between the Akyem peoples and their neighbours for almost the next two hundred years were already present.

NOTES AND REFERENCES

1. The Akyem, like other Akan or Twi peoples, are divided into seven major and seven minor *mmusua* (matri-clans), Asona and Agona being two of the seven major. There

is the assertion that the rulers of Abuakwa, Kotoku and Akuapem were all of the Agona *abusua* (sing.) Cf. Wilks I. "The Mossi and Akan States 1500–1800", in Ajayi, J. F. A. & Crowder, M. (Ed.), 1976. *History of West Africa*, Longman, London. Vol.I, p.438. This is misleading. While it is true that Kotoku rulers were, and still are, of the Agona matri-clan, those of Abuakwa and Akuapem have always been of the Asona *abusua*.

2. Population Census of Ghana 1960 Vol.1, *The Gazetteer*, p.xxii.
3. Chart 743: Dutch Map of the Gold Coast, 1629, done on 25th December 1629 at Mouree, The Leupen Collection. The Chart is reproduced in this work as Map No.2.
4. Anville, M. D., 1729. "A Map of the Gold Coast from Issini to Alampi", April. It is reproduced in this work as Map. No.3.
5. Nicolas Villaut, 1670. "A relation of the coast of Africa called Guinea" (Trs. 2nd ed., London, cited by Boahen, A. A., 1973. "Arcany or Accany or Arcania and the Accanists of the sixteenth and seventeenth centuries European records), in *Transactions of the Historical Society of Ghana (THSG)* Vol. XIV Part 1, pp.100–112.
6. Heerman Abramsz to the Assembly of Ten, Holland, 23 November 1629, in Albert van Dantzig, Dutch Documents Relating to the Gold Coast and the Slave Coast (Coast of Guinea) Part I: 1680–1710, Department of History, Legon, p.5.
7. Boahen and Addo-Fening have arrived at the same conclusion. Cf. Boahen, "Arcany . . ." in *THSG* Vol.XIV Pt. I p.106; Addo-Fening, R. 1988. "The 'Akim' or 'Achim' in 17th Century and 18th Century Historical Context: Who Were They"?, in *Institute of African Studies Research Review*, New Series Vol.4 No.2, Legon, pp.2 – 8.
8. *Guineiske Journaler (GJ)* 1840–1844: entries No.329 dd. 18 December 1842 & No.367 dd. 10 February 1843, Royal Archives Copenhagen; Simon Sus (Gyadam) to Basel, 11 March 1859, Basel Mission Archives – Paul Jenkin's Abstracts (BMA-PJA), The Balme Library, Legon (1970); Petition of Quabina Fuah, King of Insuaim (Oda) to the Governor, Cape Coast Castle (CCC), 17 July 1871, CO 96/88, PRO, London; Precis of Akim Claims to Ashanti-Akim. Kotoku, MP 212/93, MP 5718/94, Confidential MP 105/96; MP 559/96, MP/6974/96, MP 8661/97, MP 4964/98, MP 1588/00, MP 1206/01, Acting Colonial Secretary (Accra) to the Chief Commissioner (Kumasi), 2 June 1908, all in File No. D 46, Kumasi Archives; Willcocks (Fumso-Ashanti) to Chamberlain (CO, London), 17 July 1900, CO 96/361, PRO London; K. Ameyaw, Akim Oda (Kotoku) Tradition, IAS acc. No. KAG/7, Institute of African Studies (IAS), Legon 1966; Akyem Kotoku Tradition, (AKT); Awisa as told the present author by Awisahene & Elders (1968); NAG Adm. 11/1/1095 Akyem Abuakwa Native Affairs No. 171/07; Letter from Kwabena Atcherry, 17 November 1908, NAG Adm. 11/1/1075 Statements by Attafua, King of Kotoku . . . & Kwabena Kesse of Insuaim 24 July 1888, NAG Adm. 11/1/1126; H.M. Hull, Travelling Commissioner (TC) to Ag. Governor, 26 October 1893, & NAG 11/1/1126: Moses Williams, Solicitor for Attafua, to Colonial Secretary, 7 June 1901, all cited by Addo-Fening, R., in *Research Review* NS Vol. 4 No.2, pp.5–6 notes 52, 53, 55, 57, 58 & 59.
9. Precis of Akim Claims: Abuakwa Conf. 345/00, 1900, para. 6, File D 46, Kumasi Archives.
10. H. Abramz to the Assembly of ten, 23 November 1679, in van Dantzig, Dutch Documents, p.5
11. Daaku cited by Boahen, "Arcany . . .", in *THSG* Vol. XIV Part (i), p.106
12. *Ibid.*
13. Reindorf, C. C., 1895. *The History of the Gold Coast and Asante*, Basel Mission Book Depot, Basel, 2nd edn. p.61; AAT: Kukurantumi, Begoro, Kwaben Wankyi,

Pamen etc. (1925/6); AAT: Kyebi (1968); Ward, W.E.F. 1969, *A History of Ghana*, George Allen & Unwin Ltd., Edition, London, pp. 109–110; NAG. Adm. 11/1/1126: Statement of Cudjoe Kotamoah of Insuaiam, 15 June 1887, cited by Addo-Fening in *Research Review* NS. Vol.4 No.2 p.1 notes 3 & 5.
14. Dompoase, Akrokyere, Fomena & Ayaase Traditions, recorded by Daaku, K. Y., 1969, *Oral Traditions of Adanse*, IAS, University of Ghana, Legon, pp. 5ff.
15. Fage, J. D., 1969, *A History of West Africa*, Cambridge University Press, Cambridge, p.40.
16. Wilks, I., 1957, "A Note on Akwamu and Twifo", in *THSG*. Vol.III Part III, p.217.
17. The 1629 Dutch map of the Gold Coast.
18. Addo-Fening, "Akim or Achim", *Research Review* NS. Vol.4, No.2, p.1.
19. Stromberg, Kyebi to Basel, 24 January 1863, No.Akim 17. BMA-PJA.
20. Reindorf, *The History of Gold Coast*, Appendix C. p.348.
21. Addo-Fening, R., 1980, "Akyem Abuakwa c. 1874–1943: A Study of the Impact of Missionary Activities and Colonial Rule on a Traditional State", Ph.D. Thesis, University of Ghana, Legon,(unpublished) p.8.
22. Reindorf, *The History of Gold Coast*, pp. 48–49.
23. Kumah, J. K., 1965. "The Rise and Fall of Denkyera", M. A. Thesis, IAS, University of Ghana, Legon (unpublished); Kumah, J. K. "The Rise and Fall of the Kingdom of Denkyera", in *Ghana Notes and Queries (GNQ)* No.9, 1966, pp. 33–35.
24. Valckenburg's Report, September 1659 cited by Daaku, K. Y., 1970. *Trade and Politics on the Gold Coast 1600–1720*, Oxford University Press, Oxford, p.156.
25. Reindorf, 1966. *The History of the Gold Coast*, p.49; Kumah, "The Rise of Denkyera", *GNQ* No.9, p.35.
26. Ward, *A History of Ghana*, p.54; Daaku, Oral *Traditions of Adanse*, pp. 8 & 25,
27. Meyerowitz. *Akan Tradition*, p.91: Akwamu Tradition, in Field, *Akim Kotoku*, p.2.
28. Reindorf, *The History of the Gold Coast*, p.49.
29. *Ibid.*
30. Rattray, R. S., 1929, *Ashanti Law and Constitution*, Oxford University Press, Oxford, Chapter XIV, pp. 107–109.
31. Ameyaw, 1966. "Akim Oda (Kotoku) Tradition", IAS Acc. No. KAG/7, January, pp. 2–6; Asante-Akyem Traditions (As-Ak. T): Juansa, collected by the present author in 1968/9.
32. Ward, *A History of Ghana*, p.110, also Ameyaw, Akim Oda (Kotoku) Tradition, p.34 & Addo-Fening, "Akim or Achim", *Research Review* NS. Vol.4 No.2 p.4.
33. Reindorf, *The History of the Gold Coast*, pp. 55 & 61; AAT: Kukurantumi, Begoro, Wankyi, Kwaben & Pamen (1925/6); AAT: Kyebi (1968/9); in Meyerowitz, *Akan Traditions*, p.91; Ward, *History of Ghana*, pp.109–110, Danquah, *Akan Laws*, pp. 2–3. Adanse (Sodua) tradition attributes the Abuakwa migration from Adanse to a defeat the Kokobiante suffered at the hands of Asante. Cf. Daaku, *Oral Traditions of Adanse*, p.363.
34. Field, *Akim-Kotoku*, pp.2–3.
35. AAT: Banso (1925/6) & Kyebi (1968/9).
36. AAT: Kukurantumi (1925/6).
37. AAT: Kukurantumi, Begoro, Pamen & Wankyi (1925/6) & Kyebi (1968/9); NAG Adm. 11/1/1095: Award published at Nsawam, September 1929, cited by Addo-Fening, "Akim or Achim", *Research Review* NS. Vol.4 No.2 n.67.
38. Reindorf, *The History of the Gold Coast*, p.49.

39. Addo-Fening, "The 'Akim' or 'Achim' in *Research Review* NS Vol.4 No.2, p.7.
40. Addo-Fening, 1980, "Akyem Abuakwa c. 1874–1943", Ph.D Thesis, Legon, (unpublished), pp. 7–8.
41. Doutreleau (Accra) to Director-General H. H. Haring (Elmina Castle), 10 October 1715, *NBKG* 82.
42. Van Alzen (Accra) to EC, 30 October 1717; Letter from Apam to EC. 5 November, EC. Journal: entry for 7 November 1717, *NBKG* 84.
43. Reindorf, *The History of the Gold Coast*, pp. 65–66.
44. Ward, *A History of Ghana*, p.39.
45. Kwamena-Poh, M. A., 1973, *Government and Politics in the Akuapem State 1730–1850*, Northwestern University Press, London, p.125.
46. As-Ak T: Bompata and Juansa (1968/9).
47. Boahen, A. A., 1966, *Topics in West African History*, London, p.70, & in Ajayi & Espie (Eds), 1966. *A Thousand Years of West African History*, Macmillan, London, p.168.
48. See the 1629 Dutch map of the Gold Coast, reproduced as map No.2 in this work.
49. Ozanne, Paul, 1971, "Ghana" in Shinnae, P. (Ed.), *The African Iron Age*, Oxford, p.49.
50. 1629 Dutch map of the Gold Coast.
51. Director-General Rohart & Council (EC) to Holland, 10 March 1700, WIC 124.
52. Bosman, W., 1967, *A New and Accurate Description of the Gold Coast of Guinea*, Frank Cass & Co. Ltd., London, p.78.
53. H. Abramsz to the Assembly of Ten, 23 November 1679; Van Dantzig, *Dutch Documents*, p.5.
54. Bosman, *A New Accurate Description*, p.78; Romer, L. F.. *Tilforladlig Efterring om Kysten Guinea*, Copenhagan 1760 (English Tr.), p.164; *Atlas Maritime de l'Asie et de L'Afrique*, No.104, Paris 1764, cited by Macdonald, G., 1896. *The Gold Coast Past and Present*, London, p.121; Butler, W. F. (Major), cited by Brackenbury, H., 1874. *The Ashanti War, A Narrative*, London, Vol.II, p.357.
55. Fage, *A History of West Africa*, p.40; Daaku, *Trade and Politics*, pp.145–146.
56. Addo-Fening, "The 'Akim or Achim'" in *Research Review*, NS Vol.4, No.2, p.2.
57. Daaku, *Trade and Politics* pp. 170–173; Fynn, J. K., 1971, *Asante and Its Neighbours 1700–1807*, NUP, London, 1971, pp. 22–23.
58. Kea, R. A. 1971. "Firearms and Warfare on the Gold Coast and the Slave Coast from the Sixteenth to the Nineteenth Century", in *Journal of African History (JAH)*, Vol.XII, No.2, p.188.
59. Day Journal (1670–1703) of Christiansborg Castle, Osu (CCO): entry for 21 May 1700, VgK, cited by Fynn, *Asante*, p.40 n.1.
60. Wilks, I, "Akwamu 1650–1750", M.A Thesis, p.22.
61. Reports of Director-General Jan van Sevenhuysen, 21 June & 1 July 1700, WIC 97.
62. Wilten, R. M. *Gold Coast Mission History 1471–1880*, p.40, cited by Debrunner, C. H., 1967, *A History of Christianity in Ghana*, Waterville, Accra, p.16 n.2.
63. See Van Dantzig, Albert, 1980, *Forts and Castles of Ghana*, Accra.
64. De Marees, P., *Beschryvingh ende Historiche Verhall van hat Gout Koninchrik van Guinea enders de Gout Custe de Mina . . .*, pp. 95–96, cited by Kea, *Op. cit.*, p.187 n.16.
65. Burns, S., 1624. *Schifferten Welcher in ettjehen Ewe Lander . . .* (Basel), p.86f., cited by Debrunner, *History of Christianity*, p.30 n.3.

66. Letter from Elmina Castle to the Assembly of Ten, Holland, 8 March 1681, WIC 124, in Van Dantzig, *Dutch Documents*, p.28; also Kea, *Op. cit.*, pp. 192–194.
67. Bradley & Council, Cape Coast Castle (CCC) to the Royal African Company (RAC), 7 December 1680, T 70/20/20, Public Record Office (PRO), London.
68. Petition against the importation of Dutch Guns, 17th October 1684, (T 70/22/1 PRO), cited by Daaku, *Trade and Politics*, p.157, n.4.
69. Dalby Thomas (CCC), to the RAC, London, 26 August 1705, T 70/22/1 PRO.
70. Gray, R., 1974. "Portuguese Musketeers on the Zambezi", in *JAH*, Vol.XII, No.4, pp. 531–533.
71. Van Sevenhuysen, EC, to the Assembly of Ten, 21 June 1700 WIC 124.
72. Fynn, *Asante*, p.39.
73. Heerman Abramsz, EC, to the Assembly of Ten Holland, 23 November, 1679, Van Dantzig, *Dutch Documents*, p.6.
74. Boahen, *Topics*, p.71; also Boahen, in Ajayi & Espie, *A Thousand Years*, p.166; Fynn, *Asante*, Chapter two; Fynn, "The Rise of Ashanti" in *GNQ*. No.9, p.25.
75. Reindorf, *The History of the Gold Coast*, p.49.

Chapter 2

THE SEARCH FOR SUPREMACY AND SECURITY 1700–1727

Commotion and a general sense of insecurity were the hallmarks of the Akyem country during the eighteenth century.[1] In the first ten years immigrants fleeing from enemies in Asante arrived to found the state of Bosome. During the same period and the next seventeen years the older states, Abuakwa and Kotoku, engaged in a search for political supremacy over their neighbours and avenues to increase their material well-being through trade. At any rate they were determined not to fall victim to others who were equally bent on the pursuit of political aggrandisement. Alliances were as often and conveniently contracted as they were rejected. The various peoples of the Gold Coast were participants, as it were, in an inter-state game of supremacy and survival of the fittest.[2] For Abuakwa and Kotoku the period, as a whole, was one of unfulfilled hopes.

THE FOUNDING OF AKYEM BOSOME

During the first decade of the eighteenth century, Bosome was founded in the western sector of Akyem. Like the older states, it was monarchical. Bosome thus increased the number of organized states in the Akyem country from two to three.

The founders were immigrants from Boaman, a small state in the lacustrine district around Lake Bosomtwe in southern Asante. Conflict with Kumasi, the foremost of the states which formed the Asante confederation, triggered off the migration. Boaman had supported Denkyira in a war with Asante during 1698–1701 and had suffered a defeat with that power.[3] The defeat did not discourage Boaman: it continued to support Denkyira in guerrilla warfare against Asante.

Clan ties may have been a reason for the Boaman stand; its ruling lineage and that of Denkyira were of the Agona *abusua*. Preservation of its independence was probably another reason. According to Wilks, Boaman was a small but an ambitious state.[4] Boaman offended Asante in another way: its inhabitants were in the habit of infesting trade routes with a view to raiding and robbing traders as well as travellers plying the routes. In or about 1706 Asantehene Osei Tutu organized an armed expedition against Ntow Kroko, King of Boaman. The immediate objective of the expedition was apparently to put an end to the banditry and predatoriness of Boaman, but in reality to politically subdue that small but ambitious state. Ntow was defeated. To escape further punishment, he and a section of his subjects fled to western Akyem south of river Birem and there founded a new state which was called Bosome.[5]

That section of the Boaman citizenry who did not emigrate remained in Asante till the 1818-1825 period when, as shown in Chapter 5, yet another clash with Kumasi forced them to migrate, again to western Akyem, to join their kinsmen already settled there.

Until the 1820s Bosome remained a backwater to Akyem politics in particular and the Gold Coast generally. Virtually nothing is heard of it until the crisis in the nineteenth century. Even then, Bosome, from the point of view of European observers, did not draw much attention up to 1860 when it became engulfed in an Abuakwa-Kotoku conflict.

Foreign Policy objectives of Abuakwa and Kotoku

Cordiality and sometimes cooperation characterized relations between Abuakwa and Kotoku during the first half of the eighteenth century. This was particularly the case in the area of foreign policy. Right from the beginning of the century both generally pursued similar foreign policy objectives, sometimes cooperating and coordinating their efforts to achieve those goals. Their aims included

(i) acquisition of imperial domination over neighbours, where possible, or at least the preservation of their independence and territorial integrity, and
(ii) the achievement of full and unimpeded participation in the European trade on the coast.

Which of these two foreign policy objectives was to be given priority attention, however, was an issue on which they were never totally agreed during the first twenty-seven years of the eighteenth century.

One Abuakwa monarch and two Kotoku Kings reigned during that period. The two Kotoku rulers were Apenten and Frimpon Manso. The latter's reign actually went beyond 1727. It is not certain when exactly Apenten ascended the Kotoku stool. European traders on the coast noted that he was Kotokuhene in 1715.[6] They also recorded his death in 1717.[7] Reindorf, possibly using oral traditional evidence, says that the King of Asante-Akyem (as he sometimes calls Kotoku) in 1702 was called Ofosuhene Apenten, adding that this Kotokuhene was taken prisoner in a war with Asante.[8] It is not unreasonable to suggest that Ofosuhene Apenten of the traditions and Apenten of the European records of 1715-1717 may be one and the same person. We can therefore fix the reign of Apenten between 1702 and 1717.

Contemporary to Apenten was Abuakwahene (or Okyenhene) Ofori Panin.[9] The exact date of his accession to the Abuakwa stool is not clear. His name, however, appears, apparently for the first time, in the European records in 1704. In that year the Dutch traders on the coast sent him gifts which included guns, gun-powder, and a scarlet cloth.[10] Perhaps the presents symbolised Dutch congratulations to him on the occasion of his enstoolment. The evidence available, both documentary and traditional, marks him out as being completely different from the Abuakwahene whom Bosman in 1702 described as "young and betraying but too palpable signs of cruel nature," to the extent that part of the government of his chiefdom was taken away from him.[11] It is not unlikely that this young and callous chief was deposed altogether in or about 1704 and Ofori put in his place. Most probably Ofori of the European records is the same as the Ofori Panin whom Abuakwa traditions remember so much.[12]

During his reign Ofori pursued a dynamic foreign policy. He was, or was made to appear, aggressive to several of his neighbours, including the states of Agona, Fante, Assin, Gomoa, and above all Akwamu. His aims were to achieve hegemony over these neighbours, and to gain unimpeded access to the European trade on the coast. His Kotoku counterpart, Apenten, espoused similar goals, and generally showed a willingness to cooperate with Ofori to achieve those objectives. But in 1727 when Ofori died neither Abuakwa nor Kotoku had achieved those aims.

The basic cause of the failure of the two states was disagreement between them as to which of the two objectives was to be pursued first. Jointly they were faced with a dilemma. They had to choose between ensuring the territorial integrity of their kingdoms and a quick achievement of imperial as well as economic greatness. Circumstances, in terms of time and place, made it impossible for them to concurrently pursue both goals with confidence. For, relations with neighbours were such that the two states never had enough room to manoeuvre together.

Geography essentially vitiated their concerted effort. The location of each in relation to their immediate neighbours influenced the thinking of each most of the time. For example, Abuakwa, located in southern Akyem, had comparatively weaker neighbours. These were Akuapem, Agona, Fante and Akwamu, all of whom stood between the Akyem and the coast trade. In contrast Kotoku, based in northern Akyem, had the rising power of Asante for a neighbour. Thus while Abuakwa thought that the southern peoples should be attacked and defeated to achieve not only imperial supremacy over them but also gain easy access to the coast trade, Kotoku was primarily concerned with the protection and preservation of its very independence and identity in the face of Asante aggression. This was the dilemma in the Abuakwa-Kotoku foreign policy in the first three decades of the eighteenth century.

Abuakwa Attitude towards Akwamu

By the beginning of the century, Akyem Abuakwa was already hostile to Akwamu. In 1699 and 1700 reports reaching the coast spoke of Abuakwa attacks or impending attacks, on Akwamu.[13] The general view on the coast was that the Abuakwa hostility was to compel Akwamu to pay a debt it owed to the rulers of Banso (the Abuakwa capital). According to the Danes the amount involved was about 3,000 oz of gold.[14]

Opinion is divided as to how Akwamu contracted the debt. One view is that the money represented an annual tribute which Akwamu had to pay the Banso court because Abuakwa rulers, as Bosman puts it, "pretended a feudal right" over Akwamu.[15] Bosman goes on to say that the pretension generated differences between the two because

> the Aquamboans will by no means submit to [it], as knowing very well that a concession of that nature may in time cost them their whole country.[16]

There is also Romer's view that the debt was in connection with a compensation Akwamu was duty bound to pay to Abuakwa on account of a marriage arrangement between the two which had apparently fallen through.[17] The third and final view said the debt resulted from a loan which Abuakwa had given to Akwamuhene Ansa Sasraku in 1677, when the Akwamu were about to go to war against the Ga (Accra); Ansa died without paying the loan and so bequeathed it to his successors.[18]

Of the three opinions, Bosman's is the most difficult to accept. It raises questions as to when Abuakwa imposed its overlordship on Akwamu and how the imposition was effected. The evidence in hand suggests no Abuakwa conquest of Akwamu in the seventeenth century to bring about feudal relationship between the two. Romer's view is equally difficult to accept. There certainly was a marriage between the two courts. In 1922, Kwaku Amoa, then the Ohene of Asamankese, recalled that Adu Daaku, a brother of Akwamuhene Ansa Sasraku, married Oforiwaa, sister of Okyenhene Ofori Panin.[19] The Asamankese tradition does not say that this marriage broke down. Even if it did, it is Abuakwa which should be expected to pay compensation, or make a refund to Akwamu because according to Akan custom, if a marriage breaks down the woman would have to refund the bride-money which the husband paid for her hand.

The loan theory is thus the most acceptable. Commenting on the cause of the Akyem (Abuakwa) – Akwamu conflict, Rohart, the Dutch governor at Elmina Castle, in March 1700 said:

> The disruption of the trade in Accra has its origins in the claims the Akim Negroes pretend to have on the Aquamboes concerning gold and men supplied by them some time ago to Aquamboe King called Ahinsang [i.e. Ansa] to help him defeat the Accra Negroes.[20]

Rohart states further that the Akyem Abuakwa kept on extracting monies from the Akwamu, though the latter had made several payments to the former in respect of the loan. Apparently, to the Abuakwa, the Akwamu court had merely been servicing the loan. Hence the pressure on them to pay the principal.

Another source of conflict between the two was the coast trade. Akwamu was in the habit of denying Akyem traders easy access to the coast trade. Between 1700 and 1703 Akwamu organised a tight blockade of the trade routes to the Ga-Adangbe coast against the Akyem states.[21] The closure was so effective that the European traders also found it quite detrimental to their interest. The Dutch had to intercede to get the sanction lifted.[22] The raising of the ban did not last long. In 1709 Sir Dalby Thomas, the English governor at Cape Coast Castle, observed that

> Akim is a rich country [which] lies mostly on the backside of the Quamboe country and Unguine [i.e. Agona] and are hindered by them from making trade they would do.[23]

While the Akwamu often blocked Akyem access to the Ga-Adangbe sector of the coast trade, the Agona closed the route to the European trade on the Senya Bereku-Winneba-Apam coast. Since the Akyem were great traders, they found the conduct of Akwamu and Agona most intolerable and irritating. To get rid of this inconvenience became a cardinal objective in the foreign policies of both Abuakwa and Kotoku.

Barriers to the Coast-bound Trade of the Akyem

During the first fifteen years of the eighteenth century, rumours continually circulated on the coast that the Akyem, especially the Abuakwa, were about to attack either Akwamu or Agona. But all the rumours turned out to be mere barking and no biting on the part of the Akyem. The European traders on the coast found the Akyem inaction quite disappointing. In 1705, the English, for example, longed for the day "the Akims" would actually descend "on the young and hair-brained King of Quamboe"; that, they said, would be "the best thing done on the [Gold] coast for several years".[24] In 1706 the Dutch also expressed almost similar sentiments on hearing of an impending Akyem invasion of Akwamu.[25]

But the expected attack did not materialize. Lack of a concerted effort and cooperation between Abuakwa and Kotoku lay at the root of the Akyem inaction. Abuakwa was bent on taking the south, especially Akwamu, by storm, but Kotoku was unenthusiastic. Daa (or Oda), the Kotoku capital, had two main reasons for not backing Banso against Nyanoase (the Akwamu capital). First, Kotokuhene Apenten was not sure as to what Asante reaction would be should he made a hostile move against Akwamu, a traditional friend of Kumasi. Second, Apenten's more immediate concern was his marital links with Akwamu: one of his wives was an Akwamu royal. Perhaps she was one of the "gifts" and "fair words" with which, according to Bosman, Akwamu succeeded in creating differences among the Akyem. At any rate the marriage was bound to nullify any talk of an Abuakwa-Kotoku concerted move against Akwamu. Among the Akan, as among other peoples of the Gold Coast and elsewhere in Africa, a marriage was regarded as a bond between not only the two individuals involved but also between the families, towns, and states (in the case of royal marriages) of the man and the woman. That the marriage was a barrier to Abuakwa-Kotoku cooperation against Akwamu was underscored by events in 1715. In that year Apenten divorced his Akwamu wife. Immediately after this divorce there was a joint Abuakwa and Kotoku move to invade Akwamu.[26]

Reaction from the south was electrifying. Anxiety gripped several of the southern states and peoples. Akwamu and Agona put their forces in a state of alertness. Trade on the eastern sector of the coast was seriously affected. During the last months of 1715 and the first months of 1716 European traders here bitterly complained that trade was no longer "as voluminous" as it used to be, "which is caused by [the fact that] the Quamboes and Agonnas are on the alert [against the Akyem]".[27] The Dutch gave 24th December as the zero hour for the "Akim" invasion of the south. But at this crucial point in time, tension with Asante forced the Akyem to put the "southern" venture on hold.

Abuakwa's Relations with Assin and Fante

Relations with "Akanny" and Fante also gave Okyenhene Ofori a chance to spread the focus of his aggressive foreign policy. Opinion is divided on the true identity of Akanny. Some identify it with Adanse,[28] others with Assin.[29] The second view seems to be more acceptable. The reason is that until the end of the first quarter of the nineteenth century the Assin inhabited the territory between the river Pra and the Kwisa section of the Adanse hills. It is therefore fairly easy to confuse them with Adanse.

In the first half of 1715 Ofori threatened to attack Assin.[30] Two views have been proffered as the causes of the Abuakwa-Assin conflict. One attributes the cause to Assin's friendship with Asante, an enemy of the Akyem.[31] The other viewpoint stresses a clash of economic interests, mutual animosity, and bickerings usually characteristic of close neighbours.[32] The hegemonial ambition of Abuakwa seems to have been a third and most probably the most accurate cause. Akwamu for example found this aspect of Abuakwa's foreign policy so worrying and disturbing that it fortified parts of its border with Akyem Abuakwa.[33]

Whatever the cause, or causes of the Abuakwa aggression against Assin, it led to the forging of alliances among several of the Akan ethnic groups against Akyem Abuakwa. The Assin concluded that they would not be able to face Abuakwa single-handed. They appealed to the Fante for assistance and protection.[34] The Fante responded favourably to the Assin appeal.

The Assin request for Fante help seriously affected Ofori's immediate war plans because of the seeming military strength of the Fante. Up to the end of the seventeenth century, the Fante were divided into petty states, some of them not even larger than a single town or village; they were individualistic in many ways and also warred among themselves.[35] By the first two decades of the eighteenth century, however, they had achieved a degree of unity, having formed themselves into a kind of confederation.[36] The union gave them a semblance of formidability; which was why the Assin in their hour of need turned to them for help.

But the Fante unity must not be overemphasized, because some of the old elements of disunity and petty squabbling were still prevalent among them during the 1710s. The Assin request brought this side of the Fante into full glare. They all agreed that a general meeting of the confederation should be held to formally respond to the Assin request. But where to meet became a subject of a protracted debate amongst them. One Dutch report said that

> the Caboceers of Abrah summoned the Braffo to them, saying that they constituted the most powerful Fantyn and therefore the meeting must be held there.[37]

The 'Braffo' was the Commander-in-Chief and may well have been based at Mankesim, the religious capital of all Fante. Abora and Mankesim were thus vying for political leadership of Fante. For some time the controversy over the place of meeting remained unresolved inspite of the urgency which may have surrounded the Assin appeal for help. Eventually, it was agreed that Abora should be the venue.

Once the controversy was resolved, the Fante worked with alacrity and purpose. At the Abora assembly the confederation decided to help the Assin, not necessarily because of the appeal but because, as they put it, "if the Akannists were defeated, they [themselves] would not go free".[38] Ofori's aggression against Assin thus brought on Abuakwa a possible war with Fante. This additional hazard he tried to avert through diplomacy. He despatched an official embassy to tell the leaders of the Fante Confederation that he had no quarrel with Fante, therefore they should not go to the aid of the Assin. Had the Okyenhene stopped there, perhaps this diplomatic move would have yielded dividends. Unfortunately, he tried to combine persuasion with intimidation: he warned that if the Fante insisted on going to the aid of the Assin, they would be doing so at the risk of an Akyem invasion of the Fante country itself.[39] The threat annoyed the Fante leaders. They issued a terse and unequivocal reply; they said that they and the "Akannists were and are still one. If the Akims ... wanted to come and fight they will welcome them."[40]

Abuakwa-Agona Relations

Ofori now had an uphill task containing the Fante. But he was not unduly purturbed. He was still determined to pursue the Assin venture. All he had to do was to find a counterweight to the Fante involvement. This meant that he must forge an alliance of his own to challenge the Assin-Fante one. Since Akyem Kotoku was not all that enthusiastic he decided to approach Agona even though he was very much aware of the difficulty he would encounter in making such a move. After all, his military agenda had Agona also as a major target. All the same an alliance with Agona looked a fine proposition, in view of that state's geographical position in relation to both Assin and Fante. Agona was an immediate neighbour to both. A military cooperation with her was bound to be a thorn in the flesh of those two peoples. Such a prospect might well force the Fante to reconsider their relations with Assin.

Agona in the eighteenth century appears to have been divided into two sections, each independent of the other. South Agona had Swedru as its chief commercial centre while Nsaba may have been its political capital. North Agona had Nyarkrom for its capital. The King of Nyarkrom at the time was Nyarko Eku (Nyarko Ako according to Reindorf).[41] He was the most powerful Chief in all Agona. Ofori of Abuakwa decided that Nyarko Eku must be won to his side. In June 1715 the Dutch Factor At Apam observed that

> Akim Caboceer Afory sent to the said Jacconcoe [i.e. Nyarko Eku] an empty bowl with a promise to present it to him full of gold if he will join him Afory against the Acanists and Acrons.[42]

"Akron" was no other state than Gomoa. The Okyenhene was thus clearly dangling gold and Gomoa as a bait to win an alliance with Nyarkrom. The records consulted do not show that Abuakwa was at loggerheads with Gomoa. Probably it was during this period that differences existed between Nyarko Eku and Gomoa, according to Reindorf.[43] Hence Ofori's proposition of an Abuakwa-Agona (Nyarkrom) offensive against Gomoa.

The Search for Supremacy and Security 1700-1727

But Ofori's diplomatic move in Agona had come too late to be successful.[44] Confederate Fante had already effected an alliance with Agona Nyarkrom. Neither Akyem gold nor an attack on Gomoa was tempting enough to make Nyarko Eku shift alliances. At any rate the Fante, to ensure that the Nyarkrom Chief kept faith with them, had taken from Nyarkrom securities, in the form of hostages, who included Nyarko Eku's own son.[45] Moreover, the Agona ruler was aware of Ofori's secret agenda against Agona. Consequently, in response to the Abuakwa request for alliance, Nyarko said that

(i) he had already committed himself to the Fante and the Assin (by implication) and
(ii) he was not even sure that Ofori, in his hour of success against Assin and Fante, might not turn his arms against the Agona.[46]

A false start now stared Ofori in the face. But apparently he felt that all was not lost yet. He and Apenten of Kotoku launched another diplomatic move in South Agona. The response from this part of Agona contrasted sharply with the one from Nyarkrom. As already pointed out, Swedru was the foremost commercial town in South Agona. The commercial man's instinct and desire for business and profits led Agona Swedru (and presumably all South Agona) to contract what clearly looked like a trade pact, not only with Ofori of Abuakwa, but also with Apenten of Kotoku. According to the Dutch traders, in or about May 1715.

> Agonna large *crom* Soedoe [took] oath with Caboceer Afory and Caboceer Apintin that they will not close the routes nor start any quarrel with Akim traders, but will sell to the Akims as much [gun-] powder and [as many] guns as the Akims require.[47]

Akyem diplomacy thus succeeded in prying Agona into two, one part friendly and the other hostile to the Akyem.

The Dutch and, no doubt the people of South Agona, especially Swedru, must have been enthused after the signing of the treaty which was both commercial and political in nature because soon after the agreement large numbers of Akyem traders arrived on the Senya Bereku-Winneba-Apam coast, bringing with them large quantities of gold to purchase arms and ammunition.[48] South Agona clearly did a rolling business with them.

The advantages of the Swedru Pact were not one-sided. To the Akyem states of Abuakwa and Kotoku its greatest importance lay in the alternative access (vis-a-vis the Akwamu route) which it gave them to the European trade on the coast. The Agona access rendered useless the Akwamu closure of the route to the Ga-Adangbe coast trade.

The Swedru Pact may have been the culmination of several months of tough diplomatic negotiations between the two Akyem states and South Agona. The Akyem should have felt fully satisfied with, and proud, of their achievement, but this very success in South Agona ironically led to the enlargement of the Fante-led alliance against them. The Akwamu found the Akyem diplomatic success in South Agona a useful indicator to the hostile attitude of Banso and Oda. As a precaution against Abuakwa and Kotoku, Akwamu too joined the Fante-led Alliance.[49]

That was not the end of the enlargement. Nyarko Eku sponsored Gomoa to become a member of the alliance. In the early months of 1716 it was known that he had resolved his differences with "Acron" (Gomoa) and had successfully lobbied for Gomoa's admission into the alliance.[50] This certainly was not a difficult task. All he had to do was to disclose to Gomoa leadership Abuakwa's evil designs for them. Nyarko may have done more than getting Gomoa to become a member of the Fante-led alliance. Probably he persuaded South Agona to abrogate the Swedru Pact and join the alliance. For by the end of 1715 South Agona too had joined the alliance.

Thus Okyenhene Ofori's aggressive foreign policy raised a hornet's nest in southern Gold Coast for his own people and for the Kotoku. Assin ("Akanny"), Confederate Fante, Agona, Gomoa, and Akwamu all became members of a formidable alliance poised for a confrontation with the Akyem. Could Banso and Oda cope with the situation? The Dutch, for example, doubted this. They conceded that even though

> Akim was great and powerful . . . the Fantyn, Accanists, Acrons, Agonnas and Quamboes are no less; besides these districts are so vast that it will be impossible [for the Akyem] to fight them all at once, especially when Akim . . . have no more allies than Cabes Terras and Adoms who have nothing to boast of but the mere existence of their name . . . and the Juffer [Twifo] who, with the Warsaws are expected to join the Ashantyns against Aoweens . . .[51]

Intra-Akyem Differences

Internal differences rendered the Akyem even less formidable. The May 1715 Treaty with Agona Swedru indicated that at long last Abuakwa and Kotoku had come together to form a pan-Akyem front against their enemies. The times also favoured an Akyem unity and aggression against the south, at least. The Swedru pact had given them the opportunity to buy as much war material as they would want from the European traders on the Awutu-Efutu coast. Asante, as just indicated above, seemed to have been pre-occupied with Aowin in distant south-western-most Gold Coast, thereby giving the King of Akyem Kotoku, Apenten, a chance to turn his attention to the 'southern' question. The only hindrance to an Abuakwa-Kotoku cooperation was Apenten's marital links with the Akwamu ruling house, by virtue of his Akwamu wife. This issue was resolved in late 1715 when Apenten divorced his Akwamu wife.[52] The divorce convinced the European traders on the coast that all Akyem was now poised to do battle with the southern states, particularly Akwamu and Agona. The Dutch for instance said that an Akyem invasion of the south would begin on 24th December, 1715.[53]

The year ended without the attack taking place. This inaction of the two Akyem states generated considerable speculation on the coast that probably there had been, or there was going to be, a negotiated settlement between the Akyem states and the southern neighbours.[54] The speculation turned out to be partially correct. At this crucial moment, Kotoku unilaterally decided to pull out of the southern venture to deal with Asante to the north. Abandoned unexpectedly by Apenten of Kotoku, Ofori felt that he alone could not invade the south effectively.

Instead he decided to resolve his differences with the southern states through largess and negotiation. To Akwamu he reportedly sent 200 bendas of gold as a peace price.[55] He also approached Agona. But here he met a rebuff. It is not clear why Agona adopted that uncompromising attitude. However, some plausible reasons are fairly discernible. Agona does not seem to have been too keen on a peace settlement with the Akyem states. She is said to have been flirting with Asante around this time.[56] Also Agona set high pre-conditions which Abuakwa could not agree to without feeling humiliated, or being viewed as having compromised its national pride. One of the conditions was that the Akyem (Abuakwa) should pay £800.00 sterling. Ofori rejected the terms. Moreover he concluded that the best way forward was war with Agona.

Attempted Abuakwa Invasion of Agona

In the early months of 1716 Ofori, without any allied support, invaded Agona.[57] Following the invasion, trade on the coast came to a standstill. The European traders should have found this development rather detrimental to their interest. Ironically some of them, the Dutch for example, welcomed the event. The Dutch attitude was understandable. All along they had been looking forward to seeing such an Akyem assault on the southern states. They anticipated that an Akyem victory over Akwamu or Agona would ensure a steady and unimpeded flow of the Akyem gold trade to the forts, castles and lodges. To this end they went a step further to enhance Abuakwa's chances of success against Agona. They made sure that the Ga did not go to assist Abuakwa's adversaries. The Resident Commissioner for the Ga Province of the Akwamu empire at this time was Prince Amo, a member of the Akwamu royal house. Dutch Accra was Amo's headquarters. The Akwamu resolved to go to the aid of Agona against Abuakwa. To increase his forces the Akwamu ruler sent to ask Amo to raise a Ga contingent to join the Akwamu army about to go to the aid of Agona. As soon as the Dutch learned about the instruction from Nyanoase, the Akwamu capital, they threatened to hand Amo over to the Akyem in the event of the latter's success against Agona and its allies.[58] The Dutch threat forced Amo to abandon his efforts to carry out the order from the Akwamuhene.

The instruction to Amo raises the question as to why Akwamu was anxious to go to the aid of Agona. Had not Abuakwa recently bought peace with Nyanoase with an amount of 200 bendas of gold? The evidence now available does not afford a direct and easy answer to the question. It is possible that the amount was expected to purchase for the Abuakwa a free passage to the coast trade for a stipulated period. It is equally possible that the Akwamu were out to dupe. Another possibility was that Akwamu was seemingly pretending to fulfil the obligation imposed by its membership of the Fante-led Alliance since the alliance was preparing to go to the support of Agona.[59] Faced with the apparently formidable array of enemy forces Ofori suddenly curtailed the invasion and withdrew his forces from Agona.

Dutch reaction to the news of the withdrawal was one of utter disbelief. They described Ofori's action as "very disgraceful and shameful".[60] Obviously they were completely disappointed with the Akyem Abuakwa. This mood of theirs was justifiable, in view of the moral support they had for Abuakwa. Besides, the curtailment of the Agona invasion would naturally lead to the continued blockade of the trade routes against the Akyem, be they Abuakwa or Kotoku. An Abuakwa victory in Agona would have facilitated, at least partially, the steady flow of the gold trade from Akyem to the Awutu-Efutu coast. The closure of the routes, the suspense and the general atmosphere of expectancy and anxiety would even prevent the southern states themselves from paying any attention to trade, because they had to be on the alert to defend their borders. Trade was bound to be the loser, as it actually was. The southern states tightened the blockade against the Akyem.[61]

In the eastern sector of the Gold Coast, trade without the Akyem was deprived of a most vital element. No wonder that in December 1716 the Dutch bitterly complained that

> If the Akims had attacked with gain or loss, an agreement [among the states] would have been reached. But now the prospects are remote.[62]

Hendrix, the Dutch Factor at Apam, found the situation all the more damaging because, as he put it, "Akim is the fountain from which the trade in gold flows into these countries [i.e. the coastal states]".[63]

Conflicting views prevailed at the time regarding the cause of the Abuakwa pullout from Agona. The Fante boasted that the fact of their membership of the southern alliance induced the Abuakwa withdrawal.[64] Put differently the

Akyem Abuakwa were afraid of them. Another view was proffered by the Dutch at Apam; they said the withdrawal was to enable the Abuakwa to attend to their farming.[65] A third view, also held by the Dutch elsewhere on the coast, attributed the immediate cause of the pullout to pressures from Asante on the Akyem.[66] Neither the Fante claim nor the Dutch view from Apam is convincing. Had the Abuakwa been afraid of the Fante they would not have invaded Agona in the first place, because they were already aware of the Fante membership of the southern alliance. With respect to the Dutch view from Apam it is true that from time immemorial the farming season in the Gold Coast had always been between late December and late April, but war could take place during the same period. The second Dutch view, as demonstrated below, was the most accurate.

Kotoku-Asante Relations

From the last quarter of 1715 tension between Akyem Kotoku and Asante began to rise. Reports reaching some parts of the coast said that the Kotoku were threatening Asante with an invasion.[67] This was the very period when the Akyem (Abuakwa and Kotoku) were expected to attack the south. What was happening was this: while the Southern Question continued to attract Abuakwa as a light draws a moth, the Northern Problem, namely relations with Asante, pre-occupied Kotoku. This was the reason why Kotoku in the last minute abandoned the southern venture, to the discomfiture of Abuakwa. It also explains the Abuakwa curtailment of its invasion of Agona. That move, unexpected in the south, was to enable Ofori to redeploy his forces on his northern borders against a possible spillover of a Kotoku-Asante war into his territory.

Up to the end of 1715 it was Kotoku which threatened Asante with an invasion. But from the early months of 1716 aggression rather came from Kumasi to Oda. Instead of Asantehene Osei Tutu waiting to be attacked on his own soil, he decided to carry the war to his adversary. Clearly, Asante war strategists were working on the principle that the best form of defence is attack. He recalled his army which was then campaigning in far-away Aowin and ordered it to invade Akyem Kotoku.

The tension between the two peoples dated back to the very beginning of the eighteenth century when Kotoku espoused aggression by supporting Denkyira in its offensive war against Asante during the period 1698–1701. As was the case with Boaman, clan ties appear to have partly influenced Kotoku to side with Denkyira: both were of the Agona *abusua*. Kotoku suffered defeat with Denkyira at the hands of Asante. Commenting on losses in this war, Bosman in 1701 said among other things: "Of the negroes of Akim [Kotoku] only who came to the assistance of Denkirans there were about 30,000 killed, besides, a great Caboceer of Akim with all his men were off".[68]

In spite of their defeat and heavy losses the Kotoku were never forgiven by Asante. Denkyira had been the aggressor in the Feyiase War. Therefore, Kotoku, its ally, was also guilty of that offence, and must be punished, Asante appears to have concluded. The hawks in the Asante government demanded total war with Kotoku.

In or about 1702 Asante forces invaded Kotoku, defeated it, and imposed on it war reparations to the tune of 2,000 bendas of gold; it was also forced to recognize Asante as its overlord.[69] Before long Kotoku repudiated the indemnity as well as its vassalage to Asante. Besides, during the next decade and a half Kotoku continued to align with Denkyira. In 1712 it was an ally of Denkyira.[70] Kotoku also encouraged other states such as Twifo which were hostile to Asante.[71]

There must have been a thaw in the Kotoku-Asante tension during the period between 1713 and 1715. That was why the latter could send its army to campaign in Aowin.[72] The absence of the army left Asante relatively weak. Hence the decision of Kotokuhene Apenten to invade Asante in the last quarter of 1715. Thus while in the first nine months of the year it was generally known on the coast that Ofori of Abuakwa was about to invade either Akwamu or Agona, a section of the European traders were aware in the last months of the year that "Akim Caboceer Apintin is posing himself in a position to make war against the Zaay [Osei Tutu] of Ashantyns".[73] Mr. Haring, the Dutch Director-General at Elmina Castle, was surprised at this dichotomy in the overall Akyem foreign policy objectives.[74] The general expectation on the coast had been an imminent Abuakwa-Kotoku invasion of the south. But the Asante bogey vitiated the Akyem aggression against the south.

Asante reaction to the threat from Kotoku was quick and decisive. Asantehene Osei Tutu urgently recalled his army from Aowin. In December 1715 the Dutch at Axim observed that

> all the Ashatyns, Warsaws . . . are on their way back home at the urgent request of the Zaay who has summoned them very urgently as the Akims are threatening him with a major war.[75]

For one reason or another, the war did not break out immediately. The cause of the delay is not clear. Probably Apenten had not expected Kumasi to react so quickly to his intentions. The urgent recall of the Asante army from Aowin must have taken the wind out of his sails, forcing him to delay the invasion in order to review the situation. At any rate there is evidence that both sides used the period immediately preceding the war canvassing for allies. For instance both parties sought the positive neutrality of Akwamu.[76]

The Kotoku-Asante War of 1717-1718

Hot war broke out in early 1717. In January, information reached the coast saying that "the Zaay of Ashantyn has' taken the field against Akim and Dinkiran".[77] The war raged on for many months. By the end of the year the Akyem Kotoku, Abuakwa, and their allies had defeated Asante.[78] It was the most crushing defeat Asante had suffered since the formation of the Asante Union in the last quarter of the seventeenth century and was to suffer for many years to come. Among Asante's losses were Osei Tutu himself and the cream of Asante aristocracy.[79] But the victory was almost a pyrrhic one for Kotoku especially and the Akyem in general. Apenten also lost his life in the war.[80] All the same the fact of the Akyem victory was undeniable.

Several factors contributed to the Akyem success. Over-confidence and lack of discretion on the part of Asante were some of the factors. Asante tradition recalls that King Osei Tutu and the flower of the Asante aristocracy did not set off for the war front with the main army: rather they followed it later, and "at a leisurely pace".[81] That was a dangerous thing to do especially when Asante war strategists seem to have thrown discretion to the wind by allegedly not keeping their line of march a top secret; Asante had confided their plan of movement to the Akwamu who had undertaken to show the Asante army how to surprise the Akyem forces.[82] Butler, our source on this issue, states further:

> The Ashantees depending on the friendship of the Aquamboe King, divided their forces to seek the supposed place of advantage which the Aquamboe King had chosen for them, but he in the mean time informed the Akims of it.

On the receipt of this vital intelligence from Akwamu, the Akyem organized an ambuscade: they stationed excellent marksmen at the village of Akromante on the banks of river Pra. There they succeeded in assassinating Osei Tutu and killing his retinue almost to a man.[83]

Butler's report clearly imputes a charge of treachery against Akwamu. What must have compelled Akwamu to betray Asante, "its traditional friend", as Ward puts it?[84] Since Butler's report also suggests that up to 1717 an entente cordiale existed between Akwamu and the Akyem states, the answer to the question lies in Akwamu duplicity, unreliability, and inclination to cheat. The reason is as follows. In spite of the existence of differences between them, by February 1717 the Akyem states had reached some kind of understanding with Akwamu. In that month the Akwamu not only allowed Akyem traders a passage to the Ga coast but actually assisted them to buy arms and ammunition in Accra. Prince Amo, the Akwamu Resident Commissioner for Ga-Adangbe, led a group of Akyem traders to Fort Crevecoeur, and presumably to the other two castles, to purchase war materials.⁸⁵ Also, just before the outbreak of the war, Akonnor, the Akwamuhene, allowed the Akyem Abuakwa to send some of their women and children to Akwamu for asylum and protection.⁸⁶ All these are clear proofs of an Akyem-Akwamu *rapprochement*. Taken in relation to Akwamu's friendship with Asante as indicated in the Butler report, they also show that Akwamu was playing a double game with the Akyem and the Asante. As shall be demonstrated in due course, Akwamu had no intention of keeping faith with either party but was out to dupe both. For in the course of the Akyem-Asante war the Akwamuhene sold into slavery the Akyem refugees he himself had undertaken to protect.⁸⁷

For the moment let us go back to the reasons for the Akyem victory. Essentially the war strategy of the Akyem as well as their military strength won them the war. Let us examine the first point in detail. The philosophy of the Kotoku-Abuakwa war plan was to administer surprises and shocks to achieve quick success. In a report dated 30th October, 1717, Van Alzen the Dutch factor in Accra, said the Akyem destroyed most of their farms where the invading Asante army could have foraged. The action deprived the Asante army the only source of adequate provision. As a result they were poorly fed and soon developed weak resistance to disease. And in the tropical environs of the Gold Coast, diseases often and easily broke out during wars. On this occasion a smallpox epidemic broke out among the Asante forces, taking a heavy toll on their number.⁸⁸ It is not unlikely that it was after this bitter experience that the Asante evolved the practice of carrying *nkyewe* (roasted corn) in their haversacks to war.

Then there was the ambuscade which the Akyem (Kotoku) organized on the banks of river Pra. Its success in bringing about the sudden and unexpected death of Asantehene Osei Tutu registered a rude shock to the invading Asante army, completely demoralising them to the extent of making them decide to curtail the war and return home to mourn the death of that great King. But they were not to get away so easily. According to Van Alzen as they started

> marching off, the . . . Akims . . . decided to pursue the fugitive army with energy. They got into action . . . and victory went to the Akims who did a great slaughter among [the Asante].⁸⁹

The Akyem victory over Asante had a great impact on the entire Gold Coast. It led to further violence, real and perceived, in several parts of the country, mainly against Asante. States and peoples already defeated by that power and reduced to vassalage saw in its defeat an opportunity for revenge and rebellion. Among such states were Aowin, Twifo and Wassa. As soon as the Akyem victory was known, Aowin and Wassa for example began to massacre Asante citizens found in their territory.⁹⁰ Even prevalent were rumours, perhaps exaggerated, that Aowin and Wassa had defeated Asante in set battles.⁹¹ It seemed that the Akyem had at long last broken the myth of Asante invincibility and that the moment had come for a concerted attack on Asante by states which had, in one way or another, suffered at the hands of that power, and crush it for ever. In April 1718 Barn, the Dutch factor at Komenda, reported that "Caboceer Acafo of Juffer" had sent him word saying that

> the Asantyns have gone to their country, and that Dinkira, Warsaw, and Juffer have requested Akim Caboceer Offorij to join them in an attack on Asantyns in their own country and crush them⁹²

To some extent the hostile posture of these states was understandable. They seem to have suffered considerably at the hand of Asante. As vassals they had been forced to fight the master's wars and suffered much in the process. Twifo and Wassa had to join the Asante army to fight Aowin in 1716; they most probably sent contingents against the Akyem in the just ended war. As for Aowin, beside the recent invasion of their country by Asante, they had had to pay as much as 250 bendas of gold and large numbers of slaves as war reparations and appeasement to the Asante government in 1716.⁹³ The proposed joint invasion of Asante did not materialize. But massacres of Asante subjects in those states continued up to 1721.⁹⁴

The outcome of the 1717 war had some impact on the Fante-led Southern Alliance. Fante reaction was a complete u-turn. Up to the outbreak of the war, the Fante attitude towards at least Akyem Abuakwa had been one of hostility. After the success of the Akyem over Asante, the Fante adopted a more friendly posture towards the Akyem. According to Van Alzen the war had hardly ended when the Akyem leaders sent as a present "the head of a fallen Ashantyn Caboceer to the Braffo of Fantyn".⁹⁵ By the norms of contemporary Akan military culture such a gesture was accorded only to friends. Considering the recent anti-Akyem stance of the Southern Alliance led by the Fante, they must have done something friendlier to deserve that courtesy from Abuakwa and Kotoku. Probably they had quickly sent congratulatory messages to the victorious Akyem.

This is suggested by the thinking of a section of the Fante. In April 1718 "Aussi Quansang" (i.e. Awusi Quansah) the Chief of the Fante coastal town of Kormantse, informed the Dutch factor there that the Fante

> will together march on, and defeat Agonna, Addemensa, Creman . . . so that the Akims can have free passage to help them bring gold, slaves and ivory to the forts.⁹⁶

By 'Addemensa' the Dutch at Kormantse probably meant Adamansa, and 'Cremen' a misspelling of Breman, both of which were in the Asikuma district, through which the Akyem would have to pass on their way to the Fante coast to trade. It is clear that the new and seemingly friendly Fante attitude towards the Akyem was partly actuated by the possibility of the Fante gaining commercially from the Akyem success over Asante.

The Kormante expectations did not reflect the reality of the situation. The war actually paralyzed trade on the Gold Coast. Both the warring nations as well as the coastal and near-coastal peoples suffered economically. The war threw the trade on the Gold Coast out of gear. The Akyem and the Asante were the two major pillars of the trade. Both were great producers of gold. In addition Asante was a prolific ivory producer and a powerful slave exporter. Trade without Abuakwa, Kotoku and Asante lost its vitality. Even states and peoples not directly involved in the war suspended trading in order to defend their borders against possible spillovers. In April 1718 the Dutch reported that trade on the Gold Coast had been adversely affected

> by the terrible inland war between the districts of Ashantyn and Akim which also keeps all [other] trading nations like Aowin, Warsaw, Accany, Agonna and Quamboe in continual commotion, as they dare not leave their own countries to come and trade with us on the coast because of fears of invasion [of their own coutries].[97]

The vigilance and alertness of Agona was prompted by expectations on the coast that Okyenhene Ofori now had the chance to take up once again the unfinished 1716 invasion of that country. With regard to Akwamu, speculation had started as far back as October 1717 that "Caboceer Afforij . . . will come and demand Akim natives whom Aquando [i.e. Akonnor] had robbed and sold [into slavery]".[98]

The fear of Agona and Akwamu were not borne out by the immediate development, namely the protracted nature of the Akyem-Asante war. The latter were a people of remarkable resilience.[99] They soon recovered from the initial shock which the unexpected death of King Osei Tutu had registered on them; and they also recovered from the 1717 defeat and in 1718 took the field again against Kotoku and Abuakwa. They may have done so under Opoku Ware I, successor to Osei Tutu.

Meanwhile Frimpon Manso had succeeded the late Apenten as the new Kotokuhene. He and Ofori of Abuakwa stoutly and squarely defended their kingdoms against Asantehene Opoku Ware I. By June 1718 a stalemate had set in: neither side was winning the new phase of the war. Strains and stresses apparently began to tell on both peoples, and yet neither side would throw in the towel. Of all Akan groups perhaps the Asante and the Akyem were the most tenacious. They continued to slog it out well into the third quarter of 1718.[100]

Eventually weariness and a realization that Akwamu had duped both of them forced them to recognize the need to end the war which, in all aspects, had become protracted and destructive to both sides. In November 1718 reports reached the coast that

> the Asantees and Akims, miserably duped by the Quamboes, have agreed on an armistice ... Now it is said that they are friends and have jointly decided to avenge themselves on the Quamboes.[101]

The 1718 truce was in 1719 converted to a formal peace treaty by which neither side conceded defeat nor accepted subservience to the other. In March 1719 the Dutch Director-General at Elmina Castle reported to his employers in Holland that "the long war between the Ashantees and Akims, after damage to both sides, has, at long last, been ended with a durable peace".[102]

As far as Akyem-Asante relations were concerned, the 1719 Peace Settlement proved quite long lasting. During the next twenty-two years they never went to war against each other. In the eighteenth century political milieu on the Gold Coast that indeed was a long period of peace.

With respect to the country as a whole, there was no real peace. In March 1721 reports reaching Europe said that after the Akyem-Asante peace,

> other quarrels have arisen. The Juffers, Warsaws, and Aoweens, during the aforementioned war, plundered Ashantees of their women ... and burned down an Ashantee village called Atwee. They must now account for it.[103]

Between 1719 and 1721 Asante forces invaded those territories one by one to punish them. Meanwhile rumours of an imminent Akyem invasion of the south, especially Akwamu or Agona, kept circulating on the coast. But nothing dramatic happened other than two or three feeble raids which Ofori of Abuakwa organized against Akwamu between 1720 and 1723.[104]

The result was that a state of muted tension continued to exist between the Akyem and the peoples of the south. The root cause of the over-all Akyem inaction was Kotoku's lack of interest in taking up the Southern Question again. In 1724 it was known on the coast that Frimpon Manso, the Kotokuhene, was a cautious ruler who was not keen on promoting Akyem aggression against Akwamu because he was not sure what the reaction of Asante would be.[105] Deprived of Kotoku support and cooperation, Ofori of Abuakwa could not summon enough confidence to invade either Akwamu or Agona.

He died in or about April 1727,[106] leaving the Southern Question unsolved. All his aggression against neighbouring states since 1704 came to naught. Nor was the Northern Problem also resolved definitively. Relations between Kotoku and Asante continued to remain uneasy and tense. Above all,

Abuakwa and Kotoku were yet to gain unhindered access to the coast trade. Divergent priorities in their foreign policy had militated against the achievement of these political and economic goals.

Summary

Right from the beginning of the eighteenth century the Akyem states of Abuakwa and Kotoku pursued, severally and jointly, a dynamic foreign policy meant to bring them hegemony and wealth, the latter through full and unhampered participation in the European trade on the coast. Several of their neighbours also chased after similar goals. Consequently there were inter-state wars and threats of war. Military alliances were contracted and more often abrogated lightly for apparent immediate advantages. By the early 1720s Abuakwa and Kotoku had gained some relief from the military and political pressures from Asante in the north. But the southern states continued to have a stranglehold on their political and economic ambitions in the south. The main reason for the situation was that fundamentally the two states failed to organize a sustained and concerted action against the south.

NOTES AND REFERENCES

1. Ward, W. E. F. 1957, *A History of Ghana*, George Allen & Unwin Ltd., London, p.104
2. Others have studied this period and almost the same events, though from different perspectives. See for example Wilks, I., 1957, "Akwamu 1650–1750", M.A. Thesis, Bangor (unpublished); also his "The Rise and Fall of the Akwamu Empire 1650–1710" in *THSG*. Vol.III Part 2, 1957, pp. 99–136; Daaku, K. Y., 1970. *Trade and Politics on the Gold Coast 1600–1720*, OUP, Oxford, Chapter VII; Fynn J. K., 1971. *Asante and Its Neighbours* 1700–1807, NUP, Longman Group Ltd., London, Chapters Two and Three; Kwamena-Poh, M. A., 1973, *Government and Politics in the Akuapem State 1730–1850*, NUP, Longman Group Ltd., London, Chapter One.
3. Wilks, in Ajayi, J. F. A. & Crowder, M. (Ed.), 1976, *History of West Africa*, Longman, London, Vol. One, p.374.
4. *Ibid.*
5. Elmina Castle (EC) Journal: Letter from Landman, 11 April 1707, cited by Wilks, *Op. cit.*, 374; Kyeremanten, A. A., 1966, "Ashanti Royal Regalia: Their History and Function", Ph.D. Thesis, Oxford University (unpublished), pp. 215–221.
6. Doutreleau (Accra) to Director-General H. H. Haring (EC), 10th October 1715, *NBKG* 82.
7. Report by van Alzen, 30 October 1717, *NBKG* 84.
8. Reindorf, C. C., 1895. *The History of the Gold Coast and Asante*, Basel Mission Book Depot, Basel, Second Edition, pp. 65–66; Tradition of Asumegya, as told Rattray, R. S., 1929. *Ashanti Law and Constitution*, Oxford, p.132.
9. Reindorf says Kuntunkununku was the Abuakwahene during the time of Ofosuhene

Apenten of Kotoku (cf. *The History of the Gold Coast*, pp. 65–66). Though generally an intelligent writer, Reindorf, on this occasion, seemed confused as to who the Abuakwa rulers were in the early 18th century. On p.348 of his work he fixes Kuntunkununku's reign in the 16th century.

10. Director-General William de la Palma (EC) Reporting, 9 April 1704, cited by Fynn "Akyem Abuakwa Kings".
11. Bosman, *Description*, p.78
12. See Chapter 1 p.11.
13. Christiansborg Castle Osu (CCO) Journal: entry 10 October 1699, Vgk 121, cited by Fynn, *Asante*, p.23 n.6; Minutes of Council Meeting (EC), 23 February 17000 WIC 124.
14. Norregaard, G., 1966, *Danish Settlements in West Africa 1656–1850*, B.U.P., p.64.
15. Bosman, *Description*, p.69
16. *Ibid.*
17. Romer, L. F., 1760. *Tilforladelig Efterretning om Kysten Guinea*, Copenhagen, trans. (parts) by K. Bertelsen, 1965, I.A.S., Legon, p.105.
18. Wilks, "Akwamu 1650–1750", p.10.
19. Asamankese Tradition as told by Kwaku Amoa, Asamankesehene, in 1922 to J. T. Furley of the SNA Office, 30 March 1922.
20. Rohart in Council, (EC) Council Minutes, 10 March 1700, WIC 124.
21. C.C.O. Journal: entry 21 May 1700, Vgk 121; EC Council Meeting, 10 March 1700, WIC 124; EC Journal, entry 3 April 1703, *NBKG* 98.
22. Daaku, *Trade and Politics*, p.172.
23. Sir Dalby Thomas, Cape Coast Castle (CCC), to the Royal African Company (RAC), 26 November 1709, T70/175.
24. Abstract of letters from CCC to RAC, 1 January 1705, T 70/1184/1, cited by Daaku, *Trade and Politics*, p.172.
25. Peter Nuij (Accra) to Amsterdam, 24 June 1706, WIC 115.
26. Van Dyke (Accra) to Haring (EC), 26 December 1715, *NBKG* 82.
27. Van Dyke to Haring 26 December 1715; Hendrix (Apam) to Haring (EC), 3 December; EC Journal: entry 5 December 1715, *NBKG* 82, also EC Journal: entry 5 January 1716; "Abren" (Apam) to EC, 15 & 30 January 1716.
28. Macdonald, G., 1898. *The Gold Coast Past and Present*, London, p.10; Note by Fage, in Bosman, *Description*, p.522.
29. Boahen, A. A., 1966. *Topics in West African History*, Longman, London, p.62.
30. Zelst (Accra) to Haring (EC), 17 & 30 March 1715; Van Visbeek (Kormantse) to Haring, 19 April; EC Journal: entry 20 April; Hendrix (Apam) to Haring (EC) 19 June 1715 *NBKG* 82.
31. Fynn, *Asante*, p.45.
32. Daaku, *Trade and Politics*, p.169.
33. Wilks, *Akwamu 1650–1750*, p.22.
34. Jan van Visbeek (Kormantse) to Haring (EC), 20 August 1715, *NBKG* 82.
35. Margaret Priestley, 1961, "The Ashanti Question and the British: Eighteenth Century Origins", in *Journal of African History (JAH)*, Vol.2, p.37.
36. Tenkorang, S., 1964, "British Slave Trading Activities in the Gold and Slave Coasts and their Impact on African Society". M.A. Thesis, University of London, (unpublished), pp. 145–147.
37. Jan van Visbeek (Kormantse) to EC, 20 August 1715 *NBKG* 82. Caboceer = Chief; Abrah = Abora; Braffo was the title of the Commander-in-Chief of all Fante forces.

Abrah = Abora; Braffo was the title of the Commander-in-Chief of all Fante forces.
38. Van Visbeek (Kormantse) to EC, 20 August 1715, *NBKG* 82.
39. *Ibid.*
40. *Ibid.*
41. Reindorf, *The History of the Gold Coast*, p.63.
42. Hendrix (Apam) to Haring (EC) 6 June 1715 *NBKG* 82.
43. Reindorf, *The History of the Gold Coast*, pp. 60–65.
44. Fynn (*Asante*, p.46) says that Ofori actually did sign a treaty with Nyarko Eku. This is doubtful, in view of Nyarko's cordial relations with Fante.
45. Hendrix (Apam) to EC., 6 June 1715 *NBKG* 82.
46. *Ibid.*
47. Boerhaven (Senya Breku) to Haring (EC), 28 May; also Hendrix (Apam) to Haring 6 June 1715 *NBKG* 82.
48. Boerhaven to Haring, 28 May 1715 *NBKG* 82.
49. Zelst (Accra) to Haring (EC) 17 & 30 March 1715 *NBKG* 82.
50. Van Dyke (Accra) to Haring (EC), 8 March 1716 *NBKG* 82.
51. Haring (EC) to Doutreleau (Accra) 5 November 1719 *NBKG* 82. Cabes Terra, according to Bosman (*Description*, p.77) was a state, perhaps a small one, situate between Asebu and Akanny (Assin). The "Adams" were the Etsii, and "Juffer" Twifo.
52. Doutreleau (Apam) to EC, 5 November 1715; Van Dyke (Accra) to EC, 26 December 1715, *NBKG* 82.
53. Van Dyke to EC, 26 December 1715, *NBKG* 82.
54. Van Dyke to EC; 31 December 1715, *NBKG* 82.
55. Daaku, *Trade and Politics*, p.174.
56. *Ibid.*
57. Van Dyke (Accra) to Haring (EC), 8 March; EC Journal: entry to March 1716, *NBKG* 82.
58. Van Dyke (Accra) to Haring, 13 March 1716, *NBKG* 82.
59. Van Naerssen (Senya Breku) to EC, 10 March 1716, *NBKG* 82.
60. Van Naerssen (Senya Breku) to Hendrix (Apam), 25 March; Hendrix to EC, 26 March; EC Journal: entry 1 April 1716, *NBKG* 82.
61. EC Diary: entries 10 March & 2 June; Snoek (Accra) to EC, 25 August, 26 September & 9 October 1716; Hendrix (Apam) to EC, 19 December; EC Diary: entry 23 December 1716, *NBKG* 83.
62. Hendrix (Apam) to EC 19 December 1716, *NBKG* 83.
63. *Ibid.*
64. Van Naerssen (Senya Breku) to EC, 25 March 1716, *NBKG* 82.
65. Hendrix (Apam) to EC, 6 & 10 April 1716, *NBKG* 82; see also Daaku, *Trade and Politics*, p.175.
66. Butler (Axim) to EC, 13 December 1716, Haring (EC) to Holland, 15 December 1716, *NBKG* 83.
67. Doutreleau (Accra) to EC., 10 October 1715, *NBKG* 83.
68. Bosman, *Description*, p.76.
69. Dupuis J., 1824, *Journal of Residence in Ashantee*, Frank Cass & Co. Ltd., London, pp.230–231; Fuller, F., 1921. *A Vanished Dynasty: Ashanti*, London, pp. 22–23.
70. Haring (EC) to Amsterdam, 15 August 1712, WIC 101.
71. Fynn, *Asante*, p.45.
72. Daaku, *Trade and Politics*, p.176; Fynn, *Asante*, pp. 42–45.
73. Doutreleau (Accra) to Haring (EC), 10 October 1715, *NBKG* 82.

74. Haring to Doutreleau, 16 October 1715, *NBKG* 82.
75. Butler (Axim) to Haring (EC), 13 December 1715, *NBKG* 82.
76. Landman (Komenda) to EC, 13 January 1717, *NBKG* 84; Johnson (CCC) to RAC, 26 May 1717, T 70/6/48, Snoek (Accra) to EC., 29 May 1717, *NBKG* 84; Phipps to RAC, 25 September 1717, cited by Daaku, *Trade and Politics*, p.176, n.1.
77. Van Alzen (Accra) to EC, 30 October; Letter from Apam, 5 November; EC Diary: entry 7 November 1717, *NBKG* 84.
78. Letter from Apam, 5 November; EC Diary: entry 7 November 1717, *NBKG* 84.
79. Bowdich, T. E., 1817. *A Mission from Cape Coast to Ashantee*, Frank Cass & Co. Ltd., London, p.233; Dupuis, Residence, pp. 231-232; Reindorf, *The History of Gold Coast*, pp. 66-67; Fuller, *a Vanished Dynasty*, p.23; Fynn, *Asante*, pp. 48-50. Fynn discusses the conflicting views about the dating of Osei Tutu's death. In the light of the evidence above, the present author accepts Fynn's conclusion that Osei Tutu died in 1717.
80. Van Alzen (Accra) to EC, 30 October 1717, *NBKG* 84.
81. Bowdich, *A Mission*, p.233; Dupuis *Residence*, pp. 231-232.
82. Butler to van Naerssen, 3 November, 1718, *NBKG* 85.
83. Bowdich, *A Mission*, p.233; Dupuis, *Residence*, pp. 231-232.
84. Ward, *History*, p.115.
85. Snoek (Accra) to EC, 23 February 1717, *NBKG* 84.
86. Van Alzen (Accra) to EC, 18 May 1718, *NBKG* 85.
87. Van Alzen to EC, 30 October 1717, *NBKG* 84.
88. *Ibid.*
89. *Ibid.*
90. Monninkhoven (Axim) to EC, 21 March 1718, *NBKG* 85.
91. Boerhaven (Kormantse) to EC, 9 April; van Naerssen (Sekondi) to EC, 17 April 1718, *NBKG* 85.
92. Barn (Komenda) to EC, 9 April 1718, *NBKG* 85.
93. Butler (Axim) to EC, 5 & 18 November 1715; cf also Daaku, *Trade and Politics*, p.172.
94. Muller (Axim) to EC, 15 & 18 November 1721, *NBKG* 88.
95. Van Alzen (Accra) to EC, 30 October 1717, *NBKG* 84.
96. Boerhaven (Kormantse) to Director-General Robberts (EC), 9 April 1718, *NBKG* 85.
97. EC Diary: entry 13 April 1718, *NBKG* 85.
98. Van Alzen's Report, 30 October 1717, *NBKG* 84.
99. Hence the appellation "Asante *Kotoko, kum-apem a-apem-beba*"(the daring porcupines of Asante, they fight in their thousands).
100. Van Alzen to EC, 10 May; Muller (Axim) to EC, 8 June 1718, *NBKG* 89; Director-General Butler (EC) to Amsterdam, 8 August; van Alzen (Accra) to EC, 17 August 1718, WIC 108.
101. Butler (EC) to van Naerssen (Axim) 3 November 1718, *NBKG* 85.
102. Butler (EC) to Amsterdam, 27 March 1719, WIC 108.
103. Butler to Amsterdam, 27 March 1719, WIC 108; Muller (Axim) to EC, 15 & 18 November 1721, *NBKG* 88.
104. Letter from Nortman, 7 May 1722, *NBKG* 89; de Crane & L. Beum (EC) to Amsterdam, 17 September 1723, WIC 105.
105. Beum & Council (EC) to Amsterdam, 8 January 1724, WIC 105.
106. Phal (CCO) to Copenhagen, 14 April 1727, Vgk 121: breve og dokumenter fre Guinea 1717-1732.

Chapter 3

AKYEM ASCENDANCY IN THE EAST 1728–1744

As shown in the previous chapter, the main direction of the foreign policies of Abuakwa and Kotoku during the first twenty-seven years of the eighteenth century was towards the coast, with the achievement of political hegemony in the south and easy access to the coast trade as the dual objective. But in 1727 when Okyenhene Ofori, the chief architect, died, neither goal had been realised; indeed, it looked as if the Akyem States might never be able to break the stranglehold of Akwamu and other southern states on the coast-bound Akyem trade. This situation, however, changed, almost dramatically, after 1727 in favour of Abuakwa and Kotoku.

THE AKYEM DEFEAT OF AKWAMU 1729–1730

Modification in Asante attitude towards them helped to bring about the change. Pressure from Asante had been a major element which had militated against the efforts of the Akyem to solve the Southern Question. From 1727 Asante became more and more pre-occupied with its efforts to gain access to the European trade on the Western sector of the coast.[1] The diversion of Asante attention to the west eased the pressure on the Akyem states in the east, giving them a good opportunity to tackle the southern states with greater confidence.

A change in the attitude of Kotoku towards the southern issue was the immediate outcome of the easing of the tension between the Akyem and Asante. Between 1718 and 1726 Kotokuhene Frimpon Manso had been extremely cautious about joining Ofori of Abuakwa in search of a solution to the Southern Question because he feared that such a move might arouse unfavourable reaction from Asante. From 1727 his disposition towards the subject became more positive. He may well have been the Akyem ruler who was reported in 1727 to have almost bought the neutrality of Asante in order to go to war against Akwamu.[2] By 1729, he and Baa Kwante, the new Okyenhene, had reached complete agreement to launch a joint Abuakwa-Kotoku attack on Akwamu.

Conditions prevailing at the time also favoured such a venture. Akwamu was in political crisis: it was experiencing political instability in both the metropolis and the provinces. With respect to the provinces the beginnings of the crisis could be traced as for back as 1702. In that year Akwamu leadership was obliged to send a punitive force to quell restiveness in the Ga area.[3] Though the Ga were suppressed, they continued to be jittery in subsequent years. In 1716 they refused to raise a contingent to join the Akwamu army detailed to

Akyem Ascendancy in the East 1728–1744

go to the assistance of Agona against an invading Akyem Abuakwa force.[4] The behaviour of the Ga so angered Akwamuhene Akonnor that he resolved to punish them after the storm from Akyem had subsided.[5] Unfortunately for Akonnor events overtook Akwamu before he could punish the Ga.

Among the events were two provincial revolts which broke out, one in Akuapem and the other in Ga-Adangbe. The two rebellions were to combine with Akyem hostility to eventually spell the doom of Akwamu. The tyranny of the Akwamu government was the main cause of the provincial rebellions. The government habitually ordered raids on the various provinces for slaves.[6] Akwamu provincial administrators were wont to govern harshly; this was especially the case with Amaga, the administrator for Ladoku.[7] The despotism of Akwamu rulers compelled the Akuapem and the Ga to raise the standard of rebellion in 1727 and fight a war of liberation against the overlord during the next three to four years.[8]

Had the malaise been confined to provincial Akwamu, perhaps the situation would have been containable for the Nyanoase leaders. But this was not the case. Disagreements and dissensions arose to tear the metropolis itself apart: the situation had been brought about by a succession dispute following the death of Akonnor in 1725. Two leading claimants contested for the vacant stool, one Ansa Kwao and the other Amo. For several years the latter had been the Resident Akwamu Commissioner for the Ga province. Apparently Amo had been entertaining high hopes of succeeding to the Akwamu stool after Akonnor. But it was Ansa Kwao who got the nod from the king-makers of Akwamu.

Disappointment, frustration, anger, and perhaps Dutch nudgings drove Amo into the camp of the Ga and Akuapem rebels. The Dutch influence on Amo's decision to join the rebels is suggested by the enthusiasm and joy with which those Europeans received a report from Amo in 1729 that Abuakwa and Kotoku had agreed to give military assistance to the rebels.[9] Obviously the rebels had appealed to Banso and Oda for help.

To the two Akyem states the request from Akuapem and Ga merely served as a spark in a powder magazine. They already had an axe to grind against Akwamu. The Nyanoase monarchy was yet to account for the Akyem refugees whom the late Akonnor had sold into slavery in the 1717 – 1718 period when the Akyem states were at war with Asante. Romer, the Chief Danish official at Christianborg castle, Osu, was of the view that this issue was the sole cause of the Akyem invasion of Akwamu in 1729–1730.[10]

However, there were other but less obvious causes. At the heart of the tension with Akwamu were Akyem imperial and economic ambitions. Abuakwa and Kotoku were still seeking hegemony in the south and were also searching for unimpeded access to the coast trade. But Akwamu was always blocking the trade routes against them.

The War

By mid-1729 the Abuakwa and Kotoku forces were ready to invade Akwamu. It is not clear what the military strengths of the respective belligerents were. The Akyem forces, in both real and psychological terms, must have been formidable, considering that just before the outbreak of the war, a section of the Akwamu informed Gomoahene "Kuijse Addoe" (i.e. Kusi Adu) that they were afraid to face the Akyem and had therefore decided to flee their country as soon as the fighting started. Moreover, the Akyem obtained allied support from the Assin while at some stage in the war the Fante and the Agona would express a desire to join them against Akwamu.[12] The Fante, Agona and the Assin, like the Akwamu, had all been members of the anti-Akyem Southern Alliance during the early 1710s. Why they should all now turn against Akwamu, it is not easy to explain. The evidence currently available does not offer any reason. Either Akwamu in the 1720s had offended them all or that they realized Akwamu was bound to lose the war and therefore they decided to side with the potential winner for their own security and safety. The latter proposition seems to have been the case, because in the political milieu of eighteenth century Gold Coast alliances were fleeting and transient.

However, the Akuapem and Ga appeal to the Akyem for help was a wise step. By 1729 they had their back to the wall, with imminent defeat staring them in the face. The Akuapem in particular seem to have been in greater danger. Following their request for help an Abuakwa army, under the command of an Abuakwa chief variously called Ofori Kumaa, Ofori Dua or Sa-Fori, was despatched to assist them directly.[13]

The main Akyem force, under the joint command of Frimpon Manso of Kotoku and Baa Kwante of Abuakwa assisted by his heir-apparent, Owusu Akyem, invaded Akwamu itself in September 1729,[14] not mid-1730 as some writers have said.[15] As soon as battle was joined three principal Akwamu Chiefs,

> with all their subjects fled to the Crepee country; but as they could not cross the Volta [quickly], the Hill people [ie. the Akuapem] fell on them and killed many of them.[16]

The unfortunate fugitive Akwamu may have included those Akwamu Chiefs who had earlier disclosed to the Gomoa their intention to take to flight as soon as the Akyem attacked. This early setback should have demoralised the Akwamu. But they fought on gallantly, occasionally driving the invader to near exhaustion in ammunition.[17] The war continued into 1730. But no matter how long the war dragged on, to discerning observers, its likely outcome was not in doubt. By September 1730 the Akyem forces had conquered almost all Akwamu. Only the capital, Nyanoase, was still holding out. Even here it was the Fante and the Agona who were delaying the final assault. These two had

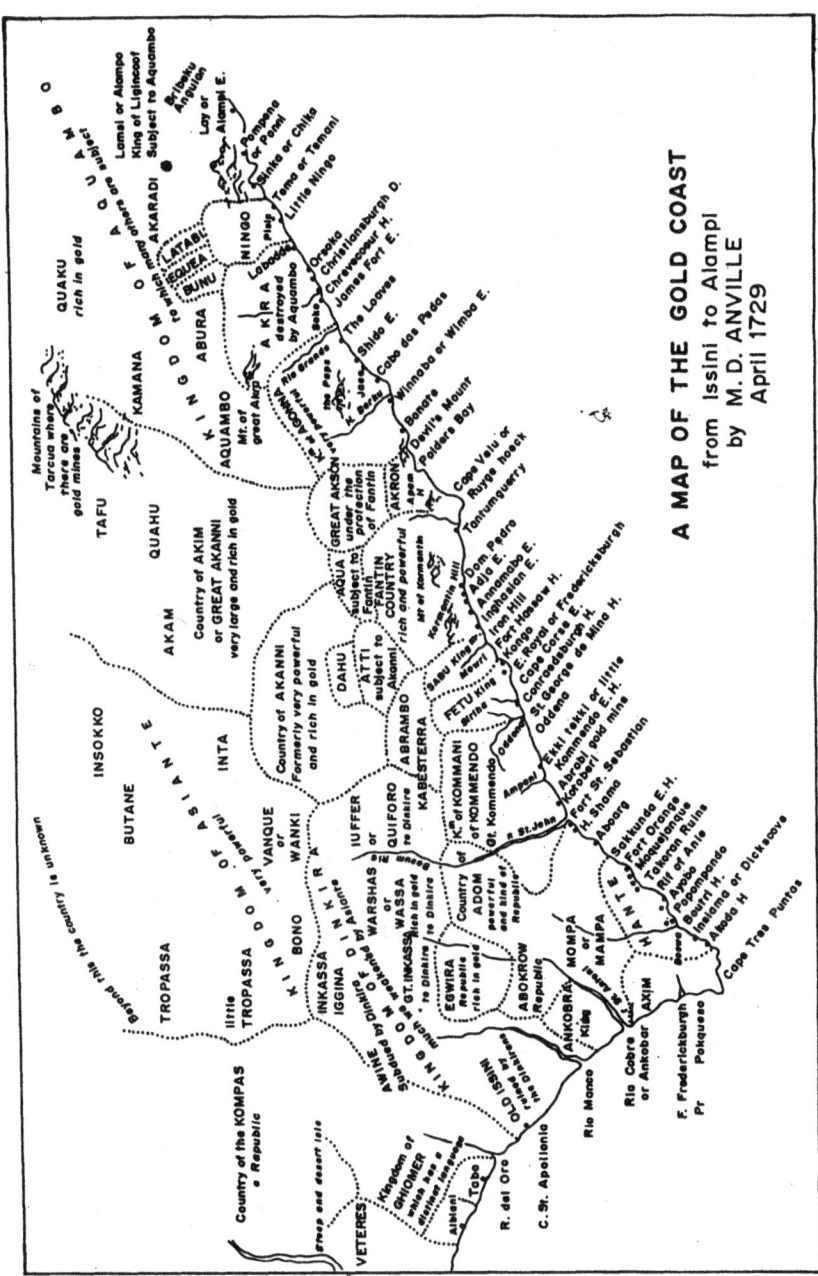

Fig. 2: Anville's Map of the Gold Coast in 1729
Source: Fynn, J. K., 1971. *Asante and its Neighbours, 1700–1807*, NUP, Longman Group Ltd., London

sent to inform the Akyem leaders of their desire to join the Akyem forces in attacking the Akwamu capital.[18] Eventually both failed to show up, a conduct which was deliberate, as shall be pointed out by and by.

The invaders stormed the Akwamu capital in the third week of September, 1730. The outcome of the assault was not in doubt. On 21 September the Dutch factor at Fort Lydzemheid at Apam thus reported to Elmina Castle authorities that

> This is just to inform you that my Foetoe [Efutu] servant has just arrived straight . . . from Aquamboe. He tells me that the whole of Aquamboe has been defeated by the Akim, and the King [of Akwamu] taken prisoner and put in irons. The whole [Akwamu] country is now in the possession of the Akims.[19]

Tradition also remembers the victory of the Akyem in what it calls the Nyanoase War.[20]

The Dutch were delighted at the outcome of the war. Their satisfaction was not without justification. Since the beginning of the century they as well as the English had been looking forward to the day Akyem arms would prevail over Akwamu to allow the smooth flow of the Akyem gold trade to the coast. They and the other Europeans were anxious to do business with Akyem who, because of their gold, a strong purchasing power, were better inclined for trade and commerce than the Akwamu.

Effects of the Nyanoase War

The impact of the Abuakwa-Kotoku victory over Akwamu was both revolutionary and evolutionary. The most immediate effect of the Nyanoase War of 1729–1730 was the founding of a new Akwamu State. To members of the Akwamu ruling house who escaped capture and death, flight was the only alternative to total submission and a concomitant vassalage to the Akyem. The 1729 flight of some of their subjects to the lower trans-Volta was there for them to emulate. They followed the example by fleeing to the same place in 1730. Here they founded a new home and state, namely the Akwamu State as we know it today, with Akwamufie as the capital. Thus the founding of present day Akwamu was a direct result of the success of Abuakwa and Kotoku in the Nyanoase War.

Politically the Akwamu were a very ambitious people. Defeat and the deprivation of their pre-1730 home did not totally dampen their spirits. From their new home they, for the rest of the eighteenth century, tried to influence the inter-state politics of the lower trans-Volta with a view to establishing a hegemony similar to what they had enjoyed west of the Volta before their downfall in 1730. But they only succeeded in worsening the conflicts already existing in, and afflicting, the region.[21]

Akyem Ascendancy in the East 1728-1744

The defeat and subsequent departure of the Akwamu ruling house for the lower trans-Volta paved the way for the ascendancy of the Abuakwa and the Kotoku in the eastern sector of the Gold Coast. By fleeing, the Akwamu leadership abandoned its imperial possessions west of the Volta. These, besides the former metropolitan Akwamu, included Kwawu, Kamana (i.e. the Guan-Kyerepon communities inhabiting what became the Begoro district of Abuakwa), Akuapem, Ga, Adangbe and Krobo. By virtue of their victory in 1730 the rulers of Akyem Abuakwa and Akyem Kotoku assumed imperial authority over all these places and peoples in addition to the pre-1730 metropolitan Akwamu (which from now on will be referred to as Old Akwamu vis-a-vis New Akwamu in the trans-Volta). This imperial authority extended virtually from the mouth of river Ayensu in the west to the Volta estuary in the east, a distance of about two hundred miles, and from the shores of the Atlantic in the south to as far north as the headwaters of river Anuru (or Anum), some one hundred and fifty miles inland. The Akyem had at long last achieved the supremacy they had hankered after since the last quarter of the seventeenth century.

The issue of empire raises the founding of Akuapem as a centralized state on the Akan model. Up to 1730 the Akuapem had consisted of petty fragmentary Guan, Kyerepon and Akan communities living independently of one another. After the Nyanoase War, they reached a consensus and invited Safori or Ofori Dua, better known as Ofori Kumaa, their immediate liberator, from Akyem Abuakwa, to be their paramount ruler.[22]

Continued fear of Akwamu seems to have been the basic reason for the Akuapem decision to make Ofori Kumaa their King. A Dutch complaint in December 1730, made probably on behalf of the Akuapem and the Ga, suggests this. The Dutch were not satisfied that the Akyem (Abuakwa) had spent "only one-fifth of the time" they had contracted to assist the Akuapem and the Ga.[23] Since by December 1730 the surviving leaders of the Akwamu and their subjects were settled in the lower trans-Volta, the Dutch complaint can only suggest a continued Akuapem/Ga fear of Akwamu. They may have entertained the anxiety that the defeated Akwamu, even from their new home beyond the Volta, were capable of attacking them. It was therefore unsafe to quickly and completely dispense with the superior military services of the Akyem. To make Ofori Kumaa the King of all Akuapem would be an insurance against their former tyrants should they attempt to re-open hostilities from across the Volta. Another possible reason is that the Akuapem made Ofori Kumaa their paramount ruler in lieu of the fee they had to pay for his military assistance to them. It is worth noting that the Ga had to raise loans from the Danish, Dutch and English trading companies before they could pay the Akyem.[24]

Whatever the reasons for his elevation, Ofori Kumaa organized the hitherto acephalous Akuapem communities into a centralized unitary state, with the Ofori Kumaa dynasty at its head.[25] Amanprobi, where Ofori initially based himself, became the capital of the new state. Later the capital was moved to Akropon where it has since remained. Thus Akuapem as an organized state owes much to Abuakwa for its origins. It is an example of what ethnic admixture and exchange of political ideas could positively lead to.

Division of the Empire

The creation of the Ofori Kumaa dynasty for Akuapem in turn raises the question as to how Abuakwa and Kotoku controlled the empire. Akuapem was placed under the overrule of Abuakwa.[26] And so were almost the whole of Ga-Adangbe which consisted of Ladoku, Ada, Krobo and all Ga except Osu. Owusu Akyem, heir apparent to the Abuakwa stool,[27] was made the absentee governor of all these places in addition to Akuapem. Old Akwamu was also placed under Abuakwa overrule.

Osu as an imperial province went to Kotoku.[28] Kotoku seems to have also received Kwawu as an imperial province. There is no contemporary evidence for this. However, Adoagyiri tradition asserts that from the time of Frimpon Manso, Kotoku rulers were accustomed to regard Kwawu Kings as their 'wives'.[29] In Akan culture, jocular marital relations such as we have here implied the existence of cordial relations in which the 'wife' regarded the 'husband' as superior. The tradition may well be referring to an overlord-vassal relations between Kotoku and Kwawu dating back to the 1730s. A strong name of the Kotokuhene is "Oko-fro-Buo" (Conqueror-of-the-Hills), possibly another allusion to Kotoku overrule of Kwawu, a hilly district.

Whether Kotoku did or did not obtain Kwawu as an imperial province, it stands out unmistakably that the division was lop-sided: Abuakwa received the lion's share of the ex-Akwamu empire. In the early 1730s Abuakwa even tried to deprive Kotoku of the Osu province.[30] Contemporary evidence currently available to the present author does not shed any light on the rationale behind the disproportion. Probably the Kotoku were still not too sure about the feelings of Asante on the Akyem defeat of Akwamu, and so did not want to saddle themselves with distant provincial administration which would have diverted much of their attention. They accepted Osu probably because of the Christiansborg castle from which they could easily and readily obtain Danish manufactured guns. The Kotoku allegedly had a great liking for "Dane guns".[31]

Akyem Ascendancy in the East 1728–1744

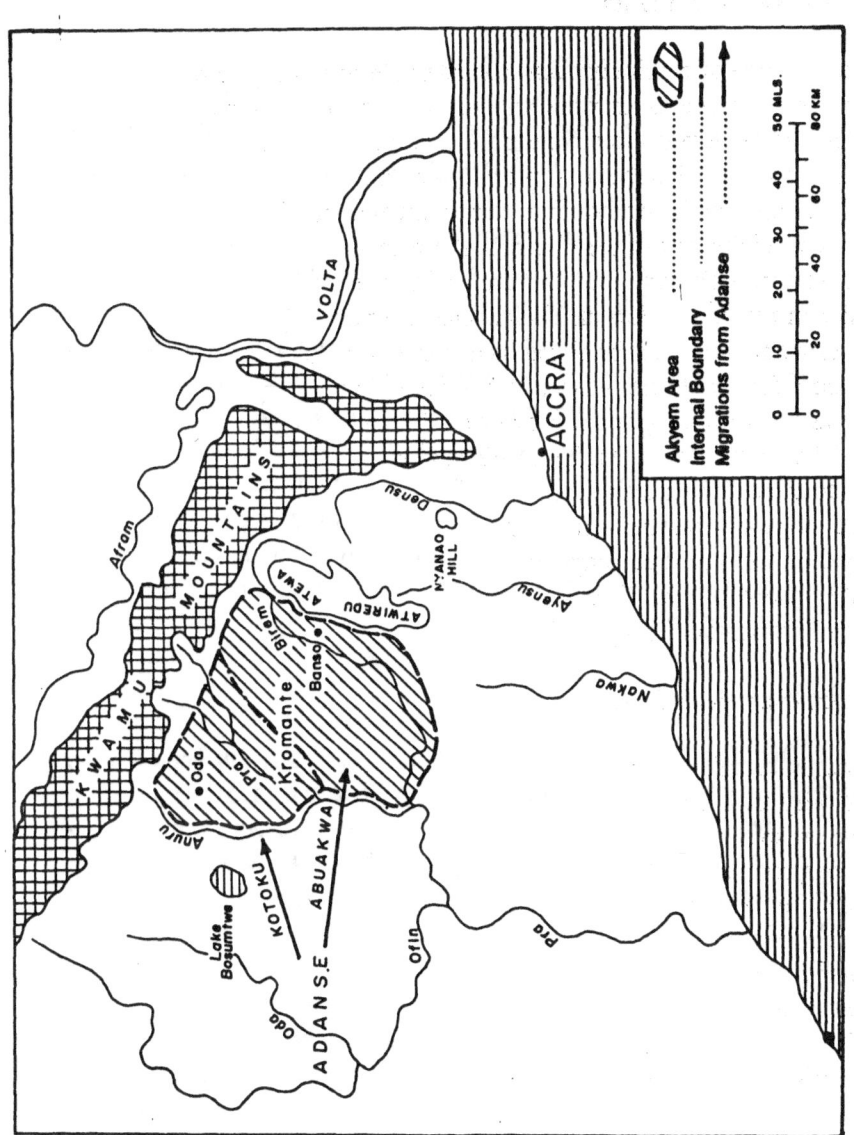

Fig. 3: Approximate Limit of Abuakwa and Kotoku at the beginning of the 18th Century.

PRIVILEGES/PROFITS OF HEGEMONY

Tributes, Taxes and Gifts

The acquisition of empire brought considerable prosperity to the two Akyem states. Tributes and taxes were undoubtedly imposed on subject states and peoples but the details are not clear. Ground rents from the castles, forts and lodges on the Ga-Adangbe coast went to the Banso and Oda courts. While the Abuakwa ruler collected those from James fort and fort Crevecoeur, the Kotoku ruler received the rent of the Christiansborg castle. The European traders on the coast habitually sent gifts, or "dashes" as they were usually described, to the Akyem rulers. In 1736 the Okyenhene received a gift of 20 bendas worth of goods from the Danes for giving them permission to build Fort Fredensburg at Ningo.[32] Prince Owusu Akyem, the official governor of the Adangbe province, must have been given a present too. Romer recalls that the Abuakwa Prince shaved the hair on his head, added 8 oz. of gold to it, and sent it to the Danes to bury it under the foundations of the fort. The English also planned to build a lodge at what they called "Prangprang" (i.e. Prampram). In all probability they too would accompany their application for permission with a gift to the Banso court. In 1740 the Danes and the Dutch jointly protested the English "Prangprang" project.[33]

The Afro-European Trade

The Danish-Dutch protest against the English in 1740 was symptomatic of the keen rivalry among the European traders for the African trade which appears to have prospered during the 1730s because of the ascendancy of the Akyem in the eastern sector of the Gold Coast. Even after 1744 when the Akyem ceased to be the overlords of the region, the Danes for example, continued to send gifts to its rulers on account of the importance of the Akyem gold trade. The practice continued well into early nineteenth century when the Danes described such gifts as regular salaries for the Akyem authorities.[34]

The Pax Akyema which Abuakwa and Kotoku established promoted prosperous trade in the eastern parts of the Gold Coast. Aside from creating congenial conditions for trade to thrive in the Akyem were themselves great drivers of trade from the interior to the coast, especially the gold trade. It has been strongly suggested that by the 1730s slaves had overtaken gold as the leading article in the Afro-European trade in the Gold Coast.[35] It might be tempting to infer from this claim that most, if not all the peoples, of the Gold Coast were participants in the trans-Atlantic slave trade. The Akyem were an exception, as they demonstrated after the 1729–1730 war with Akwamu. The

Europeans on the coast had expected the victorious Akyem to march all the Akwamu prisoners-of-war to the coast and sell them to the trans-Atlantic slavers. The Akyem, to the surprise of the Europeans, did not, rather, according to the Dutch, the Akyem sent all the captives to their own country in order to swell Abuakwa and Kotoku population.[36] Danish opinion confirms the Dutch assertion. Romer was an official at Christiansborg Castle in the 1730s. Writing in the 1760s he said most Africans sold their prisoners-of-war but the Akyem kept theirs and grafted them on native lineages by eventually manumitting them and accepting them as free-born members of Akyem society.[37]

This clearly negative attitude of the Akyem towards the Atlantic Slave Trade was indeed unique in the Gold Coast. Along the whole of West Africa a parallel could be found only in contemporary Dahomey (Benin today) where the Abomey monarchy, for reasons other than those of the Akyem, were at one time not favourably disposed towards the trans-Atlantic slave trade.[38] This is not to suggest that the Akyem were averse to the institution of slavery. Domestic slavery formed a vital part of Akyem society. To keep up the custom the Akyem usually purchased slaves from other peoples and sometimes organized armed expeditions to raid for slaves.[39]

The Gold Industry

Military and economic considerations largely promoted slavery in the Akyem states. During wars slaves were enlisted to fight for their masters. In peace time slaves were employed in long-distance trading and in the extractive industry. Indeed in the extractive industry lay the main reason for Akyem unwillingness to sell war captives into the trans-Atlantic slave trade. Such prisoners-of-war were converted into domestic slaves who provided cheap labour for the economic activities of the free-born such as the gold industry.

The gold industry provided the backbone of Akyem economy in both the eighteenth and the nineteenth centuries. The Akyem had three main methods in extracting gold. One was surface collection. After heavy rains nuggets could be found lying in gutters and gullies for the picking. The second method was the scooping of sand from the beds of rivers and rivulets. Such sand more often than not contained gold pecks and pebbles. The third method, the most popular and profitable, was digging for gold.[40] Some of the European traders on the coast tried to gather as much information on the Akyem mining methods as possible. Romer was particularly outstanding in this respect.

The information he obtained is worth quoting extensively, if only to provide a comparison between Gold Coast and European methods of mining. Römer writes:

> According to what our Accra and the Akims tell us, [the Akyem] dig holes in the ground wherever they please, making sure, however, that it is a good distance from the towns and not too close to the footpaths, so that their children and animals may not fall into them. They make landings about three feet high . . . in order that they may pass the trays or vessels (with the soil which they have dug from the ground) to each other. While Europeans dig 'streets' underground and prop them up . . . and have windlasses to hoist their ore etc., the Akims simply dig slanting holes into the ground which looks like a staircase, each step being 1½ allen high.
>
> If after having dug 8–10 allen, they find that the soil is not rich, they start digging elsewhere. Sometimes, however, they bring a trayful of soil to the water to test it. If they do not hit a rich soil by the time they have dug a hole 10 allen deep . . . or 8 landings, their effort has been in vain . . . they go to another place to start digging afresh.
>
> Yet they seldom fail to find a rich soil . . . and in most cases it is so rich that each of the workers delivers 8 oz. everyday, which is considered the minimum a master will accept.[41].

The industry was labour-intensive because a pit might require, on the average, a labour force of about forty workers. Besides diggers at the bottom of the pit, between thirty and sixty others were required to stand on the stairs to pass trays to and from the bottom of the pit; others worked as panners looking for the precious metal from the soil. On 'bonanza' mines, according to Romer's informants, still larger work forces were required. The need for slave labour in the Akyem states thus becomes clear.

Other aspects of the industry which Romer touched on included the beliefs and odd ideas of the Akyem about gold. Some of the information given him made him think that the Akyem were stupid and superstitious. He says that at one time Kotokuhene

> Frempong's men found a whole rock of gold in a mine. This was reported to the King who was asked whether they should use chisels, as the travat [ie. the rainy season] was approaching. Frempong consulted the great men and the resolution was that this rock must be the mother or father of the small gold, nobody was to touch it . . . the men should leave the mine and start at another place.[42]

Romer attributed the decision of King Frimpon Manso and his councillors to their stupidity and superstition.[43] The Akyem were certainly superstitious but not stupid. To this day there are many Akan peoples, including those of Asante-Akyem, the ancestral home of the Kotoku ruling lineage, who believe that gold is fetish or god if it occurs in a large unit such as an exceptionally large nugget. But such an occurrence did not, and still does not, stop people from exploiting it. The order to the workers to leave that bonanza mine obviously had a dual rationale behind it. The first was that the stoppage would allow the monarchy to perform rituals on the mine, rituals such as the pouring of libation and the slaughtering of sheep on the land where the deposit was.

The second, which was the real motive, was to prevent the miners, who in most cases were slaves, from acquiring part of the discovered gold.

Romer's relatively detailed information was indicative of the great interest of the European traders in the Akyem gold industry. To them the name Akyem was almost synonymous with gold. At the beginning of the eighteenth century the Dutch official, William Bosman, noted that the Akyem furnished

> as large quantities of gold as any land that I know and that also the most valuable and pure of any that is carried from this coast: it is easily distinguished by its deep colour.[44]

Between 1700 and the 1720s virtually all the European traders who operated in the Gold Coast always regretted the heavy incidence of war which disrupted the gold trade from Akyem. In the 1730s the Akyem sold only "a few slaves" but plenty of gold" to the white traders.[45] Some thirty years later the Akyem country was described as a very rich source of gold.[46]

Easy Access to the Coast Trade

Hegemony in eastern Gold Coast hugely enhanced Akyem accessibility to the European trade on the coast. This issue had been a major source of conflict between them and the intermediary states such as Akwamu and Agona. With the defeat and resultant emigration of the Akwamu ruling house to the lower trans-Volta in 1730 the Abuakwa and the Kotoku now had a fairly easy access to the coast trade; 'fairly easy' because, as shall be shown in due course, the inhabitants of Old Akwamu who did not emigrate, occasionally raised barriers against Akyem traders to the coast.

Gold put a strong purchasing power into the hands of the Akyem. That in turn made them most welcome to the European traders. The over-all effect was that the Abuakwa and the Kotoku became avid long-distance traders to the coast. In order to boost the coast-bound trade the Akyem acquired slaves to undertake, on their behalf, the task of escorting and porterage. However lowly-placed he was, the free-born Akyem normally regarded porterage as below his dignity: slaves therefore must undertake that task for him. Slaves were sometimes employed to increase the number of armed escorts for traders and travellers because the trade routes were not wholly free from the scourge of highway robbery and raiding.[47]

As another solution to that same scourge, the Akyem evolved the caravan system of travelling. An Akyem caravan could sometimes contain up to two thousand men.[48] Such a concourse of travellers could not be easily attacked. The system had another advantage. It made it possible for the Akyem traders to do collective bargaining on prices. On arrival at the coast, Akyem master traders would go to the forts and lodges to negotiate prices with the European traders who, for this purpose, usually employed African agents or interpreters. The bargaining could last up to four or more days. As long as the haggling had not formally ended no Akyem trader would purchase anything.[49] Buying proceeded briskly as soon as prices were agreed upon between buyer and seller.

The Akyem bought all sorts of items. However, they gave top priority to a few of them. These included salt, textiles, knives, iron, spirits and above all firearms and ammunition. Sometimes they bought nothing but guns and other munitions of war. For instance in 1741, the Dutch in Accra had to send express message to Elmina Castle for more guns and other war materials because the Akyem traders who had arrived in Accra were buying nothing else apart from those items.[50] The Akyem bought large quantities of spirits, especially the Danish Flensborger corn brandy for which Abuakwa Kings like Baa Kwante reportedly had a special liking.[51]

On the whole, trade in the eastern parts of the Gold Coast seems to have prospered under the Akyem imperial authority though it is difficult to measure the prosperity in statistical terms. The general testimony of some of the white traders themselves should suffice as a legitimate proof. Indeed some of them felt sad when the Akyem ascendancy collapsed in 1742–1744. Lamenting over the demise of the empire, Romer in the 1760s said:

> We Danes could have earned enough in those years [of Akyem supremacy] to cover all our costs for some fifty years. We did not [then] need to take our goods out ourselves for sale as we have had to do recently, nor did we require the services of up to forty African agents in the interior of the country as is now the practice.[52]

PROBLEMS OF HEGEMONY

Provincial Administration

Success of course creates its own peculiar problems. And so it was with the Abuakwa and the Kotoku in the 1730s and early 1740s. Provincial administration was one of the problems with which the two states had to grapple. Others were misunderstandings between them and some of the European traders, the jealousy of neighbours, and provincial recalcitrance and rebellions.

After the defeat of Akwamu, the most immediate problem which confronted the rulers of Abuakwa and Kotoku was provincial administration, an altogether new thing to Banso and Oda. Ultimately the Akyem did not evolve a uniform system as the Akwamu before them had done. In their imperial days the Akwamu used the system of residential governorship to control the component provinces of their empire. For instance Prince Amo, as already pointed out, was the Akwamu resident governor for the Ga province while Amaga, another Akwamu royal, obtained the gubarnatorial authority for Ladoku.[53] Unlike the Akwamu, the Akyem adopted non-residential governorship as well as indirect rule. Prince Owusu Akyem of Abuakwa was made governor of Akuapem and the Ga-Adangbe provinces, but in neither province did he reside. Nor was any governor, resident or non-resident, appointed for Old Akwamu. Here the Akyem (Abuakwa) adopted indirect rule. In 1730 the Dutch had hoped that the Akyem would govern it directly.[54] But Jan Pranger, the Governor-General at Elmina Castle, a shrewd observer of politics in the Gold Coast, disabused the minds of his colleagues thus:

> As regards the [Old] Quamboe country, you say you want to see the Akims assume ... the government of it, but that will never happen because it is an established custom of the nations [in the Gold Coast] that they always leave a part of the defeated enemies in their own country, one of whom they put in authority over it, whom they regard as their tribute paying vassal. The conquerors can live there, if they so wish, but they never share in the government.[55]

The Akyem did exactly that. They appointed one Kwasi Bribi to rule Old Akwamu.[56] By December 1731 Okyenhene "Bacontin [ie. Baa Kwante] and the native who will govern [Old] Quamboe country by order of the Akims" were together communicating with the Dutch in Accra.[57] Contemporary evidence thus substantiates the traditional assertion that after the Nyanoase War, Old Akwamu came under Abuakwa overrule.[58]

Relations with the European Companies

Relations with some of the European companies also presented the victorious Akyem with another immediate problem. The Dutch for instance proved particularly troublesome. They started giving difficulties to the Akyem right from 1730. The first problem the Dutch created was their refusal to help the Ga requite the Akyem for their military services against the Akwamu in the just ended war. The Ga had reportedly promised the Akyem rulers a subsidy of "360 bendas of gold [and] six strings of *contre de terre*".[59] After the war, the Ga could not raise the subsidy on their own. Consequently, they approached the European trading companies for loans to enable them pay the Akyem. The Danes and the English readily obliged, but the Dutch refused to help saying that the Ga might never pay back the loan.[60] Requiting the Akyem was of course the sole responsibility of the Ga, and how to find the money was also their own business. But the Dutch refusal to assist the Ga did not naturally augur well for Akyem-Dutch relations, considering that the Danes and the English readily helped.

A more direct friction between the Akyem leadership and the Dutch also started in 1730 and was over how much groundrent the latter were to pay for fort Crevecoeur. As overlords of the Ga-Adangbe area, the Akwamu had held "the notes" or documents which had entitled them to collect the ground-rents of the castles, forts and lodges on the Ga-Adangbe coast.[61] For fort Crevecoeur the Dutch used to pay 2 oz. of gold per month to the Akwamu rulers. But they refused to pay the same amount to the Abuakwa rulers. The evidence in hand does not make it possible to find the reason or reasons why the Dutch decided to pay less. On their part the Banso authorities refused to take anything less than the 2 oz. of gold paid to the Akwamu rulers. The dispute dragged on till 1732 when the Abuakwa rulers, for reasons best known to themselves, agreed to accept 1 oz. of gold per month as groundrent for fort Crevecoeur.[62]

Unhealthy European Competition

Unhealthy rivalry among the European companies also created headaches for the Akyem imperial presence in the Ga-Adangbe area. The companies were in the habit of trading accusations and counter-accusations which sometimes led to armed clashes. The best example was the Danish-Dutch conflict which started in 1736.[63] In that year the Danes accused the Dutch of instigating Chief Darko of "Dutch" Accra and the Mantse (Chief) of Osu against Danish interests.[64] It was the turn of the Dutch to level a similar charge against the Danes in 1737; they claimed that the Danes were intriguing with Prince Owusu Akyem of Abuakwa against them.[65] At the heart of the tensions among the European trading companies was of course unhealthy competition to grab as much of the African trade as each company could at the expense of the others. The rivalry, together with the location of the various castles, forts, and lodges, more often than not involved them in local politics which in turn intensified the commercial competition. Essentially, this was the basic cause of the Danish-Dutch tension.

The immediate cause, however, was the involvement of the Dutch in Ga politics. The Stool of Dutch Accra became vacant. The Dutch got entangled in the efforts of the Ga to fill the vacancy by supporting the candidature of Darko[66] against that of "Okaidja"; to add insult to injury they also panyarred (seized) some of Okaidja's close relatives and slaves.[67] In retaliation Okaidja fled to Osu where the Danes were only too pleased to use him against the Dutch.

As overlords of the Ga area the Akyem had a duty to impartially compose the differences between the Danes and the Dutch. On this occasion, however, the Akyem authorities, instead of acting as impartial mediators, became partisan in the quarrel of the European traders. This was the result of the effective intrigues of Okaidja and the Danes in Akyem. They informed the Akyem authorities that the Dutch had secretly been instigating the Asante to invade the Akyem states.[68] Okaidja and his Danish allies could not have struck a much better chord in the Akyem to whom relations with Asante were a most sensitive and delicate issue.[69] Already a considerable degree of tension seems to have existed between these two giants in the Gold Coast. In 1734, the Akyem had accused the Dutch of being "the friends of Poko" (ie. Opoku Ware), the Asantehene.[70] The 1737 Okaidja-Danish allegation apparently raised the level of the adrenalin in the Akyem system. The Akyem authorities took a serious view of the allegation all the more because it was partly coming from Okaidja, who was well placed to know more about the clandestine dealings of the Dutch. The Akyem immediately mobilized against the Dutch as well as 'Dutch' Accra.

To intrigue with one people against another in the Gold Coast was a Dutch speciality.[71] But on this occasion they seem to have been innocent. All the same the prospect of an Akyem attack on their establishment in Accra was something the Dutch did not want to welcome. They were determined to prevent its occurrence at all costs. They decided on high-level diplomacy as the best means to defuse the explosive situation. The Dutch Director-General himself, J. Baron des Bordes, travelled from Elmina to Accra to launch a diplomatic contact with the Akyem leadership. On 4th June 1737, barely a day after his arrival in Accra, des Bordes despatched ambassadors

> to the Great Man of the Akim Nation such as Frempong, Baquentyn and Oers [ie. Owusu Akyem] . . . to enquire from them why they have decided to attack the Dutch Company with whom they have been accustomed to trade always.[72]

Des Bordes's diplomacy paid off. On 20th July 1737 his emissaries returned to Accra accompanied by Akyem representatives who had a mandate to investigate the allegation against the Dutch. In the end the enquiry revealed that Okaidja, assisted by the Danes, was the source of the allegation and that there was no truth in it.[73] Consequently Akyem-Dutch relations were overtly normalized, or so it seemed.

Subsequent development indicated that the Akyem decision to normalize relations with the Dutch had not been unanimous. Prince Owusu Akyem, the non-Resident Governor of almost all Ga-Adangbe, was not pleased with the findings of the Accra Enquiry and unilaterally decided to side with the Danes and Okaidja.

Dutch determination to severely punish Okaidja for his conduct may have partly given the Abuakwa Prince the chance to pursue that independent line of action in the matter. Following the outcome of the Accra Enquiry, the Dutch first sentenced Okaidja to a term of imprisonment, but on the pleas and entreaties of the leading men of Dutch Accra, and possibly those of the Akyem investigators, the Dutch commuted the prison term to a fine.[74] Eventually, Okaidja managed to escape from 'Dutch' Accra, and once again fled to Osu where the Danes readily accorded him protection. Moreover, he and the Danes worked out a plan to attack 'Dutch' Accra and for that purpose invited military assistance from Owusu Akyem who quickly agreed to help.

The stand taken by the Abuakwa Prince was indicative of his capabilities and independent turn of mind. The Danish officials wondered why he was not the King of Abuakwa and rather, that high office had gone to Baa Kwante whom they considered to be a drunkard.[75] It is not clear why the Prince pursued that independent line of action contrary to the position of his superiors, namely his own King of Abuakwa and the Monarch of Kotoku. Could it have been principle or presents that had the better of him? It certainly couldn't have been principle since Okaidja had been found to be of dubious character. Gifts from the Danes may have influenced Owusu to be anti-Dutch.

Whatever his reason or reasons, Prince Owusu Akyem first sent a force of 8,000 strong in late 1737 to assist the Danes and Okaidja.[76] This contingent first moved into Akuapem in November 1737 and arrived in the Accra District in December.[77] In early January 1738 Owusu Akyem himself, with another force of 8,000, joined the earlier contingent.[78] The presence of the sixteen thousand strong Akyem force in the Ga area caused great panic in the district. Thousands of its inhabitants frantically looked for asylum, many of them fleeing into Fort Creveoceur for protection.[79]

Suddenly the situation changed in favour of the Dutch. Prince Owusu Akyem unexpectedly withdrew himself and his invading force from the Ga District and quartered himself in Akuapem. From there he and his forces left for Akyem Abuakwa. The Danes attributed the withdrawal of Owusu Akyem to shortage of water in the Ga region.[80] Scarcity of water could be bad for an army on campaign. But lack of water does not seem to provide all the reason for the pullout, because several wars in the Gold Coast were fought during the dry season which was between the months of December and March.

The ultimate effectiveness of Dutch diplomacy in Akyem was probably another and a much better reason. For in December 1737 the Dutch were confident enough to say that

> "Oers is not assisted with proper force by his brother [ie. Baa Kwante] to begin formal war; his advance is entirely contrary to the views of his brother.[81]

Kotokuhene Frimpon Manso may also have disapproved the conduct of Owusu Akyem. At any rate in February 1738, Starckenburg, the Dutch factor in Accra, repeated his 1737 assertion.[82] It is clear from Starckenburg's report that the Dutch had been in touch with the courts of Banso and Oda. It is not unlikely that their protests against Owusu Akyem may have compelled the two Akyem rulers to order Owusu Akyem to put a stop to his Accra venture.

The withdrawal of Owusu's forces had no immediate effect on the Okaidja – Dutch conflict.[83] Nor did the warnings of the Akyem authorities have any positive impact on him. He continued to block some of the routes leading to Dutch Accra and proved quite elusive to Dutch attempts to apprehend him and bring him to justice.[84] And the Akyem rulers were not in a position to do anything to suppress him because, this was about the time when the Akyem were very pre-occupied with problems in other parts of the empire, particularly Old Akwamu. Okaidja rightly calculated that the Akyem authorities were not in a good position to deal with him immediately. This point needs to be emphasized because in the latter half of 1738 when the Akyem became less distracted by problems elsewhere, not much was heard of him again. He must have scaled down his hostile activities against the Dutch when information reached Tema in July 1738 that the Akyem were about to despatch a punitive force against him.[85] Moreover, by then the Danes had somehow patched up their differences with the Dutch. Without Danish cooperation and support from Owusu Akyem, Okaidja had reached the end of his tether.

It must be pointed out, however, that in spite of the Danish-Dutch peace settlement in 1738, the commercial rivalry and bickering among the European trading companies continued, though not on a scale to warrant the attention of the Akyem states. In 1740, when the English indicated their intention to build a lodge at Prampram, both the Danes and the Dutch protested to the Akyem rulers against the English move.[86]

Troubles from Old Akwamu

As indicated above, Okaidja was able to defy the Dutch for as long as he wished because of the preoccupation of the Akyem with matters in other parts of the empire. Old Akwamu was one of the trouble spots. From 1731 the Old Akwamuans made themselves a great source of nuisance and irritation to the Akyem imperial presence in their country.

In 1730–1731 when they accepted vassalage to Akyem Abuakwa, they seem to have been playing for time. Continual recalcitrance on their part became the main feature of relations between them and their Akyem overlords. In 1732, they blockaded the trade routes to the Ga coast against Akyem traders.[87] From then on Old Akwamu dislike for the Akyem hegemony usually expressed itself in this form of economic sanction.[88] The Akyem, both Abuakwa and Kotoku, found it a great source of irritation; and the European trading companies naturally regarded it as an unwelcome disruption of the gold trade from the Akyem territories, and so tried to persuade the people of Old Akwamu to stop it. In 1733 the Dutch attempted to mediate between them and the Akyem.[89] The attempt was virtually a nonstarter because the Old Akwamu would neither send representatives to deliberate nor make known their immediate grievances against the Akyem.[90]

Indeed the attitude of Old Akwamu was such that sometimes the governments in Abuakwa and Kotoku could exploit it as a smoke-screen for their designs in other directions. For instance in 1734, the Akyem (Abuakwa) disclosed that they were about to send a punitive force to Old Akwamu but the target turned out to be the lower Volta basin. However, in late 1738, the Akyem took a definite decision to tackle the Old Akwamu problem once and for all. In October 1738 they successfully invaded the province to confirm their authority there.[91] But the victory did not eliminate Old Akwamu hatred and dislike for the Akyem supremacy. Between 1740 and 1742 they would receive with great delight the news of an impending Asante attack on the Akyem, much in the same way as the Voltaic or New Akwamu would welcome the projected Asante assault.

Akyem Attitude Towards New Akwamu

Continued harassment by the Akyem was the cause of the Voltaic or New Akwamu dislike for the Akyem. Since 1730 when the Akwamu ruling lineage and a section of their subjects fled to and settled beyond the lower Volta, the Akyem had scarcely left them in peace. In 1731 Akyem forces under the command of Owusu Akyem invaded the Lower Volta. These attacks were actually glorified slave raiding ventures targeted primarily against the Krepi.[92] All the same the raids must have sent shivers down the spine of Voltaic Akwamu as a neighbour to Krepi on account of old enmities.

The fear of the New Akwamu was justified in 1737: a direct Akyem invasion of New Akwamu took place. The Akyem invaders reportedly killed and captured many of the inhabitants; those of them who managed to escape death or capture fled in boats to an island in the Volta for safety.[93] From that safe haven they appealed to the Dutch at Kéta to either give them direct protection or at least plead with the Akyem to stop harassing them.[94] King Agaja of Dahomey (Benin today) invaded the Keta district about this time.[95] The Dahomey assault on Keta gave rise to a strong speculation among the Dutch that probably the Akwamu had sent to invite Agaja to their aid and that the attack on Keta could be the first phase of a grand Akwamu-Dahomey secret plan. The Dutch therefore began to put their defences in the Ga-Adangbe area on good footing in anticipation of the expected assault.[96] But the perceived attack never materialized to worry the Akyem as overlords of the Ga and Adangbe provinces.

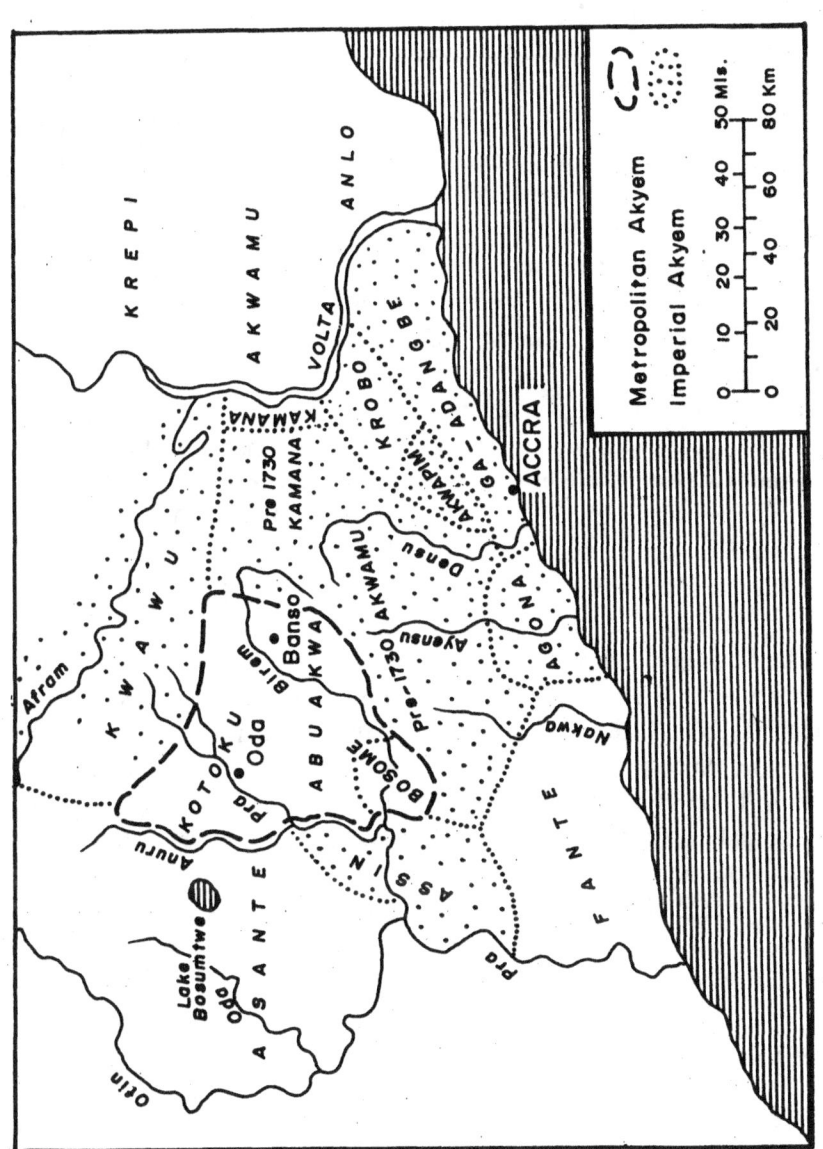

Fig. 4: Approximate Limit of the Political Expansion of Akyem 1730–1742

Headaches from Agona and Fante

Agona and eastern Fante also increased the worries of the Akyem ascendancy. The source of the tension could be traced to the 1729–1730 period. The duplicity and cheating of these two peoples were the root cause of the tension. During the second half of 1730 when the Nyanoase war had reached its most critical stage, when defeat was staring Akwamu right in the face, the Agona and the eastern Fante, sent to inform the Akyem leaders of their intention to join in the final assault on the Akwamu capital. To that end the Agona and the eastern Fante allegedly raised a force of 20,000 strong.[97] But they did not go to join the Akyem. Rather they positioned themselves on the periphery of the hot war zone, seized fleeing Akwamu refugees, and sold them straight to European slavers lying in wait.[98]

The conduct of the Agona and the eastern Fante so angered the Akyem that immediately after the fall of Akwamu, Frimpon Manso of Kotoku and the mighty Abuakwa Prince, Owusu Akyem, resolved to march on these two peoples. Gomoahene Kusi Adu (Kusa Adu, according to Reindorf) tried to mediate between the two sides but apparently failed.[99] By 1732 hot war was raging between the two sides.[100] Elet, the Dutch Factor in Accra followed the progress of the war. He reported that the Akyem received allied assistance from an Assin Chief called "Doddi Thibo". This Chief may not have been any other person than Assin Tannosuhene Oduro Tsibo. Assin Twifo tradition recalls that Oduro Tsibo assisted the Akyem against the Agona and the Fante.[101] The tradition goes on to say that even long before the Akyem were ready for the war, Oduro Tsibo had declared his preparedness to make the first move against the Agona and the Fante. Obviously he too was appalled by the behaviour of those two peoples.

The outcome of the war is not known for certain; it may have been indecisive since the tension between the two sides persisted up to 1738 when the Akyem finally defeated the Agona and the Fante.[102]

Relations with Asante

Perhaps the most sensitive of all the problems which success caused the Abuakwa and the Kotoku was relations with Asante. Relations between those inland giants hinged precariously on the personality of Kotokuhene Frimpon Manso. Unfortunately for the Akyem this ruler died two years after the 1738 war with Agona and eastern Fante, Romer and Reindorf date the death of Frimpon to 1741.[103] There is reason to think that the event occurred in 1740. In the first place, during the first eight months of 1740 the Dutch noticed that Akyem traders had been conspicuously absent at the coast, and also that a planned Akyem re-invasion of Agona had been abandoned.[104] Perhaps the Akyem were mourning the death of this great Kotokuhene. Secondly, Asantehene Opoku Ware I was poised for war against the Akyem in 1740. In the 1720s, as noted in Chapter 2, Opoku Ware had sworn that he would never take up arms against the Akyem as long as Frimpon lived. If in 1740 he was at the point of going to war against the Akyem, then Frimpon Manso must have died about that time. Frimpon's demise had obviously absolved him from the promise made in the 1720s. Thirdly, the Akyem themselves leave us in no doubt; they feverishly and frantically made preparations against Asante from 1740. From the Danes alone they bought 6,000 lbs. of gun-powder, several thousands of flint, and 6,800 ankers of Flensborger brandy.[105] It is reasonable to assume that they must have also bought hundreds of Dane guns.

The tension with Asante dated back to the very beginning of the Akyem ascendancy. In spite of Opoku Ware's promise just referred to, rumours of impending Asante invasion of the two Akyem states were prevalent in 1730, 1731, 1734, and 1737. It was perhaps proof of the strong influence which the personality of Frimpon exercised on the Asante court that war did not break out between the Akyem and Asante earlier than 1740. Part of the credit must go to the Asante monarch: no matter what, Asantehene Opoku Ware was determined to make good his promise to the Kotokuhene.

It must have been a painful determination, for the ascendancy of the Akyem on the whole seems to have caused considerable unease at the Asante court. The story is told that while he had great respect for Frimpon Manso, the Asantehene was inclined to regard Okyenhene Baa Kwante as a man of poor qualities, at least when Baa was a prince,[106] The logic is that Baa, as King was not expected by Asante to achieve imperial status and thereby be at par with the Asantehene.

At any rate Asante had some grievances and grudges against Abuakwa and Kotoku. One was the final outcome of the Nyanoase War. King Opoku Ware is said to have been of the view that the Akyem had not been fair to the Akwamu ruling lineage, by depriving it of its pre-1730 kingdom. Consequent to this view Opoku Ware reportedly cherished the hope of one day restoring the Akwamu rulers to their Nyanoase home.[107] The Asante government was also not happy with the Akyem for often supporting and sympathising with Wassahene Ntsiful, a rebel vassal.[108] Moreover, the Asante government regarded the Akyem states as a barrier to Asante communications with the eastern sector of the Gold Coast, and was also envious of the Akyem rulers as holders of "the Notes" for the forts and castles on the Ga-Adangbe coast.[109] Finally, it appears that the Dutch secretly instigated Asante against Abuakwa and Kotoku.[110] As early as 1734 the Akyem grumbled that the Dutch were "the friends of Poko".[111] The charge of Dutch intrigues is reinforced by the fact that in 1741 when it became clear that there was going to be war between the Akyem and Asante, the Dutch tried to persuade the Ga not to side with the Akyem.[112]

The 1742–1743 Akyem-Asante War

The war broke out in 1742. The immediate cause was Asante bellicosity. Apau (or Apaw) succeeded to the Kotoku stool[113] in 1740. Not long after his accession the Asantehene sent to tell him and Abuakwahene Baa Kwante that Asante forces would soon descend on them.[114] It is possible that in sending the message Opoku Ware expected the two Akyem rulers to get frightened and voluntarily sue for peace, accept vassalage, and thereby avoid war. The Akyem chose to fight.[115] Throughout 1741 they continued the war preparations which they had started in 1740.[116] Both the Kotoku and the Abuakwa were involved in the war, not the latter alone as is sometimes suggested.[117]

Battle was joined in early 1742, with the Asante carrying the war to the Akyem. It appears that the Asante were determined to make amends to their 1717–1718 debacle. They took the field with a 20,000-strong force under the command of a Commander-in-Chief whom Romer called "Ursue Afrie" (ie. Owusu Afriyie).[118] The Akyem countered with a much greater force: aside from 10,000 apiece from Abuakwa and Kotoku, contingents are said to have joined the Akyem from Ada, Akuapem, and Dutch Accra.[119] Kwawu too may have sent a contingent to assist the Akyem who were their overlords. The Akyem were allegedly confident of success.[120]

The two sides keenly contested the war. Opinion is divided on the number of battles fought. Romer says there were three.[121] Reindorf on the other hand claims that only two battles took place.[122] Contemporary evidence available to the present author is silent on this subject.

By March 1742 the Akyem had been defeated.[123] They sustained heavy and tragic losses. Kotokuhene Apau was killed, and so was Prince Owusu Akyem of Abuakwa; Okyenhene Baa Kwante and several other Akyem leaders, when they saw that the war was lost, committed suicide; and about ten thousand of the Akyem were taken captive, among whom were Asare, an Abuakwa Prince, and Broni, A Kotoku royal.[124] Chief Darko of Dutch' Accra lost his life: the Akwamu were said to have captured and beheaded him.[125] The sources consulted are silent on Asante losses. Whatever they were, the fact was that at long last Asante military might, brutally dented in 1717–1718, prevailed over the Akyem in 1742.

The Akyem troops who escaped death and capture blamed their defeat on the defectiveness of the Dane guns which they had used in the war. The faulty firearms may have indeed contributed to the defeat of the Akyem be-

Akyem Ascendancy in the East 1728–1744

cause on receiving the complaint the Danes examined the guns and actually found them to be defective.[126] All the same it must be conceded that the greater factor was the effectiveness of the Asante military machine.

Defeat was quite disheartening. But the Akyem did not allow it to deflate their spirits to the point of immediate submission to the Asante. For the next two years they stubbornly resisted the Asante invading force by resorting to guerrilla warfare. General Owusu Afriyie found it difficult to deal with this new development, forcing Asantehene Opoku Ware I to take the initiative to resolve the stalemate. He reportedly sent to inform both the Abuakwa and the Kotoku of his willingness to live peaceably with them provided

(i) they would enstool the captive Akyem princes, Asare and Broni as Okyenhene and Kotokuhene respectively;
(ii) They would ensure safety to Asante traders who would pass through Akyem territories to and from the Ga-Adangbe coast;
(iii) they would surrender to Kumasi "the Notes" for the forts, and castles and lodges on the Ga and the Adangbe coasts;
(iv) they would send accredited representatives to Kumasi to formally negotiate with the Asante government.[127]

The Asante monarch was anxious to reach a peace agreement with Abuakwa and Kotoku because he needed a "free passage for his subjects and traders through the Akim countries to Accra, as that was more accessible to him than Elmina".[128]

Abuakwa and Kotoku reacted differently to the terms of peace offered by Asante. Kotoku accepted them. They may have taken this decision under severe psychological pressure. They were much nearer to Asante and therefore more likely to bear the brunt of the military pressure from Asante During the two years of resistance between 1742 and 1744, the ruling house was virtually homeless as they had to keep shifting bases to avoid further disasters at the hands of Asante. The evidence shows that after the 1742 defeat they enstooled Ampem as the new Kotokuhene.[129] But when they accepted the peace terms which Asante proffered, they replaced Ampem with Broni.[130] In contrast, the Abuakwa rejected the offer, leaving Asantehene Opoku Ware in no doubt as to their determination to pursue the path of resistance.[131]

But no matter what choice each of them made, whether submission or resistance, the 1742 defeat brought the Akyem hegemony in eastern Gold Coast to an end. All their former subject states turned to Asante as the new overlord; nor were the European companies slow in according Asante that recognition, for they quickly started paying their groundrents to the Asantehene.[132]

Summary

After defeating Akwamu in 1730 and Agona and eastern Fante in 1738, Akyem Abuakwa and Akyem Kotoku stood on a proud pinnacle of imperial power and prestige. Success also conferred economic prosperity on them. But this achievement created its own problems. They had the ability to, and did, solve many of them. But in 1742 when they were called upon to militarily solve the perennial problem of tension with Asante, they were found wanting. By their failure they lost an empire that was barely ten years old.

NOTES AND REFERENCES

1. Fynn, J. K., 1971. *Asante and its Neighbours 1700–1807*, NUP, Longman Group Ltd., London, pp. 63–67.
2. Roem (Apam) to Elmina Castle (EC), 10 January 1727, *NBKG* 94.
3. Wilks, I. *Akwamu 1650–1750*, MA Thesis, Bangor, 1959, p.80.
4. Van Dyke (Accra) to EC, 13 March 1716, *NBKG* 82.
5. Hendrix (Apam) to EC, 26 March 1716, *NBKG* 82.
6. Romer, *Tilforladlig* pp. 106, & 121–122; Norregaard, G., 1966. *Danish Settlements in West Africa 1658–1850*, Boston University Press, Boston, pp. 57–59 & 65–75.
7. Phal (CCO) to Copenhagen, 14 April 1727 Vgk.122; de la Planque (Accra) to EC, 30 July & 13 September 1729, *NBKG* 95. Wilks, *Akwamu 1650–1750*, pp. 89–90.
8. The Akuapem rebellion is discussed fully by Kwamena-Poh. Cf his *Government and Politics*, Chapter 1.
9. De la Planque (Accra) to EC, 13 September 1729, *NBKG* 95; Phal (CCO) to Copenhagen, 30 August 1730, Waroe (CCO) to EC, 30 August 1730, Vgk 122.
10. Romer, *Tilforladlig*, p.151.
11. Gawron (Apam) to EC, 6 October 1729, *NBKG* 95, Reindorf, *The History of the Gold Coast*, p.63, calls the Gomoahene Kusa Adu. It is clear that friendly ties existed between Akwamu and Gomoa.
12. Blittersdorf (Accra) to Director-General Pranger (EC), 3 September; Gawron (Apam) to Pranger, 17 September 1730, *NBKG* 97.
13. Wilks, *Akwamu 1650–1750*, p.92.
14. De la Planque (Accra) to EC, 13 & 21 September 1729, *NBKG* 95.
15. Wilks, *Akwamu 1650–1750*, pp. 109–110.
16. De la Planque (Accra) to EC, 10 October 1729, *NBKG* 95
17. Gawron (Accra) to EC, as noted in EC Journal: entry 11 August, 1730 .
18. Gawron's Report, as noted in EC Journal: entry 17 September 1730, *NBKG* 97.
19. Quoted in EC Journal: entry 21 September 1730, *NBKG* 97.
20. The Tradition of Kyebi, as told Missionary Stromberg, cf his letter from Kyebi to Basel, 24 January 1863, BMA-PJA; AAT: Asafo (1925/6); Kwamena-Poh, *Government and Politics*, pp. 37–38.
21. Kea, R. A., 1969. "Akwamu-Anlo Relations 1730–1813", in *THSG*, Vol. X, pp. 29–64.
22. Anonymous, *Twi Kasamu Akuapem ne Eho Nsem anase Abasem*, Akropon, 1913;

Akuffo, Ahemfie, p.5; Wilks in Vansina, J., etc. (Ed.), 1964. *The Historian in Tropical Africa,* OUP, Oxford, p.405; AAT: Kyebi (1968/9); Kwamena-Poh, *Government and Politics,* pp. 45–49.

23. Director-General Pranger (EC) to Blittersdorf (Accra), 13 December 1730, *NBKG* 97.
24. Pranger to da la Planque (Accra), 1 November 1730, *NBKG* 97.
25. This subject has generated debate among scholars. Wilks (in Vansina, etc. *Op. cit.*) contends that an organized state existed in pre-1730 Akuapem. Kwamena-Poh *Government and Politics,* opines that it was the Abuakwa who created Akuapem as a unitary state. The present author is of the same view as Kwamena-Poh.
26. Romer, *Tilforladlig,* p.158.
27. De la Planque & Blittersdorf (Accra) to EC., 30 October 1730, *NBKG* 97; Waroe (CCO) to Copenhagen, 24 & 28 December 1730 & 27 September 1731 Vgk. 122; Minutes of Council Meeting, EC., 15 May 1732, *NBKG* 98; Romer, *Tilforladlig,* p.158; Biorn, *Beretning,* p.208. Biorn and Romer as well as Abuakwa traditional historians claim that Owusu Akyem was one of the eighteenth century Abuakwa rulers. This is not correct, Romer appears to have been the first observer to create this impression. He was confused on the subject. Sometimes he referred to Owusu Akyem as heir to Baa Kwante (cf. *Op. cit* p.168) at others, as King. Reindorf (op.cit 348) and Danquah (*Akan Law,* Appx.D) seem to have based their views on Romer's
28. Romer, *Tilforladlig,* p.161.
29. AKT: Adoagyiri (1968/9).
30. Norregaard, *Danish Settlements,* p.80; Letters from CCO to Copenhagen, dd. 24 April 1733 & 30 April 1734 VGK., cited by Fynn, J. K. (Asante and Akyem Relations 1700–1831", in *Institute of African Studies Research Review,* vol.9 no.1, 1973 (Legon), p.69, n.45.
31. Romer, *Tilforladlig,* p.213.
32. Romer, *Op. cit.,* p.158; Norregaard, *Op. cit.,* p.97.
33. Kuijl (Accra) to EC, 4 & 19 December 1740, Breve og Papieren van der Kust van Guinea (BPKG) 1740–1741.
34. Norregaard, *Danish Settlements,* p.208.
35. Rodney, Walter, 1969, "Gold and Slaves on the Gold Coast", in *THSG,* Vol. X, pp. 13–38.
36. Pranger & Council (EC) to Amsterdam, I March 1731, Furley Collection Legon.
37. Romer, *Tilforladlig,* p. 138.
38. Akinjogbin, I. A., 1967. *Dahomey and Its Neighbours 1708–1818,* CUP, p.24, Politically the ruler of Dahomey, Agaja, was at loggerheads with the Dutch, who were the foremost European traders on the Dahomey coast.
39. Romer, *Tilforladlig,* p.167.
40. Danquah, *Akim Abuakwa Handbook,* p.8.
41. Romer, *Tilforladlig,* p.197.
42. Romer, *Op.cit.,* p.197.
43. *Ibid.*
44. Bosman, *Description,* p.78.
45. Romer, *Tilforladlig,* p.164.
46. *Atlas de l'Asie at l'Afrique 1764,* cited by Macdonald, G., *The Gold Coast Past and Present,* p.121, footnote.
47. Dutch Reports in March 1714, Furley Collection.
48. Romer, *Tilforladlig,* p.164.
49. Romer, *Op.cit.,* p.165.

50. Kuijl (Accra) to Director-General Baron des Bordes (EC), 13 September 1741, *NBKG* 105.
51. Romer, *Tilforladlig*, pp. 165–166.
52. *Ibid.*, p.171.
53. For a more detailed Akwamu provincial administration see Kea, R. A. *Trade, State Formation and Warfare on the Gold Coast 1600–1826*, Ph.D. University of London 1974 (unpublished), especially, pp. 223–275.
54. De la Planque (Accra) to EC., 10 November 1730, *NBKG* 97.
55. Pranger (EC) to de la Planque & Blittersdorf (Accra), 17 November 1730, *NBKG* 97; also quoted in Fynn, *Asante*, p.41.
56. Wilks, *Akwamu 1650–1750*, p.115.
57. Elet (Accra) to EC, 3 December 1731; EC. Journal: entry 9 December 1731, *NBKG* 97.
58. AAT: Asafo & Maase (1925/6); Ameyaw, K., *Asamankese Tradition*, IAS Acc.No.KAG/4 & *Akwatia Tradition*, IAS Acc.KAG/2, Legon, 1963.
59. De la Planque & Blittersdorf (Accra) to EC, quoted in EC Journal: entry 30 October 1730 *NBKG* 97. *Contre de terre* was the Portuguese name for a type of beads (cf. Bosman, *Description*).
60. Director-General Pranger (EC) to de la Planque (Accra), 1 November 1730, *NBKG* 97.
61. "The Note" was a document which the authorities of a castle or fort or lodge gave to an African ruler owning the land on which such structures were built. It entitled the African ruler to collect groundrent for the structure.
62. Minutes of Council meeting (EC), 15 May 1732, *NBKG* 98.
63. Norregaard discusses this subject: cf. *Danish Settlements*, pp.97–99
64. E. N. Boris (CCO) to Copenhagen, 6 July 1736 VgK 123, Breve og dokumenter fra Guinea 1732–1745.
65. Camper (Accra) to EC., 8 May 1737, *NBKG* 102.
66. This may be the Chief whom Reindorf refers to as Darko Panyin of Otu Street of Dutch Accra, cf. *The History of the Gold Coast*, p.80.
67. Des Bordes's *Journal: de Voyage au Accra*: entry 22 July 1737, *NBKG* 190.
68. Des Bordes's Journal: entry 21 July 1737, *NBKG* 190.
69. This subject is fully discussed on p.62.
70. Augier (Accra) to EC., 28 October 1734, *NBKG* 101.
71. Daaku, K. Y., 1965. "The European Traders and the General States 1630–1720", in *THSG*, Vol.III, pp. 11–23.
72. Des Bordes *Journal de Voyage au Accra*.
73. Des Bordes' Journal
74. *Ibid.*
75. Romer, *Tilforladlig*, p.181; Reindorf, *The History of the Gold Coast*, p.80.
76. Norregaard, *Danish Settlements*, p.98.
77. Starckenburg (Accra) to EC., 11 December; EC. Journal: entry 16 December; Resolution of Brummer, Janse & Starckenburg (Accra) 23 December; Starckenburg to EC., 23 December; des Bordes (EC) to Raams (Shama), 28 December; Raams to des Bordes, 27 December; EC. Journal: entry 29 December 1737, *NBKG* 103.
78. Starckenburg (Accra) to EC., 16 January 1738, *NBKG* 103.
79. Starckenburg to EC., 29 January & 15 February; EC Journal: entry 22 February; Resolution of Council, Fort Gevecoeur, quoted in EC. Journal: entry 6 March; des Bordes

(EC) to Accra, 8 March 1738, *NBKG* 103.
80. Norregaard, *Danish Settlement*, p.98.
81. Starckenburg to EC., 11 December 1737 *NBKG* 103.
82. Starckenburg to EC, 26 February 1738; EC. Journal: entry 7 April 1738 *NBKG* 103.
83. Starckenburg to EC., 28 March; EC. Journal: entry April 1838, *NBKG* 103.
84. Starckenburg to EC, 11 June 1738; Starckenburg (Tema) to EC, 10 July 1738 *NBKG* 103.
85. *Ibid.*
86. Kuijl (Accra) to EC., 4 & 19 December 1740, copies in *Breve og Pepieren van der Kust van Guinea, (BPKG)* 1740–1741.
87. Director-General Pranger (EC) to Amsterdam, 3 April 1732, Furley Collection, Balme Library, Legon.
88. Campier (Accra) to EC, 16 & 22 September 1736, *NBKG* 101; Starckenburg (Accra) to EC. noted in EC Journal: entry 5 March 1738 *NBKG* 103.
89. Council Minutes, EC, 10 July 1733; EC. Journal: entry 14 July 1733, *NBKG* 99.
90. Pranger (Accra) to EC, 3 August; EC. Journal: entry 6 August 1733, *NBKG* 99.
91. Starckenburg (Accra) to EC., 7 October 1738, *NBKG* 103.
92. Waroe & Council, CCO, to Copenhagen, 25 March 1731, VgK 122; Romer, *Tilforladlig*, p.169.
93. "From" (Vroom), Keta, to EC., 10 June 1737, *NBKG* 103.
94. *Ibid.*
95. Akinjogbin, *Dahomey*, p.106.
96. Director-General des Bordes (Accra) to EC, 21 July 1737.
97. Blittersdorf (Accra) to EC, 5 September 1730; Gawron (Apam) to EC, noted in EC. Journal: entry 17 September 1737, *NBKG* 97.
98. Blittersdorf (Accra) to EC, 14 December 1730, *NBKG* 97.
99. *Ibid.*
100. Roems (Senya Breku) to EC, noted in EC Journal: entry 4 February 1732, *NBKG* 98.
101. Daaku, K. Y., *Assin Twifo Tradition*, p.7; cf, also AAT: Asafo, which refers to Oduro Tsibo wrongly as Denkyerahene.
102. Kuijl (Accra) to EC., 15 & 20 September 1738; Starckenbury to EC., 20 September & 7 October 1738, *NBKG* 103.
103. Romer, *Tilforladlig*, p.181; Reindorf, *The History of the Gold Coast*, p.80.
104. Green (Accra) to EC., 8 April; Smith, A.L. (Mouree) to EC, 19 October; EC. Journal: entries 26 April & 19 October 1940, *NBKG* 104, Norregaard, *Danish Settlements*, p.101, Fynn, *Asante*, p.73.
105. Boris (CCO) to Copenhagen, 25 May 1740 VgK. Fynn, citing a Dutch source, says that Frimpon Manso died in 1741. Cf *Asante*, p.74 note 4. His source is "*NBKG.* 85, Kuijl, Accra, 5 and 9 December 1741".
106. Romer, *Tilforladlig*, p.167.
107. Richard Graves (CCC) to RAC, 3 April 1742, T 70/1515, PRO.
108. Director-General Pranger (EC) to Blittersdorf (Accra), 13 December 1730, *NBKG* 97.
109. Romer, *Tilforladlig*, pp.188–189.
110. Norregaard, *Danish Settlement*, p.101.
111. Kuijl (Accra) to EC., 5 December 1741, *NBKG* 105.
112. Kuijl (Accra) to EC., 5 December 1741, *NBKG* 105.
113. Norregaard, *Danish Settlement*, p.102; Fynn, Asante, p.74, Reindorf, *The History of*

the Gold Coast, p.80, says that the immediate successor to Frimpon Manso was Ampem.
114. Romer, *Tilforladlig,* p.182.
115. *Ibid.*
116. Kuijl (Accra) to EC., 13 & 26 September and 4 & 5 December 1741, *NBKG* 105.
117. Wilks, "The Mossi and Akan States 1500–1800", in Ajayi & Crowder (Eds), *History of West Africa,* Vol.1, p.446.
118. Romer, *Tilforladlig,* p.185.
119. *Ibid,* pp.182–183; Kuijl (Accra) to EC, 5 December 1741, *NBKG* 105.
120. Kuijl (Accra) to EC, 4 & 5 December 1741, *NBKG* 105.
121. Romer, *Tilforladlig,* pp. 183–4.
122. Reindorf, *The History of the Gold Coast,* p.81.
123. Kuijl (Accra) to EC., 18 March, Minutes of Council Meeting (EC), 22 March; Journal of Raems & Verscheuren on a Journey to Accra: entries 25 March & 4 April 1742, *NBKG* 106; Governor & Council (CCO) to Copenhagen, 19 March 1742, VgK 123; Richard Graves (CCC) to RAC, 3 April 1742, T 70/1515; Norregaard, *Danish Settlements,* p.102, Fynn, *Asante,* p.74.
124. Romer, *Tilforladlig,* pp. 183–185.
125. Janson (Apam) to Kuijl (Accra) n.d., Fynn, *Asante,* p.74.
126. Romer, *Tilforladlig,* p.213.
127. *Ibid.,* pp. 188–189.
128. Romer, *Tilforladlig,* pp. 187–189.
129. Reindorf, *The History of the Gold Coast,* p.80; Fynn, *Asante,* p.75.
130. *Ibid.*
131. The Abuakwa resistance is fully discussed in Chapter 4.
132. Fynn, *Asante,* p.75, The Danes started to pay in May 1742.

Chapter 4

THE FORTY YEARS WAR 1744–1784

The 1742 debacle together with the subsequent unsuccessful two-year resistance brought home to Abuakwa and Kotoku the reality of Asante power. There is the view, first expressed in the early 1820s and repeated more recently, that by 1750 all Akyem had submitted to Asante imperial domination.[1] The claim is not wholly correct. The Kotoku indeed yielded to Asante even before the 1750s, as pointed out in Chapter 3. But the Abuakwa, under Pobi (1742–1765) and Obirikoran (1765–1784), resisted Asante power[2] up to 1783.

Reasons for the Kotoku Submission

Geography and leadership had much to do with the contrasting positions of the two Akyem states. As indicated in the previous chapter, proximity to Asante militated against the desire and ability of the Kotoku to resist Asante with any appreciable effect. Consequently in or about 1744 when Asante took the initiative to offer peace terms,[3] Kotoku accepted them, and accordingly submitted to Kumasi.

It must have been after the submission that Asante political thinkers and war strategists recommended the unprecedented measure of forcing the Kotoku to remove their capital, Oda, on the east bank of river Pra and relocate it at Dampon on the west bank.[4] The relocation of Oda deprived the Kotoku of the Pra as a barrier to, and a bastion of defence against, Asante.[5] Besides, the measure pulled the Kotoku ruling house much nearer to metropolitan Asante. That gave the Asante government a much easier access to Kotoku, and thereby increased the prospects of closer and more constant Kumasi surveillance on political climate in Kotoku. The slightest indication of recalcitrance and restiveness there could easily and quickly bring a punitive armed expedition from Asante, as it was to happen in 1781.[6]

There is an indication that the Kotoku experienced an even more subtle transplantation weapon against them, as Asantehene Opoku Ware I was reported to have given the name "Asante-Akyem" to them.[7] If the assertion is true, then it suggests an Asante policy aimed at making the Kotoku forget themselves as Akyem. Wilks may well be correct in saying that Kotoku was actually incorporated into Asante and exempted from paying tribute to Kumasi.[8] These measures taken by Asante were so effective that between 1744 and 1783 when Abuakwa also submitted to Asante, Kotoku staged only one revolt against Asante. That was in 1781 and it was not successful.[9]

It is therefore to be wondered why Asante, as later events would show, ultimately failed in its bid to absorb Kotoku. It is all the more surprising because besides geographical proximity and the overall Kotoku inclination to be loyal, several other factors favoured the course of integration between Kotoku and Asante. In language, culture, manners, religious outlook, ethnic affinity as well as social and political systems, the Kotoku were every bit akin to the Asante. Indeed, to varying degrees, others such as the Abuakwa, Kwawu, Assin, Twifo, Denkyira, Wassa, Akuapim (The Twi section), Agona, Fante, Ahanta, and the Nzima were all akin to the Asante. The government in Kumasi should therefore have found it fairly easy to form all these peoples into one large Akan (Twi) kingdom with the Asantehene as the head.

It appears that Asante political thinkers did not have the ability to conceive such a scenario. Excellent at military conquests, the Asante of the eighteenth and nineteenth centuries were incapable of forging a good policy on provincial administration with close integration of all conquered territories as a desirable and ultimate goal.[10] Asante just limited itself to the exaction of tributes from, and imposition of taxes on, conquered states and peoples. This limitation, together with its tendency to be harsh in the exaction of vassal obligations, often created in conquered states a disposition for rebellion, especially those of them fortunate enough to be further removed from metropolitan Asante, and still fortunate enough to have leaders with indomitable spirit. Akyem Abuakwa had these two advantages.

Pobi's Resistance

Situated to the south of Kotoku, Abuakwa by that very fact was further removed from Asante. Besides, Kotoku served as a buffer between her and Asante. Banso also looked to Oda as an unfailing source of military as well as political intelligence on events in Asante.[11]

Abuakwa's greater fortune, however, lay in the enstoolment of two daring and dynamic rulers after 1742. The first of these was Pobi Asomani. He ascended the Abuakwa stool after Baa Kwante. Pobi soon evinced the same fighting and forceful spirit as had characterized Prince Owusu Akyem. He and the Kotoku leadership together suffered defeats at the hands of Asante in 1743-1744. But unlike the Kotoku leaders, he refused to give in. To continue his resistance he adopted two major strategies: contraction of alliances with others who had axes to grind against Asante and the adoption of guerrilla warfare. Probably he and his forces were that section of the Akyem who, after the March, 1742 disaster, were reported to have fled "eastwards".[12] Flight gave him a breathing space to reorganize his forces. He gave battle to the invading Asante army a month later and suffered his first defeat as Okyenhene.[13] It was after this battle that the Asante managed to get through to Ga-Adangbe to formally announce their victory over the Akyem. But opinion on the coast in July 1742 was that there would be more fighting between the Akyem and Asante.[14] Asante inability to gain access again to the Accra coast until mid-1743[15] suggests continued Abuakwa and Kotoku resistance till the latter submitted to Asante in 1744.

Distraction of Asante Attention

The cause of Pobi was well served by problems which confronted Asante elsewhere. For example the Sefwi, to the north-west of Asante, invaded and ransacked Kumasi while the Asante army was still campaigning in Akyem; Opoku Ware I, had to double-march part of his forces back home to deal with the Sehwi (ie. Sefwi).[16] The Dagomba, to the north-east, were restive and eventually revolted in 1744.[17] Probably it was these other problems which partly compelled the Asante monarchy to offer the peace terms which Kotoku accepted and Abuakwa rejected.

The peace move was all the more necessary for Asante to make because the war with Abuakwa and Kotoku had led to strained relations between her and the Fante. Greed and cheating had actuated the Fante in 1742 to help themselves to booty from the defeated Akyem even though they were no allies of Asante.[18] Besides, the Fante executed an Asante Chief who fell into their hands.[19] Asante turned on Fante.

Pobi Adopts Guerrilla Tactics

The diversion of Asante attention to Fante and other problems gave the Abuakwa a much needed respite to reorganize themselves. Up to 1746 the ruling house did not have a permanent base, though it generally preferred to crouch on what the Danes described as "the hill country".[20] "The hill country" could be a reference to Akuapem, Krobo or Kwawu or the hilly parts of Akyem Abuakwa itself especially the Begoro District. The last named was the most likely place a defeated Abuakwa ruler would immediately flee to for safety. The terrain was fairly impregnable; it would not be easy for an enemy to storm. The Abuakwa ruler must have used it as a base from which he organized his guerrilla warfare against Asante.

The Abuakwa resistance was hugely successful. The success can be measured in several ways. The failure of the Asante to restore the Voltaic Akwamu to their pre-1730 inheritance was one yardstick. It will be recalled that the restoration had been one of the aims of Asantehene Opoku Ware I, in going to war against the Akyem in 1742. Owing to the effectiveness of the Abuakwa resistance Asante was never able to realize this goal. Instead the

Asantehene had to accept the *fait accompli* and rather treat Voltaic Akwamuhene Akonnor Kuma as a Divisional Chief and his collector of the groundrents for the forts, castles and lodges on the Ga and the Adangbe coasts.[21] That Akonnor was made to sign a treaty with the European companies can also be regarded as proof of the Abuakwa resistance. The fact of the matter was that the Abuakwa effectively blocked Asante access to the eastern sector of the coast. Even the Akwamu themselves, from their trans-Volta base, found it extremely difficult to get through to the Ga district. Pobi actually did not spare the Akwamu on both sides of the Volta. In 1747, he ruthlessly suppressed a revolt in Old Akwamu.[22] He also invaded New or Voltaic Akwamu, forcing some of its inhabitants to seek safety on Volta islands.[23] Thus the Abuakwa did not allow Asante to resuscitate the Akwamu; rather they wreaked vengeance on what was left of Akwamu on both sides of the Volta.

Pobi Incorporates Toprefu into Abuakwa

The attack on New Akwamu was a logical outcome of the crouching of the Abuakwa ruling house on the Begoro hills. The sojourn there enabled the Abuakwa rulers to subdue the area and incorporate it into the Abuakwa kingdom. Prior to the advent of the Abuakwa the area was the home of the Gyakiti who now live on the west bank of the lower Volta, almost opposite the Akwamu State today. The Gyakiti recall that their ancestral home was originally "Toprefu", as they call the Begoro district. They attribute their emigration from the area to military pressures from the Abuakwa who had been defeated by the Asante and had fled to the Osino neighbourhood.[24] The Gyakiti tradition finds confirmation from that of Begoro which names Topremanso, Ketekraa, Besease, Boso, Bosomfi, Akwaawa, Meri, Twewa and Suproso as being among the Gyakiti communities whom the Abuakwa drove out of the Begoro area.[25]

Neither tradition states exactly or roughly when the Abuakwa subjugated the area. The event may well be dated to the 1740s. "Toprefu" or the Begoro district was probably the hill country to which, according to the Danes in 1746, a section of the Akyem fled after their defeat in 1742.[26] The permanent residence of the Fanteakwa Asona clan of Begoro in the district may have begun at about this time. Perhaps it was the Abuakwa monarchy which asked them to settle there and lord it over the Gyakiti who did not emigrate to the west side of the lower Volta.

Beginnings of an Eastern Sector Alliance

Pobi did more than incorporate Toprefu into Abuakwa. He widened his influence by effecting alliances with Akuapem and Krobo. The main objective of the pact was to institute an economic sanction against Asante through a collective blockade of the trade routes against that power. The closure proved very effective, to the great discomfiture of the pro-Asante Dutch. In May 1746 the Dutch in the Gold Coast bitterly complained to their employers in Holland that they had diligently done everything in their power to get the blocked routes open to enable them to send gifts to the Asantehene, but had not been successful because the Akyem (Abuakwa), the Krobo and the Akwapem would not open them.[27] The Danes also noted the closure of the routes against Asante by the Abuakwa-led eastern alliance.[28] Up to 1749 the blockade of the eastern trade routes by the tripartite alliance against them obliged Asante traders and travellers bound for the Ga and the Adangbe coast to direct their course first to Kwawu, descend the hills to reach the Afram plains, cross the Volta to get to Voltaic Akwamu and from there gingerly work their way to the coast under Akwamu escorts and guides.[29] In fact Asantehene Opoku Ware died in 1750 without being able to subdue Akyem Abuakwa, let alone restore the Akwamu ruling house to their pre-1730 Nyanoase Kingdom. Besides, the report in that year said that the Asante had not had access to the Ga and Adangbe coasts because of "the Akim and Krobo [and Akuapem] who stay in large numbers between Quamboe and the beach".[30] Anxiety continually gripped both Africans and Europeans here as they wondered when "the Akim Caboceer Pobbie" would open the trade routes for "the Ashantees and the Quamboe people".[31]

Emergence of a Western Sector Alliance

By 1750 a western counterpart to the eastern alliance had also emerged. It embraced the Fante Confederate states, Denkyira, Twifo, Wassa and most likely the Assin. At least the Fante, Denkyira and the Wassa all had axes to grind against Asante.[32] Since the 1698–1701 War, there had not been any real peace between Denkyira and Asante. And hostility had always been the main feature of Wassa-Asante relations since 1721 when Asante aggression forced the Wassa ruling lineage to abandon their country.[33] In 1730–1731, this dynasty vainly sought refuge with the Akyem Kotoku.[34] The Kotoku could not help because this was the time when they were still busy dealing with the aftermath of the Nyanoase War. From then on the lineage moved from place to place until the 1740s when the Fante gave them refuge.[35]

In showing overt hospitality to the Wassa, the Fante had the ulterior motive of organizing them and the others already mentioned, into an alliance against Asante. Like the eastern pact the western alliance was essentially defensive: its aim was to deny Asante access to the European trade on the west coast and thereby prevent her from acquiring firearms and other war materials from that part of the Gold Coast.[36]

In 1748 the Asante felt that the western pact was the weaker of the two alliances. They decided to storm and smash it. But they failed. By 1751 the western blockade was still in place, obliging all the main European companies, Danish, Dutch and English, to lament the absence of the Asante from the western sector trade "for the past seven years" owing to what they described as quarrels with Wassa.[37]

Other Objectives of Pobi

In 1750 the Dutch attempted to subvert the eastern alliance. They resorted to diplomacy to try and wean Akuapem and Krobo away from Abuakwa. Pobi got wind of the Dutch move and quickly sent a 5,000-strong force to the Ga-Adangbe area to strengthen the blockade of the routes there against both Asante and Akwamu.[38]

Essentially Pobi's 'eastern' policy was political, but it had an economic dimension. The policy was partly in response to the dynamics of trade in eastern Gold Coast. Before 1730 the Akwamu rulers had been the pillars and promoters of the slave trade here, with Accra serving as the chief market. Their defeat and emigration to the trans-Volta in the early 1730s drastically reduced the volume of the trade in the area, judging from the complaints of all the European trading companies operating here. The situation worsened with the collapse of the Akyem ascendancy in 1742 owing to what Norregaard refers to as "the unsettled political situation"[39] in this part of the Gold Coast. The trade's centre of gravity shifted to the east of the Volta, apparently in response partly to the founding of New Akwamu. In the late 1730s and in the 1740s Krepi emerged as the most prolific source of slaves in the Gold Coast; hence the practice of the Akyem Abuakwa raiding the lower Volta basin for slaves during those decades.[40] The general rivalry among the European companies to establish themselves east of Accra, as shown in Chapter 3, was equally in response to the shifting of the slave trade eastwards as well as to its lucrativity. The heavy military presence of the Akyem Abuakwa in the Ga and Adangbe districts and their blockade of the trade routes in these areas were meant to destroy the economic opportunity which the shift in the slave trade to the east of Accra might have created for the New Akwamu and their Asante masters.

The effectiveness of the southern economic sanction against Asante should have encouraged the allies, both in the east and the west, to consider taking the offensive against that power. Such a move stood a good chance of succeeding during 1750–1751 because Asante then was in disarray. The kingdom was in the throes of a bitter succession dispute which had followed the death of Opoku Ware. The dispute divided the kingdom into two opposing factions, one supporting the candidature of Darko and the other that of Kusi Obodum.[41] The dispute did not end until late 1751 when Kusi was enstooled as the new Asantehene.[42] As long as the dispute remained, Asante was ill-prepared to face any external enemy. And yet neither the Akyem Abuakwa nor any of the other southern states seems to have ever considered carrying war to the Asante.

The lack of aggression on the part of the southern states created in Asante a superiority complex. As soon as he was enstooled, Asantehene Kusi emphasized this by announcing his intention to invade Akyem Abuakwa within the next four months.[43] That was not an empty boast: he did attack Abuakwa in the first half of 1752 and defeated it.[44] But it must be pointed out that throughout the rest of the 1750s the Abuakwa continued to be in arms, also the eastern economic sanction remained in place, quite in contrast to developments in the west.

Disintegration of the Western Alliance

The 1752 Asante invasion of Abuakwa appears to have been a very limited operation the purpose of which was to deceive the western alliance, the real target of the 1752 Asante military move. Wassa had been in rebellion for decades, and the new Asantehene, Kusi, was determined to win his spurs by subduing it. In that same year of 1752 a 90,000 strong Asante army moved against Wassa.[45]

The slow but steady disintegration of the western alliance encouraged Asantehene Kusi to make the move against Wassa. The Fante were progressively growing weary of the western blockade which they themselves had greatly helped to institute against Asante. The sanction was back-firing against them because the exclusion of the Asante from the trade on the west coast meant a great loss of Fante middle-man profit. Perhaps they did not consider this aspect of the economic blockade when they were planning it. Now they were feeling the pinch.

Interestingly they tried to put the blame on the Wassa. In 1750 the Fante secretly sent to request Asante to attack the Wassa[46] who were then living on Fante soil. Asante could not seize this opportunity because Asantehene Opoku Ware had just died, followed by the Kusi-Darko succession dispute. However, the Asante obviously took note of the Fante request: the stage was potentially set for an Asante assault on the Wassa. Eventually the Asante attacked and defeated the Wassa in 1752.

Abuakwa Seeks Peace with Asante

The Asante victory over Wassa shook Okyenhene Pobi out of his continued defiance of that power. He found it necessary to change his stance. From 1753 he joined the Wassa and others in the west in a search for an honourable peace settlement with Asante. In December 1753 Thomas Malvil, the English governor at Cape Coast Castle, noted that the Akyem Abuakwa, Wassa and the Fante had sent to inform him that they intended to send ambassadors to Kumasi to negotiate peace with Kusi and that he Thomas Melvil should kindly let a representative of his accompany the joint Abuakwa-Wassa-Fante delegation.[47] The rationale behind the request was clearly that the presence of a representative of the Governor in the southern delegation would lend it weight and convince the Asante government of the sincerity of the peace seekers. It is possible that the suggestion to involve the English came from the Fante, who since 1730 had been in secret contact with Kumasi.

However, it must be pointed out that the initiative to seek peace with Asante partly, if not wholly, came from an Akyem Abuakwa citizen. The man was said to be a member of the Abuakwa royal house.

In August 1754 the English at Cape Coast Castle recorded the role of this Abuakwa royal thus:

> A near relation of Osu, formerly King of Akim [ie. Prince Owusu Akyem of Abuakwa] went to Ashantee without communicating his design to anyone. When he came before Quishee [ie. Kusi, the Asantehene] he told who he was, on which orders were given to chop off his head. But he very cooly told the King that if he had a passion for his head, he was welcome to it, only he wished he [Ashantehene] would give him time to tell what had carried him there, this was granted. I observe, said he, that for many years you on one side and Akim, Dinkera and Warsaw on the other have kept each other at bay, neither party choosing to fight, and yet you do not make peace. It is for this reason that I have come to know your terms [for peace], if I can be the means of reconciling all your differences, I shall esteem it the greatest action of my life. If I fail, you may dispose of my head as you please. Quishee and all present applauded the resolution and good intentions of the man. A treaty was immediately set on foot and concluded on their terms. The Ashantees are to recover 1600 oz. of gold, viz from Warsaw 800 oz. from Akim [Abuakwa] 400 oz. and from Dinkera 400 oz. Of this money the Warsaws have paid 400 oz, to the King's messengers now in the camp. The other moeity is to be paid when Say [ie. Osei], heir to the Stool or Throne . . . of Ashantee takes fetish to observe what has been concluded.[48]

Reaction on the coast at the prospect of a general peace settlement between the southern states and Asante was one of a big relief. The Dutch for example were happy that the Akyem Abuakwa in particular had agreed, at least in principle, to submit to Asante; they also hoped that eventual peace would soon enable trade to pick up again.[49]

Contrary to the European expectation, the peace price or possibly some other issue, became a subject of misunderstanding between the Abuakwa and the Asante government. The details are not clear, but the disagreement was acute enough to compel the Asante authorities to detain the Abuakwa negotiators for some time while rumours flew about that the two nations might fight.[50]

The Forty Years War 1744–1784

The Abuakwa were partly to blame for the hitch. As will be shown in due course, Okyenhene Pobi does not seem to have been genuinely interested in a peace settlement with Asante. At any rate it was not until 1757 that Abuakwa and Asante finally reached a peace settlement.[51] This peace pact had an immediate impact on trade in the eastern sector of the Gold Coast. Late in 1757 both Akyem and Asante traders turned up in large numbers on the Ga-Adangbe coast to do business with the European companies.[52]

Renewal of Abuakwa-Asante Tension

The peace settlement, however, proved to be shortlived. Within three years it had broken down and the parties were back to their pre-1757 positions. The Abuakwa were primarily responsible for the breakdown. Though an Abuakwa royal may have indeed initiated the peace moves of 1754–1757 the Abuakwa monarchy as a whole does not seem to have been genuinely interested in a lasting peace with Asante. Okyenhene Pobi merely exploited the 1757 peace settlement as a breathing space to re-rally his forces. This is suggested by his re-alignment with the Wassa by 1760.[53]

The Wassa too were not sincere in the peace matter. Even though Wassahene Enimil I paid half of the peace price of 800 oz. of gold which the Asante Government had demanded in 1757, he appears to have done so either under pressure from the Fante or to immediately ease the military pressure from Asante. Whatever his reason, on the advice of a warlord of his called Asare, he was reported to have refused to ratify the treaty.[54]

Between 1758 and 1759 the Fante made every effort to persuade the Wassahene to relax his hostile stance but to no avail. They found Enimil's stubborn attitude so irritating that they threatened to throw him out of Fante land.[55] Worse for Enimil, the Fante, at a confederal meeting held at Abora passed a resolution to inform the Asantehene of their anger with Enimil for his intransigence, and actually did inform Kumasi accordingly.[56] Thus by 1759 the Fante friendship and hospitality to their Wassa guests had virtually whittled away.[57] Ostracized by the Fante, Enimil stood in need of an allied support. Okyenhene Pobi supplied it. The two rulers had a common ground in their hatred for Asante.

Meanwhile, in the eastern parts of the Gold Coast Pobi poured some of his anger against Asante on the Akwamu on both sides of the Volta. In July, 1760, he ordered an attack on Old Akwamu. The objective of the assault was

(i) to punish that province for its restiveness, and
(ii) to round up all Asante subjects resident in or passing through that province.[58]

The assault was successful. Thus neither their own revolts nor Asante efforts could save the people of Old Akwamu. The province was indeed on its way to becoming incorporated into the Abuakwa state.[59]

Pobi Organizes a Broader-Based Southern Alliance

After the suppression of Old Akwamu, Pobi was now free enough to turn his attention to the question of forging stronger ties with all anti-Asante peoples from the west. He concentrated more on the Wassa, Twifo and the Denkyira, all of whom he won in 1760-1761.[60] Thus by 1761 the Okyenhene had brought into being a grand Southern Alliance whose membership included Abuakwa, Akuapem and Krobo in the east, Wassa, Twifo and Denkyira in the west. Pobi seems to have spread his tentacles beyond the Gold Coast. For it was about this time that the Oyo state of Dahomey, according to Dupuis, promised the Akyem, Kwawu and others military assistance in their conflict with Asante.[61] The promised Oyo help never materialized, for what reason it is not clear. Okyenhene Pobi may have also tried to wean Kwawu from Asante, for in 1758 the Kumasi authorities had complained that the Akyem Abuakwa and others had been trying to persuade the Kwawu and others such as the Assin to rebel against Asante.[62]

The Abuakwa-led southern alliance was more defensive than offensive. Its objective, like those of earlier southern groupings, was to tighten the already existing blockade of the trade routes against Asante. The alliance may have also served as a reply of its members to what they must have regarded as Fante treachery in siding with Asante. In terms of sanction the alliance was most successful, to the chagrin of the Dutch for example. As a reprisal the Dutch took a decision in 1760 not to sell firearms and other munitions of war to the Akyem Abuakwa, Wassa and Denkyira.[63] Asante itself fumed and threatened to punish Abuakwa,[64] the pivot of the Grand Southern Alliance. But it was all an empty boast on the part of Asante.

There is substance in the view that Asantehene Kusi Obodum was a mediocrity in statesmanship,[65] though some observers think otherwise.[66] The assertion is quite valid, at least in terms of his foreign policy towards the southern states. Between 1759 and 1760 rumours kept circulating that he would soon take the field against his enemies.[67] At one stage he actually sent to warn the English at Cape Coast and elsewhere in the west that he would take a serious view of it if they continued to sell guns to the Wassa, as they had allegedly been doing, because he was about to attack the Wassa.[68] The English treated the warning as a joke, saying that Asante under Kusi Obodum would never take up arms against the Wassa or any others in the south.

Abuakwa and Asante at War 1764–1765

Contrary to the English assertion just referred to, Asante took the field against Akyem Abuakwa in 1764. But the Asante army was not under the personal command of Kusi: the Juabenhene was the Commander. The present author has not found sufficient evidence on this war. The little evidence available indicates that Okyenhene Pobi and his forces did not fare well in the clash. For it said that "the residue of Akim" planned to emigrate across the Volta and seek protection with "Ashampoe, King of Popo".[70] "The residue of Akim" is a clear reference to the Abuakwa. However, in spite of defeat, Pobi and his subjects had no plans or intentions to abandon their country and migrate to Popo or any other part in trans-Volta. The 1764 encounter may have been a limited action in which Abuakwa lost a battle not the war. Subsequent developments point to this conclusion: the Abuakwa tightened the southern sanction against Asante. The result was that Asante traders could hardly have access to the coast trade between the mouth of river Tano in the west and the Volta estuary in the east, largely on account of the closure of the routes by Abuakwa and others. The general view on the coast during the 1764–1765 period was that Asante would never have easy access to the coast trade unless she first succeeded in smashing the Grand Southern Alliance.[71]

Disintegration of the Alliance

Luckily for Asante, the situation was not to remain so for long. Since 1763, signs had appeared pointing to the imminent collapse of the grand southern alliance. Strains and stresses had set in as a result of the private policies of Denkyira and Akyem Abuakwa.

In 1764, a dispute arose between Abuakwa and Wassa over what Wassahene Enimil I regarded as Okyenhene Pobi's interference in Wassa internal affairs. The dispute started in 1763. In that year a Wassa warlord called Asare, organized against Enimil, a palace coup which aborted.[72] In or about early 1764, Asare fled to Abuakwa where the Okyenhene accorded him protection.[73] Enimil applied to Pobi for Asare's extradition to face justice, but the Okyenhene would not extradite Asare; the refusal plummeted Abuakwa-Wassa relations to an all time low.[74] The strained relations also adversely affected the solidarity of the Grand Southern Alliance.

A much greater harm to the alliance occurred in 1765. Denkyirahene Owusu Bore withdrew his membership and went over to Asante. The Denkyira had secretly been communicating with the Asante government. The other members of the alliance discovered this activity of Denkyira some time in 1765 and resolved to punish it. Governor Mutter of Cape Coast Castle tells the story thus:

The Warsaws, Dinkerahs, Akims and Tufferoes [Twifos] who have been in league for many years to prevent the Ashantees from cutting them off separately have at last quarrelled among themselves. Ousbody [Owusu Bore] King of Dinkerah was suspected by his allies above mentioned of carrying on a correspondence privately with the Ashantees and of having formed a design of abandoning his own country in order to assist the Ashantees in destroying the other nations in alliance with them. Accordingly when the Warsaws pannaiared some Ashantees, Ousbody insisted on their being set at liberty. The Warsaws and their allies refused to do this, and being now convinced of Ousbody's underhand practice, were more determined to put him to death, and fixed upon the next Saturday for putting their scheme into execution. However, Ousbody, on the Thursday morning preceding, fell upon them at 5 o'clock, and as they had not the least intention of his design, nothing could save them but their heels; a considerable number were killed and many taken prisoner; who, it seems, afterwards made their escape; and it is thought that the booty in gold and agree [ie. agore] beads will be considerable . . . The King of Dinkerah and his people immediately set out, and have fixed their camp about half way between Warsaw and Ashantee. The Ashantees now give out that they will join the Dinkerahs and then attack the Warsaws, Akim, and Tufferoes in which case they [the Asante] will, in all probability, become masters and consequently force trade to the waterside [ie. the coast].[75]

The Benna War

The Asante declaration reflected a change in leadership at Kumasi. Kusi had been deposed and replaced by Osei Kwadwo, often referred to by the Europeans as "Zay Commah". The new Asantehene was described as "young, warlike and enterprising".[76] He was committed, according to the Europeans on the coast, to a policy of total destruction of all the enemies of Asante, especially the Akyem Abuakwa, the Wassa and the Twifo. In mid-1765 he declared war overtly on all these three but covertly against only Abuakwa.[77] For, as shall be demonstrated presently, he had reached a secret understanding with the Wassa and the Twifo.

The forces of all the allies except Denkyira assembled at a place which, according the English at Cape Coast, was called "Benda", some sixty kilometers north of Cape Coast.[78] As far as Akyem Abuakwa was concerned they were all going to make a collective stand against Asante. It was here that the fate of the Abuakwa and the southern alliance in general was sealed. Precisely at this point Asante diplomacy worked extra hard to inflict a greater damage on the alliance than the Denkyira perfidy had done. The Wassa and Twifo forces suddenly left Benna, allegedly at the prompting of Asante, and encamped at a place called "Ahiman".[79] Thus by July 1765 the twenty-three-year old southern alliance had totally disintegrated, a destruction brought about by effective Asante diplomacy, first targetted at Denkyira, and later at Wassa and Twifo. As for the Fante they had become pro-Asante as far back as 1750. Akyem

Abuakwa was left as the stump of the erstwhile southern alliance to face the full brunt of Asante fury. The situation was all the more dangerous for Abuakwa because Osei Kwadwo, a young and virile Asantehene was as anxious and determined to win his spurs as Okyenhene Pobi was keen to re-establish the pre-1742 Abuakwa hegemony in eastern Gold Coast.

Before the Asante army marched out against Abuakwa, the Fante first moved in on Pobi and his forces in June 1765. The Fante soon realized that it was one thing declaring war and quite a different thing winning it. The Abuakwa forces met them squarely and fought so well that the Fante soon had their back to the wall; defeat was staring them in the face. This imminent danger may have partly compelled them to reach a definite understanding with the Asante.[80] For the latter took the field against the Abuakwa at about this time.[81]

The Benna War, as it was called by the Abuakwa, was now on. The situation proved too much for Okyenhene Pobi. The earlier clash with the Fante had naturally reduced the size of his army, though by how much it is difficult to say. The sources consulted are silent on the strengths of the opposing forces. What is certain is that the war was a joint Asante-Fante action against the Abuakwa whom the Denkyira, the Wassa and the Twifo deserted in the eleventh hour. Consequently the Abuakwa, in the words of Governor Mutter of Cape Coast Castle.

> fell an easy prey into the hands of their enemies [though] a considerable number [of them], it is said, . . . escaped and are at present [July, 1765] in or near their own country.[82]

The war proved to be quite disastrous for the Abuakwa.[83] Okyenhene Pobi, the bugbear of Asante since 1742, lost his life in the war. Contemporary evidence is conflicting on the manner of his death. In June 1765 the Dutch claimed that it was the Asante who captured and killed him.[84] The English on the other hand said thus in July 1765: "Pobi . . . is a prisoner among the Fantees".[85] An early nineteenth century view toes the Dutch line: it says that Okyenhene Atta Owusu (1807–1811) hated the Asante because Asantehene Osei Kwadwo killed a predecessor of his.[86] This is a clear reference to Pobi. The matter is made more complicated by another contemporary Dutch view which indicates that neither the Asante nor the Fante killed Pobi; but that he and several of his leading lieutenants committed suicide when they realized the war was lost.[87]

Whether Pobi committed suicide or was taken captive and killed by his enemies the fact remains that Akyem Abuakwa lost the war. Hundreds of them were taken captive out of whom Asantehene Osei Kwadwo allegedly executed "more than four hundred".[88] Hundreds of them were also sold to the European slavers.[89] The English at Cape Coast said that following the Benna war there was a glut in Fante slave markets, a situation which brought down the price of a male slave to 6-7 oz. of gold and female to 4-5 oz.[90] The Abuakwa defeat seemed so total that the view prevailed in 1766 that it was now a destroyed nation.[91] This was an exaggeration, because the battles had not been fought in their own country. Nor did they have any immediate intention of submitting to the Asante. As Governor Mutter pointed out in his 20 July 1765 report, the remnant of the Abuakwa army retreated into their own country. From there they continued to resist the Asante.

Collapse of the Asante-Fante Cooperation

The chances of the Abuakwa resistance succeeding were bright for two main reasons. The first was that the Benna War had not been fought on Abuakwa soil. Therefore contrary to the view of Hippesley in early 1766, they were not a destroyed nation. They surely lost troops at Benna but not to the extent of being wiped out as a state. The second reason was the quick collapse of the Asante-Fante understanding and cooperation which obviously contributed to the defeat of Abuakwa at Benna. The cause of the hitch between the two recent allies has been traced to unwarranted Asante entry into Fante territory immediately after the Benna War.[92] There were at least two other and more serious causes which, when taken together, amounted to Fante treachery and betrayal of trust. Firstly, during the war, the Fante, in addition to the Abuakwa whom they captured, seized many Asante subjects and sold them together with the Abuakwa prisoners-of-war to the European slavers lying in wait in Fante waters; secondly they refused to allow the Asante to sell their own war captives directly to the European slavers, without Fante middlemanship.[93] The dispute over these two issues degenerated into armed clashes between the two peoples for several weeks until an outbreak of small-pox among the Asante forces obliged Asantehene Osei Kwadwo to withdraw from the Fante territory.

In anticipation of a possible Asante renewal of hostilities, the Fante, as a precaution, attempted to resuscitate the moribund southern alliance, or at least part of it. To this end they approached the Wassa and the Twifo. The two refused to have anything to do with the Fante, even though the latter were prepared to give up important personages as hostages to back their word.[94] The Wassa and Twifo may have come to the conclusion that the Fante were fickle and unreliable. Dutch promptings are also said to have partly induced the Wassa and Twifo rejection of the Fante move.[95] These are all proofs of selfish interests and particularism which made the southern states incapable of forging a genuine and lasting united front against Asante. Little wonder that up to the 1770s many, if not all, of them, were always in imminent danger of being attacked one by one by the Asante.[96]

Fortunately for Abuakwa and other anti-Asante states, divided opinion in Kumasi gave them some respite. The division was over the wisdom in a

The Forty Years War 1744–1784

continuous war with the south. One view, held by the youth and favoured by Osei Kwadwo and the Queenmother, Konadu Yiadom, deemed continuation very necessary; in contrast "the oldest councillors", as Hippesley put it, "endeavoured to divert [the King] from [that] design".[97] The debate in Asante prevented the Kumasi government from immediately following up its victory at Benna with a more direct invasion of Abuakwa. The decimation of the Asante army, by violence, capture and disease, may have discouraged the more matured government advisers from wanting to continue the war with the south. Also developments in Akyem Abuakwa may have supported the policy of discontinuation.

Obirikoran's Temporary Submission to Asante

Meanwhile Obirikoran succeeded to the Abuakwa Stool.[98] His was an unenviable inheritance. Between 1742 and 1765, Akyem Abuakwa had suffered two major disastrous defeats and several minor ones at the hands of Asante. Continued resistance seemed to promise nothing but further debacles. On the other hand, submission to Asante was bound to compromise the independence of Banso, probably to the extent of being incorporated into Asante proper, as had happened to Akyem Kotoku. Obirikoran, like his immediate but unlucky predecessor, Pobi, chose the path of resistance. But unlike Pobi he was prepared to temper stubbornness with temporary submission so as to gain time to muster his forces for further resistance in his own good time. His strategy was to wage a continual, not a continuous war against Asante.

The military situation at his accession was quite gloomy for Abuakwa. He decided to submit to Asante. Fortunately for him, Osei Kwadwo too needed peace. The Fante were now his enemies. The dust from the Benna war had hardly settled when Wassa and Twifo revolted. All these peoples closed against Asante the trade routes passing through their territories.[99] Therefore, Asante had no access to the European trade on the west coast. Peace with Abuakwa might open to Asante the routes to the eastern sector of the coast trade. It is not unreasonable to expect Asantehene Osei Kwadwo taking the initiative to coax Abuakwa, just as Opoku Ware I, had done in 1744, into agreeing to a peace settlement with Asante. At any rate in or about February 1766, Obirikoran submitted to Asante in principle; promising to go to Kumasi at the appropriate time to formally swear the oath of allegiance to the Golden Stool.[100] Hippesley at Cape Coast Castle, was probably, referring indirectly to the Abuakwa submission when he noted in March 1766 that the war materials the Abuakwa were purchasing at the time were "professedly for their new masters".[101]

The submission to Asante did not seriously dent the prestige of Akyem Abuakwa in eastern Gold Coast. In late 1766 both blacks and whites in the

Ga-Adangbe area anxiously awaited a visit of the new Okyenhene to the area,[102] an indication of his importance.

Obirikoran Renews the Resistance

The submission in February 1766 was actually a ruse on the part of Obirikoran: the objective was to enable him to gain enough time to prepare adequately for Abuakwa's next round of hostilities with Asante. The strength of this contention derives from the fact that in 1767, barely a year after his so-called submission, he renewed the conflict with Asante.[103] He closed the eastern trade routes against Asante, and to ensure maximum effect he renewed alliances with Akuapem and Krobo. With the help of those two allies he invaded New Akwamu.[104] He defeated Akwamuhene Darko who, with some of his subjects rowed to an island in the Volta for safety.[105]

The resilience of Akyem Abuakwa under Obirikoran alarmed Asantehene Osei Kwadwo. He sent to remind the Okyenhene of his vassalage to the Golden Stool and requested him and the Akwamuhene to proceed to Kumasi for a resolution of their differences.[106] Obirikoran disobeyed the order. To show that he was a force to reckon with, he, in 1768, demanded that all the European companies pay to him the ground rents for the forts and lodges in the Ga and Adangbe districts.[107] That put the white traders in a dilemma. A blunt refusal to pay would surely anger the Okyenhene; to concede to the Abuakwa ruler's demand was bound to lead to misunderstandings with the Asantehene. The Danes got round the problem by paying but they described the payment as commission to the Okyenhene for his ability to drive trade to the coast.[108] The other companies probably took the same precaution, considering that the English for example had both the Okyenhene and the Asantehene on their payrolls.[109] Clearly the European trading companies were responding to Abuakwa resurgence in Eastern Gold Coast.

The Abuakwa-Asante War of 1768

Asantehene Osei Kwadwo became worried and decided to suppress Obirikoran. An Asante army marched out against Abuakwa in or about mid-1768.[110] The war raged on up to November the same year. Once again Abuakwa arms proved no match against the Asante military machine and Obirikoran, attempting his first armed confrontation with Asante, had to take to his heels. He fled to a place which the Danes vaguely said was between Akuapem and Asante.[111]

Two defeats in three years obviously proved quite disheartening for the Abuakwa. Consequently, Obirikoran submitted to Asante. This time he was very sincere. In early 1769, he went to Kumasi to swear the oath of allegiance to the Asantehene.[112]

Obirikoran's submission in 1769 produced ripples in Akuapem and Krobo. They too went on their knees to acknowledge Asante supremacy. In January 1770, the Okyenhene, accompanied by some of his own Chiefs, Akuapem and Krobo delegations, and two Asante envoys or commissioners, "Etja Corrie and Dekje" (i.e. Atakora and Dekye or Odekye) arrived in Accra. The visit had a dual purpose. First, the Okyenhene hoped to raise a loan of "100 bendas" of gold from the European companies in Accra to help him defray the expenses incurred during his 1769 visit to Kumasi.[113] On being informed of the loan request from the Okyenhene, the Dutch Director-General of Elmina Castle advised against advancing the loan; deGraft, the Dutch factor in Accra, thought the advice was unfortunate since, according to him, the Danes and English readily gave the Okyenhene loans without any pre-conditions.[114] DeGraft was clearly worried about the possibility of the Abuakwa driving all their trade to the Danish and English companies.

This interpretation is based on what the English said was the purpose of Obirikoran's visit which was clearly the second purpose of the visit. They said that

> Abricoan [Obirikoran], King of Akim . . . came with a good number of Ashantees, Hill country [Akuapem] and Crobbo Caboceers to clear the paths from pirates and get trade down to the water side [coast] in safety.[115]

Eastern Gold Coast continued to hold the Okyenhene in high esteem and still looked up to him for guidance in at least their foreign relations; and Ada allegedly regarded him as their overlord.[116] Besides, there is no indication of Asantehene Osei Kwadwo ever attempting to deprive Abuakwa of Old Akwamu. The Asante government even pampered Obirikoran. Barely four months after his submission, the Asante monarchy assisted him with an army of seven thousand strong to raid the lower Volta basin, possibly Krepi, for slaves whom he could sell and recoup some of the expenses incurred during his 1769 visit to Kumasi, and also to meet his financial obligations to the European companies.[117]

The Volta venture had another objective: it was meant to assist the Ada against Anlo.[118] Panic seized several peoples in the lower Volta basin. The Dutch pleaded with Obirikoran not to molest their local supporters and allies.[119] In July 1770, he crossed the Volta, stormed two Anlo towns, and threatened to lay siege to the Anlo capital itself and later to invade Voltaic Akwamu. But the Anlo, assisted by the Akwamu,[120] gallantly defended themselves, repulsed Obirikoran, and took about five hundred of his troops captive.[121] In spite of the setback, the Okyenhene continued the campaign against Anlo, intending to attack the Akwamu later. However, an order came from Kumasi asking him to stop forthwith his armed activities in the lower Volta.[122] It is likely that the Asantehene feared Obirikoran might invade New Akwamu, a vassal to Asante and collector of the groundrents from the European Companies for the Asantehene.

Abuakwa Rebels Again

The command from Kumasi, coming soon after his discomfiture in Anlo, so irritated Obirikoran that he decided to vent his spleen on the Asante government. In 1771, assisted by Atiemo, the Okuapemhene, he revolted against Asante by reorganizing a new economic blockade of the eastern trade routes against that power;[123] he ignored an order from Kumasi asking him to proceed to Accra and swear to the Dutch that he would keep the trade routes open.[124]

Once again Asantehene Osei Kwadwo had no choice but to take the field against Obirikoran. In early 1772, an Asante army of thirty thousand under the command of General Adusei marched on Abuakwa.[125] According to an English report in January 1773, Obirikoran and his ally, Atiemo of Akuapem, initially had the upper hand in the opening skirmishes but in the course of the war, they lost heart, on account of the sheer numerical superiority of the adversary, and resorted to guerrilla warfare. Obirikoran sent his women, children and the aged to Krobo for safety while the Abuakwa army headed southwards.[126] Lack of adequate allied support was also a reason for the flight of the Okyenhene from his own country. He had sounded the Krobo for military support but the latter merely agreed to shelter the Abuakwa women, children and the aged.[127] In the months of October and November 1772, he had sent emissaries to Accra to publicise Asantehene Osei Kwadwo's passion for his head and to solicit military assistance from the Ga.[128] The Ga refused to help because they did not want to get entangled with the Asante; they rather advised Obirikoran to look for help from the Fante.[129] He took the advise. He and his army headed for Fante where, it was said, the Asante were unlikely to pursue him for fear that he might strike an alliance with the Fante.[130]

In spite of the departure of the Abuakwa army for Fante, the Asante general, Adusei, subjected the Ga to serious questioning, apparently to find out where the loyalty and sympathy of the Ga lay, with Akyem Abuakwa or Asante. On 10th December 1772 the English at James Town, Accra, reported that:

> Ancrah, one of the Say's captains, with two other captains, and upwards of seven thousand soldiers, came to this and other forts, desiring to know what they had to expect from Accra in general and at the same time demanding every Akim and Hill [Akuapem] people that were about, and requesting presents for the Commanding Officer, Adoocei, who, by Ancrah, gave assurance of his good disposition towards the English.[131]

What the Ga and others in the Accra area said or did in response to the demands of Commanding Officer Adusei and Captains Ankrah and others may never be known. Whatever they were, Captain Ankrah and his colleagues appear to have found them satisfactory. But the inhabitants of the district did not altogether go scot free. They were made to pay *apea-tuo* (war-tax) which Captain Ankrah cleverly described as "presents"; the district was also denuded of its food supplies and provisions by the Asante army.[132] Actually, General Adusei and his forces quartered themselves in the district for about four months before they left for Old Akwamu,[133] the first stage of their return journey home. The inhabitants of the area must have suffered in several other ways during the stay of this 'occupation' army. General Adusei left without accomplishing his main mission: the capture and decapitation of the Okyenhene.

Asantehene Osei Kwadwo was never able to solve the Abuakwa Question before he died in 1777. That Asantehene was faced with a myriad of problems in the area of foreign affairs. Aside from the conflict with Akyem Abuakwa, adverse developments in the west were quite overwhelming. The Wassa were still in arms. The Twifo may have been no different. The Fante were unpredictable: since 1765 they would today pretend to be friendly and tomorrow become hostile. For example, between 1772 and 1774 they pretended to be favourably disposed toward the Asante, but in 1775 when the Asante attacked the Wassa they turned coat by supporting Wassa to beat back the Asante assault.[134]

The success of Wassa in the west and the hostile Abuakwa activities in the east meant a total blockade of Asante access to the coast trade between Takoradi and Ada. Between 1775 and 1780 Asante had to re-establish contact and communication with Nzima further west of Takoradi, from which place only, Asante could procure European goods, particularly munitions of war. Even here they were not left in peace: by 1785 the Wassa were reported to be challenging that access too.

Abuakwa Divided Over Asante

Asante preoccupation in the west gave Obirikoran considerable freedom in the east. After General Adusei and his army had left Old Akwamu, he, in 1773 moved into that province.[135] He was still there in 1774.[136] He was constrained to stay on there because there had been a change in Asante strategy to bring him on his knees. The military approach as a solution to the Abuakwa Question had clearly failed and the Asante government had resorted to diplomacy as an alternative. This new strategy succeeded. The government in Kumasi managed to win the Abuakwa prince Twum Ampofo (or Ampofro), to their side. In the first quarter of 1775, it was known on the coast that Ampofo, the youngest brother of Ebicoram [Obirikoran] who is the Head Chief of Old Akim, has reconciled with the King of Assiantyn, and that the same [has] sent im much help and made him King of Akim" [137]

Twum Ampofo had obviously allowed himself to be persuaded into denouncing Obirikoran so that he could gain power in "Old Akim", as the Europeans on the coast were beginning to call the Banso metroplis vis-a-vis "New Akim" ie. the Old Akwamu District. Here he seems to have either founded or made Kyebi his temporary residence and capital.

But to discerning observers on the coast Obirikoran was still a force to be reckoned with, not only in Akyem Abuakwa but in the whole of eastern old Coast. Asante traders could hardly get through to the eastern coast trade, owing to the blockade of the trade routes by Obirikoran and his Akuapem and Krobo allies.[138] The Danes for instance doubted if Asante would ever have it easy in Akyem Abuakwa and the rest of eastern Gold Coast as long as Obirikoran lived. The fact of the matter was that in spite of his so-called deposition by the Asante government, and in spite of the fact that Twum Ampofo was in power at Banso, Obirikoran still wielded greater power. He now had a political base in Old Akwamu which was being integrated into the Abuakwa state complex through his residence at Kyebi.

All the same the split in the state was unfortunate. It made it possible for others to exploit the Abuakwa. During the 1776–1778 period, the Danes and the Dutch were at loggerheads in the Ga and the Adangbe districts. While the Danes solicited military assistance from Twum Ampofo, King of Old Abuakwa, the Dutch turned to Obirikoran, King of New Abuakwa.[139] The house of Abuakwa was divided against itself. Had Asante found it convenient to exploit the division fully, the Abuakwa would have perhaps paid a great price for the disunity. Luckily for them, Asante was very much preoccupied with

(i) the death of Osei Kwadwo in 1777, and
(ii) affairs in western Gold Coast.[140]

In 1780, Obirikoran visited Accra in his capacity as Okyenhene. His main objective was to attend the funeral of the Ga Mantse who had just died. On account of what they described as his friendship and services to them, the Dutch and English companies showered on Obirikoran, gifts which included guns, ammunition and clothing.[141] In return he promised to unblock the routes to allow trade to flow to the Dutch and English Forts.[142] The Asante government, their Banso collaborators, and the Danes might choose to regard him as deposed, but to the people of "new Akim" (ie. Old Akwamu) and most of the eastern Gold Coast he was still "the King of Akim" Abuakwa. The Asante government eventually had to concede that fact in 1783. Besides, Asante needed to come to some form of accommodation with him. The truth was that based in Old Akwamu, Obirikoran, in alliance with Akuapem and Krobo, could at will always close the eastern trade routes against Asante. Since the Wassa were still challenging Asante access to the west coast trade, a peace settlement with Obirikoran could give Asante some opening to the trade in the east.

The early 1780s favoured such an arrangement. Asantehene Osei Kwadwo had died in 1777 and had been succeeded by Osei Kwame who was a minor. The Kumasi monarchy was actually in the hands of Kwame's mother (the Queenmother) and the great Councillors. The Kumasi government could therefore open negotiations with Obirikoran without any loss of face and dignity. In 1783, they opened peace talks with him. They offered to recognize him as the Okyenhene provided he would in return acknowledge the Asantehene as his overlord.[143] He agreed and paid *mpata* (appeasement money) to the Kumasi court.[144] The Asantehene then "reinstated" him as the Okyenhene.[145] The disunity in Abuakwa which had emerged in 1775 was thus healed in 1783.

Death of Obirikoran, 1784

In 1784, roughly one year after his reconciliation with Asante. Okyenhene Obirikoran died. The English factor at James Fort in Accra on 5th January, 1784 recorded the event thus:

> [Envoys] sent by Biramquoy's successor the King of Akim ... came to inform me of Biramquoy's death and to assure me that he [the new Okyenhene] had despatched messengers to Ashantee to acquaint that King that [Asante] traders will not be molested in their passage to the waterside.[146]

The new Okyenhene was no other person than Twum Ampofo, the old protégé of the Asante. His despatch of messengers to Kumasi to announce formally the death of Obirikoran to the Asante authorities was indeed customary. But it is clear that the message was also meant to leave Asante in no doubt that he was now in charge and that a new era in Abuakwa-Asante relations had dawned. For Ampofo, as shall be shown in the next chapter, replaced his predecessor's policy of continual resistance to Asante with one of total submission to that power.

The effect of Obirikoran's death was not limited to Abuakwa; it went beyond its confines. Deprived of the superior cooperation with, and alliance of Obirikoran, with the enstoolment of Twum Ampofo as the new Okyenhene who had long advocated a policy of peaceful relations with Kumasi, Okuapemhene Atiemo had no choice but to rush and tender his submission to the Golden Stool. The Krobo may have done the same, because they too had always been allies of Obirikoran.

Abuakwa, Akuapem and Krobo were sincere in their new relations with Asante. From 1784 continued Wassa hostility to Asante and the latter's military campaigns in Nzima and Aowin disrupted trade in the western sector of the Gold Coast. In contrast, trade flourished in the east, with the Asante sharing substantially in it.[147] But for the submission of Obirikoran to, and his acceptance, of Asante authority, such a peaceful economic atmosphere in eastern Gold Coast would have been impossible.

Considering the number of decades of the Abuakwa resistance to Asante, the careers of Pobi and Obirikoran were a failure. Forty years of war with Asante came to naught. However, it is worth pointing out that but for that very resistance, perhaps Kyebi would not have been founded, and the process of integration between Abuakwa and Old Akwamu would not have taken place.

NOTES AND REFERENCES

1. Dupuis, J., 1824, *Journal of a Residence in Ashantee*, Frank Cass & Co. Ltd., London, p.234; Boahen, A. A., 1966, *Topics in West African History*, Longman, London, p.74, and in Ajayi & Espie (Eds), 1966, *A Thousand Years of West African History*, Macmillan, London, p.164.
2. Wilks, I., 1975, *Asante in the Nineteenth Century*, OUP, Oxford, 1975, p.24.
3. Romer, *Tilforladlig Efterretning on Kysten Guinea*, Copenhagen 1760 (transl.), pp. 188–189.
4. Reindorf, C. C. 1896, *The History of the Gold Coast and Asante*, Basel Mission Book Depot, Basel, pp.82 & 89.
5. As shown in Chapter 2, p.36, they made use of the river to defeat the invading Asante army in 1717–1718.
6. Dupuis, *A Residence*, p.244.
7. "Precis of Akim Claims: Confidential Report, No.345/00", dated 7th January 1903. File No. D.46, Kumasi Archives.
8. Wilks, *Asante*, p.69.
9. Bowdich, T. E., 1819, *A Mission from Cape Coast to Asantee*, Frank Cass & Co. Ltd., London, p.237; Dupuis, *A Residence*, p.244; Reindorf, *The History of the Gold Coast*, pp. 133–134.
10. For useful discussions on the subject of Asante provincial administration and policy, see Wilks, I., 1967, "Ashanti Government", in Ford, D. & Kaberry, P. N. (Eds) *West African Kingdoms in the Nineteenth Century*, OUP, Oxford, pp. 206–238; Wilks, Asante, esp. Chapter 4, 5, & 7; Hagan, G.P., 1971, "Ashanti Bureaucracy", in *THSG*, vol.ix, pp. 43–62.
11. In 1716 when it became clear that Kotoku and Asante were about to clash in war, Okyenhene Ofori curtailed his invasion of Agona in order to redeploy his forces in defence of his own country and give some assistance to Kotoku.
12. Kuijl (Accra) to Director-General de Petersen (EC.), 18 March 1742, *NBKG* 106.
13. Richard Graves (Accra) to CCC, 3 April 1742, T 70/1515; Tenkorang, S., "The im-

portance of firearms in the struggle between Ashanti and the Coastal States", in *THSG* Vol.IX, 1968, p.5 notes 22 & 23.
14. Director-General de Peterseen (EC) to the Assembly of Ten, Amsterdam, 9 July 1742, WIC 488.
15. Jorgesen to Dorph, 25 May, 1743; Dorph (CCO) to Copenhagen, 11 July 1743, VgK 123: breve og dokumenter fra Guinea, 1732–1745.
16. Reindorf, *The History of the Gold Coast*, pp. 81–82.
17. Letters from Billsen, 30 March & 21 July 1744, VgK 123.
18. Janson (Apam) to Kuijl (Accra), 30 March 1742, enclosed in Raems & Verscheuren (Accra) to de Petersen (EC), ? April 1742, *NBKG* 106.
19. Report from de Peterseen, 9 July 1742, WIC 488.
20. Governor & Council (CCO) to Copenhagen, 21 July 1746, VgK.863.
21. Fynn, *Asante*, p.76.
22. Governor & Council (CCO) to Copenhagen, 18 January 1747, VgK.883.
23. Governor & Council (CCO) to Copenhagen, 6 February 1747, VgK.833.
24. Gyakiti Tradition, as recorded in the Gold Coast Gazette Extraordinary No.6 (1956), p.91. The Gazette contains the Report of a Commission appointed to look into a land dispute involving Abuakwa, Akwamu and Manya Krobo.
25. AAT: Begoro, (1925/6).
26. Governor & Council (CCO) to Copenhagen, 21 July 1746, VgK.883.
27. Director-General de Petersen (EC) to Amsterdam, 20 May & 15 November 1744, (Furley Collection, Legon).
28. Governor & Council (CCO) to Copenhagen, 21 July 1746, VgK.833.
29. Governor & Council (CCO) to Copenhagen, 23 May 1748 & 26 November 1749, VgK.124: breve og documenter fra Guinea 1746–1750; also Brummer (Accra) to EC, 10 November 1749, *NBKG* 110.
30. Brummer (Accra) to van Hoorst (EC), 10 April and 11 & 29 May 1750, *NBKG* 111.
31. Brummer to EC, 17 March 1750, *NBKG* 111; also Letters from CCO, 23 May, 10 August & 17 September 1750 VgK.883.
32. Fynn, *Asante*, Chapter 4; also his article "Asante and Akyem", *Research Review*, Vol. 9, No.1, 1973, Legon, p.73.
33. Thomas Melvil (CCC) to the Committee in London, 9 & 26 August 1751, T 79/29, PRO.
34. Pranger (EC) to Blittersdorp (Accra), 13 December 1730, *NBKG* 97; Pranger to the Assembly of Ten in Amsterdam, 1 March 1731, (Furley Collection, Legon).
35. Thòmas Melvil (CCC) to the Committee in London, 9 August, 1751, T. 70/29, PRO.
36. Tenkorang, "Firearms", in *THSG* Vol.IX, p.5.
37. Thomas Melvil (CCC) to the Committee, London, 9 & 26 August 1751, T. 70/29, PRO.
38. Brummer (Accra) to EC, 11, 18 & 29 May, and Brummer (Kponni) to EC, 13 December 1750, *NBKG* 111.
39. Norregaard, G., 1966, *Danish Settlements in West Africa 1658–1830*, Boston University Press, Boston, p.108.
40. Romer, *Tilforladlig*, p.169.
41. Brummer (Accra) to EC, 3, 11, 18 & 29 May 1750, *NBKG* 111.
42. Director-General & Council (EC) to the Assembly of Ten, Amsterdam, 17 November 1751, WIC 490.
43. *Ibid.*

44. Norregaard, *Danish Settlement,* p.109.
45. Bascot (Axim) to EC, 16 January 1752, *NBKG* 113.
46. J. Roberts to Halifax 28 September 1750, cited by Tenkorang, S., "The importance of Firearms in the Struggle between Ashanti and the Coastal States", 23 November 1750, T 70/1476; Fiscal von Dadelbeek (EC) to Amsterdam, 16 September 1757, WIC 490.
47. Thomas Melvil (CCC) to the Committee (London), 26 December 1753, also same to same, 4 April 1754, T 70/30; "A Narrative of Transaction with the Fantees on the death of Intuffero [ie. Ntsiful], King of Warsaw", 1752, T 70/30, pp.11f.
48. Thomas Melvil (CCC) to the Committee (London), 7 August 1734 T 70/30. This English version of the peace move contradicts the Dutch who give the impression that they initiated the peace move, and that their agents actually led the Abuakwa-Wassa-Fante Delegation to Kumasi. (See Fynn, *Asante*, pp. 89-92). Clearly, as Fynn rightly points out, there was some degree of Anglo-Dutch rivalry in the matter.
49. Pieter Woortman (Apam) to EC, noted in EC Journal: entry; ? July 1754, *NBKG* 115.
50. Woortman (Apam) to EC, 13 May 1755; de Graft (Accra) to EC, 14 June 1755, *NBKG* 116; CCO Day Journal: entries 3 June 1754 & 5 March 1755, VgK: Sekretprotokoller 1755-1762.
51. Governor & Council (CCO) to Copenhagen, 15 August 1757, Diverse Arkivaler fra Guinea, DAFG. I am grateful to Mr. Ole Justesen of the University of Copenhagen who drew my attention to this source.
52. Governor & Council (CCO) to Copenhagen, 22 October 1757, DAFG.
53. Blyenburg (Accra) to EC, 17 July 1760; EC Journal: entries 26 & 28 November 1760, NBKG 121.
54. Tenkorang, "Firearms", *THSG* Vol.IX, p.7.
55. Nassau Senior (CCC) to the Committee (London), 15 June & 5 July 1758, T 70/30.
56. Senior (CCC) to the Committee (London), 5 January, 22 May & 3 June 1759, T 70/30.
57. Senior (CCC) to the Committee, 23 September 1759; Mutter (CCC) to the Committee, 15 October 1760, T 70/30.
58. Blyenburg (Accra) to EC, 17 July 1760, *NBKG* 121.
59. The incorporation is fully discussed in Chapter 5.
60. Blyenburg (Accra) to EC, 9 September 1760, *NBKG* 121; Pieter Erasmi (EC) to Amsterdam, 22 March 1761, WIC 115.
61. Dupuis, *A Residence,* pp. 237-238; see also Claridge, *History,* Vol.I, pp. 210-211.
62. Fynn, *Asante,* p.90.
63. Blyenburg (Accra) to EC, 17 July 1760; EC Journal: entries 26 & 28 November 1760, *NBKG* 121.
64. Erasmi (EC) to Senya Breku, 28 November 1760, *NBKG* 121.
65. Fuller, *A Vanished Dynasty,* p.31.
66. Fynn, *Asante,* p.86.
67. Senior (CCC) to the Committee (London), 29 September 1759, 3 February & 20 May 1760, T 70/30.
68. Mutter (CCC) to the Committee, 15 October 1760, T 70/30.
69. Senior to the Committee, 27 November 1760, T 70/30.
70. Gilbert Petrie (CCC) to the Committee, 20 August 1764, cited by Kea, R., "Akwamu-Anlo Relations", in *THSG,* Col.X, 1969, p.37.
71. Huydecoper & Council (EC) to Amsterdam, 15 October 1764, WIC 115.

72. EC Journal: entry 9 February 1763, *NBKG* 124.
73. Mutter (CCC) to the Committee (London), 27 May 1764, T 70/31.
74. Mutter to the Committee, 21 January 1765, T 70/31.
75. Mutter to the Committee, 25 April 1765, T 70/31.
76. Mutter to the Committee, 20 July 1765, T 70/31.
77. *Ibid.*
78. *Ibid.*
79. *Ibid.* "Ahiman" is no doubt Heman. The choice of Heman by Asante as the place where the Wassa and Twifo forces should quarter themselves reveals the workings of the Asante mind. Heman, though surrounded by Twifo did not form part of it. It was more or less a 'city' state whose inhabitants had links with Akwamu. As such Asante in 1765 could entrust the policing of the Wassa and Twifo forces to their care while slugging it out with the Abuakwa army.
80. Margaret Priestley, "Richard Brew; an Eighteenth Century Trader at Anomabu", in *THSG*. Vol. IV, Part I, p.38.
81. EC Journal: entry 13 June 1765, *NBKG* 126.
82. Mutter (CCC) to the Committee (London), 20 July 1765, T 70/31.
83. AAT: Pamen (1925/6) Reindorf (*The History of the Gold Coast*, p.81) is therefore wrong in giving the name to the 1742 war. Contemporary evidence confirms the Pamen tradition.
84. EC Journal: entry 17 June 1765, *NBKG* 126.
85. Mutter (CCC) to the Committee (London), 20 July 1765, T 70/31, see also Priestley, M., "The Ashanti Question and the British: eighteenth century origins", *Journal of African History (JAH)*, Vol.2, 1961, p.43.
86. The reign of Okyenhene Atta Owusu is discussed in Chapter 5.
87. Director-General Huydecoper (EC) to Amsterdam, 8 May 1765, WIC 116, cited by Fynn, *Asante*, p.100 note 1.
88. Mutter (CCC) to the Committee (London), 20 July 1765, T 70/31.
89. *Ibid.*
90. *Ibid.* Mutter did not say what the pre-Benna War prices were.
91. John Hippesley (CCC) to the Committee (London), 2 March 1755, T 70/31.
92. Priestly, M. and Wilks, I., "Ashanti Kings in the eighteenth century, a Revised Chronology, *JAH*, Vol.I, No.1, 1960, p.94; also Priestly in *THSG*, Vol.IV, Part I, 1959, p.38 & in *JAH* Vol.II, 1961, p.43.
93. Mutter's 20th July 1765 Report, T 70/31.
94. Mutter (CCC) to the Committee, 25 October 1765, T 70/31.
95. *Ibid.*
96. Hippesley to the Committee, 13 July 1766; Gilbert Petrie to the Committee, 13 September, 20 October 1765, 31 January, 9 October 1767, 31 March, 27 August and 21 October 1768; and David Mill to the Committee, 22 June 1772, T 70/31.
97. Hippesley to the Committee, 20 March 1766, T 70/31.
98. AAT: Pamen (1925/6).
99. Tenkorang, " Firearms", *THSG*, Vol.IX, 1968, pp. 11–12.
00. EC Journal: entry 29 February 1766; Pieter Woortman (Accra) to EC referred to in EC Journal: entry 16 March; Woortman to EC, 12 April; EC Journal: entry 15 April 1766, *NBKG* 127.
01. Hippesley (CCC) to the Committee (London), 20 March 1766, T 70/31.
02. EC Journal: 12 September, P. Woortman (Accra) to EC, 17 September 1766, *NBKG* 127.

103. Petrie (CCC) to the Committee (London), 20 August 1767, T 70/31.
104. EC Journal: entry 28 February, Director-General Huydecoper (EC) to Woortman (Accra), 4 March; EC Journal: entry 21 March 1767, *NBKG* 123.
105. Woortman to Huydercoper, 16 March 1767, *NBKG* 128.
106. Woortman (Accra) to Huydercoper (EC), 15 April; EC Journal: entry 20 April 1767 *NBKG* 128.
107. Lise M. Johannese (CCC) to Copenhagen, 4 December 1768, VgK; EC Journal entry 3 April 1768 *NBKG* 129
108. Governor & Council (CCO) to Copenhagen, 4 December 1768 VgK.
109. James Fort (Accra) Daybook: entries January, September, November and December 1768, T 70/979.
110. Governor & Council (CCO) to Copenhagen, 21 July 1768, VgK.
111. Governor & Council (CCO) to Copenhagen, 1 November 1768, VgK.
112. Governor & Council (CCO) to Copenhagen, 9 March 1769, VgK, deGraft (Accra) to EC, 13 January 1770, *NBKG* 121.
113. DeGraft (Accra) to EC, 24 January, EC Journal: entry 29 January 1779, *NBKG* 131.
114. P. Woortman (EC) to deGraft, 3 February 1770; deGraft to Woortman, 23 February 1770, *NBKG* 131, see also Norregaard, *Danish Settlements*, p.126.
115 James Fort (Accra) Daybook; entry 18 January 1778, T 70/979.
116. Pieter Woortman (Accra) to EC, 15 June 1770, *NBKG* 131.
117. Woortman to EC, 4 June; EC Journal: entry, 9 June 1770.
118. Woortman to EC, 15 June 1770, *NBKG* 131; Kea, R. A., "Akwamu-Anlo Relations c 1750–1813", in *THSG*, Vol.X, 1969, pp. 37–38.
119. Woortman to EC, 9 & 27 June; EC Journal: entry 30 June 1779, *NBKG* 131.
120. A. Gijl (Ponni) to EC, 22 July; N. W. Krugger (Tema) to EC, 26 July 1770 *NBKG* 132; Kea, *op. cit*, p.37.
121. Governor & Council (CCC) to Copenhagen, 26 July 1770, VgK, Krugger (Tema) to EC. 26 July; Froelick & Woortman (Accra) to EC, 27 July, Gijl (Ponny) to EC, 27 July 1779, *NBKG* 132.
122. Krugger (Tema) to EC, 28 July 1779, *NBKG* 132, Kea, *Op. cit.*
123. Woortman (Accra) to EC, 11 December 1771, *NBKG* 134.
124. *Ibid.*
125. Woortman to EC, 12 January 1772, *NBKG* 136; James Fort (Accra) Daybook: entry 29 November 1772, T 70/979.
126. David Mill (CCC) to the Committee (London) 30 January 1773, T 70/31.
127. Kioge (Ada) to CCO, Osu, 21 December 1772, VgK: Sekrèt-protokoller.
128. James Fort (Accra) Daybook: entries 17 October & 27 November 1772, T 70/979.
129. James Fort (Accra) Daybook: entry 27 November 1772, T 70/979.
130. David Mill (CCC) to the Committee in London, 30 January 1773, T 70/31.
131. James Fort (Accra) Daybook: entry 10 December 1772, T 70/979.
132. Vanderpuije (Accra) to EC, 1 May 1774, *NBKG* 139.
133. Aaerestrup (CCO) to Copenhagen, 7 March 1773, VgK.
134. Fort William (Anomabo) Daybook: entry 10 November 1775, T 70/990; CCC Daybook: entries 16 & 22 November 1775, T 70/1037; Richard Miles to CCC, 24 November 1775, T 70/1534, all cited by Tenkorang, "Firearms" *THSG*, Vol.IX, p.14 note 64.
135. Pieter Woortman (Accra) to EC, 24 April 1773, *NBKG* 137.
136. Vanderpuije (Accra) to EC, 1 May 1774, *NBKG* 140, James Fort (Accra) Daybook: entry 18 March 1774, T 70/978.

137. Letter from Senya Breku to EC, 16 March 1775, *NBKG* 141, See also Governor & Council (CCO) to Copenhagen, 28 May, 1775, VgK.
138. Fynn, *Asante*, p.111.
139. Reindorf, *The History of the Gold Coast*, p.94; Norregaard, *Danish Settlements*, p. 136.
140. Vanderpuije (Accra) to EC 29 June 1780, *NBKG* 151.
141. James Fort (Accra) Daybook: entry 29 June 1780, T 70/980.
142. *Ibid.*
143. James Fort (Accra) Daybook; entry 29 January 1783, T 70/980.
144. *Ibid*; J. Kioge (CCO) to Copenhagen, 15 March, 1783 VgK, cited by Kwamena-Poh *Government and Politics*, p.83 note 4.
145. Kystdokumenter paa Guinea: entry 15 March 1783 VgK.
146. James Fort (Accra) Daybook: entry, 5 January 1784, T 70/980.
147. James Morgue (CCC) to the Committee (London), 9 July 1785, T 70/32.

Chapter 5

FROM SERVITUDE TO SOVEREIGNTY 1784–1831

The Abuakwa resistance to Asante described in the preceding chapter was not altogether an unprofitable exercise. It paved the way for the eventual integration of Abuakwa and Old Akwamu. The submission to Asante in 1783 did not reverse the integrational process. However, vassalage to Asante imposed on the Akyem states considerable disabilities and limitations which given their ambition, they could not tolerate for long. From 1810, Akyem Abuakwa revolted in an effort to recover its sovereignty and potentially carried Akyem Kotoku along in the rebellion. Cooperation with other subject states, the British and the Danes was to be their major strategy.

Incorporation of Old Akwamu into Abuakwa

A long term and a most significant effect of the Abuakwa resistance was the eventual incorporation of Old Akwamu into the Kingdom of Akyem Abuakwa. The restoration of the Voltaic Akwamu to their pre-1730 inheritance had been a major objective of Asantehene Opoku Ware I in going to war against the Abuakwa and the Kotoku in 1742. By 1783 when Abuakwa finally submitted to Kumasi, Asante leaders had lost interest in the restoration idea. No evidence has been found to show that between 1744 and 1784 the Asante government ever attempted to implement it. By the 1780s old Akwamu had become or was on its way to becoming, an integral part of the Akyem Abuakwa state. In fact during 1775 Old Akwamu, which included what is now the Kyebi district, was described by the European traders on the coast as "New Akim" as against the Banso area which they referred to as "Old Akim"[1].

The integration was accelerated by the movement of the important section of the Abuakwa leadership from "Old Akim" to the Old Akwamu territory. The paramount lineage moved from Banso to settle at Kyebi, and the Adonten lineage left Takyiman to reside at Kukurantumi.[2] That these two places once formed part of Old Akwamu is vouchsafed by both Abuakwa and Akwamu traditions.[3]

To date there have been two suggestions as to when the paramount lineage settled at Kyebi. One says 1812[4] and the other suggests 1815 or about that time.[5] There is a strong reason to believe that neither view is correct and that the event may have occurred long before the 1810s. The Kyebi-Kukurantumi area was linked to the Ga-Adangbe coast by a trade route which passed through Akuapem. For several decades after the 1729–1730 Akyem-Akwamu war, the route, according to Marion Johnson, fell into disuse; but it bounced back into use in the 1780s.⁶ It is possible, as Johnson rightly suggests, that the reopening of the route had something to do with the establishment of the paramount and Adonten lineages at Kyebi and Kukurantumi respectively.

In the case of Kyebi the settlement occurred probably between the second half of the 1770s and the early 1780s. It is not unlikely that Obirikoran was the first Okyenhene to have made Kyebi his official capital. He may well have done so from the second half of the 1770s when the Asante government used his younger brother to oust him from Banso.⁷ By origin Kyebi was an Akwamu town, and though it was not too far from Banso, he could live there quietly and feel safe. He probably decided to make Kyebi the new capital for Abuakwa after 1783 when he settled his differences with Asante.⁸ The shifting of the capital did not mean a total abandonment of Banso. It was made the final burial grounds of deceased Abuakwa royals.⁹

The absorption of Old Akwamu into Abuakwa increased the size of that state. Its southern boundary shifted from the western confines of the Atewa-Atwiredu mountain range to as far south as the Nyanao hill in the Nsawam-Adoagyiri neighbourhood. The incorporation appears to have also led to some constitutional changes in Abuakwa. It became necessary to create a new category of chiefs who would have nominal divisional status. Among the leading Old Akwamu chiefly lineages were those of Tafo, Asamankese, Akwatia and Otwereso. Tafo and Asamankese for example were great land owners.¹⁰ The horn-blower of the Tafohene intones thus: *Kuro-wo-asaase* (literally Tafo is a great landowner).¹¹ Such powerful entrants were accorded the status of divisional chiefs without controlling divisional areas separate from the five already in existence i.e. Adonten (the Vanguard). Nifa (Right), Benkum (Left), Gyaase, and Oseawuo.¹² The Otweresohene for instance was made a member of the Benkum Division and regarded as being of the same rank as the substantive Benkumhene, alias the Begoro-or Fanteakwahene; the Asamankesehene was made to stand in a similar relationship with the Oseawuohene, better known as the Wankyihene.¹³

Disabilities of Vassalage

If vassalage to Asante did not disturb the integration between Abuakwa and Old Akwamu it did entail some serious disadvantages to Abuakwa and Akyem Kotoku also. One of these was the mandatory visit a vassal chief had to pay to the Asante capital, three years after his installation, in order to formally swear the oath of allegiance to the Asantehene. Subject rulers were also required to participate, either in person or by representation, in the annual Odwira festival held always in Kumasi. They also had to take part in Asante royal funerals: on such occasions they were expected to provide human sacrificial victims whose blood would 'water' the grave of the dead Kumasi royal. Additionally, subjection imposed on vassal states payment of annual tributes and prescribed taxes such as *apea-tuo* (war tax). In this respect Abuakwa and Kotoku as gold producing states, would normally pay in gold. But in the 1860s the Abuakwa recalled that they had to pay part of the obligatory tribute in slaves, obtained from among themselves, and that so burdensome was this obligation that their population got depleted.[14]

To ensure that subject states faithfully discharged their vassal obligations and responsibilities, the Asante government stationed Resident Provincial Commissioners in such states. These Resident Commissioners appear to have had other duties, such as preventing the subject peoples from insulting Asante citizens. A. R. Biorn, the Danish Governor at Christiansborg Castle, Osu, in 1788 noted this in relation to Akuapem.[15] An even more important duty which a Resident Commissioner was expected to perform without fail was to report to the government in Kumasi the least signs of possible insurrection on the part of the subject state to which he was accredited. Akyem Abuakwa suffered considerably on this score during the 1810-1811 period.[16]

Abuakwa and Kotoku also experienced a degree of interference in their foreign policy. They could not wage war on their own initiative without obtaining prior permission from the Asantehene. Permission was not always granted, as Abuakwa bitterly experienced in the 1790s. At that time Abuakwa was regarded as a powerful state in the eastern sector of the Gold Coast. The Danes had the Okyenhene on their payroll much in the same way as the Asantehene and the King of Popo were.[17] In 1791, Governor Biorn of Christiansborg Castle appealed to Okyenhene Twum Ampofo for military assistance against the Krepi, promising the Abuakwa ruler a subsidy to the tune of twelve slaves and two thousand rigsdaler. Twum Ampofo agreed, but when he applied to the Asantehene for permission to undertake the assignment, it was not given.[18]

The Danes attributed the refusal to Asante fear that Ampofo and his subjects were probably contemplating emigration to the lower trans-Volta.[19] The Asante suspicion suggests that Ampofo, once so enthusiastic on Abuakwa subservience to Kumasi,[20] was now finding the subordination intolerable. Anlo intrigues with Kumasi have been suggested as another reason for the Asante government's refusal to grant the permission; the Anlo feared that the Abuakwa might give military assistance to the Ada who were their traditional enemies.[21] A third reason for the refusal was that the Asante government wanted to deprive Abuakwa of the subsidy which the Danes had promise to Ampofo. This is suggested by the fact that the Asantehene offered to assist the Danes himself provided they would pay him a much bigger subsidy.[22] After all, in the event of Asante going to war against Krepi, or any other state for that matter, Abuakwa and Kotoku, as vassals, would be required by Asante imperial law to join the Asantehene's army. Abuakwa thus suffered a triple loss: it was denied an opportunity to rake in revenue, it was deprived of a chance to increase its political prestige and military standing; and at the same time it was expected to sacrifice its citizens in Asante imperial wars. Only a weak ruler like Ampofo could tolerate such a situation for as long as he did. It is possible, however, that Asante provincial administration had so improved that it gave subject states no chance to rebel. All the same, viewed from the angle of Abuakwa's dignity, sovereignty and national pride, the reign of Twum Ampofo was indeed a dark age in the history of Abuakwa. On this score alone his death in 1794[23] should have been a good riddance for the state, had his immediate successor been more enterprising.

But Apraku who reigned from 1794 to about 1807 was not: he was as submissive to Asante as Ampofo had been. He and Ampoma, the Kotokuhene, apparently discharged their vassal obligations to the letter, especially in the area of fighting the master's wars, as exemplified by the Assin-Asante war of the 1800s. Contemporary evidence shows that this war began in or about 1800.[24] Just before the Asante forces left for the war front, Ampoma of Kotoku died. His nephew Kwadwo Kuma was the most legitimate candidate for the Kotoku Stool. But at the time of his uncle's death Kuma was allegedly in Abuakwa, having gone there much earlier to represent his late uncle during an Abuakwa royal funeral.[25] In his absence, Opoku was enstooled as the new Kotokuhene.[26] It was Opoku and Apraku who personally led the Akyem contingents to join Asante against Assin Tanosu (Atandansu) and Fante.[27]

The immediate cause of the war was conflict between the two sister states of Assin Atanosu and Assin Apemanim, and the former's rejection, in a most insolent and rude manner, of the efforts of the Asantehene, their overlord, to mediate between them.[28]

The war had a far reaching effect on relations between the Akyem States on the one hand and Asante on the other. Immediately, it led to further changes in the ruling personnel of Abuakwa and Kotoku. While on the field, Apraku of Abuakwa is said to have unjustifiably executed four of this subjects and the rest resolved to destool him on their return home. The resolution was actually carried out even though the Asantehene objected to the deposition.[29] On a similar charge the Kotoku also deposed Opoku,[30] and Kwakye was put in his place. The enstoolment of Kwakye meant that Kwadwo Kuma had missed the Kotoku stool twice in succession. He was still residing in Akyem Abuakwa where Atta Owusu, later to be nicknamed *Yiakosan*(The Valiant) had replaced Apraku. Atta had a rather short reign(1807–1811).

Atta Owusu's Rebellion against Asante

The accession of Atta Owusu to power in Abuakwa led to a radical change in Akyem-Asante relations. Within three years after his enstoolment, he revised the vassal-overlord relations with Asante which Twum Ampofo and Apraku before him had submitted to with humility. He already bore Asante a grudge: he simply could not stomach the fact that Asantehene Osei Kwadwo had captured and killed Okyenhene Pobi Asamanin in 1765.[31] To worsen his dislike, in 1807, the very year of his enstoolment, Asantehne Osei Bonsu imposed a heavy burial tax on him. A relative of his reportedly fell in the Assin/Fante-Asante war in which Atta himself was said to have fought with distinction. He applied to the Asantehene for permission to give his deceased relative a formal burial. He had to apply for the permission because according to Akan custom a formal funeral was not accorded to a person who did not die a natural death. According to Governor White of Cape Coast Castle, Osei Bonsu, the Asantehene, demanded from Atta Owusu "a large sum of gold" before granting the permission.[32] Governor White goes on to say that "this, together with other acts of oppression so irritated Atta that he determined on taking the first opportunity of resenting them".[33]

"The first opportunity" came his way in 1810. By then he had been on the Abuakwa stool for three years, and was expected to have visited Kumasi to formally swear the oath of allegiance to the Asantehene. He refused to discharge that obligation. In or about 1811 the Asante government sent to find out why he had not as yet done so. At the same time the Asante government combined with the query a request that Atta should arm his subjects and join an Asante army which was about to take the field against Assin Tanosu and Fante. The request was accompanied with the customary gift of 4 oz of gold. Continued Tanosu and Fante intransigence had forced the Asantehene to make this new military move. In spite of defeat in the 1807 war and the acceptance, on their behalf, of Asante overlordship, by Governor Torrane of Cape Coast Castle in June 1807, the Assin Tanosu and the Fante refused to acknowledge their subservience to Asante. Between 1808 and 1810 these two demonstrated their hatred for Asante by attacking Elmina and Accra, the only two coastal peoples genuinely friendly to Asante. Hence the Asante anxiety to go to the rescue of those two places. Besides, they were the only places on the coast from which Asante could easily purchase European goods, especially firearms and ammunition.[34]

The request from Kumasi gave Atta Owusu the chance to leave the Asantehene in no doubt about his thinking. He calmly accepted the customary gift of 4 oz. of gold and told the emissaries from Kumasi, for onward transmission to Manhyia (the Asante palace) that the Abuakwa would surely arm, not against Assin Tanosu or Fante but against Asante itself.[35] To emphasize his seriousness, Atta Owusu followed this open declaration of rebellion with the arrest, detention, robbing and execution of all but one Asante traders and travellers, including royal messengers returning home from Accra who happened to be passing through Akyem territory.³⁶ There is no doubt from both contemporary and other sources that Atta Owusu's rebellion in 1811 was carefully planned, premeditated as it were, awaiting the appropriate time for its execution. The assertion of Ward that it was fortuitous, triggered off by the Asante request for military assistance,³⁷ is not borne out by the facts.

The period between 1808 and 1811 was most suitable for launching the Abuakwa revolt. Asante was experiencing almost universal provincial rebellions. Assin Tanosu and Fante, as already pointed out, were in arms. Wassa was a rebel state; in 1809 she joined the western Fante against Elmina.³⁸ Agona also revolted in 1810 by siding with the eastern Fante against Accra.³⁹ Akuapem raised the standard of rebellion in 1809.⁴⁰ Information reaching Elmina Castle in February 1811 said Denkyira too had turned against Asante.⁴¹ At least Abuakwa, Akuapem and Denkyira had all fought for Asante in the 1800–1807 wars against Assin Tanosu and Fante. It was surely no coincidence that in a space of four years they should all be in rebellion against the overlord. It seems that most, if not all, of the subject states were unhappy with their subservience to Asante. Atta Owusu must have been aware of this overall situation. In deciding to rebel he may have considered the possibility of striking alliances with some of the states already in rebellion. The times were indeed conducive for a successful revolt in Abuakwa.

But internal disunity nearly marred the chances of success for Atta. The state was divided on the subject of loyalty to Asante. There was a strong pro-Asante party in Abuakwa. It is not absolutely clear who and who were members of this party, but its existence was not in doubt. Meredith, the English factor at Winneba, was clearly referring obliquely to it in 1812 when he said Atta "governed [Abuakwa] in conjuction with Tando".⁴² We know from Bowdich that Tano was the Resident Asante Commissioner for Akyem Abuakwa at the time of Atta Owusu's revolt.⁴³ Meredith goes on to say that Atta "refused obedience to the King's orders by not going against the Fantees, which produced a dispute between himself and Tando who drove him out of Akim ..."⁴⁴ It was not the duty of a Resident Commissioner to wage war against the leadership of the state to which he was accredited. Therefore Commissioner Tano apparently instigated the pro-Asante party in Abuakwa to challenge Atta's rebellion.

That was high patriotism on the Commissioner's part. But to that extent he clearly exceeded the parameters of his commission. His conduct and action were later examined in Kumasi. The result of the enquiry was that

> though Atta was adjudged to be at fault . . . the Ashantee government thought it politic to [replace] Tandoh, though he had become disagreeable only for his vigilance and fidelity.⁴⁵

The recall of Tano failed to deflect Atta Owusu in his resolve to revolt. He pressed ahead with it, mustering a force that was variously estimated to be between three thousand and five thousand.[46] The Asante government was equally determined to suppress the Abuakwa rebellion; it despatched against Atta an army of ten thousand strong under the command of Adusei Kra.[47]

The first battles of the Abuakwa-Asante war were fought in or about September 1810.[48] Two battles were fought and Atta won both, an outcome which forced General Adusei Kra to send to Kumasi for reinforcement.[49] In response, Asantehene Osei Bonsu sent express instructions to General Opoku Frefre (or Fredefrede) initially detailed to go to the rescue of Accra with a force of twenty-five thousand, to divert his course to Abuakwa and take over from Adusei Kra. Opoku Frefre's arrival in Abuakwa increased the formidability of the invading Asante force. Atta countered this development with an alliance with Akuapem. This was not difficult to achieve. In the first place, Akuapem was already in revolt and secondly, clan and historical ties existed between Kyebi and Akuropon.

In the face of the increased Asante force, Atta Owusu retreated southwards into Akuapem to join forces with Okuapemhene Kwao Safro Twe. The allies met Opoku Frefre in a battle at Mampon. Opinion is divided on the outcome of the battle. Reindorf says that victory went to the Asante General.[50] Cruickshank and others, however, claim victory for the allies, adding that Opoku Frefre was so hardpressed that he had to appeal to the Ga for assistance.[51] What is common to both views is that they suggest a keen contest between the two warring sides. Probably the outcome of the Battle of Mampon was indecisive.

The Ga entry into the war widened its scope for the allies. They decided to counter this new development with the adoption of guerrilla warfare. The two rebel Chiefs separated; Kwao and his forces headed first to Krobo, and later to Ada on the east coast, with Opoku Frefre in hot pursuit. Atta Owusu on the other hand went westwards to Agona and Fante in search of another invading Asante army of about four thousand under the command of General Appia Dankwa. Atta Owusu arrived in Agona in the early months of 1811. By then he had established a reputation as a redoubtable warrior. The Agona and the eastern Fante rushed to join forces with him.[52] It was also indicative of this reputation that Opoku Frefre chose to pursue Kwao Safor Twe and not Atta. At any rate Appiah Dankwa too got scared when Atta arrived in Agona and tried to take to his heels. But the Abuakwa warrior chief caught up with him in the vicinity of Tantum and defeated him.

The European Companies and the War

The war with Asante made the Abuakwa hostile to all those who were friendly to, or who in any way, showed sympathy with and support for that power. Sections of the European presence in the Gold Coast had become partisan in their African relations. Since the eighteenth century, the Danes were generally inclined to sympathize with the Akyem and the Akuapem, the Dutch on the other hand were pro-Asante. The English tried to be as much non-aligned as was politically possible, deciding which African group to support according to the demands and dictates of the moment. Atta extended his hatred for and hostility to Asante to the Dutch fort of Lydzemheid at Apam, destroyed a greater part of it, put the Dutch there to flight, and freed all Africans held in prison in the fort.[54] Finally he threatened more destruction and damage to the Dutch after he had fully settled scores with Asante.[55]

Parallel to the Akyem Abuakwa maltreatment of the Dutch was Opoku Frefre's manhandling of the Danes, on grounds of the latter's sympathy with the Akyem and the Akuapem. Opoku chased Kwao Safro Twe from Krobo to Ada, hoping to engage him there, but Kwao always eluded him.[56] The frustrated Asante General vented his spleen on Mr. Flindt, the Danish factor at Ada, for allegedly helping Kwao to escape; he seized and detained Mr. Flindt for several weeks before releasing him.[57] At the foot of the Akuapem hills, Opoku Frefre ordered the destruction of Danish coffee plantation jointly owned by Governor Schioning and a Mr. Meyer.[58] He too vowed to wreak more havoc on the Danes.[59] The cause of Opoku's anger towards the Danes was the latter's support for and sympathy with the Akyem and the Akuapem. Danish Governor Schionning, however, attributed it to Anglo-Dutch intrigues with Asante.[60] The English denied the charge and pointed to Danish sale of arms and ammunition to the Akyem Abuakwa and the Akuapem as the cause of the Asante anger; they went on to advise the Danes to be more discreet and circumspect in their local relations.[61]

The English advice to the Danes was the product of bitter experience. During the 1800–1807 war the English supported Assin Tanosu and Fante and suffered terribly for that action. For two consecutive days the Asante laid siege to fort William, the English base at Anomabo. With that experience at the back of their mind, the British, in the 1810–1811 upheavals, resolved not to formally side with any party. Atta Owusu tried to force them to declare against Asante by asking the English at Winneba to pay war-tax. Meredith, the English factor at Winneba, politely refused to pay the tax as such, arguing that payment would imply British sympathy with Akyem Abuakwa. To soothe the Abuakwa ruler Meredith sent him presents "as a token of friendship", with an assurance of British desire to support strict neutrality.[62] The warring parties respected the stand of the British. Neither of them inflicted any injury on British persons or property.

The Untimely Death of Atta Owusu

Success in Agona and Fante encouraged the Okyenhene to turn eastwards in order to attempt another confrontation with Opoku Frefre who was believed "to be at the back of Addah".[63] Misfortune, however, struck the cause of Abuakwa at this time. Atta Owusu died unexpectedly. The Abuakwa army had hardly gone beyond the Agona town of Kwanyarko when the Okyenhene contracted small pox and died a few days later.[64] Abuakwa tradition vividly recalls the misfortune.[65] The exact date of Atta Owusu's death is not known. He must have died between 20th August and 7th October 1811. On the first date Governor White of Cape Coast Castle bitterly regretted the adverse effect the Akyem-Ashante war was having on trade; on the second he recorded the arrival of an official Abuakwa delegation at Cape Coast to inform him of Atta's death.[66]

The Abuakwa liberation movement sustained an irreplaceable loss in the demise of King Atta Owusu. Under him the Abuakwa, according to Governor White of Cape Coast Castle, had fought with "great courage"[67]. Thirty-five years later, it was said of Atta that he was a genius of a military leader whose patriotism, courage and implacable hatred for the Asante hegemony would have enabled him to rescue his people from the clutches of Asante imperialism but for his untimely death.[68] In the 1850s the Basel missionaries working in Akyem Abuakwa were told that the whole Abuakwa state deemed Atta Owusu's death as a national tragedy and so commemorated the sad event with the oath "Kwanyarko".[69]

Though the oath invoked bitter memories, it was a fitting and honourable tribute to the memory of a great leader. Atta had been a real thorn in the flesh of the Asante, as their reaction in Kumasi to the news of his death showed. On the receipt of the information, the Asante government recalled the armies of Opoku Frefre and Appiah Dankwa, because with Atta dead, it was felt that serious Akyem Abuakwa resistance was over.

The analysis of the Asante government was very correct. Atta's death had a great demoralising impact on the Abuakwa liberation movement. The two immediate successors to the stool, Asare Bediako (1811–1812) and Kofi Asante (1812–1816)[70] lacked Atta's charisma, dynamism and drive to successfully continue the liberation movement.

Asare Bediako indeed tried to emulate the late Okyenhene's political and military exploits. He, Safro Twe of Akuapem and King Aduku of Mankesim organized a joint attack on the Ga, on account of the latter's friendship with Asante. There couldn't have been a much greater misadventure for the Abuakwa. The Ga gallantly defended themselves by inflicting defeat on the aggressors.[71] But for the alleged bravery of Doku Sra of Pamen, the Ga would have captured the paramount stool of Abuakwa.⁷² Reindorf states categorically that the Ga did capture the stool.⁷³ He might well be right, considering the disastrous effect the war had on the Asare Bediako line of the Abuakwa ruling house. The Abuakwa are said to have declared him an ill-fated leader, deposed him and asked him as well as other members of his line to commit suicide, which they did.⁷⁴

Kofi Asante who succeeded to the stool, was just slightly better than his immediate predecessor, as shall be shown in due course. The poor and lacklustre leadership qualities of these two rulers of Abuakwa made it possible for Kwadwo Kuma, a Kotoku Prince, to come into the lime-light of the Akyem freedom movement. Kuma was not the successor to Atta Owusu, as several writers have thought.⁷⁵ He was a Kotoku Prince during Atta's reign in Abuakwa, and ascended the Akyem Kotoku Stool in or after 1812.⁷⁶

Kwadwo Kuma's Accession to Power in Kotoku

As pointed out earlier, Kwadwo Kuma missed the Akyem Kotoku stool on two occasions, 1794 and 1807. On both occasions he was allegedly residing in Akyem Abuakwa. Precisely what attracted him to Abuakwa may never be known. Judging from his later exploits, he was apparently the adventurous type, cut in the mould of the late Okyenhene Atta Owusu whose personality and policy in relation to Asante seem to have fascinated him. Consequently, during the Abuakwa-Asante, war even though the Kotoku State fought on the side of Asante, he threw in his lot with Atta Owusu. He paid dearly for this. According to Reindorf, his closest relatives, consisting of his mother, his sister, his mother's sister and daughter, were sent in chains to Kumasi where they were all executed.⁷⁷

The Asante government clearly meant these executions to be a reprisal against Kwadwo Kuma for siding with rebel Abuakwa. It is equally possible that the victims were sent to Kumasi on the initiative of Kwakye, the Kotokuhene, with a view to wiping out Kwadwo Kuma's branch of the Kotoku ruling house.

Kwakye's collaboration with Asante and the cruelty of the Kumasi government as demonstrated by the executions just referred to eventually proved counter productive. Kwadwo Kuma grew more determined to liberate his people from the Asante yoke. His first step was to secure power in Kotoku. After the failure of the 1812 Abuakwa-Akuapem-Mankesim adventure in Accra, he informed the Kyebi leadership of his intentions to return to Akyem Kotoku and claim the stool there. Okyenhene Kofi Asante and the Queenmother, Dokuaa, agreed and reciprocated his services by providing him with men and war material. The gamble succeeded: Kuma defeated Kwakye in the Battle of Dampon.⁷⁸ Apparently aware of the fate that would befall him should Kwadwo

Kuma get hold of him, Kwakye grabbed the Kotoku Stool, gathered his closest relatives who included his nephew Kofi Agyeman,[79] and fled with them to Asante. There the fugitive Kotoku royals were made the guests of the King of the small state of Bosome near lake Bosomtwe. Kwakye reportedly died a month after his arrival in Asante.

Kwadwo Kuma was installed as the new Kotokuhene. But he was a King without the stool of his ancestors. To the Akan, that was a serious detraction from his authority. He therefore made every effort to get the stool back from Asante. Reindorf, our main source in these matters, says that Kuma approached the important palatine state of Juaben to intercede with Kumasi on his behalf for the stool of his ancestors to be returned to Daa. But all he got back in reply was a message to go to Kumasi and collect it. Of course he needed no one to warn him not to set foot on Asante soil. He abandoned the efforts to retrieve the stool of his ancestors from Asante. Instead, he mustered all resources and made Asante pay for its tyranny and cruelty. With this determination Kwadwo Kuma was poised to launch the Kotoku phase of the Akyem freedom movement.

The Kotoku Phase of the Akyem Liberation Movement

From 1813 Kwadwo Kuma of Kotoku became the pivot of the Akyem liberation struggle. Between 1813 and 1814, he effectively closed against Asante all trade routes passing through Kotoku and Abuakwa to the Ga-Adangbe and the Eastern Fante coasts. So tight was this sanction that it gave a welcome relief to several southern states which in diverse ways had suffered from Asante political and military pressures.[80]

The economic blockade generated great animosity in Asante. Besides, the Asante government saw in Kwadwo Kuma another Atta Owusu. In several ways this Kotokuhene indeed resembled the late Abuakwahene. Like Atta Owusu, Kuma was daring and dynamic. He also espoused some of Atta's military and political strategies. He did not limit his activities to the confines of the Akyem territory. In 1813 he sent Akyem (Kotoku) war mongers to Fante, to whip up against Asante, Fante hatred which was said to be on the wane.[81]

Rebellion by Kotoku was criminal enough for Asante to deal with. But for rebel Kotoku to incite revolt in others was something Asante could certainly not tolerate for long. The Kotoku phase of the Akyem rebellion, together with Kwadwo Kuma's incitement of insurrection in others, rather than the failure to suppress Atta Owusu,[82] was what compelled Asantehene Osei Bonsu to put a ten-thousand-strong army in the field against the Akyem in 1815.[83] Other estimates put the number of the Asante army even higher: twenty thousand.[84] It has also been said that the Asante government put a much smaller force in the field, under the command of old Appia Dankwa, with instructions to block a possible retreat of the Akyem forces into Fante.⁸⁵ Contemporary evidence shows that Appia Dankwa was to go and suppress the Denkyira and the Wassa who were still in revolt.⁸⁶ Six years on, the provincial rebellions were still raging, but it was the uprising in the Akyem country which engaged the greatest attention of Asante.

Kwadwo Kuma adopted the two main methods and moves the late Atta Owusu of Abuakwa had used: formation of alliances and guerrilla warfare. First, he forged alliances with Abuakwa and Akuapem. Second, he and Okyenhene Kofi Asante retreated southwards into Akuapem to join Kwao Safro Twe. At Adweso (? Adawso) in Akuapem the allies in or about September 1815 made a stand against the ten thousand strong Asante army of General Amankwa, nicknamed *Abunyiwa*("The Leg-breaker").⁸⁷ Observers are not agreed on the outcome of the Battle of Adweso. Some say that the allies lost it.⁸⁸ Others claim the contest was indecisive.⁸⁹ The second view may be nearer to the truth because after the battle the Agona and the Fante sent to invite the allies to join hands with them against Asante.⁹⁰ Had the allies lost, the Agona and the Fante certainly would not have extended an invitation to them. Also, the severity of the battle obliged the "Leg-breaker" to rest his army in the Ga district for three months before resuming hostilities.⁹¹

In response to the invitation of the Agona and the Fante, and of course in consonance with Kuma's guerrilla strategy, the allies retreated westwards. The three allied Chiefs proved so elusive that Amankwa Abunyiwa went as far west as Cape Coast in March 1816, looking for them.⁹²

Kwadwo Kuma's Fall

At this juncture ill-luck and treachery appear to have afflicted the Akyem-Akuapem war of independence. Some of the lesser chiefs of Kotoku, such as one Amoako, became war-weary and deserted Kwadwo Kuma. Others, joined by a section of the Fante, worked to betray him to the Asante.⁹³ The Fante share of the treachery is suggested by the rigorous ordeal which "The Leg-breaker" subjected three Fante Chiefs to. He seized the three Fante Chiefs, detained them and threatened to send them in chains to Kumasi if the Fante did not disclose the whereabouts of the two Akyem and the Akuapem rebel chiefs to him. But for British and Dutch intervention the Asante General would have carried out the threat. At a meeting in Cape Coast Castle, the two European trading authorities successfully pleaded for the release of the three Fante Chiefs.⁹⁴ The Fante had to pay a fine and a peace price of 100 oz. of gold to Amankwa Abunyiwa.⁹⁵

longer be counted on for support. Still applying the guerrilla tactics, they apparently decided to slip out of Fante and return to their own countries. But, according to Acting Governor Dawson of Cape Coast Castle, Kwadwo Kuma in particular was 'pursued so closely that he put an end to his own existence rather than fall into the hands of his enemies'.⁹⁶ Reindorf asserts (though he does not indicate his source of evidence) that treachery was partly responsible for Kuma's fall. He writes:

> Kwadwo Kuma, having discovered that the Fante could not protect him, fled from the country with Gyadam Kyei and Amoako Hene, intending to return to his own capital Dampong. Osaka, the mother of Aduanam Apea, with her daughter Badua having been taken prisoners by the Asante, Apea and Kwamena Asamanin despatched eight messengers after Kwadwo Kuma, who was overtaken by them at Nkwatanan, and was urgently asked to return, as the Asantes had fled from the Fante country. They persuaded him to return, and then delivered him up to the [Asante] generals at Nkum . . .⁹⁷

Effect of Kuma's Death

Reaction in Kumasi to the news of Kwadwo Kuma's fall was one of relief. Huydecoper, a Dutch agent was in Kumasi at that time. From Kumasi he reported to Elmina Castle authorities on 7th June, 1816 that the whole of Asante had gone wild with jubilation.⁹⁸ In contrast to the euphoria in Asante a blanket of gloom and grief settled on the two Akyem states and Akuapem. The defeat and death of Kwadwo Kuma, like the tragic demise of Atta Owusu in 1811, deflated the Akyem and Akuapem struggle for independence. In Akuapem, some members of the Akuropon ruling house betrayed Kwao Safro Twe into the hands of the Asante who decapitated him.⁹⁹ The collusion failed to satisfy General Amankwa Abunyiwa. He imposed a fine of four hundred slaves on the entire Akuapem State.¹⁰⁰ The Akuapem submission to Asante occurred in or about November 1816.¹⁰¹

Akyem Abuakwa also lost heart, submitted to General Amankwa at about the same time as Akuapem, and a fine of 100 oz. of gold was slammed on the state.¹⁰² In addition, the Leg-breaker beheaded Okyenhene Kofi Asante.¹⁰³ It is possible that other male members of the Kyebi ruling house were executed. The absence of male candidates to the stool in 1817 suggests this. Consequently, in that year, Queenmother Dokuaa was enstooled the new Okyenhene.

Punishment meted out to the state of Akyem Kotoku was as harsh as those of Akyem Abuakwa and Akuapem, if not harsher. According to Reindorf, our only source, almost all chiefs who had supported Kwadwo Kuma up to the time of his fall were beheaded, only Chiefs like Amoako who had deserted Kuma were pardoned and spared their lives.¹⁰⁴ Reindorf states further that

(i) the Kotoku Prince Afrifa Akwada, a son of Amoako, his mother and his sister would have all been decapitated had not Amoako paid a fine of three *pereguans* of gold to the Asantehene,
(ii) the Kotoku were not allowed to enstool a new ruler.

The gravity of the punishment for Dampong, as Reindorf calls Daa (or Oda), proves the importance of Kwadwo Kuma in the Akyem liberation struggle during its 1813–1816 phase.

Post-1816 Akyem-Asante Relations

Political life in Akyem after 1816 experienced interference from Kumasi. It has just been pointed out that the Kotoku were not allowed to enstool a new paramount ruler. Rather Chief Amoako, who had deserted Kuma when the going became difficult, was made Regent of the State.[105] Vassal obligation became burdensome and more painful to discharge. In 1818 both Abuakwa and Kotoku had to fight for their master during the Asante-Gyaman war.[106] Abuakwa losses in this war were said to be very heavy.[107] The States suffered in several other ways, such as in the matter of taxes and tributes. By 1822 the Asante government had decreed that only gold and European goods, and not slaves, would have to be paid by subject states in discharging their tax and tribute obligations.[108] As gold-producing countries, Abuakwa and Kotoku should have found the new decree a welcome piece of news. But during the 1810s and early 1820s the gold-gigging industry in Akyem, according to Dupuis, was not a profitable job to engage in.[109] Dupuis may well be right, considering that the first quarter of the nineteenth century was a period of incessant wars. The people could hardly devote sufficient time and energy on economic pursuits. Without enough gold, the Abuakwa and the Kotoku would obviously lack a strong purchasing power to buy European goods from the coast. The Asante yoke was becoming more and more unbearable and intolerable for subject states.

Civil War in Abuakwa

One such state was Akyem Abuakwa. By the early 1820s she had become jittery and unenthusiastic about the subservience to Asante. A quiet but a strong sense of dislike for Asante pervaded that country. This new mood showed itself in 1820. By that year Okyenhene Dokuaa had been on the Kyebi Stool for three years. Asante imperial law required that she should proceed to Kumasi in order to formally swear the oath of allegiance to the Asantehene. The entire state split into two over the issue. One faction questioned the wisdom in Abuakwa's continued subserviance to Asante. This group consisted of lesser chiefs, the most vociferous of whom, according to Reindorf, were Okru of Apapam, Oben Ayekwa of Apedwa, and Kwasi Asimen of Tete.[110] These openly objected to the Okyenhene going to Kumasi. The other faction, made up mainly of the Divisional Chiefs such as the Nifahene of Abuakwa (Asiakwa) and the Gyaasehene of Abuakwa (Kwaben), supported continued association with Asante; Dokuaa herself was inclined to side with this latter faction.[111]

The issue degenerated into civil war in Abuakwa, probably during the 1820–1822 period. The anti-Asantists won and forced the Okyenhene not to go to Kumasi.[112] In this way Akyem Abuakwa renounced its allegiance to Asante. Abuakwa was once more in revolt. The Asante would, no doubt, have descended on her were they not preoccupied with strained relations with the British.

Relations between Asante and the British had been deteriorating since 1820. Asante suzerainty over Fante was essentially the cause of the Anglo-Asante tension. A British mission to Kumasi in 1817 had recognized both the Asantehene and the British mercantile administration at Cape Coast Castle as joint overlords of Fante.[113] This arrangement was hardly suitable. The unsuitability was underlined in late 1818 and early 1819 when the Asante government, in connection with the Gyaman war, tried to levy war tax at Komenda and met with Fante opposition to the tax. The Asante government turned to hold the Cape Coast Castle administration responsible for the Komenda conduct – misconduct from Asante view point. The British would not accept the blame.

The issue remained unresolved up to 1820. When Dupuis in that year went to Kumasi as the official representative of the British Home Government, not; he resolved the problem by conceding the Asantehene's sole rights over Fante. That was a realistic solution, but when he returned to Cape Coast, Hope Smith of the British traders' administration in the Castle refused to endorse the decision of Dupuis.[114] That was too bad for Anglo-Asante relations. But the worse was to come. From 1821 when the British Crown made a move to take over British possessions in West Africa from the Committee of African merchants, Anglo-Asante relations plummeted further. The tension worsened from 1822 when Governor Charles MacCarthy arrived in the Gold Coast to formally take over the British possessions here. He at once adopted a hostile attitude towards the Kumasi Government. Asante retaliated contemptuously with

(i) the execution in March 1823 of an African sergeant in British employ at Fort William Anomabo and
(ii) a limited but successful armed confrontation against the British at Abora.

Immediately, Governor MacCarthy plunged into serious preparation for a full-scale war with Asante. Joined by the Danes, the British launched a campaign for local allies.[115]

Okyenhene Dokuaa was one of the Gold Coast rulers whom the British and the Danes approached. The contact was presumably made in July 1823, when the dust of the civil war in Abuakwa had not fully settled. The civil war in Abuakwa had significant effects on both Abuakwa itself and the Gold Coast in general. Immediately, the success of the anti-Asante party appears to have led to constitutional changes in the state. It is most likely that it was from about this time that the three chiefs of Apapam, Apedwa and Tete were constituted into the Amantuo-Mmiensa Council (the Council of the three Counties as Danquah called it), and made the Fourth Estate in the Akyem Abuakwa constitution.[116] The three Chiefs came to be regarded as the custodians of the Kyebi Stool and protectors of its occupant as well as the general interest of the Abuakwa state.[117]

The Liberation Movement in Akyem: The Final Phase

The success of the anti-Asantists in the Abuakwa Civil War also ushered in the third and, what was to turn out to be, the final phase of the Akyem war of liberation against Asante.

In terms of the Gold Coast as a whole, perhaps the most significant effect of the Abuakwa Civil War was the change it brought in the attitude of the Kyebi ruling house towards relations with the British. Dokuaa was compelled by circumstances to respond positively to the campaign of the British-led alliance which was fast forming in the Gold Coast against Asante. In or about August 1823, she travelled to Accra to announce Abuakwa's membership of the alliance.[118] Aside from the pressure from her own anti-Asante subjects, the British and the Danes were using calm diplomacy, bribery and intimidation in their campaign for local allies. Finally, in view of the Abuakwa rebellion it made sense to join the alliance, as it would be an insurance against a punitive expedition from Asante.

Political and war strategists in Kumasi took a serious view of the hostile developments in the Gold Coast and recommended that Asante should go on the offensive and stamp its authority on all territories to the south. In January 1824, the main Asante army took the field against the British, Wassa and Denkyira in the west, defeated them all, captured and beheaded Governor MacCarthy in the Battle of Nsamankow. Kumasi despatched another and a much smaller force, under the command of one Kwaku Bri (or Bribi),[119] to punish and suppress rebel Abuakwa. The Akyem Kotoku, on account of vassal obligation, most probably joined the Bri expedition against Abuakwa. They however, secretly played a double game to tilt the war in favour of Abuakwa.

It must have been they who, while Bri was encamped in their country, sent to warn Abuakwa that an Asante force was marching on Kyebi.[120] On the receipt of this intelligence Dokuaa quickly solicited allied assistance from her kinsman, Okuapemhene Addo Dankwa, who readily obliged.[121] The Kotoku seem to have rendered yet another useful service to Abuakwa; they apparently revealed to Abuakwa and Akuapem the war strategy and movements of the Bri army. The fact that the allies carried the war to the Asante in Kotoku suggests this.

A stiff battle was fought some time in 1824 near Asene in the neighbourhood of the present-day Asante-Akyem town of Obogu; the allies won the war.[122] An Abuakwa tradition gives greater credit to the Akuapem in this battle. The tradition has it that at one stage in the battle, the Asante had almost defeated the allies. But the Akuapem force cleverly outflanked the enemy and attacked them from behind; panic seized the Bri forces who were totally routed.[123]

The success of Akyem Abuakwa and Akuapem arms, aided by secret Akyem Kotoku moral support in the east, had a radical impact on the general war situation in the Gold Coast. It is not clear whether the Abuakwa and the Akuapem received any direct support from the Danes, but it seems that the Abuakwa-Akuapem victory at Asene was somehow proclaimed as Danish success in the east[124] vis-a-vis British defeat in the west. Rumours actually circulated that the Danes and some sections of eastern Gold Coast, led by Governor Richelieu of Christiansborg Castle, were advancing on the eastern provinces of Asante through Akyem territory,[125] if indeed the Danes made any moves at all. As Claridge rightly points out, these were mere Danish bluffs[126] if indeed the Danes made any move at all. All the same with the defeat of the Asante army under Kwaku Bri by the Abuakwa and the Akuapem, such rumours were bound to have a ring of truth. Consequently, consternation seized sections of the Asante army fighting in the west, forcing the whole army to curtail the war and return home,[127] undoubtedly to contain the alleged Danish threat in the east. Ivor Wilks touches on the Asene war but does not concede the impact of the Akyem-Akuapem victory. Commenting on the curtailment of the war in the west he writes:

> However, due in part to the onset of the rains and a serious outbreak of smallpox among his troops, and in part to the concern of the Asantehemaa in Kumase that both Gyaman and Akyem might take advantage of the situation to attack Kumase itself, Osei Yaw [i..e., the Asantehene] decided to withdraw his army from the southern provinces in August [1824]. Another smaller army which had been posted to the border of the Akyem provinces, apparently commanded by the Atwoma-Agogohene Kwaku Bene [i.e.. Bri] was also pulled back; it had been under heavy attacks organized from Christiansborg . . .[128]

It is clear from all the available evidence that the success of the Abuakwa and the Akuapem in the Asene War was a major, if not the sole, factor in ending the MacCarthy War.

Another important effect of the Asene War was the emigration of the paramount lineage of Kotoku from Northern to Southern Akyem. The lineage anticipated a possible Asante invasion in the-not-too-distant future owing to their secret role in helping the allies to win the Asene War. They seem to have calculated that the best way to avoid that possible blow was to emigrate southwards into Akyem Abuakwa. Once there, they would be sure not only of Abuakwa and Akuapem support but also that of the greater Southern Alliance led by the British and the Danes.

Amoako was still the Regent of Kotoku. He refused to be party to the emigration movement. With a small following he is said to have left Daa for Agogo whose inhabitants were very pro-Asante.[129] But "his son, Afrifa Akwada", writes Reindorf, "cousin of the late Kwadwo Kuma", was enstooled Kotokuhene and led the migration to Akyem Abuakwa.[130] The departure from Northern Akyem is said to have taken place in 1825.[131] By virtue of the emigration, the State of Akyem Kotoku formally joined Akyem Abuakwa in the final phase of the liberation movement against Asante.

This was about the time when the State of Bosome began to arouse itself from its over one century slumber, stand up, and be counted among the comity of states and peoples in the Gold Coast. Migrants from lacustrine Bosome in Asante arrived to swell its population and forge a strong link between her and the State of Kotoku. On the basis of the destination of the migrants, namely western Akyem, it is reasonable to suggest, as a remote cause, that since the 1700s the 'lake' Bosome had always cherished the hope of one day migrating southwards to reunite with their kinsmen who, as we saw in Chapter 2, migrated to settle in western Akyem in the first decade of the eighteenth century. What immediately brought about the 19th century migration, however, was tension between the rulers of the 'lake' Bosome and the State of Kumasi.

During the 1818–1819 Gyaman War the Bosome fought for the Asante government. Their losses in the war were so heavy that their feeling was that in a way Kumasi was using its imperial wars to exterminate them.[132] As compensation for their losses, the Bosome allegedly secured a large war booty. Unfortunately, the loot became a bone of contention between Bosomehene Koragye Ampaw and Asantehene Osei Bonsu who demanded that it be surrendered to the central government. Koragye refused to oblige, and since he knew what the refusal entailed, he and his subjects emigrated to western Akyem.[133]

The migration may well have taken place in the 1824–1825 period when several other peoples, including the Kotoku (as already noted above), Denkyira, and the Assin Apemanin, all migrated southwards in response to either the

Abuakwa-Akuapem success in the Asene War or the Anglo-Danish campaign for allies against Asante, or both. Reindorf indicates that there was a degree of consultations and coordination among some of the migrating lineages. He says that the MacCarthy War convinced the vassal states

> that by uniting their forces with those of the British Marines, Akras, and Fantes, they could protect themselves from the power of Asante, which they perceived was declining, while, on the other hand, the power [of] the Gold Coast tribes under the protection and guidance of the White Men was increasing. Before Kwadwo Tiboo escape from Kumase to Denkyera, he informed Dampong Amoako [Regent of Kotoku] of his intentions; and later Tibo Panyin of Asen [Tanosu] did the same. Queen Dokuwa [of Abuakwa], after declaring in favour of the British and Danish Government, sent . . . to find out the intentions of Amoako [of Kotoku].[134]

It is not unlikely that it was Dokuaa's message which partly encouraged the Kotoku ruling house to migrate into Akyem Abuakwa.

The South-bound migrations profoundly affected the social and political setups in some of the states in the Gold Coast, as well as relations between the British and the Danes on the one hand, and the Southern States on the other. Immediately, the movements led to kinship and family reunions among the Kotoku and the Bosome. In western Akyem, the Koragye Ampaw-led migrants joined their kinsmen settled there since 1706. Also the nineteenth century immigrants from lacustrine Bosome naturally increased the population of Akyem Bosome, though by how much, it is not easy to say.

The 1824–1825 Bosome migration to western Akyem prepared the ground for yet another family reunification, this time among the Kotoku. Joining in this migration were the relatives of the late Kwakye, the fugitive ex-Kotokuhene who, it will be recalled, had fled his kingdom for Asante in 1812. One of these relatives was Kofi Agyeman; he was nephew to Kwakye. Both the Kotoku and Bosome migrants had hardly settled down in their respective locations when Kotokuhene Afrifa Akwada died through accident, killed by a failing tree during a rainstorm in eastern Akyem Abuakwa.[135] His subjects quickly sent an embassy to Western Akyem to fetch Kofi Agyeman from Soadru, the Akyem Bosome capital, and enstooled him as the new Kotokuhene at Gyadam which was their main settlement in eastern Akyem.[136] The 1825 enstoolment of Kofi Agyeman thus healed the split which had occurred in the Kotoku ruling house since 1812. Besides, the installation of Agyeman and the migrations in general, quietly but undoubtedly, forged close contact and communication among the Akyem states of Abuakwa, Kotoku and Bosome. Even more importantly, the migrations into southern Akyem put all three states into the mainstream of Gold Coast politics. For the Kotoku and the Bosome were not now expected to emigrate southwards without Asante putting up a fight to stop them from having their way. Nor were the Abuakwa to go unpunished for

(i) defeating the Kwaku Bene army at Asene, and
(ii) inciting others to throw off their allegiance to Asante as they were clearly doing with the Kotoku.

All three Akyem peoples must have realized that sooner than later, they would have to face a punitive armed expedition from Asante. What was probably preventing the Asante government from making an immediate move against them was the death of the great Osei Bonsu, an event which appears to have occurred in 1823, [137] but kept secret till after the MacCarthy War. There was every reason for the Akyem peoples to prepare against a potential major danger from Asante. This awareness must have made them more anxious than reluctant[138] to seek or strengthen alliance with the British. Certainly it was due to the importance they attached to the British-led Gold Coast alliance that Okyenhene Dokuaa, and possibly the new Kotokuhene, Agyeman, travelled all the way to Accra to reaffirm their membership in, and commitment to that alliance by giving up hostages to back their word.[139] Almost all states and peoples south of Asante joined the Anglo-Danish promoted Southern Alliance. It appears that only Kwawu remained loyal to Asante.[140] The European presence in the Gold Coast was also divided on the subject of relations with Asante: while the British and the Danes, as has been made clear already, were anti-Asante, the Dutch continued to maintain their centuries-old friendly relations with that power.

The Akantamasu War

Asante forces took the field in early 1826, this time heading for the eastern sector of the Gold Coast. It is claimed that the main objective of the invading Asante force was to punish the Ga for renouncing their friendship with Asante.[141] It is true that the Ga had been seizing, robbing and killing Asante subjects they could lay hands on. However, the Asante did not have to look that far for peoples and states which had offended them in that manner. The Akyem were perhaps the most guilty offenders. The main object of the Asante was to punish the Akyem and force them to return to their allegiance to Kumasi. At any rate an invading Asante army heading for eastern Gold Coast just could not get through to Ga-Adangbe without first having to subdue the Akyem, the Akuapem and the Krobo.

For that very reason Akyem Abuakwa and the Akyem Kotoku (now in Abuakwa) were the first to face the invader. They fought the enemy in several battles and suffered as many reverses.[142] They were forced to retreat southwards, first into Akuapem, and later further south to join the troops of other members of the Alliance. The main battle between the Allies and Asante was fought in August 1826 at Akantamasu. The Allies won it. The Akyem later inflicted further defeats on the already battered invader in minor actions.[143]

With Asante defeated, the Akyem States, like all others which had joined the Alliance, were now poised to regain their independence from Kumasi. The formal and final act of liberation was undertaken on their behalf by the British and the Danes. After the hot war the British in particular made every effort to reach a peace settlement with Asante as soon as possible. But peace did not come till November 1831 when a final Peace Treaty was signed between the Alliance and Asante.

The almost five-year delay was due mainly to the opposition of some African members of the Alliance, especially the Akyem. As one British official in the Gold Coast was to observe in 1871, in terms of ethnic affinity, culture as well as social and political systems and geography, the Akyem of all the peoples of the Gold Coast were perhaps the closest to the Asante, and yet they were the most hostile to them.[144] They were not prepared to come to peace terms with their former overlords without first wreaking vengeance of some sort on that power, in order to square the ills they had suffered from them for decades.[145] For instance they refused to endorse the Peace Treaty unless certain Asante prisoners-of-war and hostages, including Akyaa,[146] daughter of the Asantehene, were handed over to them. On the other hand the Asante negotiators at the peace talks showed considerable contempt for the Akyem peoples as their former vassals.[147] Feelings and animosities between the two parties were so bitter, especially, during the peace signing ceremony that, according to Reindorf, it needed all the tact and temperament of "Governor Maclean to maintain peace".[148] By virtue of the 1831 Treaty of Peace all the Akyem states, like several others in the Gold Coast, recovered their independence from Asante.[149]

Summary

For the Akyem peoples the recovery of sovereignty was a consummation of a cherished and long standing desire dating back to at least 1783. In that year the Akyem Abuakwa reluctantly accepted vassalage to Asante, following the Akyem Kotoku who had done so forty years earlier. The two peoples had been compelled to remain subservient to Asante for lack of dynamic leadership. But in 1807 when Atta Owusu ascended the Abuakwa Stool and in 1812 when Kwadwo Kuma mounted that of Kotoku, the Akyem launched a liberation movement which was to enable them to sever their servitude to Asante. With the help of the British and the Danes and the cooperation of other subject peoples Abuakwa, Kotoku and Bosome regained their sovereignty in 1831.

NOTES AND REFERENCES

1. Letter from Senya Breku to Elmina Castle (EC), 16 March 1775, *NBKG* 141; Governor & Council, Christiansborg Castle Osu (CCO) to Copenhagen, 28 May 1775 VgK.
2. AAT: Kukurantumi (1925/6).
3. Crowder, F., Papers laid before the West African Lands Commission 1913, cited by Marion Johnson, *Migrants' Progress*, Part I, p.10 n.31; AAT: Maase (1925/6); Akwamu Tradition, as recorded by Field, *Akim-Kotoku*, pp. 2–3.
4. Johnson, *Op. cit.*, p.8.
5. Ward, *A History of Ghana*, p.208, n.2.
6. Johnson, *Migrants' Progress* Part II, p.11.
7. The subject is discussed in Chapter 4.
8. Addo-Fening on the other hand thinks that Kyebi was founded before the 1750s (Cf. his Ph.D. Thesis," Akyem Abuakwa 1874–1943", Legon 1980, pp. 22 & 26). He does not say who the founders were and why the capital was removed from Banso to Kyebi.
9. Personal communication from the Palace, Kyebi in 1968/9.
10. Field, *Op.cit.*, pp. 2–3.
11. Personal communication from Tafohene Nana Okru Banin, in 1968/9.
12. Danquah, *Akan Laws*, pp. 30–33.
13. *Ibid*, p.22.
14. Kyebi Tradition as told missionary Stromberg by Opanyin Apietu described by the missionary as "a grey haired elder" of Kyebi, Cf Stromberg (Kyebi) to Basel, 24 January, 1863 No. Akim 17; see also Lotholtz (Kyebi) to Basel, 13 October 1869, No. Akim 16, Basel Mission Archives-Paul Jenkins' Abstracts (BMA-PJA).
15. Biorn, Beretning, p.204. Biorn was Governor of Christiansborg Castle in the 1790s.
16. Norregaard, *Danish Settlement*, p.155.
17. Norregaard, *Op. cit*, p.153.
18. Guineiske Journaler: entry 6 February 1791, VgK; Sager til VJ, No. 23 1792; cf also Fynn, *Asante*, p.130, n2, and Kea, in *THSG* Vol.X (1969), p.42.
19. Fynn, *Asante*, p.130.
20. Letter from Senya Breku to EC., 16 March 1775, *NBKG*.141.
21. Fynn, *Asante*, p.130.
22. Fynn, *Op. cit.*, p.132.
23. Fynn, "Abuakwa King List".
24. James Fort (Accra) Daybook: entries 10 & 26 February and 17 August 1800. T 70/98; Archibald Dalzel (CCC) to Committee of African Merchants (CAM), London, 13 October 1800, T 70/34 PRO, London.
25. AKT: Awisa (1968/9).
26. Reindorf, *The History of the Gold Coast*, p.139.
27. Reindorf, *Op. cit.*, pp. 138–139 & 141.
28. Governor Torrane (CCC) to CAM, 20 July 1807, T 70/35, also reproduced in Metcalfe, G. E. Metcalfe, 1964, *Great Britain and Ghana: Documents of Ghana History 1807–1957*, Suffolk, pp. 7–12, Meredith, H., 1812, *Gold Coast of Africa*, London, pp. 132–133, Hutton, W., 1821, *A Voyage to Africa*, London, p.337; Cruickshank, Vol.I, Chapter IV; Reindorf, *The History of the Gold Coast*, pp. 138–139; Ward, *A History of Ghana*, p.148.
29. Reindorf, *The History of the Gold Coast*, p.141.
30. *Ibid.*

31. Claridge (Vol.I, p.98) is clearly wrong in calling this Abuakwahene "Ofosu". No Abuakwa ruler before Atta Owusu ever bore that name.
32. Governor White (CCC) to CAM, 25 March 1811, T. 70/35. This source is reproduced in Metcalfe, Documents, pp. 17-18.
33. Ibid.
34. White (CCC) to CAM, 5 May & 26 December 1809, T 70/35; Governor de Veer (EC) to White, 7 May 1810, T 70/35; Hutton, A Voyage, p.342.
35. White (CCC) to CAM, 25 March 1811, T 70/35.
36. Cruickshank, Vol.I, pp. 92-93; Ellis, A. B., 1893, A History of the Gold Coast of West Africa, Negro University Press, New York, p.123, Reindorf, The History of the Gold Coast, p.153; Claridge, Vol.I, p.263.
37. Ward, A History of Ghana, p.157.
38. White (CCC) to CAM, 26 December 1809, T 70/35.
39. A. de Veer (EC) to White (CCC), 7 May 1809, T 70/35.
40. Meredith, The Gold Coast, p.167.
41. De Veer's Diary: entry 1 February 1811, WIC 124A.
42. Meredith, The Gold Coast, p.167.
43. Bowdich, A Mission, p.123.
44. Meredith, The Gold Coast, p.167.
45. Bowdich, A Mission, p.123.
46. Vanderpuije (Senya Breku) to de Veer (EC), 15 March 1811, WIC 124A; Meredith, The Gold Coast, p.167.
47. Reindorf, The History of the Gold Coast, p.153.
48. Vanderpuije to de Veer, cited in EC Journal: entry 17 September 1810 WIC 124A.
49. Reindorf, The History of the Gold Coast, p.153.
50. Ibid., p.154.
51. Cruickshank, Vol.I, pp.93-94; Ellis (1893), p.124; Claridge, Vol.I., p.264; Ward, A History of Ghana, p.155.
52. Meredith, The Gold Coast, pp. 168-169.
53. Governor White (CCC) to CAM, 25 March 1811, T 70/35.
54. Nicro (Kormantse) to de Veer (EC) cited in EC Journal: entry 11 March 1811, WIC 124^A.
55. Vanderpuije (Senya Breku) to de Veer (EC) cited in EC Journal: entry 15 March 1811, WIC 124^A
56. Kwamena-Poh, Government and Politics, pp. 86-87, Kwamena-Poh discusses fully the Akuapem aspect of the conflict.
57. Ibid.
58. W. Hoitman (Accra) to EC., 17 March 1811, WIC 124^A.
59. Dawson (James Fort Accra) to Governor Schionning (CCC), 17 June 1811, DAFG No.50.
60. Schionning to Dawson, 17 & 20 June 1811, DAFG No.50.
61. Dawson to Schionning, 21 June 1811, DAFG No.50.
62. Meredith, The Gold Coast, p.176.
63. Governor White (CCC) to CAM, 23 May 1811, T 70/35.
64. White to CAM. 13 October 1811, T 70/35.
65. AAT: Pamen (1925/6).
66. CCC Daybook: entry 7 October 1811, T 70/1099; White to CAM, 13 October 1811, T 70/35.
67. White (CCC) to CAM, 25 March 1811, T 70/35.

68. Cruickshank, Vol.I, pp. 97-98.
69. Christaller's Report for the Third Quarter of 1865, dd. 30 September 1865, No. Akim 250, BMA-PJA.
70. AAT: Pamen (1925/6); Reindorf, *The History of the Gold Coast*, p.157.
71. Reindorf, *Op. cit.*, pp. 156-157.
72. AAT: Pamen (1925/6).
73. Reindorf, *Op. cit.*, p.157.
74. *Ibid.*
75. Cruickshank, Vol.I, p.99; Ward, *A History of Ghana*, p.159.
76. See Appendix D for the Kotoku King List.
77. Reindorf, *The History of the Gold Coast*, p.153.
78. Reindorf, *Op. cit.*, p.157.
79. Agyeman would feature prominently in Gold Coast politics from the 1820s onwards.
80. Cruickshank, Vol.I, p.101.
81. CCC Daybook: entry 23 April 1813, T 70/1103.
82. Ward, *A History of Ghana*, p.159.
83. Governor de Veers' Diary (EC): entry 8 August 1815, WIC 124A.
84. Cruickshank, Vol.I, p.101; Claridge, Vol.I, p.274, Reindorf, *The History of the Gold Coast*, p.158.
85. Ward, *A History of Ghana*, p.159; Cruickshank, Vol.I, p.101.
86. CCC Daybook: entries 1 & 11 September and 24, 29 December 1815, T 70/1107.
87. J. Hoern (Accra) to de Veers (EC), cited in EC. Journal: entry 30 September 1815, WIC 124^A.
88. Reindorf, *The History of the Gold Coast*, p.158, Claridge, Vol.I, p.274.
89. Ward, *A History of Ghana*, p.159.
90. Hope Smith (CCC) to CAM, 26 May 1817, T 70/40.
91. Flindt (CCC) to Copenhagen, 30 October 1816, Guineiske Journaler (GJ).
92. Van Neck's Report on Asante-Fante-Anglo-Dutch Meetings at Cape Coast Castle, 26 March 1816, *NBKG* 349; Acting Governor Dawson (CC) to CAM, 26 March & 21 April 1816, T 70/36.
93. Reindorf, *The History of the Gold Coast*, pp. 159-160.
94. Van Neck's Report on the CCC Meetings, 25 March, 1816 *NBKG* 349, & Ag. Governor Dawson to CAM, 21 April 1816, T 70/36. Reindorf (*Op. cit.*, p.159) gives the names of the three Fante Chiefs as "Kwaw Agyiri, Opentri, and Amisa".
95. Van Neck's Report; Dawson to CAM, 21 April 1816, T 70/36.
96. Ag. Governor Dawson (CCC) to CAM, ? June 1816, T 70/36.
97. Reindorf, *The History of the Gold Coast*, pp. 159-160.
98. Huydecoper (Kumasi) to Governor-General Daendels (EC) 7 June 1816, *NBKG* 369.
99. Anonymous, *Akuapem ne Eho Amansem anase Abasem*, Akropon 1913, pp. 39-40, cited by Kwamena-Poh, *Government and Politics*, p.89. Reindorf, *The History of the Gold Coast*, pp. 160-161.
100. Reports of Roelessen (Accra) to EC, in *NBKG* 561. The reports are several. See also Reindorf, *The History of the Gold Coast*, p.160, where the peace price imposed on the Akuapem is put at "1,500 heads of cowries and 200 slaves" as well as the surrender of all chiefs who had supported Kwao Safro Twe.
101. Roelessen (Accra) to Governor-General Daendels (EC), 6 November 1816, *NBKG* 501.
102. *Ibid.*
103. Reindorf, *The History of the Gold Coast*, p.161.

104. Reindorf, *Op. cit*, p.160.
105. *Ibid*.
106. AAT: Kukurantumi (1925/6).
107. *Ibid*.
108. Major Chisholm (CCC) to Sir Charles MacCarthy (Sierra Leon), 30 September 1822, CO 267/56, reproduced in Metcalfe, *Documents*, pp. 77–80.
109. Dupuis, *A Residence*, Part II, p.viii.
110. Reindorf, *The History of the Gold Coast*, p.175; also AAT: Kwaben (1925/6).
111. Reindorf, *Op. cit*, pp. 175–176.
112. *Ibid*.
113. Bowdich, *A Mission*, Chapter 111–VI.
114. Dupuis, *A Residence*, Chapter III
115. Metcalfe, *Maclean*, p.41.
116. Danquah, *Akan Law*, p.11.
117. *Ibid*.
118. Reindorf, *The History of the Gold Coast*, p.176.
119. Ivor Wilks, (Asante, p.18) identifies Bri as Kwaku Bene, the Chief of Atwoma-Agogo in Asante.
120. Reindorf, *The History of the Gold Coast*, p.189.
121. Reindorf, *Op. cit*, p.190.
122. *Ibid;* AAT: Kukurantumi, Begoro, Asiakwa & Pamen (1925/6).
123. AAT: Kukurantumi (1925/6).
124. Wilks, *Asante*, p.180.
125. Ellis, A B., *A History of the Gold Coast of West Africa*, p.176.
126. Claridge, Vol.I, pp. 375–376.
127. Ellis, *Gold Coast of West Africa*, p.176.
128. Wilks, *Asante*, p.180.
129. Reindorf, *The History of the Gold Coast*, p.192.
130. *Ibid*.
131. GJ (1840–1844): entries No.329 dated 18 December 1842 & No.367 dated 10 February 1843; Simon Sus (Gyadam) to Basel, 1 March 1859, BMA–PJA; "Petition of Quabina Fuah, King of Inswarmoon [Nsuaem] to the Governor (CCC), 17 July 1871, CO 96/88; Dr. Gouldsbury's Report on a Mission to Akyem, 29 June 1874, CO 96/112; "Precis of Akim Claims to Ashanti-Akim; Kotoku, MP 212/93, MP 5718/94, Confidential MP 105/96, MP 559/94, MP 694/96, MP 8661/97, MP 4964/98, MP 1588/00, MP 1209/01; Colonial Secretary (Accra) to the Chief Commissioner of Ashanti, 2 June 1908, all in File No.D46, Kumasi Archives; also Governor Hodgson (Accra) to Chamberlain, Colonial Office, London, 17 July 1900, CO 96/361; Colonel Wilcocks (Fumso, in Asante) to Chamberlian, 4 July 1900, CO 96/374.
132. Ward, *A History of Ghana*, p.142, n.15.
133. Ward, *A History of Ghana*, p.220; Afua Sutherland, D., 1954, *State Emblems of the Gold Coast*, p.15; Wilks, I., his Review of *Danish Settlements in West Africa*, (by Norregaard), in *JAH* Vol.IX (1968), p.163; Akyem Bosome Traditions (ABT): Soadru gathered by the present author in 1968/9.
134. Reindorf, *The History of the Gold Coast*, pp. 191–192.
135. Reindorf, *Op. cit*, 192.
136. *Ibid*.
137. Wilks, *Asante*, p.174.
138. Reindorf, *Op. cit*, p.176.

139. *Ibid.*
140. Kwawu severed her links with Asante in 1888.
141. Cruickshank, Vol.I, p.161; Reindorf, *Op. cit.*, 193; Claridge, Vol.I, p.285; Ward, *A History of Ghana*, p.183.
142. Reindorf, *The History of the Gold Coast*, pp. 198–199.
143. *Ibid.*
144. CS. Salmon, Acting Administrator (CCC) to Kennedy, Chief Administrator of the British West African Settlement (Freetown, SL.) 3 October 1871, CO 96/89.
145. Metcalfe, *Maclean*, pp. 93–94.
146. The name occurs in the records as 'Akyianwa' etc
147. Metcalfe, Maclean, pp. 93–94.
148. Reindorf, *The History of the Gold Coast*, p.251.
149. See Clause 3 of the Treaty. The Treaty is reproduced by Metcalfe, Documents, No.83 pp.114–115.

Chapter 6

THE AKYEM, JUABEN, THE BRITISH AND THE DANES 1832–1850

The pre-1831 upheavals had far reaching effects on the subsequent history of the Akyem country and the Gold Coast as a whole. The ruling lineage of Kotoku with a considerable following and migrants from lacustrine Bosome had fled their homes in Northern Akyem and Asante respectively to seek safety in Akyem south of the Birem. Though the 1831 Treaty of Peace had retrieved their independence for them the treaty failed to stipulate whether these two groups could return to their ancestral country without let or hindrance from Asante. They themselves resolved the issue by opting to reside permanently in their new homes. The decision, coupled with the arrival in 1832 of Juaben refugees from Asante, turned Akyem south of the Birem into a haven for fugitive chiefs and refugees. Preponderant European role in the pre-1831 convulsions and subsequent European economic interests also turned Akyem into a source of Anglo-Danish rivalry for the district as a sphere of influence. All these issues affected intra-Akyem relations, as well as relations with their various neighbours, and with European trading powers on the coast.

The Permanent Residence of the Kotoku and the Bosome Migrants

At present there is no direct evidence on the motives which prompted the refugees from northern Akyem and 'Asante' Bosome to settle permanently in Akyem south of river Birem. However, it is not too difficult to speculate the reason. Continued fear of Asante hegemony was most probably the main, if not the only reason. Denkyira's experience suggests this.

Prior to 1824–1825 the Denkyira inhabited the territory around the middle reaches of river Ofin with their capital at Abankesieso. But the ruling lineage and a section of their subjects migrated southwards, into Fante territory, in order to foster alliance with the British against Asante. In 1829, that is two years before the signing of the 1831 Treaty of Peace, they decided not to return to their native land. Accordingly, they asked the British to negotiate with the Fante on their behalf for land on which they could settle permanently. The final outcome was the founding of a new Denkyira State with its capital at Jukwa, some nineteen kilometres north of Cape Coast.[1] Apparently, the Denkyira leadership thought it was impolitic to return to their original home where they would be close neighbours again to Asante. That would have amounted to a rejection of the recovery of independence because proximity was likely to tempt Asante to reassert its pre-1831 hegemony.[2] The Kotoku and the migrants from 'Asante' Bosome seem to have made similar calculations. It was safer to remain in Akyem south of the river Birem.

With respect to Kotoku the decision had an adverse side. Politically, the decision rendered Northern Akyem a no-man's-land from the 1830s onwards. By the 1850s the district was regarded by the British protecting authority as forming part of Asante[3] while the Kotokuhene continued, vainly, to claim juridiction over it up to the 1900s.[4] What was left of the Akyem country became varied in its population pattern and township distribution. The arrival of the lacustrine Bosome naturally increased the population of Western Akyem, though to what extent it is not easy to tell. Bosome tradition gives the impression that Soadru[5] was founded by the nineteenth century immigrants.[6] But it is more reasonable to imagine these migrants joining their eighteenth century counterparts to found a new capital, or even the former settling in the chief town of the latter and expanding it into a much larger capital.

Changes also occurred in the population pattern of eastern Akyem i.e. Akyem Abuakwa proper. Up to 1825 the Abuakwa had been the sole inhabitants of the district. The arrival of the Kotoku naturally increased its population both in numbers and ethnic variety. What was more, the two Akyem peoples got mixed up socially and in township distribution. Reindorf recalls that in the 1820s when the Kotoku arrived in Abuakwa, Okyenhene Dokuaa asked them to choose any of the following towns for settlement: Gyadam, Adasewase, Muoso, Mampong, Odubi and Asafo; the Kotoku selected Gyadam as their capital.[7] Other Abuakwa towns like Muoso seem to have received substantial doses of the immigrant Kotoku element.[8] The Kotoku probably founded a few towns or settlements from scratch. Among these may have been Asuboa and Moseaso. In the 1850s, Asuboa for instance would be described as a suburb of Gyadam.[9] The Abuakwa would completely destroy Moseaso in 1860, presumably because it was founded by the Kotoku with whom they were at war in that year.[10] On the whole the arrival and residence of the Kotoku in eastern Akyem complicated the political map of the area, to the extent that by the 1850s some outsiders would regard parts of it as 'native' Kotoku territory.[11]

Abuakwa-Kotoku Relations in the 1830s and 1840s

The permanent residence of the Kotoku ruling lineage in East Akyem eventually strained the pre-1825 good relations between the two Akyem peoples. As the years passed by familiarity began to breed contempt between the two. But the greater cause was the enstoolment of Kofi Agyeman as Kotokuhene.

Following the accidental death of Afrifa Akwada in or about 1825, the Kotoku, as pointed out in Chapter 5 recalled Kofi Agyeman, nephew of ex-Kotokuhene Kwakye, from Soadru, the Bosome capital, and enstooled him at

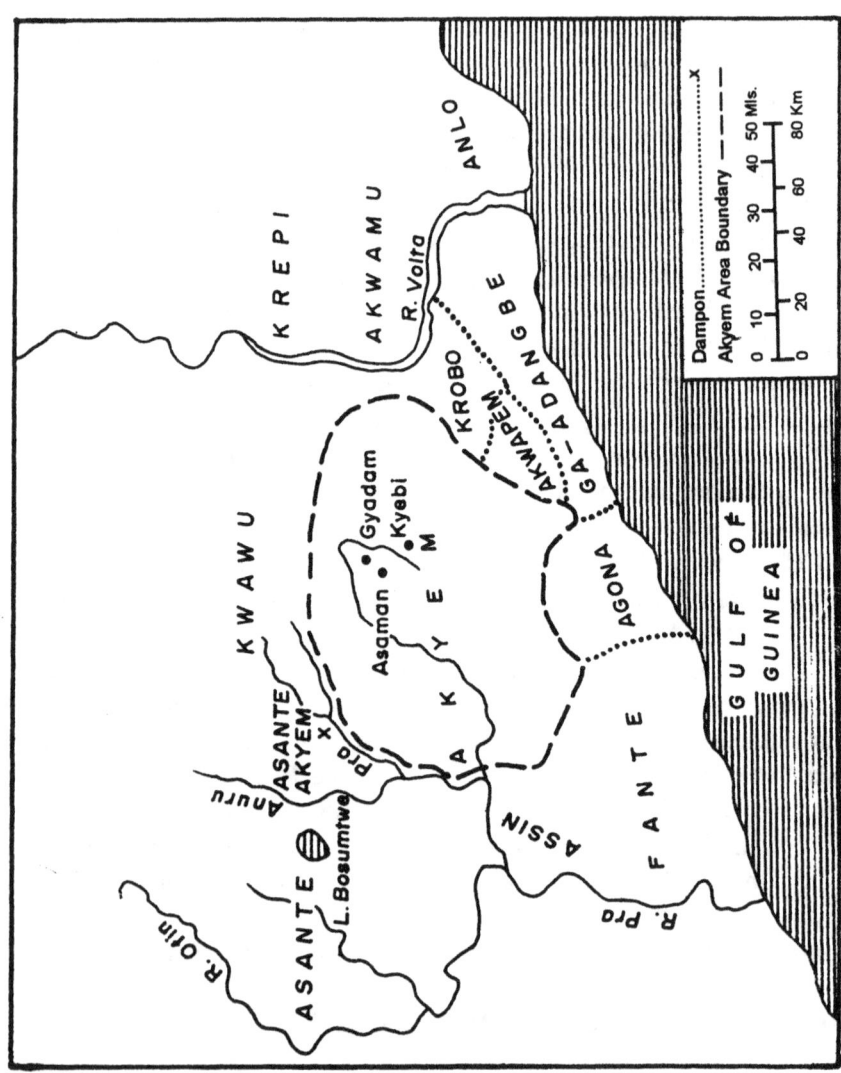

Fig. 5: Approximate Extent of Akyem Area after 1831

Gyadam as the new Kotokuhene. In the words of Reindorf

> a better election could not have been made, but it offended Queen Dokuwa, not personally, but on account of his late uncle's conduct towards the royal family of Kotoku.[12]

It will be recalled that during the 1810-1812 period, Kwakye, uncle of Agyeman, tried to exterminate the Kwadwo Kuma line of the Kotoku royal family because Kuma, as a Prince, had sided with Abuakwa in its rebellion against Asante to which Kwakye as Kotokuhene, was loyal. Besides, Kwakye in 1813 fled to Asante, taking the royal stool along with him thereby depriving Kwadwo Kuma of his ancestral stool when he became Kotokuhene that year. The Abuakwa Court never forgave Kwakye for these crimes against his own people. Hence Dokuaa's displeasure with the enstoolment of Agyeman as Kotokuhene in 1825.

The muffled but real dislike of Dokuaa for Agyeman, as nephew of Kwakye, persisted into the 1830s and 1840s, leading to the straining of relations between the hosts and the guests. Available evidence does not shed much light on the details of the tension. But the certainty of it is not in doubt. It was palpable enough for the Danish missionary Andreas Riis to notice it in 1839 when he visited eastern Akyem from his base at Akuropon, capital of Akuapem.[13] At one stage so hostile was the Kyebi ruling house to Agyeman that he reportedly had to seek safety with the Danish authorities at Christiansborg Castle for awhile.[14] Reindorf therefore may well be right in claiming that in the 1830s the Abuakwa would have gone to war against the Kotoku but for Juaben intervention.[15]

The Juaben as Refugees in Akyem Abuakwa

The mediation was made possible by the presence of the Juaben in eastern Akyem as refugees and the guests of Okyenhene Dokuaa. A civil war in Asante was the immediate cause of the Juaben flight to Akyem Abuakwa. Since the creation of the Asante Confederation (or Union) in the second half of the seventeenth century, there had always been a muted rivalry between the states of Kumasi and Juaben.[16] The rivalry resurfaced and intensified after the defeat of Asante in the Akantamasu War of 1826, and finally developed into an open war between the two states in June-July 1832. Kumasi forces invaded and defeated the Juaben. The latter, led by their Chief, Kwasi Boaten, his brother Kofi Boaten, and their mother Oseiwa, and Oseiwa's sister, Afrakuma I, who was then the *Juabenhema* (Juaben queen mother), fled to Eastern Akyem to seek asylum with Okyenhene Dokuaa.

The choice of Akyem Abuakwa seems to have been the outcome of a careful and cool calculation. Already Abuakwa was playing host to the Kotoku refugees. A Fante Chief and some of his subjects had also fled thither for protection.[17] So, the Juaben were sure that they would be welcomed. They may have had other reasons for going to Akyem Abuakwa. The Abuakwa had a dislike for Kumasi. They had been much opposed to the 1831 Treaty of Peace with Asante without first having a chance to wreak vengeance on Kumasi.[18] Moreover, they, in spite of their dislike for the Asante in general, had a soft place in their hearts for the Juaben. In 1813, the Kotoku for example had singled out the Juaben from amongst the Asante confederate states as a friend to negotiate with Kumasi for the return of their ancestral stool taken to Asante by fugitive Kotokuhene Kwakye.[19] On the basis of all these, they must have calculated that they could easily strike an alliance with the Abuakwa and the Kotoku against Asante. The Juaben were not disappointed. Okyenhene Dokuaa cordially welcomed them, hosted the Juaben royal family at Kyebi for some time before she allowed them to go and settle at Saman near Osino.

Owing to easy communication between eastern Akyem and the Ga Coast, some Accra merchants reportedly sent to the refugee Juaben messages of sympathy, moral support, and material relief.[20] Some neighbours of the Akyem were equally sympathetic and supportive. Long before the final outcome of the Kumasi-Juaben civil war was known in the Protectorate, the Assin for instance had begun seizing Kumasi subjects in support of the Juaben.[21] The Denkyira despatched a delegation to Abuakwa to assure the Juaben of their allied support should Kumasi dare to attack them in Akyem.[22] Indeed it does seem that only the fear of the castle authorities, especially Maclean of Cape Coast castle, prevented the Akyem and other Gold Coast peoples from offering immediate military assistance to the refugee Juaben against Kumasi.[23] Even then, the Akyem quietly participated in the predatory activities of the Juaben which included the disruption of Kumasi lines of communication with the coast.[24] The Abuakwa and the Kotoku also took part in armed expeditions which the Juaben organized against parts of provincial Asante, including Krachi (Krakye) and Namonsi, in 1833.[25]

Anglo-Danish Reaction to Developments in Akyem

The Akyem paid a high price for aiding and abetting the Juaben against Kumasi. European supervision over them increased. The Abuakwa and the Kotoku and probably the Bosome, in assisting the Juaben in their predatory activities, hardly took into consideration the possibility of the castle authorities disapproving of their conduct. To promote the smooth flow of trade between the forts and the forest, had been the ultimate goal of the British mercantile administration at Cape Coast Castle in meticulously guiding the process which had led to the peace settlement of 1831 between the Gold Coast Alliance and

Asante. This administration, headed by Maclean, the chief architect of the 1831 Treaty of Peace, just could not countenance any activity likely to disturb and disrupt trade. Besides, the predatory activities of the Juaben and their Akyem supporters could provoke a Kumasi invasion of the Akyem territory. Such an eventuality would not be the concern of the Akyem peoples alone, but the British and Danish trading administrations also; in short, as Maclean put it in August 1832, "the entire British alliance, by virtue of the Queen [Dokuaa of Abuakwa] being a member of the alliance . . ."[26]

It has been argued that the violation of the 1831 Treaty of Peace and the consequential political implications of such violation more than anything else obliged Maclean to intervene in Akyem affairs during the Juaben sojourn.[27] This proposition is not entirely accurate. Should Asante respond to the violent activities of the Juaben and the Akyem with an invasion of any part of the nascent Protectorate, trade, to the thinking of the British, would of course be the first casualty. On this basis we contend that the loss of opportunities for trade and profits was the main concern of Maclean. After all the Europeans were in the Gold Coast primarily to trade.

Luckily, the British, by virtue of the 1831 Treaty, could intervene in Akyem affairs. Clause 5 of the Treaty empowered British mediation between the states of the Gold Cost and Asante in the event of strained relations. The clause stipulated:

> To prevent as much as possible future war, it is agreed that in case of the parties subscribing to these articles [of the Treaty] committing an act of aggression and complaint being made thereof to the Governor-in-Chief of His Britannic Majesty's possessions on the coast . . . any satisfaction which the circumstances of the case may require will be adjudged to the aggrieved party by the said Governor-in-Chief . . .[28]

By actively encouraging and assisting Juaben hostility against Kumasi, the Akyem states committed aggression against Asante. Therefore the British could intervene even though the Asante government had not yet lodged any official complaint. Maclean threatened the Juaben and the Akyem with a collective Anglo-Danish-Dutch punitive expedition if they did not put a stop to the predatory activities, release all Asante subjects they were holding in detention, and submit the dispute with Kumasi to arbitration presided over by the castle authorities; Maclean's next move was that he and the Danish Governor of Christiansborg Castle each despatched a platoon of six troops to Kyebi to undertake a surveillance of the movements of both the Akyem and the Juaben; finally he sent a force to clear the trade routes, particularly the Assin section of the Kumasi-Cape Coast route, of all Juaben and Akyem marauders.[29] Basically all these measures were intimidatory, but they had the desired effect. In or about September, 1832, the Juaben agreed in principle to the idea of European arbitration as a means of settling the conflict with Kumasi.

The quick Juaben submission to the European authorities must be seen as also reflecting Akyem acceptance of that fiat. The speed with which the Abuakwa and the Kotoku made their submission is fairly surprising, considering that at that distance and in the primeval forest, they and the Juaben refugees could have defied, for some time, the authority of the Europeans on the coast and the latter would have found it relatively difficult taking full-scale military reprisal against them.

With respect to the Akyem, four factors appear to have dictated the rate of the submission. The first was most probably the fear of a possible European military action against them. The presence of uniformed troops in Kyebi was a novelty which Akyem leaders must have seen as a pointer to sterner measures the castle authorities in general, and the Cape Coast Castle administration in particular, were capable of taking against whoever tried to displease them. The second was the possibility of European economic sanction which could take the form of stoppage of sale of firearms to the Akyem. Thirdly, the castle authorities could withhold, or completely stop, payment of whatever stipends and "dashes" they had hitherto been making to the Akyem courts. Fourthly and finally the fear of European withdrawal of their protection of the Akyem against Asante apparently played a part. This was perhaps the most influencing factor, because Clause 6 of the 1831 Peace Treaty said:

> If any of the allied Kings and Chiefs shall be the aggressor or aggressors [against, Asante] . . . and if such aggressor or aggressors shall refuse to abide by the decision of the Governor [of Cape Coast Castle] or his representative . . . in that case he or they will no longer be considered as a confederacy, and must arrange his or their dispute as they best can.[30]

The Akyem peoples might want to annoy Asante in small ways, but not to the extent of inviting a full-scale war with that power. It was still too soon after the sufferings they had experienced at the hands of Asante in the recent past. In the face of the perennial Asante bogey, the Akyem states, like all other inland states of the Gold Coast, were forced to seek continued alliance with the militarily and technologically superior Europeans by submitting to their terms, even though such a submission compromised their own sovereignty. The submission averted the immediate danger of war with Asante..

But another problem arose to delay the process of reconciliation between the Juaben refugees and Kumasi. This was the emergence of an Anglo-Danish scramble to win the territories of Akyem, Akuapem and Krobo as a sphere of influence. This issue will be discussed in due course. Suffice it to say now that it was this rivalry which made it possible for the Akyem to actively participate in the 1833 Juaben assaults on parts of provincial Asante to which reference has already been made. The attacks were quite provocative to Asante which in the early months of 1834 actually threatened to invade Akyem in retaliation.[31] But the death of Asantehene Osei Yaw Akoto in March 1834 saved the Akyem states and the Juaben from war with Kumasi.

From March 1834 relations with Kumasi improved, because the new Asantehene, Kwaku Dua I, was favourably disposed towards the Juaben. He worked untiringly in an effort to get the Juaben refugees in Akyem back to Asante. This enabled the Cape Coast and Christiansborg Castle authorities to effect a peace settlement between Juaben and Kumasi in November 1835,[32] not May 1835 as Reindorf claims.[33] The full text of the clauses of the treaty is worth quoting, in view of the direct bearing the peace settlement had on subsequent Akyem-Asante relations:

> *Article 1:* All differences of whatever kind so ever which may have existed or do now exist between the aforesaid parties are hereby declared to be an end, and shall not be revived by either party.
>
> *Article 2:* Boatyn and his people or any portion of men, shall be, from this time forth, at perfect liberty to return to their former country of Djuabin without let, hindrance or molestation from the King of Ashantee or his people.
>
> *Article 3:* The subjects of Boatyn or Boatyn himself, if so inclined, shall be at perfect liberty to visit any part of Ashantee without being subject to molestation on account of past differences and quarrels, and in like manner, Ashantees shall be at perfect liberty to visit any part of Djuabin or Akim without being subject to any molestation or insult.
>
> *Article 4:* In order to guarantee this Treaty of Peace, and to ensure to both parties the most perfect security for their persons and property, the Governments of Cape Coast, Elmina, and Christiansborg do hereby declare that they will look upon as enemies and treat as such either party infringing the Treaty.

The Delay in the Juaben Departure

In view of this peace settlement between Kumasi and the Juaben, the Akyem Abuakwa apparently expected the latter to return to their country immediately. But the Juaben did not do so till about 1841 when they finally left. The delay in the Juaben departure must have been a source of worry and irritation to the Abuakwa. The fact of the matter was that with the passage of time the initial enthusiasm with which the Kyebi Court had welcomed Juabenhene Kwasi Boaten and his family in 1832 was fast wearing thin, giving way to a slow but steady deterioration of relations between the hosts and the guests. Scuffles are said to have occasionally broken out between the people of Kyebi and the Juaben,[34] who initially lived exactly where the Basel missionaries were to establish their mission station in 1861.³⁵ Some of the Abuakwa princes reportedly had love affairs with the wives of the Juaben royals, the most guilty being Prince Atta Obiwom (or Buom); on the other hand the Abuakwa government occasionally accused the Juabenhene of aiding, abetting and shielding Abuakwa criminals.³⁶ Further more, the Akyem royals are said to have been inclined to be jealous of what Reindorf calls the munificence, magnificence, and skill of the Juabenhene in the art of ruling "in the Twi manner".³⁷

Clearly the Juaben had over-stayed. Strains and stresses were setting in with regards to their relations with the Abuakwa. It was about time they left. With the peace settlement of 1835, they no longer had any excuse to continue to stay on in Akyem Abuakwa. What then prevented their immediate departure after 1835?

In May 1838 Mr. Topp of the Cape Coast Castle administration, gave continued existence of differences with Kumasi as the cause of the delay in the Juaben departure.³⁸ Topp's assertion was contradictory to an observation of the Elmina Castle authorities in April 1838 that the Juaben would return to their country in the dry season, that is between December 1838 and March 1839; and to assist the Juaben to leave for home during that time frame, Asantehene Kwaku Dua I, had sent Chief Kwasi Boaten one hundred *pereguans* of gold to help him defray whatever debts he might have incurred in Akyem Abuakwa.³⁹ Reindorf even says the amount was "800 peredwans".⁴⁰ The Dutch claim suggests that Chief Boaten was pleading impecuniosity as the reason for his inability to return to Asante quickly.

Neither the Dutch claim nor the British assertion can be set aside lightly. The very friendly relations between Elmina Castle and the Manhyia Palace gave considerable credibility to the Dutch claim. On the other hand the British would not make the allegation if they were not sure of the evidence, in view of their anxiety and great efforts to bring peace and harmony between Kumasi and Juaben.

Reluctance of the Juaben to leave Akyem with its excellent economic opportunities seems to offer the best explanation to the delay in the Juaben departure. The trading activities of Juabenhene Kwasi Boaten and his subjects give force to this contention. Andreas Riis, the Danish missionary working for the Basel Mission in the Gold Coast, was highly impressed by these activities when he visited eastern Akyem in 1839.⁴¹ He noted that the Juaben Chief dealt avidly in arms and ammunition the sale of which was controlled in Asante. Here in Akyem Abuakwa, he did rolling business in those items without any restraint whatever. But for the deaths of the Juabenhene and his brother Kofi Boaten in or about 1840,⁴² the Juaben surely would have still stayed on longer than 1841 when they finally left, led by Amma Oseiwaa, mother of the deceased Chiefs.

Effect of the Juaben Residence in Akyem

By 1841 the Juaben had lived in Akyem for nearly ten years. That decade old contact left lasting marks on both the Akyem and the Juaben. Ethnic admixture was one of the effects. Inter-ethnic marriages had taken place between the two peoples. On familial grounds, some of the Akyem may have joined the returning Juaben to Asante. By the same token many of the Juaben opted to stay on in Akyem. In the early 1840s it was estimated that about one thousand of them remained in the Protectorate.[43] Obviously many of these must have chosen to live in Akyem. Reindorf claims that some of the Juaben returnees, on reaching Kwawu, actually changed their minds and went back to Akyem and Akuapem.[44]

Exchange of political ideas may have been another outcome of the contact. Reindorf asserts categorically that the Akyem learned state-craft from the Juaben. Reindorf is normally a shrewd writer who, besides, seems to have made good use of documentary and, more importantly, oral traditions. But on this occasion his assertion is open to doubt. The Asante were perhaps the best exponents of government in the Akan or Twi fashion. However, even if the Akyem were not so good, they certainly would have acquired the essentials of the Akan form of government from Asante long before the arrival and residence of the Juaben in Akyem. The Abuakwa for example could make the acquisition between 1784 and 1807. As for the Kotoku and the Bosome they may have done so much earlier.

In terms of future Akyem-Asante relations, perhaps the greatest impact of the contact was the re-establishment of cordial relations between the Akyem and the Juaben before the latter finally left for Asante. Abuakwa leaders are said to have put the Juaben on oath never to disclose to the rest of Asante any Akyem secrets they might have come to know.[46] The Juaben made another promise, most likely on oath, never to take up arms against the Akyem.[47]

Finally the sojourn of the Juaben fueled, to some extent, an Anglo-Danish scramble for the Akyem district as a sphere of influence. It was indicative of the rivalry that in 1832 each of them stationed a platoon of six troops at Kyebi to monitor the movements and activities of the Juaben refugees and the Akyem, in as much as they affected relations between the Gold Coast and Asante.[48] Also both were signatories to the 1835 Treaty of Peace between the Juaben and Kumasi, which in a way concerned the Akyem also. Governor Maclean of Cape Coast Castle signed for the British and Governor Morch of Christiansborg Castle appended his signature on behalf of the Danes.[49]

The Anglo-Danish Scramble for Akyem

The prime cause of the scramble was Danish pretensions to jurisdiction over the territories of Akyem, Akuapem and Krobo. The earliest open Danish claim known to the present author is that made by Governor Schionning in 1811.[50] The English wasted no time in rejecting the Danish claim: they pointed out that no European trading power possessed any jurisdiction rights over any part of the Gold Coast.[51] The issue seems to have fizzled out for awhile. It appears to have resurfaced in 1817 with the Danes apparently reviving the claim, but the Danish Customs Board pointed out that there was no legal basis for the claim which the Danish officials in the Gold Coast were making.[52] The matter remained dormant until the 1830s when Mr. Morch arrived from Denmark to assume the governorship of Christiansborg Castle.

Between 1834 and 1838 Mr. Morch openly revived the so-called Danish jurisdiction over Akyem, Akuapem and Krobo. It was to insist on the Danish claim that in 1834 he despatched troops to escort a group of Asante subjects through eastern Akyem.[53] The British could not tolerate what they described as Danish "attempt to assert, even enforce, an exclusive right to the extensive districts of Akim and Aquapim . . . [and] . . . Crobbo".[54] Maclean led the British challenge. He invoked the 1831 Treaty of Peace to emphasize the independence of the Akyem and the two others.[55] Each of the administrators in the Gold Coast took such an uncompromising stand on the issue that it had to be taken up at high diplomatic level by their Home Governments. A protracted correspondence took place between Copenhagen and London.[56] Eventually the Danish Home Government which had initially supported Morch backed down, and advised its officials in the Gold Coast not to advance claims to exclusive jurisdiction over the three territories.

More recently a prominent Danish historian has taken Mr. Krabbe-Carisius, the Danish Foreign Minister in the 1830s, to task for ordering the clamp down. He insists that the Danes possessed a jurisdiction over Akyem, Akuapem and Krobo.[57] With respect to Akuapem and Krobo, the Danish claim has been proved to have no basis whatever.[58]

Nor has it any substance with regard to Akyem. The weight of the evidence on Akyem-Danish relations since 1730 is on the side of friendship with, and not subservience of the Akyem peoples to, the Danish mercantile administration at Christiansborg Castle, Osu in Accra. As shown in Chapter 3, between 1730 and 1742 the Akyem Kings of Abuakwa and Kotoku, in their capacity as overlords of the Ga-Adangbe area, collected groundrents from the European forts, castles and lodges there. The two Akyem states lost that right to the Asante who defeated them in 1742. In spite of that loss the Danes continued to make payments to both Abuakwa and Kotoku, describing such payments as "dashes", so that the two Akyem peoples might be induced to drive their gold trade to the Danes. As the Danish Customs Board rightly pointed out in 1817, such "dashes" (i.e. gifts) did not entitle the Danes to lay jurisdictional claim to Akyem.[59]

Danish officials in the Gold Coast were clearly not happy with this decision of a department of their own Home Government. That is why they revived the claim in the 1830s. Governor Morch was very obsessed on the issue. But Morch met his match in Maclean. In June 1838 Maclean, after carefully dismissing the Danish claim in relation to Krobo, pointed out that the Akyem peoples and the Akuapem had been subjects of Asante until 1824 when they

> upon promises of support from the British, threw off the Ashantee yoke, hoisted the British flag, and were received into British pay. Their independence having been achieved by the powerful aid of the British Government, upon what grounds can the Danish authorities come forward and claim [over Akyem and Akuapem] territorial rights which never had any existence. If the people themselves, if the Chiefs and inhabitants of Aquapim, Akim, and Crobo, wish to place themselves under the Danish protection, the case would be different, but they do not wish, and they have repeatedly appealed to the British authorities for protection against the unjust claims of Governor Morck.[60]

To claim exclusive rights for the British over the territory of Akyem and those of Akuapem and Krobo would have been logical in Maclean's argument, but he did not. Rather he declared: "the British authorities wish for no exclusive rights" over the three territories.[61]

Why then were the British and the Danes scrambling for the three areas as spheres of influence: Maclean provides the answer:

> The British merely wish the trade [in Akyem, Akuapem and Krobo] to be free and open to all, but they do badly complain that the Danish authorities should, under no pretext of exacting allegiance [from the three peoples] stop trade, seize their goods and throw the whole country into confusion.[62]

The Economy of Akyem in the 1830s and 1840s

The economies of the three territories were prosperous during the 1830s and 1840s. Krobo and Akuapem during that period were the two main pillars of the palm oil industry in the Gold Coast.[63] As for the Akyem economy neither the British nor the Danes, like the refugee Juaben, could afford to lose the chance to benefit from it. This economy is best seen through the eyes of missionary Andreas Riis who, as already pointed out, visited the eastern parts of Akyem in 1839. He observed that the Akyem economy had four main sectors: agriculture, hunting, gold-digging and long distance trading (mainly to and from the coast).[64]

From agriculture the people produced plantain, bananas, maize or corn, and several varieties of yam.[65] These were of no great benefit to international trade. During the 1830s and several decades after, palm oil was the agricultural product which the Europeans trading in the Gold Coast sought after most. But, as Riis put it "the useful palm tree is less at home [in Akyem] than in Aquapim".[66] Hunting in Akyem, like agriculture, was also of no serious benefit to the Akyem-European contact. The reason was that game in Akyem did not provide valuable furs or elephant tusks to promote international trade. Hunting, like agriculture, was therefore, done on subsistence basis.

As far as international trade was concerned, the Akyem found adequate compensation in the gold digging industry. The extractive industry in this part of the Gold Coast seems to have been in the doldrums during the 1810s and 1820s. Dupuis in 1819 said that in Akyem it was not a profitable venture.[67] He may well be right, considering that 1800–1830 was a period of great instability and flux in Akyem as well as several other parts of the Gold Coast due to incessant wars. The industry, however, experienced a boom during the relatively calm years of the 1830s and 1840s, because people could devote much of their attention to economic matters. Besides, European demand for Akyem gold was exceptionally great because of what was described as its "extraordinarily fine" quality.[68] Consequently the Akyem made every effort to increase production, for example, they supplemented free-with slave-labour, a situation which is said to have pushed up the price of slaves in the district.[69]

Gold and Long-Distance Trade

As was the case in the eighteenth century, gold placed a strong purchasing power in the hands of the Akyem. This in turn gave them the motivation to pursue long distance trading, especially to the coast. Missionary Riis underlined the link between the Akyem gold-digging industry and the coast trade in 1839 when, as an explanation to the addiction of the Akyem to gin, he said:

> There in the gold-digging we find the explanation. It provides the means and makes it possible for anyone who tries to purchase gin from the coast. On the road from Accra to Akim [via Akuapim] one meets many [Akyem] people loaded with gin.[70]

Of course the Akyem bought many other items from the coast: textiles, machets, knives, iron, lead, and above all guns and ammunition. As has been pointed out already, Juabenhene Kwasi Boaten, while residing in Akyem Abuakwa in the 1830s, greatly dealt in firearms. Thus on the basis of export and import the Akyem economy from the 1830s was as attractive as those of Akuapem and Krobo to both African and European traders. This seems to explain why (at least partly) contrary to the decision of the Danish Home Government in 1835, Danish officials in the Gold Coast in the 1840s could not resist the temptation to claim jurisdiction over Akyem.

Continued Anglo-Danish Competition for Akyem

Once again the Danes tried to do this by demanding allegiance from the Akyem Abuakwa. In 1842, Okyenhene Dokuaa abdicated in favour of the elder of her twin sons, Atta Panin, because the twins had achieved their majority. She, however, continued to be the Ohemaa (Queen) till her death in 1856.[71] In the very year of his mother's abdication Atta Panin was proclaimed the new Okyenhene. In August 1842 Edward Carstensen, the Danish Governor at Christiansborg Castle, sent his representatives to Kyebi "to supervise" the enstoolment of Atta Panin.[72] Carstensen's efforts to oversee the installation of the new Okyenhene implied a renewal of Danish claim to jurisdiction over Akyem. The British found the Danish move quite intolerable and irritating and protested strongly against it.[73] Once again the Danish Home Government, on the basis of the British objection, advised its officials in the Gold Coast to refrain from claiming exclusive rights over the Akyem country. In spite of the understanding between the two Home Governments, the local Anglo-Danish scramble for Akyem continued up to 1849,[74] barely one year before the Danes pulled out of the Gold Coast.[75]

The Akyem themselves were partly to blame for the British-Danish rivalry. They encouraged both parties, sometimes inadvertently though. For example they were not judicious in their relations with both the British and the Danes, In the 1826 war against Asante, they received arms and ammunition indiscriminately from both parties.[76] In 1831 when she was in Accra to assent to the Treaty of Peace with Asante, Okyenhene Dokuaa willingly received honours and hospitality from each of these powers. Kotokuhene Kofi Agyeman may not have behaved differently. In 1832 Dokuaa submissively allowed the British and the Danes to station troops on her soil to monitor Akyem-Juaben activities in relation to Asante. In 1835 the Akyem allowed both powers to be signatories to the Juaben-Kumasi Treaty of Peace, which also concerned them, without bothering to insist on knowing which of them was actually running the show.

Perhaps the Abuakwa and the Kotoku deliberately so behaved in the hopes of exploiting both European powers. In 1834 and 1842 the Akyem rulers accepted gifts from the Danes without questioning the significance of the presents. In view of the great respect they had for Okyenhene Dokuaa, the British too, especially Maclean, may have occasionally sent her gifts. Maclean may well be correct in claiming that the Akyem and other peoples in eastern Gold Coast often appealed to the British for justice in their judicial matters. There may be some truth in Ward's assertion that Abuakwa and some divisions of Kotoku adhered to the Bond of 1844.[77] In view of all this it was natural that both the British and the Danes should each think that they had at least some supervisory authority over Akyem.

The conduct of Okyenhene Atta Panin provides a proof that the Akyem deliberately played one European power against the other. In 1849 information reached Cape Coast Castle that he allegedly indulged in human sacrifice. Acting Governor Fitzpatrick invited him to Cape Coast to answer the allegation. Atta Panin immediately claimed that he was under Danish jurisdiction, not that of the British.[78] The Danes backed him.[79] However, Fitzpatrick insisted on British right over Abuakwa, and he declared that Atta Panin's

> case ... is so clear that when a fitting opportunity offers itself I will have him arrested and see that he gives a good security for his conduct in the future.[80]

The acting Governor could afford to boast because since Maclean's time, British influence in the Gold Coast had been growing steadily, turning the whole country virtually into a British Protectorate. This was especially so after the signing of the Bond of 1844 which according to Ward, the Akyem Abuakwa and some sections of the Akyem Kotoku accepted.[81] It is not surprising that when the Danes left the Gold Coast for good in 1850 the Akyem readily acknowledged British over-rule.

Summary

From the 1830s Akyem south of the Birem became a haven for politically and militarily hard-pressed ruling lineages, thanks mainly to the hospitality of the Akyem Abuakwa rulers. The lineages included those of the Kotoku and the Juaben. The Kotoku had arrived in the district in about 1825, and the Juaben in 1832. The latter returned to their original country in about 1841, but the former stayed put, even though with the passage of time relations with their hosts got strained. The attractive economy of the district and certain policies of the paramount rulers encouraged an Anglo-Danish scramble for the district as a sphere of influence. The competition ended only when the Danes left the Gold Coast for good in 1850.

NOTES AND REFERENCES

1. Metcalfe, G. E., 1963, *Maclean of the Gold Coast*, Oxford University Press, Oxford, p.127.
2. As late as 1853 Asante tried to do this in relation to Assin.
3. Memorandum of Sir George Barrow to the Colonial Office, London, 21 December 1855, CO 96/35.
4. W. C. F. Robertson, Secretary for Native Affairs, to the Omanhene of Akyem Kotoku,

June 1908, Case No.1073/07; also "Precis of Akim Claims to Ashanti-Akim: Akim Kotoku, MP 212/93 etc., File No.D 46, Kumasi Archives.
5. This form of the name is used to distinguish it from the Swedru of the Agona State.
6. Akyem Bosome Tradition: Soadru, as told the present author by Bosomehene Nana Oware Agyekum in 1968/9. – This tradition is referred to as ABT: Soadru.
7. Reindorf, *The History of the Gold Coast*, p.192.
8. AAT: Mmuoso (1968/9).
9. Report of Mr. T. B. Freeman on a mission to Akyem in 1857, dated 28th December 1857, CO 96/57, PRO, London.
10. Hass' Quarterly Bericht (from Gyadam) dated 2 May 1860, BMA-PJA.
11. For example some of the Basel missionaries who worked there in the 1850s.
12. Reindorf, *The History of the Gold Coast*, pp. 192–193.
13. Evangelische Mission Magazine (EMM) 1840 Part I p.96f, cited by Marion Johnson, *Migrants' Progress*, Part I, p.16.
14. Norregaard, *Danish Settlements*, p.206.
15. Reindorf, *The History of Gold Coast*, pp. 293–294.
16. Juaben Tradition, as recorded by Rattray, *Ashanti Law*, pp. 127–169, Bowdich, *A Mission*, p.279; Dupuis, *A Residence*, p.138, Cruickshank, Vol.I, p.50, Ward, *A History of Ghana*, p.207; Metcalfe, *Maclean*, pp. 124–125.
17. EMM 1840 Part III, cited by M. Johnson, *Migrants'*, Part I, p.15. The identity of the Fante Chief is not given.
18. Metcalfe, *Maclean*, pp. 93–94.
19. Reindorf, *The History of the Gold Coast*, p.157.
20. Reindorf, *The History of the Gold Coast*, p.284.
21. Governor Maclean (CCC) to Governor-General van Legen (EC), 13 July 1832, *NBKG* 360.
22. Reindorf, *The History of the Gold Coast*, p.284.
23. Metcalfe, *Maclean*, p.125.
24. Minutes of Council Meeting (CCC) 27 August 1832, CO96/1A; Maclean (CCC) to van Legen (EC), 28 September 1832, *NBKG* 360.
25. Reindorf, *The History of the Gold Coast*, p.285.
26. Maclean to CAM, 27 August 1832, CO 267/117.
27. Metcalfe, *Maclean*, p.125.
28. Metcalfe, G. E., 1964, *Great Britain and Ghana: Documents of Ghana History 1807–1957*, Nelson & Sons Ltd., London No. 83, pp. 114–115.
29. Metcalfe, *Maclean*, pp.125–126; Reindorf, *The History of the Gold Coast*, p.287.
30. Metcalfe, *Documents*, No.83, pp. 114–115.
31. EC Journal: entry 9 February 1834, Furley Collection, Legon.
32. Treaty of Peace Between Asante and Juaben, dated Accra, 16 November 1835, CO 267/136.
33. Reindorf, *The History of the Gold Coast*, pp. 285–286.
34. Reindorf, *Op. cit.*, p.286.
35. Affrifah, K., "Christianity and the Akyem of Ghana 1766–1887" (forthcoming).
36. Reindorf, *The History of the Gold Coast*, p.286.
37. *Ibid.*
38. Topp & Council (CCC) to CAM, 8 May 1838, reprinted in the House of Commons Papers, cited by Metcalfe, *Maclean*, p.130, n.1.
39. EC Journal: entry 11 April 1838, Furley Collection.
40. Reindorf, *The History of the Gold Coast*, p.289, one *pereguan* was about £8.25, ac-

cording to Reindorf's calculation(Cf, *op. cit*, p.294).
41. EMM 1840 Part III, cited by M. Johnson, *Migrants' Progress*, Part I.
42. Reindorf, (*Op. cit.*, page 294) says Kwasi Boaten died in 1839. His brother Kofi Boaten was made Juabenhene but died in Kwawu, in 1840 en route to Juaben.
43. Freeman, T. B., *Journal of Two Visits to the Kingdom of Ashanti*, London, 1843, pp.156–158.
44. Reindorf, *The History of the Gold Coast*, p.295.
45. Reindorf, *Op. cit.*, p.286.
46. Juaben Tradition, as recorded by Rattray, *Ashanti Law*, p.173
47. Boahen, A. A. "Ashanti Research Conference", in MacEwen, P. J. (ed.) *Nineteenth Century Africa*, OUP, Oxford, 1968, pp.56–57. The effect of this undertaking will be discussed fully in Chapter 10.
48. Metcalfe, *Maclean*, pp.125–126.
49. Two representatives each from Kumasi and Juaben put their marks to the treaty on behalf of their Kings.
50. Schionning (CCO) to Dawson (James Fort, Accra), 20 June 1811, Diverse Arkivaler fra Guinea (DA fra G), No.50.
51. Dawson to Schionning, 17 June 1811, DA fra G. No.50.
52. General told Kammer (i.e. Customs Board) to DFUA, 19 July 1817, DFUA alm. korres (1804–1848).
53. Norregaard, *Danish Settlements*, p.206.
54. Council Minutes (CCC), 1 March 1836, CO 98/1A; Maclean to CAM, 8 August; CAM to Colonial Office, 5 December 1838, CO267/136; GJ 1838: entries Nos. 442 & 480.
55. Council Minutes (CCC), 15 March 1836, CO98/1A.
56. Mr. Wynn, British Ambassador to Denmark, to Krabbe-Carisius, Danish Foreign Minister, 6 September 1837; Gkt: Minutes, 5 December 1837; DFUA draft letter to Mr. Wynn, British Ambassador, 3 March 1838; DFUA to Danish Ambassador, London, 29 March 1838; DFUA to Gkt, 29 March; Gkt to Mr. Morch (CCO), 29 June 1838; Resolution of DFUA, 8 August 1838, all in DFUA am korres. Intra G. Korres. ediide, establishmenter paa Guinea; also CAM to Colonial Office London, ? March 1838; Mr. Wynn (Copenhagen) to Foreign Office, London 12 April 1838, CO 387/150; FO to Wynn, 24 July 1838, copy in FO 211/33.
57. Norregaard, *Danish Settlement*, pp. 207–208.
58. Kwamena-Poh, *Government and Politics*, Chapter 4.
59. General told Kammer to DFUA, 19 July 1817, DFUA alm.korres. (1804–1848).
60. Maclean to CAM, 4 June 1838, CO 297/150.
61. *Ibid.*
62. *Ibid.*
63. George Barnes, M. Foster & Rev. Brown to R. W. Hay, 29 February 1832, CO 367/117; British Parliamentary Select Committee Report (1842) Appendix 36; CAM to CO., 8 December 1849, CO 267/162; Fitzpatrick (CCC) to Earl Grey (CO, London) 10 June 1849, CO 96/15; Metcalfe, Maclean, p.200.
64. EMM Part III, p.96 f, cited by Johnson, M., *Migrants' Progress*, Part I, p.15.
65. *Ibid.*
66. EMM 1840, Part III, p.90f; cited by Marion Johnson, *Migrants' Progress*, Part I, p.15.
67. Dupuis, *A Residence*, Part II, p.viii.
68. EMM 1840 Part III

69. *Ibid.*
70. *Ibid.*
71. Baum (Gyadam) to Basel, 14 July 1857 No.Gyadam 7, BMA-PJA.
72. Carstensen (CCO) to Copenhagen, 6 September 1842, GJ, Norregaard, *Danish Settlement,* p.210.
73. President & Council (CCC) to the Colonial Office (CO) London, 17 December, 1842; W. Hutton to James Stephens, 23 March 1843; Joseph Reid, Hutton & JG Nichols (Accra) to CCC, 8 June; Hutton to CO, 27 July 1843, all in CO 96/2, Foreign Office (FO), London to His Excellency Mr Wynn, British Ambassador, Copenhagen, 31 July; Wynn to FO, 21 August 1843, FO 84/474; CO to FO, 16 November 1843, CO 402/1.
74. Fitzpatrick (CCC) to Carstensen (CCO), 5 June 1849, Guineiske Sager: 1860–1893.
75. The Danes withdrew finally from the Gold Coast in 1850
76. Reindorf, *The History of the Gold Coast,* p.196.
77. Ward, *A History of Ghana,* p.199.
78. Fitzpatrick (CCC) to Earl Grey, London, 10 June 1848, CO 96/15.
79. Guineiske Journaler (GJ) 1849: entries 824 & 825.
80. Fitzpatrick to Earl Grey, 10 June 1849, CO 96/15.
81. Ward, *A History of Ghana,* p.199.

Chapter 7

INTRA-AKYEM RELATIONS AND THE BRITISH 1850–1860

Hostility and violence characterized intra-Akyem relations during the period between 1850 and 1860. Efforts of the British protectorate administration at Cape Coast Castle to calm the conflict promoted acceptance of British authority in Akyem. It is, however, true to say that the British took the initiative to persuade the Akyem peoples to accept that authority.

THE INTRODUCTION OF THE POLL TAX

The departure of the Danes from the Gold Coast in 1850 meant that the peoples of Akyem had no choice but to accept the British supervisory authority. But the first concrete proof of Akyem acceptance of this authority occurred in about mid-1852 when Abuakwa and Kotoku rulers travelled all the way to Accra to endorse and accept a poll-tax ordinance[1] which the British Protectorate administration had promulgated earlier in the year and which the Chiefs and peoples of the western sector of the Gold Coast had already accepted in April 1852.[2] The two Akyem rulers actually joined other eastern Chiefs to approve and accept the Ordinance.

Sources consulted by the present author do not indicate the presence of the Bosome either at the Accra assembly or the Cape Coast gathering. Living in extreme Western Akyem the Bosome may have decided not to bother about an issue which was going to impose a tax on them. For the Ordinance was to legally allow the British, as the protecting power, to levy a poll tax of five pence on every individual in the Protectorate, adult or child. Income from the tax was partly to help defray administrative costs and partly to enable the administration to provide social amenities for the people.[3]

To facilitate collection of the tax the whole Protectorate was divided into districts. Akyem was one of the four districts into which the eastern part of the Gold Coast was divided. The other three were Ga (Accra), Adangbe and Akuapem. All four were collectively designated the Eastern Districts. The headquarters of the tax collector for the Akyem district was Kyebi.

Who the first Tax Collector for the Akyem District was it is not clear. However, in 1855 the tax collector, according to the Basel missionary Simon Sus then residing at Gyadam, the Kotoku capital, was called "Vether". This man, Sus says, had been a member of a British Niger Expedition and later a printer in Sierra Leone before coming to the Gold Coast; and prior to his appointment as tax collector he had been resident in Cape Coast.[4] The presence of the tax collector at Kyebi was indicative of the growing influence of the British in the Akyem country, at least the eastern section of the District.

The Akyem as Good Tax-payers

The first returns of the tax, besides emphasizing the Akyem acceptance of the British authority, showed that they were conscientious taxpayers. Abuakwa and Kotoku together paid £1204.00 sterling during the 1852-1853 financial year.[5] This amount was double that paid by any of the three other Districts.[6] Considered in relation to the entire Protectorate the amount paid by the Abuakwa and the Kotoku was second only to that of the Anomabo District.[7]

Nor did the Abuakwa and the Kotoku default in paying during the subsequent years as several other districts did. During the 1853-1854 financial year, some of the districts, especially the coastal ones, refused to pay the tax on grounds that they were deriving no benefit from it. The Ga and the Adangbe rioted to stress their refusal. But the Akyem, and also the Akuapem, obediently paid. Perhaps this was partly due to the persuasive tongue of Mr. Brodie Cruickshank who following the disorders in the Ga and the Adangbe Districts, went to Akyem to exhort the people to continue to pay the tax.[8] There can be no doubt, however, that the main reason was the willingness of the Akyem to pay the tax. Acting Governor Henry Connor emphasized this point in April, 1855.[9]

After the 1855-1856 financial year, the eagerness of the Akyem began to wane. This was not because taxation did not go with representation,[10] but because they realized they were receiving no benefits in return. Kotokuhene Kofi Agyeman underlined this fact in 1857. He told visiting Mr. T. B. Freeman that he and his subjects had paid "the tax three times but [we] have not received a single piece of cloth or anything in return".[11] By this statement the Kotokuhene was actually reminding the Protectorate Administration to make good its promise in 1852 to return part of the tax to the people in the form of social amenities. In spite of this indirect protest of Agyeman's, for the 1857 financial year, Abuakwa paid £288.00 and Kotoku £216.00 as their tax.[12]

Up to 1859 when some of the states and peoples had long stopped paying the tax Abuakwa and Kotoku appear to have continued paying it, even though they had still not derived anything from it in return. They stopped paying in 1860. The reason for the stoppage can be inferred from remarks made by T. B. Freeman in June that year. He noted that the Akyem, like all others in the Protectorate, were made to understand that a portion of the proceeds from the **tax would be returned to them in the form of direct social services.** But, Freeman observed further:

the only really direct and social benefits which the Akims have since 1852-3 received were my successful visit there in 1857 to put peace between the two [Akyem] Kings and prevent a civil war, and Mr. Hesse's appointment there as a clerk of the District to assist the Kings in their intercourse with the Government. This was positively all the direct benefit they received from their large payments into the public chest.[13]

Though Freeman was immediately protesting against the misuse of the Poll Tax fund on behalf of the Akyem peoples, his comment emphasized the fact of Akyem acceptance of British authority.

Abuakwa-Kotoku Quarrels in 1857

British mediatory role in convulsive intra-Akyem relations provides another yardstick for measuring Akyem recognition of the British authority. The visit to Akyem in 1857 spoken of by Mr. Freeman was actually brought about by political tension between the monarchies of Abuakwa and Kotoku.

The origins of the tension dated as far back as 1825. It started with the enstoolment of Kofi Agyeman as Kotokuhene. The Okyenhene (alias Abuakwahene) at that time was Dokuaa. As pointed out in Chapter 5, she was not happy with the choice of Agyeman by the Kotoku who had just arrived from Northern Akyem as refugees fleeing the wrath of Asante. Since the Kotoku were a sovereign people Dokuaa could do nothing to stop them. The tension continued to exist, generally in a muted form, during the rest of the 1820s and throughout the 1830s.

It worsened from 1842 when Dokuaa abdicated as Okyenhene in favour of her son Atta Panin. In 1855 the report from Gyadam was that Atta Panin was allegedly trying to bring the Kotoku under his political control.[14] It is clear that by the 1850s Atta Panin had turned his mother's personal dislike for Agyeman into an official Abuakwa policy to incorporate the Kotoku into the Abuakwa State complex. That was not a judicious thing for the Okyenhene to do because even though Agyeman and some of his subjects were residing on Abuakwa soil, they were an independent and sovereign people. Admittedly the temptation for an Abuakwa ruler to adopt such a policy was too great to resist. Europeans in and outside the Gold Coast were wont to regard the Abuakwa ruler as King of all the Akyem. In 1831 Maclean talked of consulting the Kyebi ruler, not the Gyadam King nor the monarch of Bosome before concluding the Treaty of Peace with Asante. In the 1840s the Danes usually referred to the Abuakwa ruler as *Kongen* i.e. the King, and the Kotokuhene as *Caboceer*, namely Chief.[15] The implication was that the former was superior to the latter. There is a suggestion that the British encouraged, presumably unwittingly the absorption of Kotoku into the Abuakwa Kingdom.[16]

In the 1850s the impression that Kotoku was under Abuakwa received greater emphasis. In 1852 when the rulers of the states in the Eastern Districts met in Accra to assent to the Poll Tax Ordinance, the Kotokuhene was described as though he was subordinate to the Abuakwahene who was referred to as "the King of Akim".[17] Europeans in their home country toed the line with their counterparts in the Gold Coast. In 1855 Sir George Barrow of England called the Kotokuhene a "Captain of the King of the Akims".[18] "The King of the Akims" was in reference to the Okyenhene. In 1857 Governor C. C. Pine aluded to the Kotokuhene as "a very powerful vassal, a kind of an African Duke of Burgundy", in comparison with the Abuakwahene.[19] It would be absolutely unrealistic to imagine that the Abuakwa were unaware of the greater recognition Europeans accorded their King vis-a-vis the Kotoku ruler.[20] Such a recognition was bound to inflate the ego of the Okyenhene and make him regard his Kotoku counterpart as being inferior to him. An attitude of this nature could, and actually did, encourage the Abuakwa leadership to adopt a policy to incorporate the Kotoku into the Abuakwa state system. Such a policy of absorption was all the more tempting because of the residence of the Kotoku on Abuakwa soil.

But while it was possible in theory to adopt this policy, it was not easy, in practice, to implement it. Agyeman, as later events would show, was not the type of leader to tolerate such a pretension on the part of the Abuakwahene. His unwillingness to tolerate the Kyebi policy was probably behind the decision of the people of Gyadam in 1855 to emigrate from eastern to western Akyem.[21]

Two issues prevented the immediate implementation of the emigration plan. The first was the discovery later in 1855 of new and very rich deposits of gold. The discovery compelled them to shelve the migration move and stay on to exploit the auriferous deposits.[22] The second issue was strained relations with Asante.

Kotoku-Asante Relations

The immediate cause of the tension was a territorial dispute between the Kotokuhene and Asantehene Kwaku Dua I. According to Sir George Barrow

> the King of Ashantee complained that a captain of the King of the Akims [i.e. the Kotokuhene] had called land in Ashantee his own, and taken gold from it, and sworn the great Ashantee Oath that the Ashantees living on that land should leave it . . . It would appear that on each bank of the Prah river, which is the boundary between Akim and Ashantee, there is a crom [i.e. town] the inhabitants of which are in the habit of digging gold dust, the Ashantees paying tax to King Aggaman [i.e. Agyeman] for the privilege . . . King Aggaman sent his messengers to the Ashantee side of the

river to collect the tax, but his [messenger's official] cap was torn from his head, one half sent to the King of Ashantee, the other to King Aggaman with a message that if he sent 100 people with such caps they would do the same . . . and King Aggaman swore by his sword that if he had not bound himself to the English Government, he would march that day to fight the Ashantees.[23]

The sources do not make clear which piece of land was the subject of dispute between the Kotokuhene and the King of Asante. It must have been a place in the abandoned Northern Akyem, i.e. Asante-Akyem today, the ancestral home of the Kotoku ruling house prior to their emigration from there in 1825 to settle in Southern Akyem (Akyem Abuakwa).

Wherever the piece of land in dispute was, the passions it generated were not one-sided. The Asantehene also fumed against Agyeman of Kotoku for swearing "the great Ashantee Oath". The Asante monarch protested in very strong terms to the British in their capacity as the overlords of the Kotokuhene.

In order to resolve the dispute in a peaceful manner, the Cape Coast Castle administration invited the Asantehene to send his representatives to Cape Coast to assist the Governor in an enquiry into his grievances against Agyeman.[24] But the Asantehene did not oblige.[25] The failure of the Asantehene is not easy to fathom. It is possible that the Asantehene merely wanted the British administration to warn the Kotokuhene to refrain from claiming ownership to lands on the west bank of the Pra, most probably present day Asante-Akyem. The Asantehene apparently did not want to go to war over that district. The firm stand which the British took in 1853 when Asante tried to regain Assin,[26] must have been too fresh to be forgotten so soon in Kumasi. That experience was there to remind the King of Asante that the British were capable of taking a tough action against him should he go to war against the Kotoku. All the same the land dispute showed that Asante hostility against Kotoku was not in doubt. Nor was that of Abuakwa.

Continued Abuakwa-Kotoku Quarrels

So real were the tensions between

(i) Kotoku and Abuakwa, and
(ii) Kotoku and Asante that in 1855 missionary Simon Sus, then resident at Gyadam, summed up the situation thus:

On this side [to the north of Gyadam] the great Ashantee tiger growls; and on the other side [to the South] Atta shows cat's claws here and there.[27]

The fact of the matter was that the Kyebi absorption policy was not the only source of friction between Abuakwa and Kotoku. Others were a clash of jurisdiction, the missionary presence in Akyem, and economic rivalry. Let us examine these in detail one after the other. First the economic friction: the consensus of Basel missionary eyewitness accounts was that Gyadam in the 1850s was by far the largest town in all Akyem. It reportedly pulsated with brisk agricultural and commercial activities quite in contrast to Kyebi which the missionaries said was dull and its inhabitants generally lazy.[28] The Kotoku were also said to be avid gold miners.[29] It was largely the economic buoyancy of Kotoku which influenced Simon Sus in 1853–54 to select it as the Mission Station for the missionary enterprise in Akyem.[30]

That economic prosperity may have excited the jealousy of Abuakwa. The Akan proverb says *Ɔhɔho nni nkɔ ye ɔmani mfonee* (i.e. the stranger grows fat at the expense of the native). Strictly speaking the Kotoku, though Akyem, were strangers in Abuakwa; they were, as has been pointed out already, immigrants from Northern Akyem otherwise called Asante-Akyem today. The Abuakwa could not afford to see them prosper without feeling uneasy in their minds.

This muted tension was worsened from 1853–1854 when the Basel missionaries sited their Mission Station at Gyadam, the Kotoku capital. The Mission started its enterprise in Akyem in 1853 when missionary Sus went to settle at Gyadam.[31] The choice of Gyadam as the site for the Mission Station for all Akyem hurt the feelings of the Abuakwa monarchy. The reason was that before 1854 the Okyenhene had passionately appealed to the Society to start its work in Akyem from Kyebi, his capital. On several occasions he had demonstrated his enthusiasm and eagerness for the enterprise. In January 1852 he extended an invitation to the Basel Mission Society, through visiting missionary Simon Sus, to come and base themselves at Kyebi, and that once they were settled Sus himself should teach him how to read and write.[32] He renewed the invitation a month or so later when missionaries Mader and Widman also visited eastern Akyem.[33] During his visit to Accra in July 1852 in connection with the Poll Tax Ordinance, he attended a Church Service held by the Mission at Osu.[34] In or about May 1852 he sent two of his sons to school at the seminary which the Basel Mission had opened at Akuropon, the Akuapem capital.[35] He did this in fulfilment of a promise he had made to Sus in January during the missionary's visit. The missionaries at Osu in Accra were highly impressed by the Okyenhene's eagerness.[36]

In view of all his enthusiasm, he was rudely shocked, jolted as it were, when the Basel Mission chose to go to Gyadam in 1854. The Okyenhene felt so slighted that he immediately banned all his subjects from entertaining or having anything to do with the Mission's work in Akyem. He also withdrew his two sons from the school at Akuropon. Above all he secretly regarded the Kotokuhene as the person who had upset his apple-cart. Agyeman added insult to injury. Without any reference to the Kyebi monarchy, he sold to the missionaries at Gyadam land on which they planned to build the Mission station.[37] The Kotokuhene as a refugee had not made any outright acquisition of the Gyadam land or any other part of eastern Akyem Abuakwa where they had settled. The Kotokuhene, therefore, had no right to sell any piece of land in Abuakwa to anybody. In 1859 when the Okyenhene referred to that piece of land as his,[38] he was in reality giving vent to his anger at the sale.

The land sale also symbolized a clash of jurisdiction. This subject was the greatest source of conflict between Abuakwa and Kotoku. By December 1857 relations between the two states over this subject had so deteriorated as to draw them to the brink of war. At that time, Governor C. C. Pine was on a visit to the Akuapem capital, Akuropon. From there this was how he reported on the tension in eastern Akyem to the British Home Government:

> The powerful Kingdom of Akim which borders this [Akuapem] is . . . in a very disturbed state. The sovereignty of it is divided between the King and a powerful vassal [i.e. Agyeman], a kind of an African Duke of Burgundy, and on account of supposed insults, those two potentates are at the point of coming to blows. As each party can bring a large force into the field, the result of such a war might be very serious, more especially as the country borders on that of the Ashantees who might perhaps interfere in the quarrel.[39]

Pine had to do something to prevent the situation in Akyem from getting out of hand. From Akuropon he despatched Mr. T. B. Freeman, the Chief Civil Commandant of the Eastern Districts, to Akyem with instructions to do everything in his power to resolve the crisis there in a more peaceful manner.

The tension had both immediate and remote causes. With respect to the latter the Abuakwa, since 1855, had instituted a blockade of the trade routes against the Kotoku. Pursuant to that policy, they had cultivated the habit of waylaying, seizing, detaining and robbing Kotoku traders and travellers plying to the coast.[40] The immediate cause was what Freeman vaguely described as "unnecessary demands" which the Okyenhene, Atta Panin, was making on Kotokuhene Agyeman. Freeman in his report did not elaborate directly on what he meant by "unnecessary demands", but his report was detailed enough to explain it. According to him the stool of Muoso became vacant when the chief, Abrokwa, died. Muoso, to the thinking of Freeman, was a Kotoku town. Abrokwa's successor was a minor called "Obriar" (i.e. Obri Yaw). Therefore the people of Muoso appointed Pepra, a relative, to act as Regent until Obiri Yaw came of age. Pepra was asked to pay a debt of 8oz. of gold or 4 pereguans, which Obiri had incurred. Pepra refused to pay the debt and in his refusal, he had the backing of his two brothers, Kofi Nyame, a rich man who had earlier declined the regency, and Badu who happened to be a son-in-law to the

Kotokuhene. The three brothers would still not cooperate even when the towns people of Muoso undertook to pay two-thirds of the debt. The Kotokuhene himself pleaded with the three brothers, but to no avail. Whether or not Agyeman went beyond mere pleas Freeman did not say; what he said is that all the three brothers left Muoso for Kyebi and lodged a complaint with the Okyenhene against the Kotokuhene.[41]

By this act the three Muoso men brought about a clash of jurisdiction between the two sovereign authorities. Not only that: they had, by their conduct, suggested the subordination of Gyadam to Kyebi, unless they were claiming to be citizens of Abuakwa, which they were not, as later events would show. The Okyenhene capitalized on the complaint from Muoso to demonstrate his perceived superiority over the Kotoku ruler, by summoning Agyeman to appear before a Kyebi court to respond to the complaint of Pepra, Kofi Nyame and Badu against him.[42]

In terms of Akan diplomatic culture and etiquette, the summons on a sovereign ruler would amount to an "unnecessary demand", even an insult, to the Kotokuhene who was an independent sovereign irrespective of the fact of his refugee status in Akyem Abuakwa. On the other hand, the Abuakwa ruler was in a real dilemma. The Kotoku were living on his land. By virtue of that fact all of them were his guests. As their host, nothing should prevent him from seeking their collective welfare by composing misunderstandings and petty quarrels amongst them. But since the King of Kotoku himself was involved, Atta Panin of Kyebi ought to have been more discreet and circumspect in his handling of the Muoso affair in order not to offend the sensibilities of his Kotoku counterpart.

As it was, Atta Panin, no doubt, felt that Agyeman was not his equal. That was why he summoned the Kotoku ruler to appear before him at Kyebi. It is reasonable to imagine the Kotokuhene not only refusing to go to Kyebi for arbitration between him and the three Muoso men, but also getting angry with Atta Panin for implying that he, Agyeman, was his inferior. And Agyeman, according to Ward, was "a man of overbearing character likely to inflame any bad feeling rather than sooth it".[43] On the basis of this tension, Ward's view is flawed. Besides, contemporary evidence does not support Ward in his view of Agyeman. T. B. Freeman in 1857,[44] J. A. Nichol Irwine in 1866[45] and J. A. B. Horton in the 1860s,[46] all spoke highly of Agyeman's personality and policies. Any ruler worth his salt and in the position of the Kotokuhene would surely have reacted the way Agyeman did.

Agyeman could not contain his anger. He resolved on war with Atta Panin to preserve Kotoku independence and dignity. He was actually at the point of taking to the field when an Akyem Abuakwa chief reportedly swore an oath to stop him from firing the first shots until the British Protectorate Government had been given the chance to look into the whole issue of Kyebi-

Gyadam relations.[47] Missionary Simon Sus who is our source was then based at Gyadam. He did not disclose the identity of the Abuakwa Chief who by his oath, asked the Kotokuhene to exercise patience and restraint. Whoever he was his intervention was timely and wise. It prevented the immediate outbreak of hostilities and thereby made it possible for Mr. Freeman to leave Akuropon, the Akuapem capital, on 8th December for Eastern Akyem where he arrived on 10th December, 1857.[48]

The Freeman Mediation and Settlement

Freeman spent eight days in Akyem investigating the Kyebi-Gyadam tension. At the end of it all, his carefully considered conclusion was that the Okyenhene had been at fault in interfering in Kotoku internal affairs; that Atta Panin had also erred by detaining Kotoku subjects more than fifty-seven of whom were still in Kyebi cells at the time of Freeman's visit.[49] The Chief Civil Commandant of the Eastern Districts returned a verdict of guilty against the Okyenhene.[50]

Atta Panin did not challenge the verdict but calmly accepted the judgement of the Government official. He agreed to release all the Kotoku citizens he was holding in detention; he also agreed to restore whatever goods, property and moneys he had robbed them of. On the subject of restitution, however, the Okyenhene argued that since the three Muoso citizens, Pepra, Nyame and Badu, "had largely partaken of the property so plundered, they should also share in the restitution now to be made".[51]

Agyeman on his part unreservedly accepted the settlement of peace which Freeman arranged between the two states. He was prepared to forgive and forget. On 20th December 1857 when Freeman was about to leave Gyadam for Kyebi en route to Accra, Agyeman asked the Chief Civil Commandant of the Eastern Districts to

> tell Coffee Yammie and Pipira that I freely forgive them . . . and that I hope they will immediately return home and dwell peacefully with me; but if they do not wish at present to return, they must proceed to the coast and remain there for a time under the care of the Government until they can feel comfortable in their minds to come back.[52]

Agyeman also requested Freeman to

> tell Atta that all being [now] settled . . . between Coffee Yammie, Pipira, and Baddoo and myself . . . I hope all the past evil things between us will be forgotten; that he will no more stop the paths [i.e. trade routes] against me and my people . . . that he will open the path which has been shut for the past two years against my subjects of Essuadru.[53]

"My subjects of Essuadru" was in reference to the Akyem Bosome, whose capital Soadru was. Living in Western Akyem they too, on account of their clan ties with the Gyadam, had fallen victim to the Abuakwa economic blockade against the Kotoku. That was why the Kotokuhene was pleading with Okyenhene Atta Panin on their behalf.

To the extent that it prevented an immediate outbreak of war between Abuakwa and Kotoku, Freeman's 1857 mediatory mission to Akyem was a success. But the subsequent recalcitrance of Pepra and his brothers detracted considerably from Freeman's achievement. Contrary to expectation, they refused to restore their share of the loot, as demanded by the Okyenhene on accepting the Freeman settlement. Worse still, they fell out with their Abuakwa patron and protector over the issue and angrily left Kyebi for Akuapem. There they established a base at Mampon, and with the tacit support of many Akuapem, who included even the Okuapemhene, Kwao Dade, they embarked on terrorist activities against their own countrymen plying to and from the Ga-Adangbe coast via Akuapem.[54]

Exactly when the three Muoso marauders left Akyem for Akuapem is unclear from the available records. But by 1859 they were there and were disrupting Kotoku communication lines with the Ga-Adangbe coast.[55] Probably they left Kyebi either during or soon after the 1858 British armed expedition against Krobo.[56] For Abuakwa, Kotoku and Akuapem all showed their loyalty to the British Protectorate Administration by providing contingents to join the expeditionary force.

Once they had the permission, support as well as the active cooperation of the Akuapem, the three Muoso men, as Freeman put it in 1860.

> were determined to waylay Argiman's people on the paths in Aquapim and panyar and plunder; thus evincing [in 1859] the same perverse spirit which they had shown in Akim in 1857 and which had well nigh brought on actual hostilities [between Abuakwa and Kotoku].[57]

Strained Kotoku-Akuapem Relations

The activities of Pepra, Nyame and Badu in Akuapem led to a straining of relations between Gyadam and Akuropon. They also engendered a considerable extent of disruption in the trade from the interior to the Ga coast. To the Protectorate administration that was a far more serious matter. Closely linked with the adverse economic effect was a political side: the Akuapem support and sympathy for the three Kotoku renegades was both private and official. While the people of Mampon participated actively in the predatory activities of the Muoso marauders, Okuapemhene Kwao Dade accorded them substantial patronage. He granted Badu a legal action at his court against missionary Sus of Gyadam. Badu's complaint was that Sus had illegally seized his (Badu's) property at Gyadam.[58]

It was not correct that the missionary had impounded Badu's property. What actually happened was that when Badu and his two brothers left Akyem for Akuapem, King Agyeman anticipated future trouble from them, particularly Badu, who had left some property at Gyadam. To prevent that possibility, he asked the missionary who was based at Gyadam to be a caretaker of the property.[59] Sus agreed. The caretaker role of the missionary was what Badu construed to be the sequestration of his property by Sus. In 1859 Sus visited the Basel missionaries at Akuropon. As soon as he learned about the visit, Badu rushed to lodge his complaint against Sus at the Okuapemhene's court for unlawful appropriation of property. But for a strong warning from the Chief Civil Commandant, Kwao Dade would have indulged Badu with a court hearing.[60]

Agyeman took a serious view of the conduct of the Akuapem in supporting his rebel subjects. He warned the Protectorate government that the issue might lead to "a row between him and Aquapim".[61] In August 1859 the Kotokuhene ordered Christian Asante, an Akuapem born Catechist, out of Gyadam. The expulsion was a form of the Kotokuhene's protest against the Akuapem support for his three rebel subjects. The rest of the missionary personnel at Gyadam pleaded with Agyeman to rescind the expulsion order but he refused.[62]

There was thus a great need for the Protectorate government to take a quick and firm action to prevent a possible war between Kotoku and Akuapem. Freeman, the Chief Civil Commandant of the Eastern Districts, carefully analyzed the situation and came to the conclusion that the solution to the problem lay, not at Gyadam, but at Akuropon; that the Akuapem support for the three Muoso rebels was a major part of the problem, and so must be tackled. To that end he sent a strong warning to the Okuapemhene to the effect that Gyadam affairs were beyond Akuropon jurisdiction and therefore he must not dabble in them.[63] He also asked the Okuapemhene to immediately withdraw his support from the Kotoku rebels, and

> to warn Baddoo and those connected with him that if they attempt any interference with Argeman and his people or Mr. Sus, or any matter connected with the palaver about which I visited Akim in 1857 . . . I will call upon the Military Authorities to send a force and bring them down to the coast for punishment. And let them not fancy that I am indulging in empty and unnecessary threats. Their conduct has been so bad in creating troubles and disturbance that we can no longer bear with them if they continue such proceedings.[64]

Freeman followed words with action. In late 1859 he sent a platoon of soldiers to Akuapem to arrest the three Kotoku rebels and all those who were in any way supporting them in their predatory activities. But the Okuapemhene forewarned the Kotoku rebels who accordingly forearmed by shifting the base of their operation from Akuapem Mampon before the government troops got there. They moved to a place described as the boundary between Akuapem and Akyem; from there they continued to commit what Freeman called "greater outrages" against their own countrymen.[65]

The flight of the rebels from Mampon did not in any way exonerate Akuapem from attempting to disturb inter-state relations and throw the whole of the Eastern Districts into chaos. The administration of Acting Governor Bird decided that Okuapemhene Kwao Dade must be punished to serve as a deterrent for other Chiefs. At a court held at Asabi at the foot of the Larteh hills on the Larteh-Ayikuma route, the Governor closely examined the role of Akuapem in the terrorist activities of the Kotoku rebels and found the Okuapemhene guilty. The Chief was fined "1000 heads of cowries".[66] Thus Akyem affairs were helping, however negatively, to entrench British authority not only in Akyem but also in neighbouring Akuapem.

The Abuakwa-Kotoku War of 1860

By 1859 Kyebi-Gyadam relations had once again taken a turn for the worse. Atta Panin had died in May 1858.[67] His younger twin brother, Atta Obiwom (or Buom) had succeeded to the Kyebi Stool. Obiwom appears to have been of a more fiery character with the inclination to foment trouble. In the 1830s his love affairs did strain relations between the Kyebi monarchy and the Juaben royals who were then in Akyem as refugees.[68] Some of his councillors were wont to instigate him to take a more aggressive line with Gyadam. Among his bad advisers were Apietu, described as "Chief Adviser" and his sister, who was most probably the new Queenmother because the Old Queenmother, Dokuaa, had died in 1856. In May 1860 Captain des Ruvinges described this "sister" of Obiwom's as "a perfect firebrand" who assisted her brother with money.[69] Clearly, in character and in council, Okyenhene Atta Obiwom was not cut to promote cordial relations between Abuakwa and Kotoku.

He had hardly been a year on the Abuakwa stool when he seems to have renewed the old policy of Kyebi hostility towards Gyadam. In May 1859 Agyeman complained of Obiwom's habit of ordering the seizure, robbing, flogging and detaining of Kotoku subjects.[70] By the beginning of 1860 the two Akyem states found themselves in a state of war.[71] According to Stromberg, one of the Basel missionaries working at Gyadam, the Okyenhene declared war in January 1860.[72] The explosive situation caused Mr. Hesse, the Government agent at Kyebi, very anxious moments. Nor were the two rulers themselves happy with the situation. In January 1860 the Okyenhene complained to Mr. Hesse for the information of the Chief Civil Commandant of the Eastern

Districts about his quarrels with the Kotokuhene.[73] Freeman sent a message promising to proceed to Akyem in order to investigate the tension.[74] In February Freeman was twice informed that "Obewoom and Ageman are expecting you everyday".[75] But Freeman did not go to Akyem as he had promised, and hot war broke out in March 1860.[76] Explaining his failure to go to Akyem, he said Acting Governor Bird preferred to rely more on military men than civilians.[77]

The war had both immediate and remote causes. The remote cause was that habit of the Abuakwa in harassing Kotoku subjects as discovered by Freeman in 1857 and complained of by Agyeman in 1859. The Kotoku may have retaliated by similar methods, but there is currently no direct evidence for this. As regards the immediate cause, oral tradition ascribes it to a dispute between Obiwom and Agyeman over gold nuggets.[78] In 1882 Adolph Mohr, a Basel missionary based at Begoro was told an Abuakwa tradition which attributed the outbreak of the war to two causes:

(i) that the people of Gyadam had been working on a new gold field but refused to pay one-third of their takings to the Okyenhene as custom demanded;
(ii) that Kotokuhene Agyeman refused to allow Atta Obiwom to marry a Kotoku woman.[79]

The Abuakwa tradition which missionary Mohr gathered in 1882 and the later ones do not tie in well with contemporary evidence which gives three slightly different versions of the immediate cause of the war. The first version comes from one Major Cochrane whom the Protectorate government sc[nt] Akyem in March 1860, with instructions to mediate between Kyebi and Gyada[m] and prevent the outbreak of war between the two. He arrived in eastern Akyem on or about 4th March and fixed his mediation venue at "Ashiaquah" (i.e. Asiakwa) which was about midway between Kyebi and Gyadam. He failed in the attempt. The mediation did not even get off the ground because Atta Obiwom would neither go to Asiakwa nor send his representatives there. Only Agyeman sent his negoti[at]ors whom missionary Stromberg accompanied to Asiakwa.[80] On 8th March the war began, forcing Major Cochrane to leave Asiakwa for "Aniah Sing" (i.e. Anyinasin) so as to avoid being caught in the crossfire. From Anyinas[in] Cochrane reported that the immediate cause of the war was

> the desire [of Obiwom] to possess himself of Affram's nephews and their property amounting [to] more than a hundred persons and a considerable amount of gold and goods take[n] away from Agjeman's territory.[81]

A month later Captain des Ruvinges was despatched to Akyem to reinforce Cochrane who had reported his inability to prevent or stop the war single-handed. Des Ruvinges, who was a Swiss from Canton Vaadt, in the second week of April 1860, sent in a report part of which said:

> the whole war has been brought about by him [i.e. Atta Obiwom] to gratify a favourite of his named Affram who being a drunkard, and I consider the lowest kind, was perpetually calling on his relatives who were under the protection [i.e. jurisdiction] of Adjeman to help him pay debts incurred by him in his excesses.[82]

Captain des Ruvinges may have obtained part of his information from the Basel missionaries working at Gyadam who give us the third version of the contemporary evidence of the immediate cause of the war. According to one of the missionaries, Stromberg, the immediate cause of the war, was Kyebi interference in Gyadam internal affairs. Expounding on this the missionary said that a Gyadam elder (Affram) fled to Kyebi, from there he requested that all his relatives should leave Gyadam and join him at Kyebi.[83] According to the missionary the elder's people constituted a sizeable segment of the population of Gyadam.[84] Okyenhene Atta Obiwom backed Affram and despatched his palace messengers to Gyadam to escort Affram's people to Kyebi.[85]

Apparently Affram had decided to transfer not only his own Kotoku citizenship and allegiance but also those of all his relatives to Abuakwa. There could not have been a much greater source of friction between Gyadam and Kyebi. The issue appears to have aroused great emotions, especially on the part of Agyeman and his subjects. For Stromberg states that the Gyadamese insulted the escorts from Kyebi, manhandled them and chased them out of their town.[86] Even more foreboding was the fact that Agyeman swore to go to war with Kyebi "rather than give them [Affram's relatives] up".[87]

From the three pieces of contemporary evidence, it emerges that the immediate cause of the war was Okyenhene Atta Obiwom's attempt to claim jurisdiction over Kotoku subjects who had not willingly renounced their Kotoku citizenship for that of Abuakwa. Still at play in 1860 was the old Kyebi policy to absorb Kotoku into the Abuakwa State complex by subjecting Kotoku citizens to the Abuakwa Stool, a policy which dated back to the reign of Okyenhene Atta Panin (1842–1858). The policy was hostile to Kotoku sovereignty. It helps to explain why in 1859 Agyeman revived the idea of emigrating to western Akyem with all his subjects so as to be far removed from Kyebi, but would not move out until he had fought Atta Obiwom.[88] Thus an additional and a much weightier immediate cause of the 1860 Abuakwa-Kotoku war was Kotokuhene Agyeman's resolve to wage it.

The War

In anticipation of the emigration to Western Akyem, the Gyadamese and the few other Kotoku communities in eastern Akyem, between late 1859 and early 1860 performed intensive custom for their dead and shrines.[89] Next, Agyeman sent ahead to Western Akyem a large section of his subjects: these consisted mainly of women, children, the aged and the infirm. Agyeman had completed doing all this before Major Cochrane arrived to begin his mediation mission. The situation which the Major met rendered his mission a non-starter. As missionary Stromberg put it, the preparations which the Gyadamese had already undergone made Cochrane "powerless".[90] Little wonder that on 4th March 1860 he informed the Cape Coast Castle administration that he alone could not prevent the war from breaking out. Captain des Ruvinges was despatched with twenty troops to go and reinforce Cochrane whose troops had numbered only six.

Preliminary hostilities appear to have started on 8th March, 1860. Kyebi put in the field a force of two thousand as against the eight hundred of Gyadam.[91] The size of the Kyebi force, though about two and a half times bigger than that of Gyadam, was relatively small, considering that barely three years later the Okyenhene, at a short notice could raise a force of over five thousand. This suggests that not all Abuakwa supported Kyebi in the war. In fact it was known at the time that the Nifahene of Abuakwa, alias Asiakwahene, was not in favour of war as a means of settling differences between Kyebi and Gyadam.[92] It looks as if the war was between Kyebi and Gyadam, not between Abuakwa and Kotoku.

Obiwom carried the war to Agyeman thereby snatching aggression from the latter whose 1859 decision to fight before emigrating initially made him the aggressor. Contemporary evidence shows that aside from minor skirmishes two major battles were fought in the war, the first took place on 19th March, 1860, quite close to the Mission Station just on the outskirt of Gyadam,[93] and the other on 27th of the same month.[94]

Tradition gives conflicting views on the outcome of the war. All Abuakwa traditions touching on the subject claim victory for Kyebi, adding the detail that the Abuakwa forces totally burnt down Gyadam.[95] On the other hand at least one Kotoku tradition asserts that victory went to Kotoku, and states further that had Dompre, one of the leading Kotoku war chiefs, wished, he would have killed the Okyenhene whom he cornered on one accasion.[96]

The Kotoku tradition essentially ties in with the contemporary eye witness account of the Basel missionaries then working at Gyadam. On the 19th March battle, missionary Stromberg states that

(i) the Kyebi force was beaten;

(ii) the Gyadam force took two prisoners of war;
(iii) Agyeman himself ordered that the wounds of the prisoners of war be dressed and later had them released;[97]
(iv) that after his defeat Atta Obiwom retreated to Nsutam with the remnant of his force, and had run out of ammunition;
(v) that after the battle several contingents from other parts of Abuakwa went to join the Okyenhene.[98]

Regarding the 27th March battle the Kyebi force was again defeated.[99] Altogether three hundred to four hundred souls lost their lives in the war.[100] But the missionaries, our source on this issue, did not state in detail the losses of each side. At any rate the evidence shows clearly that the Abuakwa lost the second battle also. Consequently, Okyenhene Atta Abiwom requested the Asantehene "to come and assist him to take Adjiman's head.[101]

The Asante Role

The invitation to the Asante government was indicative of the great desperation of the Okyenhene, because it completely negated the traditional Abuakwa dislike for Asante. Obiwom must have been terribly stung by the defeats he suffered at the hands of the Kotoku. As to be expected, the Asante government obliged. The Asantehene already had an axe to grind against Agyeman who barely five years earlier (1855) had claimed jurisdiction over some lands beyond river Pra. The invitation from Kyebi gave the Asante government a chance to settle old scores with Agyeman. The Asantehene detailed the confederate states of Juaben and Kokofu as well as the province of Kwawu to go to the aid of Kyebi.[102] Proximity and old understanding were probably the criteria the government in Kumasi used in selecting the three to go to the assistance of Kyebi. Kwawu, as an immediate north-eastern neighbour could quickly send its forces into Abuakwa. Kokofu to the north-west could easily cut Agyeman's line of march to Western Akyem. As for Juaben the Asante government may have recalled to mind its friendship with Abuakwa in the 1830s and 1840s.

The Juaben and Kwawu forces arrived in Eastern Akyem in April 1860; but they arrived too late. By then Agyeman with all his subjects, civilians or otherwise, had left for Western Akyem.[103] It was the emigration and the resultant abandonment of Kotoku settlements which, according to the missionaries, enabled the Abuakwa forces to burn down Gyadam and other places such as Moseaso.[104]

The Kokofu were much luckier; they encountered the migrating Kotoku force and joined battle with it. But Kotoku defeated Kokofu.[105] The latter allegedly suffered heavy losses in the number of soldiers killed, one of whom was described as "Adarquaah of Kookoofoo".[106] Adarkwa of Kokofu was perhaps a reference to the Kokofuhene or a leading Kokofu war captain. The Asantehene tried to cover up the Asante aggression by presenting the armed clash as an unprovoked Kotoku attack on Kokofu.[107] Governor Andrews, after careful investigation, dismissed the complaint from Kumasi by telling the Asantehene that if the Kokofu had suffered any damage, they must have themselves to blame because they had chosen to go to war against Agyeman and his subjects.[108] Obviously the Asante assistance proved to be inadequate; besides, not all of it arrived in time to turn the scales in favour of Akyem Abuakwa.

The Last Stages of the War

His defeats in March and the failure of the Asante assistance in April clearly explain why the Okyenhene, Atta Obiwom, was determined to carry the war to Agyeman even in Western Akyem. It is also clear that the outcome so far had shocked him. Probably he had hoped to inflict a quick and heavy defeat on his adversary. This can be inferred from his refusal to attend the Asiakwa Mediation Meeting. He also refused to listen to the pleas of Major Cochrane not to go to war, telling the Major that he had renounced

> his allegiance to the British Government, conceiving it as merely a thing to speak of, and that the Government has no power capable of compelling him at this distance to accept its verdict, at least not one given on what he terms his own soil".[109]

This declaration shows that the Okyenhene meant his war with the Kotokuhene to be a challenge to the British protecting power also. Otherwise the outburst may be dismissed as emotionally made in a moment of anxiety.

The pain of defeat, the desire to square matters, and promptings from his advisers, especially Apietu and Queenmother Sekyiraa, goaded Obiwom on to carry the war to Agyeman in Western Akyem. In May 1860 he ordered his subjects at "Ackiasi" (i.e. Akyease) to attack Agyeman and his subjects at Soadru, the Bosome capital.[110] Next he moved his war camp westwards from Nsutam to the neighbourhood of Tekyiman.[111] Nothing positive appears to have come out of these measures. Akyease disobeyed the order to attack Agyeman in Bosome because, as Captain des Ruvinges put it, "Adjiman had secret friends amongst Attah's people".[112]

Perhaps it was this apparent divided opinion among the Abuakwa which encouraged Captain des Ruvinges to hit on the idea of taking a tough action against the Kyebi monarchy. He was of the view that bad advisers at Kyebi were largely responsible for the outbreak of the Kyebi-Gyadam war. Foremost among the bad advisers were Apietu, described as Obiwom's "Chief Adviser" and Queenmother Sekyiraa, Obiwom's sister who was described as "a perfect firebrand" assisting Obiwom with money.[113] Captain des Ruvinges recommended to Governor Andrews the arrest and detention of the two.[114] Governor Andrews had just assumed duty at Cape Coast Castle. His knowledge on Gold Coast politics was naturally limited. And yet he rejected the recommendation because such a measure, he argued, would smack of high-handedness and cowardice, since the two were unprotected.[115]

Fortunately for the new Governor, things began to sort themselves out in Akyem from the last week of May 1860. The truculence of Kyebi started to subside. Several factors contributed to the change in the attitude of the Kyebi monarchy. One of them, as already stated, was the divided opinion amongst the Abuakwa as to the propriety of the war: not all Abuakwa shared in the war excitement of Kyebi. For instance Nifahene Duodu was

> much opposed to the manner in which Atta [Obiwom] has acted in not in the first instance obeying the Governor's orders and that he Doodu has expressed his determination to meet me [Governor Andrews] at Christiansborg, and that Atta should accompany him there,[116]

and allow the Protectorate government to settle his disputes with Agyeman. Another segment which did not support the war was the Gyaase Division headed by Kwaben. The Kwaben allegedly allowed Agyeman and his migrating subjects to pass through unmolested during the journey to western Akyem; while the people of Anyinam equally remained neutral.[117] For remaining neutral the Anyinam were later punished. On this issue missionary Mohr in 1879 noted:

> Before the Kotoku people were driven away from Gyadam, the Anyinam people lived on a pretty hill the other side of [river] Berem. After the war they were commanded to come to this side by the distrustful Kibi king and forced to pay [a heavy fine] because like Kwabeng, in the war, altho' they did not fight on the side of Agyeman, neither did they join the Kibi King.[118]

The Asiakwa pressure had a salutary effect on Okyenhene Atta Obiwom. By the third week of May 1860, bellicose Kyebi had so cooled down that Obiwom sent to inform Captain des Ruvinges that he would

> no more make war with Adjeman . . . [but] will return back [sic] to Chebi by your orders to await there for the appointed time for us [to go to Accra].[119]

The change in the attitude of the Abuakwa leadership immediately eased the tension in Akyem. But it did not altogether eliminate it. As late as 1863 Obiwom claimed that the land on which Agyeman and his subjects had settled on in Western Akyem was under his jurisdiction.[120] The Protectorate government had to send an embassy of Fante Chiefs to Kyebi to plead with the

Okyenhene to revise his hostile stand against Kotoku.[121] The Abuakwa ruler agreed in principle, but it was not until 1870 that Abuakwa and Kotoku concluded a formal peace treaty at the Abuakwa town of Akaanten[122] to end the 1860 war. The deaths of both Atta Obiwom and Agyeman three years before the conclusion of the Akaanten Treaty seem to have contributed to that happy event. Both rulers died in 1867. With the two protagonists out of the scene, Abuakwa and Kotoku could arrange a peace settlement without much loss of face to either side.

The Akaanten Settlement

A considerable part of the credit, however, goes to Goerge Ekem Ferguson. Ferguson is better known in Gold Coast history as the African Surveyor through whose surveying activities the British were able to colonize the northern territories of the Gold Coast.[123] It is hardly known that he was also a good mediator. It was he who, on behalf of the Protectorate administration, brokered the 1870 Akaanten Peace. Ferguson deserves great credit because even in 1870 when ten good years had passed since the Abuakwa-Kotoku war was fought, emotions were still high. For example, the Kotoku negotiators wanted to lay down some conditions which the Abuakwa representatives could not accept. One of these was that a certain head of an ex-Gyadam family who had sworn an oath to serve the Abuakwa Stool and had been accepted by the Kyebi monarchy, should be surrendered and returned to Kotoku allegiance.[124] Perhaps this demand by the Kotoku negotiators was a reference to Affram whose transfer of his allegiance to Abuakwa had been an immediate cause of the 1860 war. Missionary Lodholtz attended the peace talks. According to him the 'surrender' condition was clearly a vindictive strain in the five Kotoku Peace negotiators because it did not have the backing of the new Kotokuhene, Kwabena Fuah.[125] Eventually the Kotoku negotiators dropped the demand to pave the way for peace to be concluded. Ferguson's tact and persuasive tongue may have played a part in compelling the Kotoku negotiators to drop the condition.

The ceremony of the peace settlement is worth describing concisely, if only to serve as an illustration of how some peoples of the Gold Coast of the nineteenth century concluded peace among themselves. Among the Akan the process leading to a peace settlement (treaty) or any other agreement was termed *nom abosom* (literally, drinking the gods or fetishes). Missionary Lodholtz said that Ferguson's interpreter first accompanied a person carrying the Kotoku Fetish, Ekyere, to the five Abuakwa peace negotiators who would "drinks" it. The fetish was contained in a small brandy bottle, placed in a brass pan and carried in absolute silence among all those present as a sign of reverence to the Ekyere god. On reaching a "drinker", i.e. an oath-taker,

Ferguson's interpreter poured out some of the fetish, set the toes of his left foot on those of the oath-taker and orated, the gist of which was that if the "drinker" was not sincere but intended treachery, the god Ekyere should kill him. After the oration the interpreter then poured again from the bottle into the mouth of the "drinker" whose head was also sprinkled with some of the fetish. In a similar manner all the five Kotoku negotiators "drank" the Abuakwa Fetish Wankobri, which was in a beer bottle. While a particular god or fetish was being drunk, horns would be intoning its praises.[126] Even though the final peace settlement took place in 1870, it is reasonable to regard the third week of May 1860 as marking the end of the war.

Immediate Effect of the War on the Protectorate Administration

The war had an immediate impact on the Protectorate administration. Apparently it incurred some expenditure in its efforts to bring back peace to the Akyem District. The records consulted, however, do not provide the evidence on the subject.

The war also compelled Governor Edward Bullock Andrews to subject the Civil Commandantcy of the Eastern Districts to a rigid examination. For there was a belief in some sections of officialdom at Cape Coast Castle that the inefficiency of Mr. T. B. Freeman, as Chief Civil Commandant of the Eastern Districts, was largely responsible for the outbreak of the war in Akyem. In June 1860 Mr. Freeman was formally charged thus: "to the manner in which you adjudicated the case between Atta [Panin] and Adjiman [in 1857] must be attributed the present disturbances".[127] He was also accused of "grossest irregularity in the mode of keeping . . . accounts".[128]

Meticulous accounting does not appear to have been a virtue in Thomas Birch Freeman. Of mixed English and African parentage, he first arrived in the Gold Coast in 1838 as a missionary of the Wesleyan Methodist Mission of England.[129] In June 1844 he had to return to England to appear before a Committee of the Wesleyan Mission to answer a charge of financial mismanagement.[130] He returned to the Gold Coast but in 1857 gave up the missionary work to take up the post of Chief Civil Commandant of the Eastern Districts during the governorship of Mr. C. C. Pine.

The Executive Council at Cape Coast on 5th and 16th July, 1860 sat as a Court to examine the two charges against Mr. Freeman. Prior to the sittings of the court, he had submitted to the Executive Council a voluminous written defence refuting the two charges.[131] He ably refuted the charge of administrative incompetence. In connection with this charge Kotokuhene Kofi Agyeman was invited to Cape Coast Castle to be a prosecution witness. The evidence of the Kotoku ruler rather substantiated Freeman's argument. As a result he was acquitted on that count. However, he was found guilty on the charge of financial embezzlement and dismissed from the Protectorate service. The July 1860 trial of Mr. Freeman emphasized the importance the Protectorate Administration attached to the Akyem District.

Summary

In the 1850s the Kotoku living in Eastern Akyem as refugees prospered economically. Gyadam, their capital settlement, grew into a thriving economic centre. From 1853 it also became the Mission Station of the Basel Mission Society's evangelical work in Akyem. These developments aroused the jealousy of the Abuakwa monarchy at Kyebi. The Kotoku leadership worsened matters by tramping on certain rights of the Abuakwa monarchy. The tension exploded into war between the two states in March 1860. To minimize the tension, if not eliminate it altogether, the Kotoku ruling house with almost all their subjects, emigrated to Western Akyem in April 1860.

NOTES AND REFERENCES

1. J. Zimmerman (Osu-Accra) to Basel, 7 July 1852, Basel Mission Archives – Paul Jenkins's Abstracts (BMA-PJA).
2. Governor Hill (Accra) to Earl Grey, Colonial Office (CO), London, 23 April 1852, CO96/25.
3. For a full and very useful discussion of this subject see Kimble, D., 1963, *A Political History of Ghana 1850–1928*, Oxford University Press, Oxford, Chapter IV.
4. Sus (Gyadam) to Basel, 16 October, 1855, No.IV.47, BMA-PJA. The British organized three Niger Expeditions, 1841, 1854 and 1857. If indeed Mr. "Vether" joined one of these then it must have been either 1841 or 1854. The 1841 one is the more likely considering that he was said to have gone to live in Sierra Leone after the expedition before proceeding to the Gold Coast.
5. Statement of Poll Tax: Income and Expenditure, CO 96/33. The Statement is reproduced in an edited form by Kimble, *A Political History*, p.177.
6. Evidence of Mr. T. B. Freeman at Cape Coast Castle on 8 June 1860 CO96/54.
7. Kimble, *A Political History*, p.177.
8. Brodie Cruickshank, was appointed the first Collector-General, and was yet to take up the post when he was made Acting Governor from 27 Aug. 1853 to 16 Jan., 1854. He was partly instrumental for the promulgation of the Poll Tax Ordinance, See Kimble, *Op. cit.*, pp. 170–176.
9. Connor, H. (CCC) to Sidney Herbert, C.O., 7 April, 1855, CO96/33.
10. Kimble, *A Political History*, pp. 175–176.
11. Freeman's Report on his Mission to Akyem in 1857, dated 28 December, 1857, CO96/33.

12. *Ibid.*
13. Evidence of Freeman at Cape Coast Castle, 8 June 1860, CO96/64.
14. Sus (Gyadam) to Basel, 1 June 1855, BMA-PJA.
15. Vgk of GTK: Sager til Guineiske Journaler, 1842–1843, No. 458.
16. Ward, *A History of Ghana*, p.199, n.17.
17. Zimmerman (Osu, Accra) to Basel, 7 July 1852, BMA-PJA.
18. Memorandum of Sir George Barrow to the Colonial Office, London, 21 December 1855, CO96/33.
19. C. C. Pine (Akuropon-Akuapem) to the Rt. Hon. H. Labouchere, Colonial Office, London, 7 December, CO96/43.
20. The Basel missionaries working in Akyem and Akuapem were the only whites who knew that the two Akyem rulers were equal in status.
21. Sus (Gyadam) to Basel, 27 May 1855, No.IV.43, BMA-PJA.
22. Sus (Gyadam) to Basel, 29 August 1855, No.IV.47, BMA-PJA.
23. Memorandum of Sir George Barrow to the Colonial Office, London, 21 December 1855, CO96/35.
24. *Ibid.*
25. *Ibid.*
26. Ellis (1893), pp.219–220; Claridge Vol.I, pp.485–493; Ward, *A History of Ghana*, pp. 209–212.
27. Quoted in Evangelische Mission-magazine (EMM) Part III, p.30 and reproduced in Johnson, *Migrant Progress*, Part I, p.17.
28. Sus (Gyadam) to Basel, 3 February 1852; Widman and Mader (Akuropon-Akuapem) to Basel, 3 March 1852; Mader's Reisebericht on a visit to Sus at Gyadam in 1854, 21 April, 1854; Zimmerman's Report on a journey to Eastern Akyem, 7 May, 1858, BMA-PJA.
29. Freeman's Report on his Mission to Akyem in 1857, dated 28 December 1857, CO96/57.
30. Sus (Gyadam) to Basel, 9 January 1854, BMA-PJA.
31. For a fuller and detailed discussion of the Basel Mission work in this part of the Gold Coast, see Affrifah, K., "Christianity and the Akyem of Ghana 1766–1887", (Forthcoming).
32. Sus (Akuropon-Akuapem) to Basel, 3 February 1852, BMA-PJA.
33. Widman & Mader (Akuropon) to Basel, 23 March 1852, Vol.V., No.47 BMA-PJA.
34. Zimmerman's Quarterly Report, 7 July 1852, No.140, BMA-PJA.
35. Sus (Akuropon) to Basel, 22 May 1852, No.55; Dieterle & Christaller (Akuropon) to Basel, 7–15 June 1854, Vol.III, No.18, BMA-PJA.
36. *Ibid.*
37. Baum (Gyadam) to Basel, 1 April 1857, No. Gyadam 14 BMA-PJA.
38. Haas (Gyadam) to Basel, 29 August 1859, No. Gyadam 14, BMA-PJA; Supplement to Freeman's Written Defence, 8 June 1860 CO96/48.
39. C. C. Pine (Akuropon) to the Rt. Hon Labouchere, 7 December 1857, CO99/43.
40. Freeman's Report on his mission to Akyem in December 1857, dated 28 December 1857, CO96/45.
41. *Ibid.*
42. *Ibid.*
43. Ward, *A History of Ghana*, p.222.
44. Freeman's "Police Memorandum made in Akim", dd. 20 December 1857", CO 96/48.

45. Nichol Irwine (Accra) to Colonel Conran (CCC), 14 May 1866, CO96/72.
46. Horton, A. B.,1868, *West African Countries and Peoples*, Frank Cass & Co. Ltd., London 1967 Ed., p.120.
47. Sus's Jahresbericht on Gyadam, 1 March 1859, BMA-PJA.
48. Freeman's Report on his Mission to Akyem, 28 December 1857, CO96/45.
49. *Ibid.*
50. *Ibid.*
51. *Ibid.*
52. Freeman's "Police Memorandum made in Akim", 20 December 1857, CO96/48. Badu, the third of the brothers, was then at Gyadam.
53. *Ibid.*
54. Freeman (Kponi) to Kwao Dade, Okuapemhene, 12 February 1859; Hesse (Kyebi) to Freeman, 10-24 May 1859; Ross (Akuropon) to Freeman (Accra), 1 September 1859, all in CO96/48; Haas (Gyadam) to Basel, 29 August 1859 No. Gyadam 19, BMA-PJA.
55. *Ibid.*
56. For a useful account of events leading to the Expedition, its course and its outcome see Freda Wolfson, "A Price Agreement on the Gold Coast – The Krobo Oil Boycott 1858-1866", in Economic History Review, 1953 Vol.VI, No.1.
57. Freeman's Written Defence dated 8 June 1860 CO96/48. As will be shown in Chapter 8 following, in 1860 Freeman, as the Chief Civil Commandant of the Eastern Districts was accused of mishandling affairs in the Akyem District, A Commission of Enquiry was set up at Cape Coast Castle to investigate the issue. To the Commission Freeman submitted a voluminous Written Defence before appearing before it in person.
58. Freeman's Written Defence, 8 June 1860, CO96/48. Sus was then on a visit to Akuropon from Gyadam.
59. Hesse (Kyebi) to Freeman (Accra), 3 May 1859, as Enclosure No.23 in Freeman's Written Defence, CO96/48.
60. Freeman (Kponi) to Okuapenhene Kwao Dade, 12 February 1859, CO/96/48.
61. Hesse (Kyebi) to Freeman, 21 May 1859, copy as Enclosure No.37, in Freeman's Written Defence, 8 June 1860, CO96/48.
62. Missionary Haas (Gyadam) to Basel, 29 August 1859, No. Gyadam 19, BMA-PJA.
63. Freeman (Kponi) to Okuapemhene, 12 February 1859, copy; also Freeman (Kponi) to Sus (Akuropon) 12 February 1859, copy both as Enclosure Nos. 23 & 24 in Freeman's Written Defence, CO/9648.
64. Freeman to Okuapemhene, 12 February 1859, CO96/48.
65. Freeman's Written Defence, 8 June 1860, CO96/48.
66. *Ibid.* "1000 heads of cowries" was valued at $600.00.
67. Testimony of Kotokuhene Agyeman before the Executive Council (CCC), Cf. Minutes dd. 16 July 1860, CO96/48.
68. Reindorf, *The History of the Gold Coast*, p.286.
69. Capt. des Ruvinges (Soadru) to Cape Coast Castle, 5 May 1860, CO96/48.
70. Kotokuhene Agyeman to Freeman (Accra), 9 May 1859, CO96/48.
71. Kromer's 4th Quarterly Report for 1859, dd. 12 January 1860, No. Gyadam 26, BMA-PJA.
72. Stromberg (Gyadam) to Basel, 20 March 1860 No. Gyadam 6, BMA-PJA.
73. Freeman's Written Defence, 8 June 1860, CO96/48.
74. Freeman (Accra) to Hesse (Kyebi), 26 January 1860, CO96/48.

75. Hesse (Kyebi) to Freeman (Accra), 15 & 23 February 1860, CO96/48.
76. Acting Governor Bird (CCC) to the Duke of Newcastle, CO, London, 2 April 1860, CO96/47.
77. Freeman's Written Defence, 8 June 1860, CO96/48.
78. AAT: Begoro & Pamen (1925/6); Ameyaw, "Oda Tradition", IAS, acc.KAG/7 pp. 12-14; Bosome Tradition, cited by Ward, *A History of Ghana* p.222, n.26, AKT: Adoagyiri & Awisa (1968/9); AAT: Kukurantumi seems to confuse events of 1857 and 1860 and so must be read with care; AAT: Asiakwa & Kwaben (1925/6) mention the war and its outcome but say nothing about the cause.
79. A. Mohr (Begoro) to Basel, 15 May 1882 No.11, 79 BMA-PJA. Adolph Mohr was born on 20 January 1851 at Akuropon. He went to Basel in August 1870 and was ordained a missionary in 1874 and returned to the Gold Coast the same year, and was sent to Begoro. His parents hailed from Grunbach, Wurttenberg.
80. Stromberg (Gyadam) to Basel, 20 March 1860, No. Gyadam 6, BMA-PJA.
81. Major Cochrane ("Aniah Sing") to Acting Governor Bird (CCC), 8 March 1860, CO96/47.
82. Capt. des Ruvinges ("Akim") to Cape Coast Castle, 13 April, 1860, CO96/47.
83. Stromberg (Gyadam) to Basel, 20 March 1860, No. Gyadam 6, BMA-PJA.
84. *Ibid.*
85. *Ibid.*
86. *Ibid.*
87. Minutes of Executive Council Meeting (CCC), 16 July 1860, CO96/48.
88. Kromer's 4th Quarterly Report for 1859, dd. 12 January 1860, No. Gyadam 26, BMA-PJA.
89. Joint Rahresbericht of Haas & Kromer (Gyadam) to Basel, 12 January 1860, No. Gyadam 1, BMA-PJA.
90. Stromberg (Gyadam) to Basel, 20 March 1860 No. Gyadam 6, BMA-PJA.
91. Stromberg to Locher, 26 March 1860 No. Gyadam 8, BMA-PJA.
92. Captain des Ruvinges (Akyem) to Cape Coast Castle, 13 April 1860, CO96/47. According to the Basel missionaries the Asiakwahene was called "Diedu", i.e. Duodo.
93. Haas' 1st Quarterly Report on Gyadam for Year 1860, dd. ? No. Gyadam 10, BMA-PJA.
94. *Ibid.*
95. AAT: Asiakwa, Begoro, Kwaben, Kukurantumi, Pamen & Wankyi (1925/6).
96. AKT: Adoagyiri (1968/9).
97. Stromberg to Basel, 20 March 1860, No. Gyadam 6, BMA-PJA.
98. Stromberg to Locher, 26 March 1860, No. Gyadam 8, BMA-PJA.
99. Stromberg to Basel, 31 March 1860 No. Gyadam 9, BMA-PJA.
100. Report from Kromer, 28 May 1860, No. Akim 12, BMA-PJA.
101. Captain des Ruvinges (Soadru) to CCC, 8 May 1860, CO96/47.
102. Stromberg to Basel, 31 March 1860, No. Gyadam 9, BMA-PJA; Freeman (Accra) to Governor Andrews (CCC) 21 April; Andrews to Freeman, 25 April; Capt. des Ruvinges (Soadru) to Andrews. 5 May; Governor Andrews (CCC) to the Asantehene, 9 May 1860, CO96/47.
103. Report from Kromer, 28 May 1860, No. Akim 12, BMA-PJA.
104. Report from Stromberg, 3 August 1860, No. Akim 19 BMA-PJA.
105. Asantehene to Governor Andrews (CCC), 25 April 1860, CO96/47.
106. *Ibid.*
107. *Ibid.*

108. Governor Andrews to the Asantehene 9 May & 20 September 1860, CO96/47.
109. Major Cochrane (Anyinasin) to CCC, 8 March 1860, CO96/47.
110. Capt. des Ruvinges (Soadru) to Governor Andrews (COC), 5 May 1860, CO96/47.
111. Report from Stromberg, 3 August 1860, No. Gyadam 19, BMA-PJA.
112. Capt. des Ruvinges to Governor Andrews, 5 May 1860 CO96/47.
113. *Ibid.*
114. *Ibid.*
115. Alphonso Cary, Acting Colonial Secretary (CCC) to Capt. des Ruvinges, 8 May 1860, CO96/47. At the time of the recommendation, Okyenhene Atta Obiwom was still in the field with his army. Apietu and the Queenmother who were at Kyebi were thus not protected.
116. Governor Andrews (CCC) to the Duke of Newcastle (CO), London, 9 June 1860, CO96/47.
117. Report of Mohr on his visit to Anyinam as an Out-Station, dd. 28 October 1879, No.161; BMA-PJA. AAT; Pomase, i.e. Abomosu (1925/6).
118. Report of Mohr on his visit to Anyinam, 28 October 1879, No.161. BMA-PJA.
119. Okyenhene Atta Obiwom (Akaantin) to des Ruvinges (Soadru), 23 May 1860, CO96/47.
120. Kromer (Kyebi) to Basel, 1 November 1863 No. Akim 18, BMA-PJA.
121. *Ibid.*
122. Lodholtz (Kyebi) to Basel, 5 January 1871 No. Akim 19, BMA-PJA.
123. Sampson, M. J., *Gold Coast Men of Affairs*, London 1969, pp. 129–146.
124. Lodholtz (Kyebi) to Basel, 5 January 1871 No. 19, BMA-PJA.
125. *Ibid.*
126. *Ibid.*
127. Mr. Lindsey, Acting Colonial Secretary (CCC) to Freeman, 2 June 1860, CO96/48.
128. *Ibid.*
129. See Harrison M. Wright's New introduction to T. B. Freeman, (Ed.), 1968, *Journal of Various Visits to the Kingdoms of Ashanti Aku and Dahomi* (1968 edn), p.xi.
130. Freeman, *Op. cit.*, p.xxxviii.
131. The Written Defence with many Enclosures can be found in CO96/48, PRO., London.

Chapter 8

IMPACT OF THE KOTOKU EMIGRATION TO AND RESIDENCE IN WESTERN AKYEM 1860–1867

The 1860 emigration of the Kotoku from Eastern to Western Akyem had far reaching effects on the Akyem states themselves and the Gold Coast in general. While the emigration released the Abuakwa from the aversion they had hitherto had for the Christian missionary enterprise in Eastern Akyem it also led to the founding of Nsuaem (later re-named Oda) and Nsawam, the one in Western Akyem and the other in extreme south-western Akuapem. Their presence in these two places enabled the Kotoku to influence events in the Gold Coast on such a scale and in such scope as they had never done before.

Expansion of Christianity in Eastern Akyem

The departure of the Kotoku for Western Akyem in 1860 resulted indirectly in the expansion of Christianity in Eastern Akyem. Since 1853 the Basel Evangelical Mission Society with its Mission Station at Gyadam, the capital of the Kotoku, had been propagating the Christian faith in Eastern Akyem.[1] But up to 1860 the conversion rate had been dismal even though by then six missionaries, two missionary wives and two African catechists had worked at Gyadam. In that seven-year period, the Mission made only five converts from among the Akyem, all five being Kotoku citizens.[2]

The main reason for this lack of progress was the boycott which the Abuakwa monarchy instituted against the Mission and its evangelical work for siting its Mission Station at Gyadam instead of Kyebi, the Abuakwa capital.[3] The emigration of the Kotoku and the destruction of Gyadam in March 1860 gave the missionaries a new opportunity to make a fresh start. They moved their base first to Kukurantumi in April 1860 and finally to Kyebi in early 1861.[4]

Almost immediately, Christianity began to experience rapid progress in Eastern Akyem. By November 1861 the Mission had gained several converts; a Christian quarter was fast springing up at Kyebi, and evangelization in the surrounding towns and villages like Tete, Pano, Apedwa, Nkronso, Wirenkyiren (now Amanfrom), Adadietam and Apapam, all within about fifteen kilometers radius from Kyebi, had learned about the Word.[5] Kukurantumi was not abandoned; it became the first out-station vis-a-vis the Kyebi Mission Station. By 1867 the Mission had won thirty-five converts at Kyebi and sixteen at Kukurantumi; it had two schools, one at Kyebi with over twenty pupils and the other, which was at Kukurantumi, had about ten on roll.[6]

This achievement was many times better than the Mission's record at Gyadam for a similar period of seven years. The reason for this comparatively rapid advance was the abandonment, by the Abuakwa, of their hostile attitude toward the Mission and its work during the pre-1860 period. Now that Kyebi was hosting the Mission Station the Abuakwa felt easy in their minds to patronize the Christian enterprise. Besides, the Mission had no immediate plans to evangelize among the Kotoku in Western Akyem and thereby incur the displeasure of the Kyebi monarchy and Abuakwa society.

Tension Between Agyeman and Dompre

In Western Akyem the Kotoku were faced with several problems, the most immediate being tension between the paramountcy and the Ankobea division headed by Chief Dompre. The cause of the crisis was what Kotokuhene Agyeman considered to be an unpardonable offence committed by Dompre, the Ankobeahene. During the March 1860 war, Dompre reportedly had an excellent chance to kill Okyenhene Atta Obiwom but refrained from doing so on grounds of clan affinity.[7] The Okyenhene, like Dompre, belonged to the Asona *abusua*. The Okyenhene was, and is still, looked upon as head of all those Akan or Twi who belong to the Asona clan, irrespective of where they came from.[8] Had Dompre killed the Okyenhene, he, according to the Akan *abusua* culture, would have committed fratricide, a heinous crime among the Akan. The Kotokuhene who was of the Agona clan, on the other hand, felt that in the circumstance of war, Dompre should have allowed Kotoku national and military interests to take precedence over *abusua* obligations by killing the No.1 enemy of the Kotoku.[9] With this frame of mind Agyeman refused to include Dompre on the honours list after their arrival in Western Akyem. Dompre's reaction was sharp, unequivocal and immediate: he left Western Akyem with his subjects, headed south-eastwards and finally settled at what is now Nsawam.[10]

Given the uncertain situation in which the Kotoku were at the time, the rift between Agyeman and Dompre was unfortunate. Dompre's subsequent exploits, as will be shown in Chapter 9 following, marked him out as indeed a genius of a military leader. His contribution to the success of the Kotoku in the Gyadam War must have been quite substantial. Agyeman should and could have dealt with him more diplomatically and retained his services. For the Kotoku were not safe even in Western Akyem; Kyebi continued to be truculent and Kumasi was hostile. As late as 1863, Okyenhene Atta Obiwom grumbled that the land on which the Kotoku had settled in Western Akyem fell within his jurisdiction.[11] Either Abuakwa or Asante could attack them in Western Akyem, in which case the services of Dompre would be needed. But there the rift was; Dompre and his followers went away leaving the rest of the Kotoku

The Founding of Oda

To find a permanent and peaceful home had been the main motive of the Kotoku paramountcy in migrating to Western Akyem. But clan ties with the Bosome monarchy was an enabling factor. In April 1860 Captain des Ruvinges found the Kotoku migrants at Soadru, the Bosome capital, as guests of the Bosomehene.[12] Tradition is therefore absolutely right in asserting that

> after the war between Akim-Kotoku and Akim Abuakwa in the middle of last [nineteenth] century, the Omanhene of Akim-Kotoku left Jyadem in Eastern Akim and sought another site. The Stool of Akim-Bosome was already established at Akim-Swedru in Western Akim . . . This Stool, like the Kotoku Stool, is of the Agona clan, and for clanship's sake the Omanhene of Bosome gave sanctuary to these homeless kinsmen in her town. . . .[13]

The Bosomehene at that time was a woman called Amoakoaa. By giving "sanctuary" to the migrant Kotoku, she was merely fulfilling an obligation of the Akan *abusua* system which enjoined all those belonging to the same clan to assist one another, particularly in times of difficulty, irrespective of ethnic, political and economic affiliations. Clan ties, as Boahen rightly points out, "completely cut across tribal and political boundaries".[14]

To Amoakoaa, Agyeman was more than a clansman. Firstly, Agyeman had been connected with the Bosome ruling lineage since 1813 when he, his uncle Kwakye (an ex-Kotokuhene) and other relatives, as pointed out in Chapter 5 arrived in Asante as refugees from Kotoku and were attached to the Bosome ruling house. Then in 1824 the Bosome ruling lineage together with Agyeman emigrated to Western Akyem to join kinsmen who had gone to settle there during the first decade of the eighteenth century. It was from Akyem Soadru in Western Akyem that Agyeman was recalled in 1825 to be enstooled as Kotokuhene at Gyadam in Eastern Akyem. Thus to Amoakoaa, Agyeman was like a relative who had returned home from a long travel. Secondly, because of the close link between Agyeman and the Bosome monarchy Abuakwa extended its hostility towards the Kotoku to the Bosome during the period between 1855 and 1860. In fact in May 1860 Okyenhene Atta Obiwom directed his western-most subjects, the Akyease, to attack both the Kotoku and the Bosome in Western Akyem. The Akyease disobeyed the order because, as Captain des Ruvinges put it in 1860, "Adjiman has secret friends amongst Attah's people"[15]

The "secret friends" of Agyeman amongst the Abuakwa were even more supportive to him in another way; they provided the Kotoku migrants with land on which to settle. As already pointed out, the main objective of the

Kotoku migrants was to find a peaceful and permanent home in Western Akyem. But the Kotoku Stool did not possess land of its own there. Nor could the Bosome rulers indefinitely play host to the migrants. Moreover the Bosome themselves did not possess enough land in Western Akyem part of which they could release to the "homeless" kinsmen of theirs. But Wankyi, headquarters of the Oseawuo Division of Abuakwa, owned large tracks of land. Amoakoaa assisted Agyeman to apply to the Wankyihene for land and the Wankyi ruler readily obliged.[16] The Wankyi land grant to Agyeman may have taken place some time between June 1860 and 1862 because by 1863 the Okyenhene was claiming that the land on which the Kotoku had settled in Western Akyem fell within his jurisdiction as the Omanhene (Paramount Ruler) of Akyem Abuakwa.[17]

Apparently, the Wankyihene did not consult with Kyebi before giving out the land. This is not to suggest that the Okyenhene could have stopped the grant. The Wankyi land gift to the Kotoku without prior consultation with the Abuakwa King merely emphasized the weak position of the Kyebi monarchy in the matter of land ownership and control in the Abuakwa State up to the middle years of the nineteenth country. Several of the lesser Chiefs were greater landowners than the Okyenhene himself and could dispose of such land as they pleased.

With his acquisition of land from the Wankyi, Agyeman founded a new capital in Western Akyem and called it Nsuaem (The Slice), perhaps in gratitude to the Wankyi who generously gave him the land. Nsuaem is called Oda today. The change of name allegedly occurred at the beginning of the present (20th) century, and was meant to put an end to the confusion people made between Nsuaem and Nsawam.[18] True as this assertion may be, it must be pointed out that the Kotoku in the 1870s sometimes referred to Nsuaem as "Akim Daa"[19] i.e. Akyem Oda.

From the evidence adduced above it is clear that the founding and crystalization of the Akyem Kotoku State as it is today resulted from the Abuakwa-Kotoku War of 1860.

Problems Arising from the Kotoku Presence in Western Akyem

The advent of the Kotoku in 1860 created ethnographic, demographic as well as political problems in Western Akyem in succeeding years. Naturally, the population of the district increased in variety and numbers though by how much it is not easy to tell. The area became relatively crowded as the Kotoku immigrants founded towns and other settlements cheek by jowl with existing Abuakwa, Bosome and reportedly stateless Atwea[20] towns and villages. The outcome today is that Abuakwa, Bosome and Kotoku towns and settlements are so mixed up that it is difficult, if not impossible, to draw clear territorial boundaries between the three types of Akyem.²¹ While it is appropriate to describe Eastern Akyem as Abuakwa, Western Akyem does not yield to such a straightforward definition: it consists of a mixture of all three Akyem types.

The admixture appears to have given rise to the practice of some communities, towns and groups transferring loyalties and allegiances from one Stool to another. For example the Kotoku Stool, in the course of time, gained Apaso, Ayirebi, Anyinam (Western Akyem), Abenase and possibly several others from the Abuakwa and Bosome states; Kotoku is also said to have absorbed some of the stateless Atwea.²² However, Kotoku was not always at the receiving end; it too appears to have lost some of its subjects to the other two states.²³ But it seems that transfer to rather than from Kotoku was the general trend. Exactly when the process began cannot be pin-pointed but in less than ten years after his arrival in the district, more or less as a refugee, the Kotokuhene was being referred to as "the King of Western Akim".²⁴

The Kotoku paid a painful price for their rise to pre-eminence in Western Akyem. By the early 1870s they had lost that cordiality and cooperation which had existed between them and the Bosome monarchy up to the 1860s; friction had replaced fraternity between the two stools. The cause of the conflict seems to have been the issue of transfer of allegiances and loyalties. The best proof of this assertion is the Bosome-Kotoku dispute over the town of Awisa which Captain Butler noted during the British invasion of Asante in 1874²⁵ but which may well have existed in the late 1860s at least. Awisa town was situated between Oda and Soadru, capitals of Kotoku and Bosome respectively, and its chief was called Kwabena Ahenkora. The Kotokuhene then was Kwabena Fuah and the Bosomehene was Kofi Ahenkora.

According to Captain Butler, Kwabena Ahenkora, the Awisa Chief

> owed a kind of divided allegiance on the one hand to Quabinah Fuah [and] on the other to Coffee Ahencora. Fuah had sent to summon [the Awisahene] to Insuaim with all his men to march under the banner of West Akim to the War [i.e. the 1874 British invasion of Asante]. But Cobra [Ahenkora], doubtless thinking that he might altogether escape service in the field, pleaded that to Coffee Ahencora, and not to Quabinah Fuah, was his fealty, if any due, and declined to obey the summons from Insuaim. Upon which Fuah had declared that he would go to war with Awisa if the refusal was persisted in. With the rifles and ammunition he had received for service against the Ashantis, he [Fuah] would, it was averred, soon carry destruction into the hamlet of Cobra Ahencora. Hence the alarm at Swaidroo, for Awisa lay only a mile distant [from Soadru].²⁶

Butler apparently managed to get Bosome and Kotoku to sink their differences over Awisa in the greater interest of the British invasion of Asante during which both states were allies of the British.

Probably the Bosome-Kotoku rivalry over Awisa in the 1870s dated back to the late 1860s and may have been an outcome of the practice of towns and communities unilaterally transferring loyalties and allegiances from one state to another without considering the implications of their actions. It is equally possible that the Kotoku leadership, having emerged as the predominant power in Western Akyem, were trying to compel lesser chiefs who were unwilling to accept their authority. The threat of King Kwabena Fuah to destroy Awisa was tantamount to intimidation if Awisahene Kwabena Ahenkora indeed did not owe allegiance to the Kotoku Stool. Whatever the cause of the Bosome-Kotoku dispute over Awisa, it seemed unfortunate when viewed against the backdrop of cordiality and cooperation which enabled them to contain an Asante invasion of their district in 1863.

The Asante Invasion of the Protectorate in 1863

Hitherto this invasion has been seen as primarily directed against the British Protectorate Administration at Cape Coast Castle. [27] This is completely wrong, but admittedly excusable, in view of the fact that at the time of the invasion a dispute indeed existed between the Administration and the Asante government. Kumasi cleverly exploited the quarrel to deceive the British on the cause or causes of the attack and its objective.

The Anglo-Asante quarrel was over the extradition of two Asante fugitives in the Protectorate, one a runaway slave boy and the other an Asante Chief called Gyani.[28] Gyani had violated a mineral law in Asante and to skip justice fled into the British Protectorate for safety. The law required that anybody who discovered a gold nugget, or nuggets, should surrender same to the King's treasury. Failure to do so carried the mandatory penalty of death.

At the time of the invasion Gyani was residing in Denkyira. On his way there, he and the runaway slave boy had reportedly been sheltered by the Kotokuhene who returned an insolent reply to the Asantehene on being applied to to surrender them.[29] This is doubtful, to say the least. Kotokuhene Agyeman could only have done this if the fugitives had arrived in the Protectorate via Western Akyem after May 1860 when the Kotoku ruler and his subjects arrived in the district as refugee immigrants from Eastern Akyem. But some contemporary reports said that Chief Gyani with about eight hundred followers had "left Ashantee several years ago".[30]

Barely two months after Richard Pine assumed the governorship at Cape Coast Castle in October 1862, the Asantehene, Kwaku Dua I, applied to him for the extradition of Gyani and the slave boy to face justice in Asante. Their execution was almost a certainty should they ever set foot on Asante soil even though the Asante King promised to spare their lives. On humanitarian grounds, therefore, Governor Pine refused to extradite the two criminals.[31] In February

Impact of the Kotoku Emigration to and Residence in Western Akyem

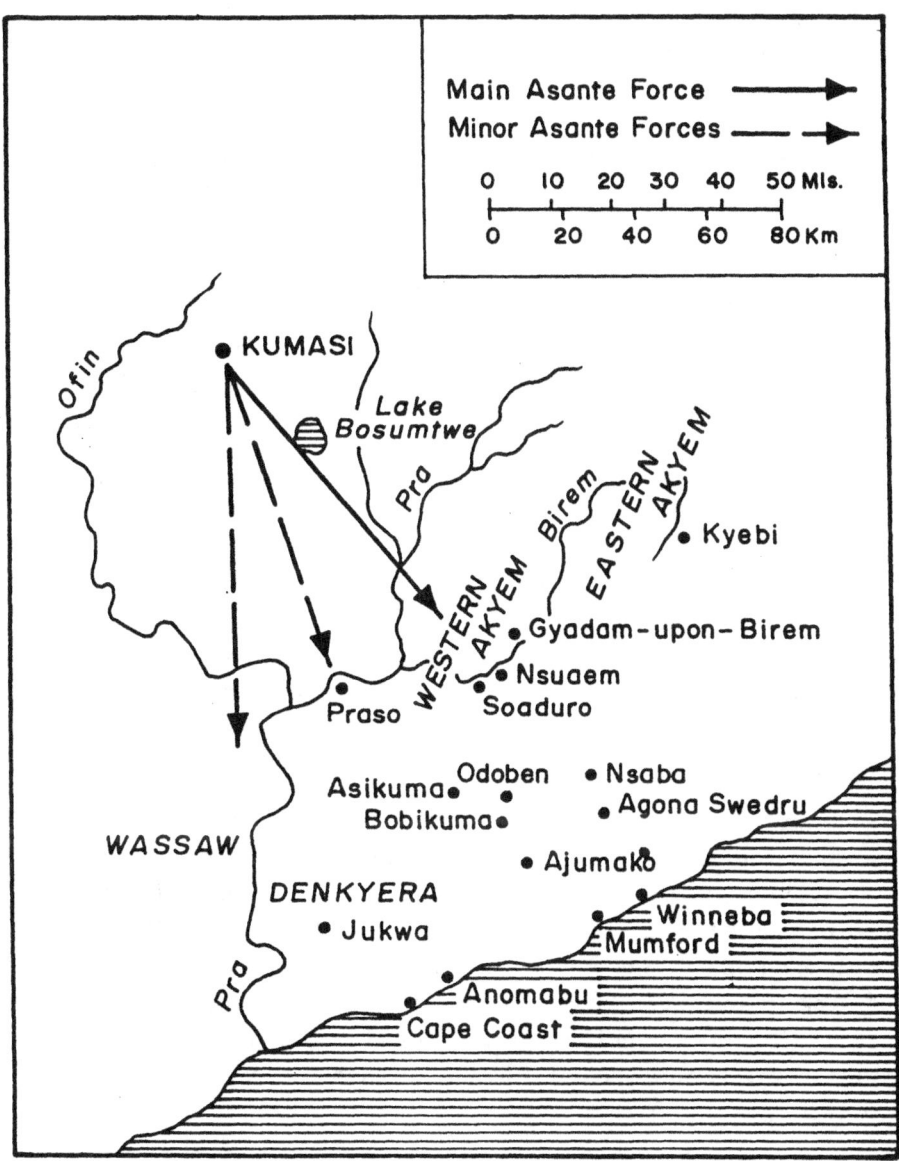

Fig. 6: The Kotoku-Asante War of 1863: Movements of the Invading Asante Army

1863 the Asantehene renewed his application for the extradition by sending a powerful delegation to Cape Coast Castle to restate his case. Still Governor Pine remained unyielding. A month later, in March 1863, an Asante army invaded the Protectorate. It is thus easy to see why since 1863 many observers have been inclined to regard the Governor-Asantehene differences over the extradition issue as the cause of the invasion.

But this view has two flaws which some, if not all, of the earlier observers should have detected. The first is that the manoeuvres of the invaders showed unmistakably that the British were note the target of the attack. The second is that the view contradicted what the Asante themselves said in and after 1863 were the causes of the invasion, namely, strained relations with the Akyem Kotoku. Let us examine the two points in detail. In relation to the manouvres of the Asante invading force, the general opinion is that the invaders adopted a three-pronged attack. J. A. B. Horton, writing in 1869, may have been the first observer to have popularized this view. Commenting on the 30,000 strong invading army he states:

> the smallest division of about 2,000 was sent to the boundary with Warsaw [i.e. Wassa] on the west [of Cape Coast] with orders to avoid, as much as possible any general engagement with the enemy, but keep the Warsaws and Denkeras in check and prevent them from joining the Fante force. The second division, consisting of about 8,000 descended, after crossing the Praah [river] on the main road to Cape Coast, pushed rapidly into the middle of the country as far as it was safe, avoiding engagement with a superior force. The third and main body [of 20,000], under the personal command of Prince Osoo Cokkor [i.e. Owusu Kokoo] marched on the eastern Fante and [Western] Akim, the most powerful and warlike people in the Protectorate, forcing everything before them . . .[32]

Some observers even say that the strength of the Asante army was 60,000 though no word is said about the division.[33] If indeed Governor Pine in Cape Coast was the target of the invasion and the aim was to punish him for his intransigence on the extradition issue then it was certainly odd that the Asante government sent only 8,000 troops against Cape Coast, 2,000 against Wassa and Denkyira where Chief Gyani was sheltering, and 20,000 against the eastern Fante (by which term Horton clearly meant the Agona and Gomoa) and the West Akyem. Ward appears to have detected this absurdity but explained it away thus:

> On this occasion the eastern most column [of the invading Asante army] was the strongest. This was apparently because Ashanti had a subsidiary object in the capture of Akim Kotokuhene Agyeman. Agyeman had sheltered the two fugitives on their way to the coast, and had returned an insulting answer when called on to surrender them.[34]

It is difficult, if not preposterous, to even imagine that an intelligent people like the Asante would send the strongest division of their invading army to chase after a subsidiary object and allow the principal ones, namely the British Governor at Cape Coast Castle and fugitive Chief Gyani in Denkyira, to get away with it by sending against them smaller divisions of 8,000 and 2,000 respectively, which even had orders, if we are to believe Horton, to avoid engagement with the enemy should it be discovered that they commanded superior forces. The truth was that "the whole war", as Captain Brownwell put it in April, 1863, "is against King Argiman and the Queen".[35] "The Queen" in question was the woman Bosomehene, Amma Amoakoaa, who was Agyeman's foremost ally on this occasion.

Captain Brownwell's assertion brings up the issue of contradiction. Within two months after the Captain had made his report, the Asante themselves left the British authorities at Cape Coast Castle in no doubt as to whom they were fighting and the reasons why they were fighting. In May 1863 Prince Owusu Ansa [36] was sent by Governor Richard Pine into the Asante war camp to find out from them who they were fighting and why. On 1st June, 1863 Owusu Ansa reported back that the invasion was against the Kotoku.[37] A day after the receipt of the Ansa report, the Asantehene himself wrote to confirm the accuracy of Ansa's report. In his letter the Asantehene queried Governor Pine as to why the British and the Fante were mobilizing against the invading Asante army because he was at war, not with the British or the Fante, but with Kotokuhene Agyeman.[38] In Kotoku-Asante relations then must be sought the cause, or causes, of the 1863 Asante invasion of the Gold Coast Protectorate.

Remote Causes of the Asante Attack

There were both immediate and remote causes. In his letter of 2nd June, 1863 the Asantehene touched on one of the remote causes. His Majesty started his letter thus:

> I should like to inform my friend [Governor Pine] about the case of Argieman Inkantoe[39] and Attah [Obiwom of Abuakwa] who fought some time ago, and at that time one man of mine named Ardaquar of Kokofoo was killed.[40]

Then in a long winding manner the Asantehene went on to tell Governor Pine how he appealed to Mr. Andrews, Governor at that time, for justice to be done him, but Governor Andrews refused to address, much less redress, his grievance against the Kotoku who had killed Adarkwa of Kokofu.[41] From this assertion of the Asantehene's it is clear that the Kumasi government was still smarting under the defeat which the Kotoku had inflicted on the Abuakwa-Asante alliance in 1860.

There were other remote causes which the Asantehene did not touch on in his letter of 2nd June, 1863 but which were equally worrying to the Asante government. One of these had something to do with a Kotoku citizen who beat an Asante priest called Busumuru at Anomabo in July 1860. Six Asante traders, including Busumuru, had gone to trade at Anomabo. They lodged in the house of the gold-taker[42] of Mr. Butler, a leading merchant in Anomabo. It was about that time that Kotokuhene Agyeman, as pointed out in Chapter 7 above, was invited to Cape Coast Castle to be a prosecution witness in the trial of Mr. Freeman. On their way back home some members of Agyeman's retinue, who included his interpreter, went to the same gold-taker's house, most likely on business too. As soon as they entered the house Busumuru shouted: "Who comes there! Is that crooked-legged Argiman's interpreter?".[43]

One of the Kotoku who could not bear to see his King insulted and derided by an Asante of all people, grabbed Busumuru and gave him a sound beating.[44] The other Asante traders saw how impetuous Busumuru had been and what the consequences would be should the Kotoku report the matter to their King. To induce the Kotoku not to report the affair, Busumuru's colleagues voluntarily gave the Kotoku "4½ ackies" of gold as bribe.[45]

The Asante traders returned home to tell their own story. The Asantehene immediately seized on the matter and formally complained to Governor Andrews against the beating of his priest. The Governor set up a Committee of Enquiry to look into the affair.[46] The Committee found the Kotoku not guilty because, as they said, Busumuru's conduct had been most provocative and therefore he deserved the beating at the hands of the Kotoku.[47] Governor drews accordingly communicated the Committee's finding to the Asante government.

Apparently the Asantehene realized that Governor Andrews was a fair-minded and firm man who could not easily be pushed about, and so quietly dropped the issue. What was more, by November 1860. His Majesty was exuberantly professing friendship with the British. In that month he sent as a present to the Queen of Britain per Governor Andrews a live hog with the following message:

> My friend. I send this [letter] to tell you plainly to send this nice hog called sanker [i.e., Sanka or Osanka in Twi] to the Queen of England as a present [from me], I am well, hoping that you are the same.[48]

It stands out clearly from the above evidence that in the last months of 1860 while the government in Kumasi was profusely professing friendship with the British, it was secretly nursing bitterness against the Kotokuhene, a British protected subject.

Tension between Kotoku and Asante continued into 1861 and 1862, as other incidents occurred to exacerbate the frost between the two. For example the Kotokuhene allegedly ordered a *panyarred* Asante citizen to be tattooed in the face.[49] The Basel missionaries based at Kyebi were of the view that this was the immediate cause of the Asante invasion of the protectorate in 1863. In view of what the Asante themselves said provoked them to embark on the invasion, the tattooing of the Asante must be deemed as one of the remote causes.

Immediate Causes of the Asante Attack

The execution of about forty Asante subjects by the Kotoku constituted the immediate cause of the invasion. On 1st and 2nd June, 1863 Prince Owusu Ansa interviewed the Asante General, Owusu Kokoo, at his war camp at Gyadam-upon-Briem. The Prince quoted the General as saying that Kotokuhene Agyeman seized sixty Asante citizens, presumably in Western Akyem, and executed forty of them. The executions so angered the Asantehene that His Majesty ordered the invasion of Western Akyem, with the capture or killing of Agyeman as the sole objective.[50] The Asantehene confirmed his General's statement. In his letter of 2nd June, His Majesty spelt the immediate cause thus:

> Argieman Inkantoe caught sixty of them [Asante citizens], killed 40 and delivered twenty to me, therefore I sent my Captain Osoo Korkor to [go and] kill him and bring his jaw.[52]

This explains why the strongest section or main body of the invading Asante army – 20,000 strong – was sent against the "Akim, the most powerful and warlike people in the Protectorate".

In their new home in Western Akyem the Kotoku appear to have cultivated the habit of seizing and killing any Asante citizens they could find. This Kotoku conduct constituted a legitimate *casus belli* for the Asante government. Perhaps the mistake the Asantehene made was that he never formally protested against the executions to the British Protectorate authority before he took the field against Agyeman.

The silence seems to have been deliberate. The 1831 Treaty of Peace had anticipated possible disputes between some of the Protectorate States and Asante, and had prescribed the procedure for resolving such disputes. The treaty was still in force in 1863. Clause 5 of the 1827 part of the Treaty stipulated that whenever any Protectorate state or states offended Asante, or vice versa, the aggrieved party should first complain to the Governor, or any official empowered to act on behalf of the Governor, who would settle the matter as justice required. Asked why the Asantehene did not complain to the Governor before embarking on the invasion of Western Akyem, General Owusu Kokoo replied that the Asantehene feared "he would be served as before".[53]

The Asante General was obviously referring to the somewhat peremptory manner in which Governor Andrews treated the Adarkwa and Busumuru affairs in 1860. Much has been made of the claim, first attributed to Asantehene Osei Bonsu (c.1800–1824), that Asante never went to war to obtain justice "while a path lay open for negotiation".[54] If indeed this was a general maxim of the Asante, then their invasion of Western Akyem in 1863 was an exception to the rule. In 1863 they did not even complain, much less resort to negotiation, before they invaded the Gold Coast Protectorate in order to capture or kill Kotokuhene Agyeman.

The Invasion

The invasion began in March, 1863, the peak of the dry season when farmers were busy clearing the bush for farming. It appears to have taken the Kotoku and their Bosome kinsmen and allies unawares. This can be inferred from the manner in which Agyeman reported the arrival of the invaders in Western Akyem. The Kotoku ruler informed a Mr. Parker of Winneba for onward transmission to Mr. Nicol, the Civil Commandant of the Eastern Districts, that

> the Ashantees have come to his town and are ready to fight, which gives him no chance to have it fair with them from the way they have surrounded his town; but as soon as he finds chance he will fire on them[55]

The surprise tactics which the invaders adopted obviously pointed to the respect they seemed to have for the Kotoku as a fighter nation. In adopting the surprise attack Asante war strategists may have had at the back of their minds the ability of the Kotoku to hold their own against the combined efforts of Abuakwa and Asante in 1860. The 1863 Asante war planners apparently worked on the principle of surprise attack to achieve a quick defeat of the enemy.

The course and outcome of the invasion are other aspects where earlier accounts seem to have considerably sacrificed truth. The impression is given that the invaders swept everything before them, winning victories in two major battles at Asikuma and Bobikuma, and withdrawing with impunity only at the approach of the rains.[56] This is not, on the whole, borne out by contemporary evidence. In the first place there were three, not two, set battles. Nor is it correct that only the rainy season forced the invaders to curtail the invasion: defeat in the three battles and the prospect of having to face the entire Protectorate force were weightier reasons for the withdrawal. But more of this later; for the moment let us take a look at the immediate reaction of the Kotoku and the Bosome. The most immediately pressing problem which Agyeman and his ally, Bosomehene Amoakoaa, had to find a solution to was how to extricate themselves from the spider's web which the invaders had virtually woven around them. A way of escape lay to the south. And so they and their subjects retreated southwards into neighbouring Agona and Gomoa. The retreat had one great advantage: it gave the Kotoku and the Bosome a breathing space to work out their war plan. But it also had an equally great disadvantage: it left their kingdoms defenceless. This enabled the invaders to loot and destroy about thirty Bosome and Kotoku towns and villages.[57] It is therefore true to say that during the initial stages of the war the invading Asante army swept everything before them.

The same however, cannot be said about the set battles which were fought later. As stated already, the Kotoku-Bosome forces retreated into the territory of the Agona and the Gomoa who quickly offered allied support. Agona Swedru became the main war camp of the Allies (i.e. Kotoku, Bosome, Agona and Gomoa} while the invaders established theirs at Odobin.

The first set battle was fought at Asikuma in the last days of March 1863. All previous accounts say that the invaders won it. We are not sure on what evidence such accounts are based. One contemporary account states that the Allies were victorious in this battle. This information came from Captain Brownwell. He had been sent by his superior, Major Cochrane, to go and study the situation in eastern Fante and report back. Brownwell went to Winneba where he arrived in the morning of 1st April 1863, just a day after the Battle of Asikuma. He was informed that the Allies won the battle.[58] Captain Brownwell actually sent two reports to Major Cochrane on the first of April, one in the morning and the other in the evening.

Both reports gave an insight into the plight of the invaders. The two reports said the Allies took many prisoners-of-war from whom the Allies learned that at the beginning of the war the Asante army numbered many thousands, though they could not give the exact figure; that besides General Owusu Kokoo, there were several other prominent war leaders who included "Adarquar" (Adarkwa), "Samanquanta" (Asamoa Nkwanta), "Eddoo Guaffoooah" (Adu Bofuo) "Yah Manee" (Yaw Amanin) and "Koyah"; that "Koya" and Adarkwa had been killed at Asikuma; that Asante losses had been so great that all was agreed the war should end there; that General Owusu Kokoo alone was opposed to the suggestion, saying he would not stop fighting until he had either killed or captured Kotokuhene Agyeman.[59] There is no serious reason to doubt the truth in this contemporary source.

The battle of Bobikuma, the second in the series, was fought in the second week of April 1863. Captain Brownwell was still at Winneba. His report on this battle said that the Allies were again victorious.[60] A third battle was fought on 1st May 1863 near Nsaba. None of the earlier accounts mentions it. Just before the battle, Captain Brownwell had gone to Agona Swedru in order to learn of the events at first hand. His report which gave victory to the Allies was an eyewitness account.[61] On 2nd May a Captain Williams joined Brownwell at Agona Swedru. His report confirmed Brownwell's.[62] Thus in all the set battles the Allies won victories. Again one cannot see any reason to doubt the veracity of the reports of Captains Brownwell and Williams.

But elsewhere in the Protectorate a general impression prevailed that the invaders were winning the war. The reason for this false impression lay largely in the poor handling of the war situation by both Governor Richard Pine (at least up to the end of April) and his military chief, Major Cochrane.

Reaction of the Administration up to April 1863

The Governor and his military chief displayed a considerable degree of incompetence, to the extent that the people, according to Pine's own testimony, accused the administration of dereliction of duty.[63] This aspect of the war has to date not received the close and careful historical scrutiny it deserves. Of the earlier accounts only that of Claridge touches on the subject, but it does so rather casually and briefly.[64]

Until about mid-May when they became absolutely sure that they were not the target of the invasion, the British were more concerned about their own safety; they showed very little, if any, concern about the security of "the Protected", especially those further inland. This stands out clearly from the early measures they took. For example by the second week of April the Administration had become fully aware that

> large parties of Ashantees have crossed the boundary [River Pra] and invaded Protectorate, pillaging and over-running the country and compelling the allies to fall back.[65]

Any yet all that the Executive Council did was to resolve that

> as ho positive (SIC) declaration of war has been made by the King of Ashantee, it was desirable to know whether the alleged incursions of his subjects were with his sanction and approval.[66]

To this end Prince John Owusu Ansa was to leave immediately for Kumasi. Ansa never even got to the Pra because the invaders had infested not only Western Akyem but the Assin country also. The Administration of Richard Pine needed no better proof that the invasion was a reality and that it was necessary to mobilize at once and go to the defence of the more inland peoples of the Protectorate. But the Cape Coast Castle authorities merely issued out arms and ammunition to their "allies", by which they meant the Fante in and immediately around Cape Coast, with strict orders, not to use the weapons "unless in case of extreme necessity.⁶⁷

Earlier, on 10th April, the Executive Council had decided that major Cochrane, Officer commanding the Gold Coast Artillery Corps, and his army of 420 troops should take the field

> not for the purpose of attacking the Ashantees but with a view of observing their movements, concentrating the Allies [i.e. the Central and Western Fante], and his little army in an advantageous position so as to command access to that point of the Protectorate the most sorely pressed.⁶⁸

"The most sorely pressed" part of the Protectorate was Western Akyem. By then too other peoples not directly affected by the war had assembled a force of "between 15,000 and 20,000" at Ajumako, and were waiting for Cochrane and his professional soldiers to come and lead them to the assistance of the Kotoku, Bosome and their Allies.⁶⁹

Major Cochrane, according to Governor Pine, made a mess of the belated efforts of the Administration.⁷⁰ On 10th April the Major and his men left Cape Coast for Anomabo. He remained there till 13th April thinking, as Governor Pine put it, that the enemy might attack Anomabo. As the enemy did not show up he moved his men to

> Mankessim, about 19 miles in the interior, in the direction of the alleged position of the enemy – where he remained until 5th May, but without meeting with any opposition although reporting to me [Pine] continually that the enemy was sometimes in one direction, sometimes in another.⁷¹

Major Cochrane never got anywhere near "the most sorely pressed" zone, even though from the reports of Captains Brownwell and Williams he knew exactly where the action was. It was not until 5th June that he went to Ajumako with his men. By then the war was virtually over. Cochrane's conduct, or misconduct, largely explained the charge of desertion from, and dereliction of, duty which, according to Pine, the people of the Protectorate levelled against his government.⁷² Pine and Cochrane engaged in a protracted argument as to which of them was to blame for the dismal performance of the administration.⁷³ Which ever way one looks at it the argument emphasizes the incompetence of the administration with respect to its handling of the war. Luckily for the Protectorate, the Kotoku, the Bosome and their Agona-Gomoa allies were able to hold their own against the invading Asante army without any support from the administration.

Effect of the Battles on the Protectorate Administration

The success of the Kotoku, Bosome and their allies in the set battles had different effects on the invaders and the Protectorate administation. By the second week of May, Governor Pine, who, at the start of the invasion, had been rather panicky and nervous, became completely transformed into a symbol of aggression. He started to advocate for a British invasion of Asante itself. Now he was determined

> that a final blow shall be struck at Ashantee power, and the question set at rest as to whether an arbitrary cruel and sanguinary Monarch [i.e. Asantehene] shall be for ever permitted to insult the British flag and outrage the laws of civilization.[74]

Pine further stated that this "final blow" could be dealt Asante if only the British Home Government could provide him with

> such a force as I fear the Governor of these settlements can never hope to command unless your Grace should be pleased to urge upon Her Majesty's Government the policy, the economy, and even the mercy of transporting to these shores an army of such strength as would, combined with the allied native forces, enable us to reach Coomassie and there plant the British flag.[75]

Governor Pine anticipated the possibility of the British Home Government dismissing as impracticable his idea of invading Asante and hurried to assure would-be sceptics thus:

> To a stranger the cause I point out may appear a visionary one, but I am convinced even with the disadvantage of climate, the expedition would not be so dangerous, fatal, or accompanied with such loss of life as have attended expeditions in other and apparently more congenial climates, and with 2,000 disciplined soldiers, followed by upwards of 50,000 native forces who require only to be led and inspired by the presence of organized troops, I would undertake (driving the hordes of Ashantees before me) to march to Coomasie.[76]

To compensate the Kotoku in particular and the Protectorate in general was the objective of the somewhat transformed Governor Pine. In advocating for the invasion of the Asante, he said that he

> was guided by the same principles with respect to the liberty of an innocent subject which your Grace was pleased to approve in the case of the Chief Gainin [i.e. Gyani] as Adjiman is not known to have committed any offence [against Asante].[77]

Pine was determined never to leave the Gold Coast "until I have gained them redress for the wrongs they have suffered . . ."[78]

Effect of the Battles on the Invaders

The success of the Kotoku and their allies had yet another transformatory

Chapter 9

DOMPRE OF NSAWAM 1867–1871

While the presence of the bulk of the Kotoku in Western Akyem was creating problems for the district and the western sector of the Protectorate in general, the Ankobea division headed by Dompre had by 1867, already started influencing the course of events in the eastern parts of the Protectorate as well as the Lower Volta region from their base at Nsawam. Trade interests got the Kotoku of Nsawam involved in the inter-state conflicts which bedevilled the Lower Volta region from about 1865. The involvement culminated in the Kotoku (Nsawam) collaborating with the Protectorate Administration in its efforts to re-establish British presence in the region from which it had been withdrawn in 1860.

The Founding of Nsawam

The founding of Nsawam by the Ankobea section of the Kotoku was a direct result of the differences between Dompre, the Ankobeahene, and Agyeman, the Kotokuhene, following the Abuakwa-Kotoku War of 1860.[1] Unable to tolerate his King, Dompre withdrew from Western Akyem altogether with his subjects, and headed south-eastwards till he reached the extreme southwestern Akuapem where they decided to settle. They appealed to the Aburihene of Akuapem to whom the site they chose belonged for the grant of it; there they founded a settlement which they called *Nsaawa-mu* (i.e. Nsawam today).[2] The founding of the town may have taken place between 1860 and 1866 when Dompre started to influence events in the Eastern Districts and the Lower Volta basin. At any rate he is not remembered to have featured in the 1863 Kotoku-Asante War in Western Akyem.

Abundance of fish in the nearby river Densu is held up as Dompre's reason for choosing the Nsawam site.[3] Other and more laudable factors seem to have influenced the choice. Political independence was possibly one of them. The withdrawal from Western Akyem meant a physical separation as well as political isolation of the Ankobea headquarters from the rest of the Kotoku polity. But Dompre does not appear to have had a desire to substitute any other power for the authority of the Kotokuhene. Since his settlement at Nsawam was on Akuapem soil, he would of course regard the Okuapemhene through the Aburihene, as his landlord.[4] But situated some twenty kilometres west of the Akuapem hills, Nsawam was quite removed from the mainstream of Akuapem political life which was located on top of the hills. Besides Akuapem, other neighbouring peoples were the Ga, about thirty kilometres to the south,

(ii) but the British would negotiate only on their own terms, not on those of Asante, as the demand for the person of King Agyeman of Kotoku suggested;

(iii) General Owusu Kokoo should send "accredited and responsible" representatives to assist the Governor in an enquiry into Asante grievances against Kotoku;

(iv) the Asante had already placed themselves in the wrong by invading a portion of the Protectorate with a view to seizing the person of a Chief under the protection of the British without a prior complaint to the Governor of Cape Coast Castle;

(v) the invaders should withdraw immediately from the Protectorate;

(vi) the Asante government should be prepared to make immediate and appropriate reparations for whatever damage the invading army had caused in the Protectorate.[84] If the Asante Commander-in-Chief refused to accept all the above stated conditions, Owusu Ansa was to end his meeting with the Asante war leadership at Gyadam-upon-Birem with the warning that the British would wage a full-scale war against Asante.[85]

Ambassador John Owusu Ansa, Catechist Bernasco and their four carriers left Cape Coast on 29th May, 1863 and arrived at Gyadam-upon-Birem on 31st May 1863. Ansa had his first interview with General Owusu Kokoo in the morning of 1st June and on the same day sent to Cape Coast Castle a report the most important part of which read:

> I have already made known your Excellency's message. The Prince [i.e. Owusu Kokoo], according to their custom, will [formally assemble] his great chiefs [tomorrow] to hear Your Excellency's message again and give an answer. [From] the little I have seen of the Prince this morning, I think he will send a proper messenger with me to Your Excellency . . . Depend on it I shall not let them take advantage of my time.[86]

But taking advantage of Owusu Ansa's time was exactly what Commander-in-Chief Owusu Kokoo did, apparently with the cooperation and collusion of Ansa himself, as the following shows. On 2nd June 1863, Ansa claimed to have despatched to Governor Pine a second report saying among other things that

(a) the Asante war leadership at Gyadam-upon-Birem claimed it was not within their competence to start peace talks with the Governor without an official mandate from the Asantehene;

(b) Owusu Ansa should therefore proceed to Kumasi and raise the matter with the King himself;

(c) but while Ansa was effecting contact with Kumasi, the Asante army would withdraw from the Protectorate and quarter themselves on the east bank of river Pra, that is outside the Protectorate.[87]

In view of all these decisions of the military leadership of the Asante, Owusu Ansa wanted to know from Governor Pine whether or not he should proceed to Kumasi.[88] Surprisingly Ansa, in a postscript to this second report wrote: "The Ashantee people are ready to start with us now [for Kumasi], which I am glad of".[89] That is to say Owusu Ansa who was seeking permission from Governor Pine to go to Kumasi felt it was no longer necessary to wait for the Governor's instruction.

The second report never even got through to Governor Pine until after 10th June when Ansa despatched it together with a third one written from an Asante village called "Akiassiwa" i.e. Akyeasewa.[90] In the Akyeasewa report he explained the delay of the second report thus:

> I sent your Excellency a letter from Gadem dated 2nd instant by three messengers [but] I am sorry indeed that they were returned to me at this place [Akyeasewa] today by the Ashantees",

because the Asante Commander-in-Chief said he was afraid they might get killed.[91] Ansa then added that he was, however, pleased because

> Prince Owoosoo Cocor has faithfully fulfilled his promise [to withdraw from the Protectorate] to my satisfaction. He is [here] now with me with all his army.[92]

It is surely indicative of the disastrous outcome of the invasion for Asante that General Owusu Kokoo who had vowed to remain in the Protectorate "for years" in order to secure the person of the Kotokuhene could not even spend a few more days on the border but marched the remnant of his army back to Asante under the cover of John Owusu Ansa's presence.

The final proof of Ansa's assistance to his countrymen was his sudden return to Ajumako on or about 19th June without reaching Kumasi. Giving a reason for his failure to reach the Asante capital he said: "I went with Prince Owoosoo Cocor as far as a day and half journey from Coomassie [and he] told me to return".[93] Ansa had clearly helped his countrymen to quietly withdraw from the Protectorate so as to avoid further pummelling. Governor Pine was mad with Prince John Owusu Ansa. For he realized that Ansa had deliberately assisted his countrymen to withdraw un-noticed from the Protectorate in order to dodge the blow which he Pine had intended for them.

Pine's Aggressive Plans against Asante

Immediately after despatching the Ansa Mission to Gyadam-upon-Birem,

Governor Pine rushed to Ajumako. His aim was to go and organize that part of the Protectorate forces assembled there for the full-scale war which he intended to wage against the Asante should they reject the conditions he had proffered for a peace settlement.[94] He arrived there on 29th May 1863 and spent about two weeks shaping the Protectorate forces there into combat readiness while he awaited the outcome of the Ansa Mission. Unfortunately he fell ill and had to be carried back to Cape Coast on 12th June.[95]

But he was still bent on satisfying the people of Western Akyem and the rest of the Protectorate by punishing the Asante in spite of their reverses in the war.[96] Besides, there was a general but erroneous, belief that the Protectorate might be re-invaded by Asante.[97] Pine felt that it was better to carry the war to the Asante on their own soil than to allow them to be on the offensive again. Having come to this conclusion he took up with greater zeal the idea of invading Asante itself. But the Colonial Office in London refused to sanction such a venture, saying that it was too serious a step to be entertained.[98] The Colonial Office, however, allowed the establishment of two military posts on the border with Asante, one at Akyem Soadru and the other, which is better known in Ghana history, at Praso in the Assin country.[99] Claridge gives the impression that the creation of the two posts was a prelude to an impending British invasion of Asante.[100] This is not correct. The posts were meant to serve as "a demonstration" of British military power, a display which, it was hoped, "would induce the King of Ashantee to proffer such [peace] terms as [Pine] could consistently accept".[101] The "demonstration" did not last long. By June 1864 the two military posts had been abandoned, overtly on account of bad weather and disease. The real reason was the dissipation of the fear of re-invasion. The anxiety started to subside from about early 1864,[102] to the extent that some of the more interior states, Kotoku and Bosome included, began to commit acts of aggression against Asante. Some of them actually raided parts of Asante, carrying off or killing Asante subjects.[103] And yet Asante did not retaliate, a restraint which Cape Coast Castle authorities found quite uncharacteristic of the Asante government. The truth, as Lieutenant-Colonel Conran rightly put it in September 1865, was that Asante's reverses "in the last war" had been quite disastrous.[104]

Reaction in Britain to the War in the Gold Coast

Viewed against this situation in the Gold Coast, the public and Parliamentary furore and fuss which the Kotoku-Asante War of 1863 produced in Britain [105] seems ironical though quite understandable. To score a political point the Opposition in the British House of Commons tabled a motion with a view to censuring the Government on the subject of the war in the Gold Coast. For in Britain as in the Gold Coast the general notion was that the Asante had invaded the British Protectorate with impunity. That cast a slur on Britain, the protecting power. The motion was defeated by 233 to 226 votes in favour of the Government.[106]

All the same the British Government was compelled to take a hard look at British presence in West Africa in general and the Gold Coast in particular. It seemed to many that the British presence in the Gold Coast was a liability rather than an asset to the British taxpayer. Aside from the expenses incurred to combat Asante in the 1863 war, the annual cost to the Imperial Treasury of maintaining the British Gold Coast possessions had risen from £5,000.00 sterling in 1850 to £12,000.00 in 1863,[107] a rise of 140%. But, it was argued, returns from the Gold Coast did not match investment. This assessment raised the issue as to whether there was a justification in the continued presence of Britain in the Gold Coast particularly and West Africa in general. Some felt there was none, others thought there was.[108]

To resolve the matter, the British Government in 1864 appointed Colonel Ord as sole Commissioner to investigate the subject of British presence in the whole of West Africa, focusing especially on the efficiency of the administration, and recommending ways and means of cutting down cost. A Parliamentary Select Committee was set up in 1865 to study the Ord Report. Its Chairman was Mr. Charles Bowyer Adderley, a free trader, and surprisingly a vociferous campaigner against extension of British protection beyond the immediate precincts of the forts and castles to neighbouring states and people.

After carefully studying the Ord Report and interviewing people knowledgeable about the Gold Coast, such as the missionary Rev. Ellias Schrenk of the Basel Mission, the 1865 Select Committee came to the conclusion that "it is not possible to withdraw the British Government, wholly or immediately, from the settlements or engagements on the West African Coast".[109] The Committee, however, recommended

> that all further extension of territory or assumption of Government of new treaties offering protection to native tribes would be inexpedient; and that the object of our policy should be to encourage in the natives the exercise of those qualities which may render it possible for us more and more to transfer to them the administration of all Government with a view to our ultimate withdrawal from all except probably Sierra Leone.[110]

The Committee also recommended for adoption by Government a suggestion that, for purposes of efficient supervision on administration, all the British West African establishments be headquartered in Freetown, the Sierra Leonean capital.[111] This then was the extent of the impact which Akyem Kotoku's strained relations with Asante in the early 1860s had on British politics at home and British policy in West Africa.

Peace Moves

Meanwhile by the last months of 1865 it had become clear that Asante was not going to re-invade the Protectorate, as many had expected. By then Asantehene Kwaku Dua himself appears to have started throwing feelers about in search of peace.[112] In September 1865 the Asantehene sent messengers to Mr. George Blankson, a well known Fante merchant at Anomabo, overtly to buy silk from him but covertly to sound him on the possibility of coming to peace terms with the Protectorate authorities, who, he apparently feared, might still be pondering on a full scale war with Asante. For their safety the royal messengers first travelled to Kwawu, descended the Kwawu hills into the Afram plains, from where they crossed the Volta into Akwamu. The Akwamuhene then provided them with an armed escort to Accra. From Accra they travelled to Anomabo by boat. This unexpected but sincere gesture on the part of the Asantehene enabled Lieutenant-Colonel Conran to reverse his predecessor's policy of war with Asante, and set in motion a process aimed at peace with the Asante government.

Credit must also be given to Mr. George Blankson. The importance of his role in the peace process has so far not been fully appreciated by historians and other writers who have touched on this issue. It was the confidence which the Asante government placed in him which helped to generate the moves toward a peace settlement.[113] Blankson worked to justify the trust which the Asante government reposed in him. For instance in order that no Asante messengers were molested on their way to Cape Coast Blankson himself travelled to Assin Praso in December 1865 to receive and lead a three-man negotiating team from Kumasi to Cape Coast.[114] In a letter to the Governor the Asantehene said:

> Your Excellency, yours by George Blankson to send . . . my ambassadors down to your honour at Cape Coast Castle for putting in order the case between me and you [has been received].
>
> I have sent, by him, one of my sword-bearer named Cofee Doro, chief Cofee Aifilfah and Cudjoe Aiboo my herald and hope to hear from you by them.[115]

The peace talks at Cape Coast Castle lasted throughout the first two weeks of January, 1866; a peace settlement was reached in principle on 12th January 1866.[116] A formal but unwritten treaty of peace was effected, not at the end of 1865 as several writers have thought,[117] but in April 1866.[118]

Post-Peace Tensions between Kotoku and Asante

The Peace settlement of April 1866 nearly foundered. Some observers state categorically that the Asantehene almost immediately denounced it because Lieutenant-Colonel Conran issued a proclamation saying that it was Asante which had sued for peace.[119] Contemporary evidence available to the present author states otherwise. The evidence shows that Conran nearly failed to achieve a lasting peace with Asante because he omitted to involve Kotokuhene Agyeman, the immediate cause of the 1863 war, as a direct party to the peace settlement. The Governor could have done this easily by simply inviting the personal assent of Agyeman. Mr. George Maclean achieved a durable peace by asking Okyenhene Dokuaa to assent to the 1831 Treaty of Peace. The omission is all the more surprising because Conran was fully aware that Akyem Kotoku was the cause of the 1863 war.[120]

On the basis of Akyem Kotoku-Asante relations alone the April 1866 Peace Settlement was almost a non-starter. In May, 1866 Kotoku and Bosome farms were raided by the Asante.[121] The raids were probably Asante reaction to similar activities of the Western Akyem which Major R. S. Jones noted in May 1865.[122] But the Kotokuhene presented the Asante raids as though they occurred without any provocation on the part of the Western Akyem. He informed the Protectorate authorities through Mr. Nicol Irwine, the acting Civil Commandant of the Eastern Districts, that the raids were probably a prelude to the expected re-invasion. The government should therefore provide him with "a small quantity of [gun-] powder and lead-bars to enable him resist any attacks which might be made on his part of the Protectorate".[123] Mr. Irwine felt it was a reasonable request and recommended it to government.

But Lieutenant-Colonel Conran's reaction was utter disbelief. In his mind's eye he could see an imminent collapse of the peace settlement he had just achieved with Asante. To him if the peace failed, the Kotokuhene would have been the cause. That Chief, he felt, should be stopped before he could cause any damage to the peace settlement. In a mixed mood of fear, anxiety and anger, Conran saw no justification for anybody, much less an Acting Civil Commandant, to encourage Agyeman. To Irwine he expressed

> his very great surprise to see or hear of your recommending that this scoundrel, Adjaman (sic) who provoked the last [1863] war, and now wants to do the same, should receive encouragement whilst the Government are at peace with the King of Ashantee.[124]

Conran went on to remind Irwine that the April 1866 Peace Settlement enjoined the Kotokuhene, and all other Chiefs in the Protectorate, to refrain from ill-treating Asante subjects "who, if wrong, will be punished by their King" through the Governor's report thereof.[125] Irwine therefore was to warn Agyeman that if he . . . by any means whatever, disturbs the peaceful relations now existing between Ashantee and the Government, Colonel Conran, with an armed force, will proceed to Akim for the purpose of bringing him down to this coast prior to transposing him beyond the seas altogether, as a most seditious and insubordinate Chief is never at rest.[126]

On his part the Acting Civil Commandant was equally surprised to learn that the Governor entertained so low an opinion about the Kotokuhene as to call him a "scoundrel".[127] In his reply to the Governor he said:

I have been resident in Accra for twelve years, and I can assure Your Excellency that this Chief has always been looked upon with such great and universal respect that he is considered by the whole Eastern Districts as the trustworthy guardian of his frontiers against Ashantee.[128]

Fortunately for Conran the "raids" did not lead to a fresh outbreak of war between the Western Akyem and Asante. The alleged raids were most probably in reply to similar activities undertaken by the Kokoku and the Bosome against nearby Asante confederate States like Bekwae, Kokofu and others. In May 1865 such activities came to the notice of Major R. S. Jones.[129]

The Conran peace settlement continued to hold as far as relations between Cape Coast Castle and Manhyia were concerned. Kotoku-Asante relations, however, remained strained up to 1867 when both Asantehene Kwaku Dua and Kotokuhene Kofi Agyeman died, the one in May and the other in July. On this score Agyeman bequeathed to his successor, Kwabena Fua, a rather difficult inheritance, the more so because the Lower Volta basin was fast emerging as the next battle ground for the Kotoku and Asante.

NOTES AND REFERENCES

1. For a much fuller discussion of this subject see Affrifah, K., "The Impact of Christianity on Akyem Society, 1852–1887", in the Transactions of the Historical Society of Ghana (THSG), Vol.XVI (i) 1975, pp. 67–86; Affrifah, K., "Christianity and the Akyem of Ghana, 1766–1887", (Forthcoming).
2. Affrifah, in THSG, Vol.XIV (i), p.68.
3. Other contributory factors included the obsession of the Akyem in general with their traditional religion and ancestor worship.
4. Missionary Stromberg's Report for the First Quarter of 1861, dd. 28 May 1861 No. Akim 8; Kromer's Report, 26 May 1861 No. Akim 9; Station Conference Protocol, 26 June 1861 No. Akim 19; Stromberg (Kyebi) to Basel, 30–31 July 1861 No. Akim 13; Kromer (Kyebi) to Basel, 29 August 1861 No. Akim 14, Basel Mission Archives – Paul Jenkins's *Abstracts of Basel Mission Gold Coast Correspondence*, (BMA-PJA), Legon 1971.

5. Stromberg (Kyebi) to Basel, 1 November 1861 No. Akim II.20 BMA-PJA.
6. *Ibid.*
7. Akyem Kotoku Tradition (AKT): Adoagyiri, collected by this author in 1868/9.
8. Personal communication from Nana Apeanyo of Kukurantumi, the Adontenhene of Akyem Abuakwa, January 1869.
9. AKT: Adoagyiri (1968/9).
10. *Ibid.* The founding of Nsawam is fully discussed in Chapter 9.
11. Kromer (Kyebi) to Basel, 1 November 1863 No. Akim 18, BMA-PJA.
12. Captain des Ruvinges (Soadru) to Governor Andrews (CCC), 5 May 1860; Alphonso Cary, Colonial Secretary (CCC) to Captain des Ruvinges (Soadru), 8 May 1860, CO 96/47. For the identity of des Ruvinges see Chapter 7 p.154.
13. Akyem Kotoku Tradition, as recorded by Field, M. J., 1948, *Akim-Kotoku: An Oman of the Gold Coast*, London, p.37.
14. Boahen, A. A., in Ajayi & Espie (Eds), 1968, *A Thousand Years of West African History*, Ibadan University Press, Ibadan.
15. Capt. des Ruvinges (Akyem Soadru) to Governor Andrews (CCC), 5 May 1860, CO 96/47.
16. AAT: Wankyi (1925/6); Ameyaw, K. Akim Oda (Kotoku) Tradition, IAS acc. No. KAG/7, Legon 1963; AKT; Awisa (1968/9); ABT: Soadru (1968/9).
17. Missionary Kromer (Kyebi) to Basel, 1 November 1863 No. Akim 18, BMA-PJA.
18. Ameyaw, *Oda Tradition*.
19. Kwabena Fuah; King of Kotoku, to Administrator C. S. Salmon (CCC), dated "Akim Daa" 24 January 1872, CO 96/92.
20. Ameyaw, *Oda Tradition*. All efforts to identify the descendants of the so-called acephalous Atwea communities have proved futile: nobody in Western Akyem is willing to freely discuss the subject much less point out the descendants of the Atwea people.
21. Field, *Akim-Kotoku*, pp.2–3, and also the map at the back of that book.
22. Ameyaw, *Oda Tradition*.
23. Field, *Akim-Kotoku*, pp.53–63.
24. Horton, J. A. B., 1868, *West African Countries and Peoples*, Frank Cass and Co. Ltd., London, pp. 132–133.
25. Butler, W. F., 1874, *Akimfoo: A History of a Failure*, London, p.179.
26. *Ibid.*, p.183.
27. Horton, J. A. B.. 1870, *Letters on the Political Conditions of the Gold Coast*, Frank Cass and Co. Ltd., London, pp. 52–57; Ellis, A. B., 1893, *A History of the Gold Coast of West Africa*, Negro University Press, New York, Chapter XVII; Claridge, W. W., 1915, *A History of the Gold Coast and Ashanti*, Frank Cass & Co. Ltd., London, Vol.1, pp. 502–503; Fuller, F., 1921, *A Vanished Dynasty: Ashanti*, London, p.91; Rev. W. T. Balmer., 1924, *A History of the Akan Peoples*, London, pp. 141–142; Ward, W. E. F., (Ed.), 1969, *A History of Ghana*,1969 edn., London, p.199; Kimble, D., A., 1963, *Political History of Ghana 1850–1928*, OUP, Oxford, p.199; Agbodeka, F. 1971, *African Politics and British Policy on the Gold Coast 1869–1900*, Longman, London, p.16; Boahen, A. A., "Politics in Ghana, 1800–1874", in Ajayi & Crowder, (Eds), 1974, *History of West Africa*, Longman, London, Vol.Two, pp. 224–227; Wilks, *Asante*, (pp. 219–222) is not sure who the invasion was against, the British or the Akyem Kotoku.
28. The name is given as Janin in the contemporary records, but in the secondary sources it takes various forms, e.g. Jenin, Gainie and Ganin.
29. Claridge Vol.I, p.510, Ward, *A History of Ghana*, p.215; Wilks, *Asante*, p.221, citing

Despatches from the Governor (CCC) – British Parliamentary Papers: Accounts & Papers LXV.
30. Report by Commodore Wilmot, ? April 1863, copy in Br. PP(1864), Vol.LXV, p.21.
31. Pine (CCC) to the Duke of Newcastle, 10 December 1862, CO96/59; Metcalfe, *Documents*, No. 230, pp. 291–292.
32. Horton, *Letters*, pp. 52–53.
33. *The African Times*, cited by Wilks, *Asante*, p.221, n.66.
34. Ward, *A History of Ghana*, p.215. But see his note 13 on the same page.
35. Captain Brownwell (Agona Swedru) to Major Cochrane (Anomabo), 1 April 1863, CO96/61.
36. John Owusu Ansa was one of the two hostages the Asante Government gave as securities to back their word in relation to the 1831 Treaty of Peace. The other was Owusu Nkwantabisa. For a detailed biography of J. O. Ansa, see Wilks, *Asante*, especially Chapter 14.
37. Owusu Ansa ("Gadam-upon-Berim") to Governor R. Pine (CCC), 1st June 1863, CO96/61.
38. Asantehene Kwaku Dua I to Governor Pine, 2 June 1863, CO96/61.
39. "Inkantoe" or *nkonto* is a Twi term which means crooked-legged, not *nkontompo* (i.e. lying) as Ward thinks.
40. Asantehene to Governor Pine 2 June 1863, CO96/61.
41. *Ibid.*
42. "Gold-taker" was a kind of a middle-man in the gold trade. Usually a Fante, his job was to introduce to the merchant on the coast the gold producer/seller from inland for a small commission from both parties.
43. Report of the Committee of Enquiry into Asante grievances against Kotoku: "Evidence from the gold-taker of Mr. Butler on Oath at Anomabo" 13th August 1860, CO96/47.
44. *Ibid.*
45. *Ibid.*
46. *Ibid.*
47. Governor Andrews (CCC) to the Duke of Newcastle, CO, 13 December 1860, CO96/47.
48. Asantehene Kwaku Dua to Governor Andrews, 20 November 1860, CO96/47.
49. Stromberg (Kyebi) to Basel, 5 April 1863 No. Akim 18, BMA-PJA.
50. *Ibid.*
51. Owusu Ansa (Gyadam-upon-Birem) to Governor Pine (CCC), 1 & 2 June 1863, CO96/61.
52. Asantehene to Governor Pine, 2 June 1863, CO96/61; Alphonso Cary, Colonial Secretary (CCC) on behalf of Lt. Col. Conran, to Agyeman 11 May 1866. CO96/61.
53. Owusu Ansa to Governor Pine 1st June 1863 CO96/61.
54. Dupuis, *A Residence*, pp. 225–226; Wilks, in Forde & Kaberry (ed), *West African Kingdoms of the Nineteenth Century*, OUP, 1967. p.218; Boahen, Topics p.79.
55. Mr. Parker (Winneba) to Mr. Irwine (Accra), 16 March 1861, CO96/61.
56. Horton, Letters, pp. 52–53, Claridge, Vol.I, p.515; Ward, *A History of Ghana*, p.215; Wilks, *Asante*, p.221; etc.
57. Pine (CCC) to the Duke of Newcastle, CO (London), 10 June 1863 CO96/61.
58. Capt. Brownwell (Agona Swedru) to Major Cochrane (Anomabo) 1 April 1863, CO96/61.

59. *Ibid.*
60. Capt. Brownwell (Winneba) to Major Cochrane, 13 April 1863, CO96/61. Horton (*Letters*, p.62) says that the Battle of Bobikuma was fought on 12 May 1863.
61. Capt. Brownwell (Swedru) to Governor Pine, 1 May 1863, CO96/61.
62. Capt. Williams (Swedru) to Governor Pine, 2 May 1863, CO96/61.
63. Governor Pine (CCC) to the Duke of Newcastle, 10 June 1863, CO96/60.
64. Claridge, Vol.I, p.545.
65. Governor R. Pine (CCC) to the Duke of Newcastle, 15 April 1863, CO96/60.
66. *Ibid.*
67. *Ibid.*
68. *Ibid.*
69. *Ibid.*
70. Claridge, Vol.I, pp. 515–519.
71. Pine to the Duke of Newcastle, 12 May 1863, CO96/60.
72. Pine to the Duke of Newcastle, 15 April 1863, CO96/60.
73. See CO96/60 which contains most of the correspondence on the handling of the war by Governor Pine and Major Cochrane.
74. Pine (CCC) to the Duke of Newcastle, 12 May 1863, CO96/60. This source is reproduced in Metcalfe, *Documents* No.225, pp. 295–296.
75. *Ibid.*
76. *Ibid.*
77. *Ibid.*
78. Pine (CCC) to the Duke of Newcastle, 12 October 1863, No.92, CO96/62.
79. Captain Brownwell to Major Cochrane, 1st April 1863, CO96/61.
80. This Gyadam is different from the former Kotoku capital in Eastern Akyem which was destroyed by the Abuakwa after the 1860 War.
81. Kromer (Kyebi) to Basel, 1 November 1863 No. Akim 18, BMA-PJA.
82. Captain Williams (Agona Swedru) to Governor Pine 21 May 1863, CO96/60.
83. Governor Pine (CCC) to J. O. Ansa (CCC), 22 May 1863, CO96/60.
84. Governor Pine to the Duke of Newcastle, 10 June 1863, CO96/60.
85. *Ibid.*
86. J. Owusu Ansa (Gyadam-upon-Birem) to Governor Pine, 1 June 1863, CO96/60.
87. J. Owusu Ansa (Gyadam-upon-Birem) to Governor Pine, 2 June 1863, CO96/61.
88. *Ibid.*
89. *Ibid.*
90. J. Owusu Ansa (Akyeasewa in Asante) to Governor Pine, 10 June 1863, CO96/61.
91. *Ibid.*
92. *Ibid.*
93. J. Owusu Ansa (Ajumako) to Governor Pine, 19th June, 1863, CO96/61.
94. Pine (Ajumako) to the Duke of Newcastle, 10 June 1863, CO96/61.
95. Pine (CCC) to the Duke of Newcastle, 11 July 1863, CO96/61.
96. Pine (CCC) to the Duke of Newcastle, 12 October, 9 & 13 November and 12 December 1863, CO96/62.
97. Pine to the Duke of Newcastle, 12 October & 13 November 1863, CO96/62.
98. Secretary of State for the Colonies to the War Office, London, 22 August 1863, CO96/61. See Metcalfe, *Documents*, No.236, p. 296 for a reproduction.
99. Pine to the Duke of Newcastle, 12 February & 11 March 1864, CO96/64.
100. Claridge, Vol.I, p.524.

101. Pine to the Duke of Newcastle, 12 December 1863, Despatch No.106, CO96/62.
102. Pine to Rt. Hon. Edward Cardwell (CO), 18 November 1864, CO96/65.
103. Report of Major R. S. Jones, 9 May 1865, CO96/88.
104. Lt. Colonel Conran (CCC) to Rt. Hon. E. Cardwell (CO), 8 September, 1865, CO96/88.
105. *The Times*, 16 & 17 June, 1864.
106. Metcalfe, *Documents*, No.241.
107. Figures quoted by O. Dike, 1956, *Trade and Politics in the Niger Delta 1830–1885*, OUP, Oxford, p.167.
108. House of Commons Debate, 21 February 1865, Hansard 3/177/535f, reproduced by Metcalfe, *Documents*, No.244, p.307.
109. Resolution of the Select Committee, 26 June 1865, HC.412 of 1865, in Metcalfe, *Documents*, No.248, p.311.
110. *Ibid*.
111. *Ibid*.
112. Wilks (Asante, p.223) suggests that it was the Cape Coast Castle administration who made the first peace moves, by inviting the Asantehene for the peace negotiations.
113. George Blankson (Anomabo) to H. M. Kwaku Dua, Asantehene, 19 September 1865, copy as Enclosure in Conran to Cardwell, 9 October 1865, CO96/68.
114. George Blankson (Praso, Assin) to Lt. Col. Conran (CCC) 20 & 25 December 1865; Blankson (Atwereboanna) to Lt. Col. Conran, 4 & 5 January 1866, CO96/70.
115. Asantehene to Governor, 19 December; Asantehene to Blankson, 20 December 1865, CO96/70. Cofee Doroo = Kofi Duro; Cofee Aifilfah = Kofi Afrifah; Cudjoe Aiboo = Kwadwo Abu.
116. "Minutes of Proceedings of Public Meeting with Ashantee Ambassadors of Peace at Cape Coast". 8 & 15 January 1866; Conran to H. M. Asantehene, 18 January; Conran to Assin Tanosuhene, 25 January (copy); Conran to Cardwell, 5 February 1866, CO96/70.
117. Claridge, Vol.I, p.543; Ward, *A History of Ghana*, p.220.
118. Conran (CCC) to Blackwell, Governor-in-Chief, Freetown, (SL) 10 May & 6 July Blackall (Freetown) SL) to the Colonial Office (London) 19 May & 3 August 1866, CO96/71.
119. Claridge, Vol.I, pp. 545–546; Ward, *A History of Ghana*, p.220; Wilks, *Asante*, p.223.
120. Alphonso Cary, Colonial Secretary (CCC) to Nicol Irwine (Accra), 11 May 1866, CO96/72.
121. Nicol Irwine, Civil Commandant of the Eastern Districts, to Lt. Col. Conran 6 May 1866, CO96/72.
122. Report of Major R. S. Jones, 9 May 1865, CO96/72.
123. Nicol Irwine to Lt. Col. Conran, 6 May 1866, CO96/72.
124. Alphonso Cary, Colonial Secretary (CCC) to Nicol Irwine (Accra), 11 May 1866, CO96/72.
125. *Ibid*.
126. *Ibid*.
127. Irwine (Accra) to Lt. Col. Conran, 14 May 1866, CO96/72.
128. *Ibid*.
129. Report of Major R. S. Jones, 9 May 1865, CO96/88.

Chapter 9

DOMPRE OF NSAWAM 1867-1871

While the presence of the bulk of the Kotoku in Western Akyem was creating problems for the district and the western sector of the Protectorate in general, the Ankobea division headed by Dompre had by 1867, already started influencing the course of events in the eastern parts of the Protectorate as well as the Lower Volta region from their base at Nsawam. Trade interests got the Kotoku of Nsawam involved in the inter-state conflicts which bedevilled the Lower Volta region from about 1865. The involvement culminated in the Kotoku (Nsawam) collaborating with the Protectorate Administration in its efforts to re-establish British presence in the region from which it had been withdrawn in 1860.

The Founding of Nsawam

The founding of Nsawam by the Ankobea section of the Kotoku was a direct result of the differences between Dompre, the Ankobeahene, and Agyeman, the Kotokuhene, following the Abuakwa-Kotoku War of 1860.[1] Unable to tolerate his King, Dompre withdrew from Western Akyem altogether with his subjects, and headed south-eastwards till he reached the extreme southwestern Akuapem where they decided to settle. They appealed to the Aburihene of Akuapem to whom the site they chose belonged for the grant of it; there they founded a settlement which they called *Nsaawa-mu* (i.e. Nsawam today).[2] The founding of the town may have taken place between 1860 and 1866 when Dompre started to influence events in the Eastern Districts and the Lower Volta basin. At any rate he is not remembered to have featured in the 1863 Kotoku-Asante War in Western Akyem.

Abundance of fish in the nearby river Densu is held up as Dompre's reason for choosing the Nsawam site.[3] Other and more laudable factors seem to have influenced the choice. Political independence was possibly one of them. The withdrawal from Western Akyem meant a physical separation as well as political isolation of the Ankobea headquarters from the rest of the Kotoku polity. But Dompre does not appear to have had a desire to substitute any other power for the authority of the Kotokuhene. Since his settlement at Nsawam was on Akuapem soil, he would of course regard the Okuapemhene through the Aburihene, as his landlord.[4] But situated some twenty kilometres west of the Akuapem hills, Nsawam was quite removed from the mainstream of Akuapem political life which was located on top of the hills. Besides Akuapem, other neighbouring peoples were the Ga, about thirty kilometres to the south, the Abuakwa, some forty kilometres to the north, and the Agona, about twenty-five kilometres to the west. To none of these did Dompre transfer his allegiance.

Economic interest may have been another, and perhaps the greatest, factor which influenced the choice of Nsawam as a place to settle. Nsawam was on crossroads, as it were.[5] A trade route linked it to Accra, by far and away the most important commercial centre in the Gold Coast. Dompre and his subjects could drive a salt trade from the coast to the interior.[6] The trade route from Accra extended northwards to reach Eastern Akyem (Abuakwa) and beyond.[7] The route would help the Kotoku of Nsawam to share in the gold digging industry in the Densu and Birem basins. A third route went westwards to Adeisu where it bifurcated, one branch going northwards to Western Akyem via Asamankese and Akwatia, and the other to Agona Swedru. Based at Nsawam, Dompre and his subjects could exploit the European trade on the Senya Breku-Winneba coast via Agona Swedru. A fourth route went eastwards to climb and descend the Akuapem hills and reach the Lower Volta region[8] in whose economy his people could fully share. The importance of this last route to the Kotoku of Nsawam seems to have been second only to the route to Accra.

The Economy of the Lower Volta Basin

The economy of the Lower Volta Basin was very prosperous during the second half of the nineteenth century.[9] The prosperity derived from agriculture and trade. Among the leading agricultural and forest products exported from or via the region were cotton,[10] palm oil,[11] and to a less extent peanuts.[12] Between 1858 and 1866 Krobo, perhaps the greatest producer of palm oil in all Gold Coast at the time,[13] exported much of its produce via the Lower Volta to the Ada-Anlo coast in an attempt to beat British monopoly and lower prices for the commodity on the coast between Prampram and Accra.[14] So abundant was palm oil from Krobo and Akuapem that the 1861 season was described as "glorious".[15] Gum copal from Akyem also reached the Ada-Keta coast through Lower Volta for sale to American merchant men.[16] Part of Akyem gold export would also go via the same channel.

These agricultural, forest and mineral products exported from or through the region turned the Lower Volta basin into one big market of brisk international trade which attracted both European and American ships.[17] The truth was that besides the commodities already mentioned slaves were still exported from or through the region in spite of the general abolition of the trans-Atlantic slave trade: Asante and the Lower trans-Volta states were the slave producers and the South American merchantmen were the buyers.[18] The other feature which made the Volta trade attractive was the non-existence of customs duties on the Ada-Keta coast.

Both African and Europeans resident in Accra and the Adangbe-Anlo coast found the Volta trade most attractive.[19] Prominent among the Accra merchants doing business in the Lower Volta basin were Nicol Irwine of the firm Foster & Smith, F. & L. Swanzy, G. S. B. Ryall, William Morris, James and Charles Bannerman, S. Brownwell, William P. Gunnel, and N. H. Luterodt; the others were William Addo, G. F. Cleland, Leberecht Hesse, and H. L. Rottman of the trading wing of the Basel Mission in the Gold Coast. Geraldo de Lima, an Ewe, was the foremost of the merchants not residing in Accra; his bases were Keta and Ada. The preponderant participation of the Accra merchants in the Volta trade was proof of the attractiveness of the trade. Non-Voltaic peoples, like the Kwawu, Akuapem, Asante, Fante and above all the Akyem vied to get a share in the Volta trade because of the availability of a wide range of European and American manufactured goods. Akyem traders carried trade to and from the Lower Volta states. Most avid among them were the Kotoku of Nsawam.[20]

The Kotoku of Nsawam and Volta Politics

But economic pursuits got them entangled in the violent inter-states politics which became the bane of the Lower Volta basin from 1865 due largely to trade rivalries and traditional ethnic animosities. The conflicts adversely affected trade in the basin.[21] In 1865 the seizure by Geraldo de Lima[22] of twelve casks of palm oil being canoed down from Kpong to Ada sparked off a dispute between him and the people of Ada. As a further reaction, the people burnt down his shop and house at Ada to stress their protest against his conduct. In reply Geraldo solicited the support of the Anlo, the traditional enemies of the Ada, and war broke out between the two peoples.[23]

No direct evidence has been found to suggest that the Accra merchants were the brains behind the arson committed by the Ada against Geraldo. The fact, however, is that the Accra merchants, apparently with a view to eliminating Geraldo's stiff competition in the Volta trade, got the crew of the British ship H. M. S. Dart to bombard some of the Anlo coastal towns. The Anlo countered with piracy on the navigable stretch of the Volta between the estuary and Kpong, some ninety kilometers upstream. The aim of the piracy was to block the Volta as a major trade route for the Accra merchants most of whom had business establishments at Kpong which Horton in the 1860s described as "the great emporium of the cotton trade".[24] In this exercise the Anlo had the solid support of the Akwamu and others like the Dafor and Volo. The Volta trade was now in total chaos.

The British Protectorate administration at Cape Coast Castle made an

Governor Pine rushed to Ajumako. His aim was to go and organize that part of the Protectorate forces assembled there for the full-scale war which he intended to wage against the Asante should they reject the conditions he had proffered for a peace settlement.[94] He arrived there on 29th May 1863 and spent about two weeks shaping the Protectorate forces there into combat readiness while he awaited the outcome of the Ansa Mission. Unfortunately he fell ill and had to be carried back to Cape Coast on 12th June.[95]

But he was still bent on satisfying the people of Western Akyem and the rest of the Protectorate by punishing the Asante in spite of their reverses in the war.[96] Besides, there was a general but erroneous, belief that the Protectorate might be re-invaded by Asante.[97] Pine felt that it was better to carry the war to the Asante on their own soil than to allow them to be on the offensive again. Having come to this conclusion he took up with greater zeal the idea of invading Asante itself. But the Colonial Office in London refused to sanction such a venture, saying that it was too serious a step to be entertained.[98] The Colonial Office, however, allowed the establishment of two military posts on the border with Asante, one at Akyem Soadru and the other, which is better known in Ghana history, at Praso in the Assin country.[99] Claridge gives the impression that the creation of the two posts was a prelude to an impending British invasion of Asante.[100] This is not correct. The posts were meant to serve as "a demonstration" of British military power, a display which, it was hoped, "would induce the King of Ashantee to proffer such [peace] terms as [Pine] could consistently accept".[101] The "demonstration" did not last long. By June 1864 the two military posts had been abandoned, overtly on account of bad weather and disease. The real reason was the dissipation of the fear of re-invasion. The anxiety started to subside from about early 1864,[102] to the extent that some of the more interior states, Kotoku and Bosome included, began to commit acts of aggression against Asante. Some of them actually raided parts of Asante, carrying off or killing Asante subjects.[103] And yet Asante did not retaliate, a restraint which Cape Coast Castle authorities found quite uncharacteristic of the Asante government. The truth, as Lieutenant-Colonel Conran rightly put it in September 1865, was that Asante's reverses "in the last war" had been quite disastrous.[104]

Reaction in Britain to the War in the Gold Coast

Viewed against this situation in the Gold Coast, the public and Parliamentary furore and fuss which the Kotoku-Asante War of 1863 produced in Britain [105] seems ironical though quite understandable. To score a political point the Opposition in the British House of Commons tabled a motion with a view to censuring the Government on the subject of the war in the Gold Coast. For in Britain as in the Gold Coast the general notion was that the Asante had in-

What immediately made the Kotoku of Nsawam a direct party in the Lower Volta politics was the desire and efforts of Dompre to rescue about forty Nsawam traders whom the Dafor and Volo had seized and detained.[33] These two peoples were inhabiting the banks of the Volta south of Akuse and were said to be a piratical set of people who were in alliance with the Akwamuhene. On the orders of the Akwamu King they, in or about April 1867, seized the forty traders from Nsawam, robbed and detained them, and even killed some of them.[34]

Dodi tradition, as recorded by Marion Johnson, says that the Kotoku traders got involved in a dispute over market tolls and the Kotokuhene, apparently Agyeman, sent Dompre to go and investigate.[35] The tradition is clearly wrong because up to July 1867 when he died, Agyeman was still not reconciled with Dompre with whom he had been at variance since 1860. Ward asserts that the cause of the Kotoku (Ankobea) presence in the Lower Volta area was strained relations between the Kotoku and the Akwamu because the Akwamu were "in the habit of waylaying Akim Kotoku traders and robbing them"[36] The maltreatment was probably Akwamu's reprisal against Dompre for assisting the Ga-Adangbe Chiefs in the 1866 expedition against Anlo, an ally of Akwamu..

The attack backfired against the Akwamu, Dafor and the Volo. According to Adoagyiri tradition, Dompre was a warrior Chief who would not let slip any opportunity to fight.[37] The tradition may be exaggerating on the subject of Dompre's innate love for fighting, but that it was his duty to rescue his subjects cannot be disputed. Ussher under-rated this obligation of the Kotoku Chief in his report of 6th September when he said that a

> more important reason for the hostile attitude of the Doffoes [and Volo] is the unnecessary and inconvenient armed presence of the Akim Captain Odum-Pira at Asuacharry.[38]

T. B. Freeman's Attempt to Solve the Volta Conflict

Ussher was perhaps playing down the seriousness of the situation in the Lower Volta basin for the benefit of his superiors in Freetown, Sierra Leone, and the Colonial Office in London. That he was really concerned showed in his appointment in June, 1867 of Mr. T. B. Freeman as Chief Civil Commandant of the Eastern Districts so that Freeman might use "his acknowledged tact" to resolve the Volta problem.[39]

Though the Colonial Office in London did not ultimately approve of the appointment, before the disapproval arrived in the Gold Coast in or about November 1867[40] Mr. Freeman had already made efforts to resolve the Volta conflict. He saw the Akyem Kotoku (Nsawam) factor as one of the two major barriers impeding solution to the problem. In this frame of mind Freeman immediately sent to ask Dompre and his army to cease all hostility against the Dafor, Volo and the Akwamu, confine themselves to only a defensive measure and wait until they heard from the government.[41] His next step was that he travelled to Akuapem and to Odumase, the Manya Krobo capital.[42] From there he sent to invite Dompre who was then at Asutsuare to come and confer with him on the subject of the Volta conflict.[43] Dompre declined the invitation for two reasons. First, he said Odumase was a town he would not visit because Odonkor Azu, the Konor (King) of Manya Krobo was intriguing with Akwamu against Akyem Kotoku (Nsawam) interests; second, he simply could not leave Asutsuare at that material time because the Dafor and Volo were threatening him with an impending attack.[44] Eventually Freeman had to go to Asuatsuare in order to meet Dompre. He went there accompanied by Rev. Zimmerman of the Basel Mission Station at Odumase.

On 15th August 1867 Freeman met Dompre formally. He was instantly captivated by the personality of Dompre. He found the Nsawam Chief "courteous and respectful".[45] The diplomatic move paid off, at least in theory, because Dompre agreed in principle to leave the redress of his grievances against the Dafor, Volo and Akwamu in the hands of the government and suspend all military operation.[46]

Part of the solution to the problem of course lay in Akwamu. Dompre's conciliatory attitude encouraged Freeman to turn to Kwafo Akoto, the Akwamuhene. Again accompanied by Rev. Zimmerman and Mr. Röttman,[47] Freeman went to Akwamufie, the Akwamu capital, on 28th August 1867, and succeeded in talking Kwafo into signing a Treaty of Amity and Commerce with the Protectorate Government.[48]

Ussher was elated at Freeman's success with Dompre and Akwamuhene Kwafo Akoto. The end to the Volta conflict, he said, was now in sight. He continued:

> The only matter now remaining which gives me some uneasiness is the probable correctness of the rumours of the death of Quaquoe Dooah, King of Ashantee. Should this really prove to be the case, I fear that his successor will be easily led by the war party of Ashantee to commit acts of aggression on the Protectorate, unless this Government, by a mixture of firmness and conciliation can avert the blow.[49]

In reality Freeman's diplomatic success in the Lower Volta basin had come too late to be lasting. To counter the armed Kotoku (Nsawam) presence in that region, the Akwamu and the Anlo had long sent to ask for Asante military assistance.[50] Only the death of Asantehene Kwaku Dua I, in May 1867 had prevented Asante from immediately responding favourably to the Akwamu-Anlo request. In anticipation of the impending help from Asante, Akwamu did not see the need and urgency to ask the Dafor and Volo to release the Akyem Kotoku traders they had seized and detained. For that reason Dompre was forced to renew hostilities from September 1868 with a view to rescuing his detained subjects. Up to June 1868 when Ussher left the Gold Coast for Britain on leave, the Volta problem, still remained unsolved.[51] It was there, for his stand-in, Mr. Simpson, as Acting Administrator, to attempt a solution to it as best he could.

The Situation as Simpson Found it

Simpson found the situation in the Lower Volta basin most worrying. In September 1868, he analyzed the situation as follows: "the Eastern Districts" (in which term he included the Lower Volta area) required greater attention than they had hitherto received because they were in a very unsettled state; the trade routes were closed; and the navigable stretch of the Volta was blocked by the ceaseless and what he termed "the petty hostilities" among the inhabitants occupying both banks of the river.[52]

To describe the hostilities as petty was surely an understatement by the Acting Administrator. By 1868 the Volta conflict had become worse than it was in 1867, because it had potentially increased in scope and intensity. Dompre had struck an alliance with the Krepi to counter the Akwamu-Anlo-Dafor-Volo axis. Viewed against this backdrop it is not surprising that the Peace Treaty which Sir Arthur Kennedy signed with the Anlo in November 1868 failed to end hostilities.

The armed presence of the Kotoku (Nsawam) as a key factor in the Volta troubles was stressed in December 1868 when the Anlo bitterly complained against what they described as "the excesses" of the Akyem Kotoku army "under Odumpeley".[54] By "excesses" the Anlo were clearly referring to Dompre's seizure and execution of two Anlo ambassadors returning from a mission to Kumasi.[55] The ambassadors had been to Kumasi, probably to represent Anlo during the funeral of the late Asantehene Kwaku Dua and also to renew the request for military aid made to the late King. The inference derives its strength from the fact that in early 1869 an Asante army of about five thousand, under the command of Asamoa Nkwanta, arrived in the Lower Volta area to assist the Akwamu-Anlo alliance against the Kotoku-Krepi pact headed by Dompre.[56] On the basis of this evidence, the view that in 1869 Asante invaded Krepi to acquire booty[57] must be received with caution, if not rejected outright. The Akwamu recall vividly that they solicited Asante military help against Dompre.[58] At play in the Lower Volta basin were clearly old animosities and antagonisms: Ada against Anlo, Akwamu against Krepi, Akwamu against Kotoku (Nsawam), and Kotoku versus Asante. The Volta conflict had widened: what Administrator Ussher had anticipated in 1867 happened in 1869.

The Kotoku-Krepi alliance joined battle with the Akwamu-Anlo-Asante axis in the first three months of 1869 i.e. in the dry season. The Asante force under the command of Asamoa Nkwanta numbered five thousand, as already noted. The strength of the Akwamu was not known, but that of the Anlo was estimated at six hundred, all armed with guns.[59] The size of the Krepi army was also not known but the Kotoku force under Dompre was reckoned to be four hundred.[60]

The importance of the Kotoku factor was again emphasized in March 1869 when Simpson, commenting on the war, said that in two battles already fought, the Krepi obtained.

> the powerful assistance of Domprey, an Akim Captain who had come to Crepee for the purpose of obtaining satisfaction from the Aquamoos for some property of his countrymen which [the Akwamu] had plundered them of whilst peaceably trading . . . This man is undoubtedly the leading spirit of these districts; his name is a terror even to the Ashantees themselves; and he has shown qualities which serve to indicate him as a man of remarkable energy, talent, and daring courage . . . He alone, unaided, at the head of 400 followers, has defeated the Aquamoos in two engagements against great odds, and at present is the barrier to a general subjection of Crepee by the Ashantees.[61]

Simpson's Military Approach

Initially Mr. Simpson, as Acting Administrator, adopted diplomacy as the means to resolve the Volta problem, just as Blackall, the Administrator-in-Chief, and Freeman in 1867, and Kennedy in 1868, had all tried to do. He singled out Akwamu as the main stumbling block to be tackled first. In the last days of February 1869 he travelled to Akwamufie in order to effect a peace settlement with Akwamuhene, Kwafo Akoto.

He arrived there on 1st March. After a protracted discussion lasting five days during which he said he was virtually a prisoner of the Akwamu, he seemingly succeeded in signing a peace treaty with the Akwamuhene.[62] But Simpson knew right from his arrival at Akwamufie on 1st March that diplomacy as a means of resolving the Volta issue was doomed to failure owing to what he called "the ominous presence of the Ashantees" in Akwamu.[63]

This realization, together with his awareness of Dompre's qualities as a first class soldier, made Simpson decide to adopt a military approach should the diplomatic track fail. To him Dompre would be the perfect tool to use. The formulation of the military approach matured finally on 8th March when he, in a strongly worded letter, requested Kofi Karikari, the new Asantehene, to withdraw Asamoa Nkwanta and his army immediately from the Lower Volta area or he Simpson would not hesitate to give material support to the Krepi in defence of their country.[64]

In anticipation of a possible refusal of the Asantehene to comply with his ultimatum Simpson signed on Dompre and his force as government troops to fight the enemy.⁶⁵ Two years earlier the Protectorate administration under Ussher had described Dompre as a disturber of peace. In 1869 he was recruited as a soldier in the employ of the same administration, headed by an Acting Administrator and charged with the pacification of the Lower Volta basin.

To help Dompre achieve success Simpson rallied support from other parts of the Eastern Districts. He began with the mobilization of the Ga.⁶⁶ He then turned to the Akyem Abuakwa: to Okyenhene Amoako Atta I, described as the staunchest and the most determined foe of Asante, he sent a gift of £100.00 sterling, a consignment of arms and ammunition, and a message that the Government relied on his loyalty to the British and the welfare of the Protectorate to render every assistance "in your power" to oppose the enemy.⁶⁷

The employment of Dompre as a government soldier, however, did not last long, because by June 1869 Simpson had been forced to abandon the policy of using a military approach to solve the Volta conflict and had stopped sending munitions of war to Dompre.⁶⁸ The change of policy was due to the disapproval of the military approach by both the Administrator-in-Chief of the British West African possessions and the Colonial Office in London.⁶⁹ In order to stress his disapproval the Administrator-in-Chief, among other things, said:

> Whatever may have been the result of your negotiation with the King of Ashantee I am averse to your committing the Government to affording material aid [to the Kotoku and Krepi] as long as the belligerents confine themselves to the distant district of Crepee.⁷⁰

Granville, the Colonial Secretary, was even much blunter and more forthright in his condemnation of Simpson. He fumed that Simpson

> had adopted a very hazardous cause without a clear apprehension of the facts or a just calculation of his powers, a serious error in an officer occupying so responsible a position.

He went on to say that the measures which Simpson had taken

> would make the British Government not a neutral, nor even an ally, but a principal in the quarrel [i.e. the Volta conflict, and that the defeat of the Kotoku-Krepi Alliance would be] the defeat or ill success of the British Government. If he [Simpson] were a less efficient and zealous public servant, I should have therefore thought it necessary to recall his commission . . . I refrain, however, from doing so, in the confident hope that he will loyally dispel the illusions his vows must have created, and that his knowledge of native character will enable him to retain that influence which this untoward affair must no doubt impair.⁷¹

Dompre Fights on without Official Support

Following the disapproval of his measures by his superiors, Simpson, from June 1869, stopped sending war materials to "Domprey and his Ackim army", who found themselves in a very grave situation. Simpson's bellicosity, as spelt out in his letter of 8th March to Kumasi as well as his preparations for armed confrontation with Asante, together with Dompre's successes against Asamoa Nkwanta, had so angered Kofi Karikari, the Asantehene, that in or about May 1869 he had despatched a much larger force of fifteen thousand, under the command of General Adu Bofuo, to go and assist the Akwamu and Anlo against Dompre.[72]

The Adu Bofuo force increased the fighting power of the Akwamu-Anlo-Asante alliance against Dompre. By May 1869 he was fighting against great odds. Numerically his own fighting force of four hundred must have thinned down; besides, he was running out of ammunition. Before the disapproval of his measures reached him, Simpson had detailed Oben Darko, a younger brother of Dompre, to convey a consignment of ammunition to Dompre.[73] When Oben Darko arrived at Battor on the Volta, Dompre had been surrounded by the adversary.[74] On 23rd May Dompre reported that he had had to beat a retreat in the face of the enemy advance owing to the numerical inferiority of his force, and requested the Protectorate authorities to send him express reinforcement.[75] On 21st June he sent out another appeal for help, and also reported the fall of the town of Anum and the capture, by the Asante, of the Basel missionary Ramseyer, his wife and baby and his colleague, Kuhne.[76]

From his save-our-souls messages it is clear that the Akyem Kotoku sub-Chief had no illusions about the fact of his being a government soldier fighting in defence of the Krepi territory which he felt was under the British jurisdiction.[77] At least the activities and pronouncements of Simpson had led him to that conclusion.[78] It was therefore unfair for Simpson to say on 16th July 1869 that Dompre had been foolish because he had not been asked to defend Krepi but to station himself at Battor on the Volta, and that Dompre should have himself to blame if the enemy was closing in on him.[79] Worse, Simpson accused Dompre of selfishness. To Oben Darko he said further:

> the Ashantees say that they fight only against Domprey and not against the British Government. Is this, as I suspect, on account of the Old palaver between them and Adjeman? If so, how can he expect me to follow him wherever he chooses to go – I am no friends with Ashantee, but neither can I justify to support one who leaves the Protectorate for selfish purposes of his own and seeks to fight over my shoulders his own independent quarrels?[80]

Simpson was absolutely correct in thinking that old enmity between

Kotoku and Asante partly accounted for the involvement of both in the Volta conflict. But he just could not deny his own responsibility in getting Dompre thus far in the current predicament for which he was now blaming the Nsawam Chief. Simpson seemed to be too honest a man to shirk his responsibility, and had to admit that his refusal to continue to support Dompre was due to the disapproval of his measures by Freetown and the British Colonial Office. He stated further:

> Domprey is a good soldier if not a good citizen, and I would gladly have made use of him to increase the defensive strength of the Protectorate. The state of the country is deplorable enough, but unless I can satisfy my Government in Great Britain that we are in the right, I risk my own position by offering aid to your brother.[81]

This then was how confused British policy in the Lower Volta basin partly helped to push Dompre deeper into war with an Akwamu-Anlo-Asante Alliance only to abandon him mid-stream. Many historical accounts on the Gold Coast are replete with accusations against the peoples and states of barbarism and love for war. There were occasions when European presence and overrule were responsible for some of the wars.

Deserted by the Simpson administration in the thick of the Volta war, Dompre and his small Kotoku (Ankobea) army had to battle with the formidable adversary as best they could. He became almost the sole target of the Asante in particular. Asantehene Kofi Karikari was determined that either the British should give up Dompre or "else he will catch him at any price".[82] In Dompre the Asante were apparently seeing the late Kotokuhene Agyeman reincarnated. Just as they had determined in 1863 to get Agyeman dead or alive, so were they resolved in 1869 to get Dompre at any price. It was proof of Dompre's prowess and quality as a first class soldier that in spite of the great odds against him, he continued to slug it out with the overwhelmingly powerful Asante force under General Adu Bofuo and their Akwamu and Anlo allies.

The Protectorate Rallies Behind Dompre

His predicament created a sense of unity in the entire Protectorate: many regarded him as a true patriot of the Protectorate. His plight, the capture of the Basel missionaries of Anum by Adu Bofuo, and the false but widespread alarm that the Asante General intended to invade the Ga-Adangbe area after subjugating Krepi, aroused the entire Protectorate into doing something in support of Dompre. The new Kotokuhene, Kwabena Fua, sent reinforcement to him in spite of the Administration's refusal to supply the Kotoku with weapons.[83] By this action the new Kotokuhene healed the nine-year-old breach which had existed between the Kotoku paramountcy and the Ankobea segment since 1860.

The Okyenhene, Amoako Atta I, also raised a force of five thousand strong to go to the aid of Dompre.[84] Though the Abuakwa assistance eventually did not reach the Lower Volta, Amoako Atta's gesture may have gone a long way to improving Kotoku-Abuakwa relations which had been strained since the 1860 Gyadam War. For just a year later (1870) representatives of the two Akyem states met at the Abuakwa town of Akaanten to perform a peace ceremony formally marking the end of strained relations between Abuakwa and Kotoku.[85] The Assin and the Fante demonstrated their moral support for Dompre by tightening up the hitherto loose blockade of the Cape Coast trade route against Asante;[86] the two peoples acted under the aegis of the Mankessim Council.[87] Finally, in Accra a group of scholars who described themselves as "Accra Gentlemen" got annoyed with Acting Administrator Simpson for describing Dompre as a marauder. They not only rejected the description but also declared Dompre as a devoted patriot who

> is really playing a very important part in the preservation of the Protectorate . . . It is essentially owing to the recent movements of Domprey that the Ashantees have hitherto been prevented from making further progress.[88]

In appreciation of Dompre's achievements, the Ga set up a committee charged with raising funds and a force to assist the patriotic Akyem Kotoku under his command.[89] In short, as Simpson himself put it in October 1869, "the whole of the Eastern Districts were in arms against Ashantee" in support of Dompre.[90] What may have partly engendered this universal and enthusiastic outburst of both material and moral support for Dompre was his signal victory over the Asante-Akwamu forces in a battle fought at the rocky hill of Gemi in the Amedzofe neighbourhood in October 1869.[91]

Before this spontaneous material and moral support could reach him, Dompre had fought gallantly and managed to reach the west bank of the Volta with the remnant of his small but daring force, some time between November and December 1869.[92]

The 1870 Volta Expedition

By then Mr. Ussher had returned from leave and resumed duty as Administrator at Cape Coast Castle. He regretted the withdrawal of Dompre from the Lower trans-Volta. The basis of his regret was a change of mind in Freetown and at the Colonial Office in London. At long last it had dawned on both that the military solution to the Volta Question which Simpson had advocated was after all the best approach. The change had occurred while Ussher was in Britain. He had, as a result, hoped to renew the government aid to Dompre immediately on his return to the Gold Coast. The departure of Dompre from the Lower trans-Volta, he feared, might inspire Asante not only to subdue but also occupy the whole of Krepi.[93] The military approach was now all the more desirable because Geraldo de Lima was just about to renew hostilities from his base in Anlo.[94] Ussher was determined to sign on Dompre once again as a government soldier. In May – June 1870 Ussher organized an armed expedition to the Lower Volta basin. Besides a small contingent from the West India Regiment, he got the Ga Chiefs and the Accra merchants to raise a force for the expedition. Next he invited support from the British Lagos establishment in Nigeria, from where came the gunboat H. M. S. Eyo with troops under the command of Captain Glover, the Administrator of the British Lagos possession.

Together with Glover, the entire regular troops, as well as the indigenous forces, Ussher sailed up the Volta to Battor with a view to consulting Dompre without whose advice he would not proceed any further with the armed expedition.[95] Both he and Glover found Dompre to be

> a competent man, and moreover most loyal to H. M. Government. The remarkable absence of ostentation and marked deference paid him to the position of the [Ga] Kings did not fail to impress me with a high idea of him.[96]

On his part Dompre did not disappoint the two Administrators. In spite of the recent British betrayal, he had no hard feelings against the Protectorate administration. He was still prepared to cooperate with it in an effort to find peace for trouble-torn Lower Volta basin. On 30th May 1870 Ussher signed an agreement with the Nsawam warrior Chief the terms of which said Dompre should:

1. Charge himself with the defence of the left or eastern bank of the Volta, keeping open the communications for trade, with the duty of expelling, to the best of his ability, attacks from hostile tribes in the trans-Volta Districts;
2. Receive instructions either from the Administrator direct, or through the Civil Commandant of Accra, and from none other. Should any interference be tempted by other Chiefs, to report at once to the Commandant;
3. Use every means in his power to protect and keep open trade and communication in the Volta, and neither on his own behalf, nor on that of any other person, to permit toll or imposts to be levied on person, merchandise or produce ascending or descending the river;
4. Confine his operations, as well as may be, strictly to the defence of his country and that of his allies, and neglect no means to effect a permanent peace, and not to refuse to accept the submission of hostile tribes or bodies. He will, above all, refrain, by any ill advised measures, from

prolonging the war, in the interest of selfish and disaffected persons.

5. In consideration of the faithful discharge of these conditions, and of his general desire to promote the welfare and foster the trade of River Volta and the Eastern Districts, Domprey shall receive from Her Majesty's Colonial Government of the Gold Coast settlements, the sum of two Hundred pounds sterling per annum, paid quarterly in advance, in addition to such assistance from time to time in munitions of war and general necessities as the Officer administering the said Government shall deem fit.
6. It shall be lawful to the said Administrator, for misconduct or disobedience of instructions on Domprey's part, or for any other cause, to suspend for a time or permanently to discontinue the stipend and assistance above-mentioned to be given to Domprey.
7. It is to be understood by Domprey that in the event of a permanent peace being established by his aid, and by his obedience to the policy of the Gold Coast Government, his position at the close of the disturbances in the Eastern Districts shall, if possible, be better than before – and that in any case, the stipend of (£200) two hundred pounds sterling per annum, shall not be discontinued, in consideration of certain future services to be rendered by Domprey to the Government in protecting the interests of the Government in the Eastern Districts and River Volta.
8. This agreement to be subject to the approval of the Legislative Council of Cape Coast and the Governor-in-Chief of the West African Settlements.[97]

Ussher signed for the Gold Coast Protectorate Government, and Dompre, on his own behalf, put his mark to it. Those who witnessed the Convention were Captain W. J. Ross, the Acting Civil Commandant of the Eastern Districts, Dr. Thomas Jones of H. M. S. Eyo, and Messrs Lebrecht Hesse, Edmund Bannerman and William Addo.

With the signing of the Battor Bond, Dompre once again became a government soldier. The stone that was rejected by the Administration of the British West African Settlements and the British Colonial Office in the first half of 1869 was made the cornerstone of British presence in the Lower Volta basin in 1870.

Dompre, Ussher and Glover laid immediate plans to implement the first clause of the Convention. The most urgent concern of Ussher was to subdue the Dafor and Volo completely in order to allow the smooth flow of trade once again on the Volta. Dompre would then be left to defend the Volta waterway and protect allies in the trans-Volta against enemy attacks.

The Dafor and Volo of course continued to enjoy the solid backing of

Akwamu, Anlo and the Asante army under Adu Bafuo. On 19th June 1870 the Government forces moved in on the enemy, with Dompre directing the land operations whilst Captain Glover took charge of the 'marine' manoeuvres of the gunboat H. M. S. Eyo. The Battle of the Volta began at 1.00 p.m. the same day, and within about three hours it was all over.

Dompre and his land forces rushed in under the cover of the gunboat. The enemy put up a stiff and spirited resistance in the initial stages but was compelled to give in to the heavy onslaught from land and mid-stream. On the basis of Ussher's account, the carnage must have been horrifying; he said that of the fighting men "of Duffo and Voloe" not a single man escaped.[98] Glover was slightly more informative than Ussher. According to him an Asante Captain, an Akwamu Chief, and all their followers, when they saw that the day was lost, "blew themselves up", adding that "of the men of Duffo and Voloe none remained", and that about three hundred of the people, mainly women and children, were taken captive.[99] On account of the alleged carnage the Colonial Office queried Mr. Kennedy, the Administrator-in-Chief of the British West African possessions, for allowing the Gold Coast Administration to wage the war in the first instance, saying that the Colonial Secretary had only permitted a demonstration, not war.[100] Had the Colonial office managed to lay hands on other sources of information, perhaps they would not have worried so much about the issue of the carnage. For it seems that both Ussher and Glover, considerably exaggerated on the subject. Winwoode Reade, a British journalist accompanied the expedition and witnessed the Battle of the Volta. He said that at the time, only about thirty men captained by an Asante Chief manned the island of Dafor, the target of the attack.[101] The losses of the Government forces were put at "a few dead" and a few wounded whom Dr. Jones of H.M.S. Eyo successfully treated.[102]

The outcome of the expedition pleased the two Administrators. Ussher enthused that at long last an end to the Volta conflict was in sight. But the leadership of the indigenous forces saw things differently, they clamoured for a direct invasion of Akwamu itself. The rationale behind the demand was that Akwamu was the real enemy and so the Government should press home its advantage with a direct invasion of that state. But Ussher refused to go that far; the people were not aware that Ussher's hands were tied by the Colonial Office's directive that the expedition should be a demonstration and not a major operation. Had it been possible for the Protectorate forces to invade Akwamu immediately, perhaps the Akwamu-Asante alliance would have suffered a more crushing defeat, and peace would have been completely restored to the Lower Volta basin. Ussher and Glover, however, could only hope that the defeat of the Dafor and Volo would be enough to do the trick. Consequently, on 27th June 1870 both men embarked on the Eyo for Accra, leaving

Dompre to begin his role as a frontier policeman.[104]

Dompre's Death

Paradoxically the success of the Volta expedition ultimately proved disastrous for the Akyem Kotoku in particular and the Eastern Districts generally. Petty internal jealousies among the Allies soon destroyed their sense of unity and cooperation, proved a barrier to Dompre in his role as a frontier policeman, and finally claimed his life barely a month after the expedition. Dompre must have lost his life some time in July because by 3rd August the news of his death had reached the Administrator-in-Chief in Freetown, Sierra Leone.[105]

How did Dompre's death come about? According to Kennedy the Administrator-in-Chief, Dompre was killed in "a skirmish", apparently with the enemy, "being the only man of his party killed or wounded".[106] Writing in 1925, Welman accepted this killed-in-battle theory. He states that "Adu Boffo succeeded in defeating Dompre who met his death in battle in November or December 1870 at Abotia".[107] A Krepi tradition claims that the Akwamu ambushed and killed Dompre.[108] Adoagyiri tradition, however, states categorically that it was the Ga who assassinated Dompre.[109] As will be demonstrated in due course, there is a strong circumstantial evidence suggesting that the Adoagyiri tradition, however biased it may seem, is probably nearest to, if not, the truth. Suffice it to say now that it seems surprising that the *African Times* in October 1870 and the *West African Herald*, the latter an Accra newspaper, in March 1871, fully commented on what they termed the untimely death of Dompre but failed to say how Dompre met his death.[110]

Whatever the manner of Dompre's death, the British administration in West Africa formally acknowledged the Akyem Kotoku warrior chief as a collaborator of the British imperial presence in the Gold Coast. In his tribute to Dompre, Kennedy, the Administrator-in-Chief, said among other things:

> the subsidy . . . promised Domprey was a judicious outlay to a tried and influential man who would have acted as a Frontier Police, and would have had an interest in keeping peace. This war-chief who had just established a character for courage and loyalty has unhappily lost his life in a skirmish, being the only man of his party killed or wounded.

Ussher was not out-done in the tribute paying exercise. He presented to Oben Darko, Dompre's brother and successor, a marble plaque with the inscription "DOMPREY" written on it.[112] The tributes were appropriate because that Kotoku Chief was indeed a loyal collaborator of the British in their efforts to establish their protectorate presence in the Lower Volta basin. No wonder they regretted his untimely death.

We have suggested that the Adoagyiri tradition might well be right in claiming that it was the Ga, led by King Tackie, who assassinated Dompre. What is the justification? The evidence is circumstantial but quite strong. The first piece of circumstantial evidence is Ussher's view of Ga Mantse Tackie. In July 1870 Ussher suspected that the Ga Mantse was capable of some foul play. The Administrator described "King Tackie" as "the hotheaded . . . Chief of Accra", dangerous and untrustworthy, and that "if any mischief arises it will be from him".[113] Ussher's view of Tackie ties in well with the Adoagyiri tradition which recalls that it was "Nkranhene Takyi" (i.e. Ga Mantse Tackie) who bribed the Ga wife of Dompre to show how her husband could be killed since Dompre appeared to have a charmed body that was bullet-and sword-proof. Dompre's wife complied, and the result was the assassination of Dompre.[114]

Now why should the Ga Chiefs want to kill Dompre? The Ga Mantse had apparently grown jealous of Dompre. There is an Akan proverb which says, literally, that no one's walking stick is taller than himself. Dompre was an Akyem Kotoku sub-Chief whom the Ga rulers had employed as a mercenary soldier during the 1866 Volta expedition. By signing the Battor Convention with him in May 1870, Ussher had unwittingly elevated Dompre above his superiors, namely the Ga Chiefs. The elevation hurt not only the status, personal pride and dignity of Mantse Takie and the other Ga Chiefs but also the ethnic feelings of the Ga. It is reasonable to imagine the elevation of the Akyem sub-chief engendering bitterness in a "hot-headed" person like Tackie to the point of driving him to contrive the assassination of Dompre.

There are other pieces of strong circumstantial evidence, but these will be dealt with later; suffice it to say now that the untimely death of Dompre adversely affected the efforts to restore peace in the Lower Volta Basin. The Anlo continued to be hostile, most probably at the instigation of Geraldo de Lima.[115] Adu Bofuo and his Asante army and the Akwamu took fresh courage from Dompre's death and renewed hostile activities. In short instead of the Battle of the Volta leading to cessation of violence and instability in the Lower Volta Basin, it worsened the situation to the extent that in September 1870 the Accra merchants declared the Volta policy of Ussher's administration a failure.[116]

In spite of this gloomy situation the Asante army under Adu Bofuo allegedly decided to give peace a chance. When leaving for Accra, Ussher appointed Mr. R. Bannerman, one of the leading Accra merchants, to act on his behalf. Bannerman somehow got in touch with the Asante General who agreed in principle to a peace settlement. About late September 1870, Bannerman informed Ussher that to back his word Adu Bofuo had delivered to him (Bannerman) "some important hostages as a pledge of his intentions to abandon hostilities and . . . as security for the rendition of the captive missionaries".[117]

Following the understanding reached with the Asante army, Mr. Bannerman ordered the demobilization of the Protectorate forces in the same month of September. By then violent relations between the Akyem Kotoku and the Ga had replaced the turbulence of the Lower Volta Basin.

Kotoku-Ga Conflict

After the demobilization the Kotoku army, now under the joint command of Oben Darko and another Chief called Asuman, pursued the Ga forces right to their country and infested it. Here the Kotoku warriors engaged in what the West African Herald described as

> a very irregular jurisdiction over the [Ga] . . . seizing and kidnapping in a very bold manner and [were] otherwise guilty of violent acts.[118]

Thus the 1870 armed expedition which had been expected to restore peace and calm to trouble torn Lower Volta ended up tearing the Eastern Districts apart. The cordiality and cooperation which had characterized Ga-Kotoku relations between 1865 and 1869 had by 1870 broken down, each was at the other's throat. Herein lies another strong circumstancial evidence that the Ga might well have been the murderers of Dompre as averred by the Adoagyiri tradition.

As their district happened to be the theatre of hostilities, it was the Ga who felt the pinch more, if information in the 31st March 1871 issue of the *West African Herald* is anything to go by. In addition to promoting insecurity to the Ga people and property, the Kotoku warriors blockaded all trade routes to the Ga District. That put them in great disfavour with the British protectorate administration which they had very recently served with all loyalty.

Captain Lees was then the Civil Commandant of the Eastern Districts. Without making any effort to look into the grievances of the Kotoku warriors he concluded that they should be suppressed militarily in order to end the conflict between them and the Ga. In the early months of 1871 he organized what was described at the time as a firm armed expedition against the Oben Darko-Asuman warriors who were now labelled "bandits".[119]

Obedience and loyalty once again played the so-called marauders into the hand of the Eastern Districts Commandantcy. They submitted to Captain Lees without a fight. The leaders gave themselves up. These included Oben Darko, Kwame Dompre Kuma, Kwame Afroten, Kwadwo Abokyi, and Kwasi Buo; they were marched to Accra and remanded in custody to await a court action against them.[120]

Exactly when they were taken to court is unclear. But the *West African Herald* of 31 March 1871 gave a vivid description of the scene at one stage of the proceedings. The paper said the prisoners were charged with a breach of public peace.[121] The paper then continued:

> After hearing the prisoners who spoke well for themselves, his honour [the Magistrate] directed the interpreter (Mr. Addo) to ask the native [Ga] Chiefs what they had to say. Upon this King Tackie, King of Ussher town . . . spoke thus to the interpreter: "Look here, tell our master (meaning the judge) that these people (meaning the prisoners) have been making war against the Ashantees and the Aquamoos, and have secured plenty of plunder, and we want a share, we must have it too, otherwise we shan't be satisfied, because we supplied the ammunition to fight. Besides the Crepees have told us all about it. Therefore let's have our share at once.[122]

It is clear from this emotional outburst of Ga Mantse Tackie that, another cause of the Kotoku-Ga conflict was a quarrel over booty from the 1870 Volta Expedition and that it was this dispute which probably led to the murder of Dompre. The judge ignored King Tackie's request, but imprisoned Oben Darko and his colleagues for breach of public peace.[123]

Akyem Kotokuhene Kwabena Fua had no doubt in his mind that the imprisonment of his subjects was nothing less than a travesty of justice. But all he could do in the circumstance was to plead leniency for his convicted subjects.[124] The Petition did not immediately receive a favourable response from the Protectorate Administration. The state of Kotoku therefore revolted to stress its protest against the imprisonment of the five Kotoku citizens of Nsawam. Luckily for both sides, in December 1871 Mr. C. S. Salmon, the Acting Administrator, detected a miscarriage of justice and accordingly ordered the release of Oben Darko and his colleagues from prison.[125] The Kotoku state reciprocated the gesture by signing a peace treaty with the Administration on 21st December 1871 to end its rebellion.[126]

Summary

The imprisonment and release of the five Nsawam citizens and the shortlived rebellion of the Akyem Kotoku State against the British in 1871 must all be seen as a long term effect of the 1860 War between Abuakwa and Kotoku. The war had produced a rift in the Kotoku leadership, with the larger section, led by the Kotokuhene, going to found Nsuaem (Oda) in Western Akyem, and the much smaller part headed by Ankobeahene Dompre, establishing Nsawam on Akuapem territory. The residence of the Ankobea Division at Nsawam ultimately got them involved in the violent trade and politics in the Lower Volta basin. Akwamu, old enemy of Kotoku, exploited the involvement as a pretext for ordering the seizure, detention and even killing of some Kotoku citizens from Nsawam trading in the area of conflict. Dompre's determination to rescue his subjects led to the emergence of the Kotoku of Nsawam as one of the leading parties in the Volta conflict. The British tried to use Chief Dompre to effect a military solution to the conflict, but he paid dearly with his life. When his subjects attempted to avenge his death on the Ga, the alleged assassins of their Chief, they aroused the anger of the very British whose proto-colonial interest in the Lower Volta area they had helped to promote.

NOTES AND REFERENCES

1. The rift is discussed in Chapter 8.
2. Nsawam Native Affairs, Case No. 76/1910, Ghana National Archives; AKT: Adoagyiri (1968/9). *Nsawa-mu means* Under-the-small-*Nsaa*-trees. *Asaa, Asoaa* (or *Nsaa*) is a wild fruit tree.
3. AKT: Adoagyiri (1968/9).
4. At the beginning of this century (20th), a quarrel with their landlords compelled the Kotoku Ankobea to abandon Nsawam to found Adoagyiri on the western bank of Densu. The land here belonged, and still belongs to the Akyem Abuakwa. Consequently the Adoagyirihene to this day pays homage to the Okyenhene on account of the land on which he lives.
5. See Map No. 9.
6. AKT: Adoagyiri (1968/9).
7. Freeman's Report on a mission to Eastern Akyem in 1857, 28 December 1857, CO96/43.
8. The Lower Volta basin may be said to have consisted roughly of the area falling within about twenty five kilometres on either side of the Volta between its estuary at Ada and the point where river Dayi joined the Volta.
9. For a study of the Lower Volta economy see Reynolds, E., 1974 *Trade and Economic Change in the Gold Coast 1807–1874*, NUP, London, especially pp.141–144 and 172.
10. Evidence of Rev. Elias Shrenk before the 1865 British Parliamentary Select Committee, Br. PP.1865, Vol.412, pp. 136, 142 & 147; Ga Mantse Cudjoe Ababeo (Ada) to Lt-Col. Conran 29 November 1866, CO96/72; Horton, Letters, pp. 75–76.
11. The *West African Herald*, quoted by the *Times* of London, 26 October 1861.
12. *Ibid.*
13. Krobo and Akuapem were great producers of palm oil in the Gold Coast at this time.
14. Wolfson, F., "A Price Agreement on the Gold Coast. The Krobo Oil Boycott 1858–1866" in Economic History Review, 2nd Series, Vol.6 No.1 (1953), pp. 68–77, Kimble, *A Political History*, pp. 6 & 187–188, Amenumey, D. E. K., "Geraldo de Lima: A Reappraisal", in *THSG*, Vol.IX (1968), pp.68–69.
15. The *West African Herald*, quoted by the *London Times*, 26 October 1861.
16. J. Muller's Report to Basel on a journey to Eastern Akyem in 1868, dated 11 March 1868 BMA-PJA.

17. The *London Times*, 26 October 1868.
18. Alfred Churchill to the Colonial Office, 20 April 1863 CO96/63; Governor R. Pine (CCC) to the C. O., London 9 November 1863, CO96/62; *African Times*, 23 January 1864; Amenumey, "Geraldo", in *THSG*, Vol.IX, pp. 65–68.
19. Memorials of Accra Merchants to Lt-Col. Conran, 31 January & 24 February 1866; Crozier (Accra) to Lt. Col. Conran, 5 December 1866, CO96/70.
20. T. B. Freeman (Odumase-Krobo) to Governor Ussher (CCC) 19 August 1867, CO96/76; Dodi Tradition, cited by Marion Johnson, "Ashanti East of the Volta", in *THSG*, Vol.VIII (1965).
21. Reynolds, *Trade and Economic Change*, pp. 143–144.
22. For a comprehensive account on Geraldo de Lima, See Amenumey in *THSG*, Vol.IX (1968).
23. Memorials of the Accra Merchants to Lt.-Col. Conran, 31 January & 24 February 1866, CO96/70.
24. Horton *Letters*, pp. 75–76.
25. The Memos. of the Accra Merchants, 31 January and 24 February 1866 CO96/70.
26. AKT: Adoagyiri (1968/9).
27. Conran to Quarter Master General, H. M. Forces, London, 8 March 1866; Conran to Cardwell, 10 March 1866, CO96/70. Claridge (Vol.1, p.549) puts the number of the guns at 1,200. He seems to have based his figure on the number mentioned by James Bannerman who gave the same figure in a letter to Horton in 1869. Cf. Horton, *Letters*, p.34 footnote.
28. Claridge, Vol.1, pp.548–552; Ward, *A History of Ghana*, pp.227–228.
29. Conran to Cardwell, 5 May 1866; Conran to the Accra Merchants, 28 May; Conran to Blackall (Freetown) 9 June; Blackall to the Colonial Office, London, 12 June; Petition of the Accra Merchants to Lt.-Col. Conran, 22 November 1866, CO96/72.
30. Blackall (Freetown) to Carnavon, Colonial Office, London, 6 May 1868, CO96/74; Treaty Opening the River Volta, 30 November 1868, reproduced by Metcalfe, *Documents* Appendix, C p.741.
31. Amenumey, "Geraldo", in *THSG*, Vol.IX (1968), p.71.
32. Ussher (CCC) to Yonge (Freetown), 6 September 1867, CO96/74.
33. By the end of 1867 the Ga Chiefs had withdrawn from the Lower Volta region.
34. T. B. Freeman (Odumase-Krobo) to Ussher (CCC), 19 August 1867, CO96/79.
35. Johnson, M. "Ashanti East of the Volta" in *THSG*, Vol.VIII, p.44.
36. Ward, *A History of Ghana*, p.230.
37. AKT: Adoagyiri (1968/9).
38. Ussher (CCC) to Yonge (Freetown SL) 6 September 1867 CO96/74. "Odum-Pira" = Odompre or Dompre; Asuacharry = Asutware or Asutsuare.
39. Ussher to Yonge, 6 September 1867, CO96/74.
40. Buckingham (CO) to the Administrator-in-Chief (Freetown, SL), 18 November 1867, CO96/74. The reason given was that Freeman had been dismissed from the Gold Coast service in 1860 for gross misconduct. See Chapter 7, p.7160.
41. Freeman's Report on a Mission to Akuapem and Krobo, 5 July 1867, CO96/74.
42. Freeman's Report on a Mission to Akuapem and Krobo, 5 July 1867, CO96/74. Freeman in going to Odumase may have been influenced by the fact that there was a Basel Mission Station at the Manya Krobo capital.
43. Freeman (Odumase) to Ussher, 19 August 1867, CO96/74.
44. *Ibid.*
45. *Ibid.*

46. Ibid.
47. Rottman was the head of the trading wing of the Basel Mission (Gold Coast).
48. "Treaty of Amity, 28 August 1867, CO96/74. Cf also Metcalfe, *Documents*, p.746.
49. Ussher (CCC) to Yonge (Freetown), 6 September 1867, CO96/74.
50. Freeman to Ussher, 19 August 1867, CO96/74, cf also Wilks, *Asante*, pp. 224–225.
51. Ussher (CCC) to Freetown (SL), 6 February 1868, CO96/76.
52. Simpson (CCC) to Sir Arthur Kennedy, 5 September 1868, CO96/79.
53. "Treaty Opening the River Volta, 30 November 1868", cf. Metcalfe, *Documents*, p.746.
54. Lawson (Accra) to Kennedy (Freetown), 17 December 1868, CO96/79. Sir Arthur Kennedy, after agreeing the November peace Treaty in principle sailed back to Freetown, leaving Mr. Lawson behind to complete the peace agreement with the Anlo.
55. Amenumey, D. E. K., 1964, "The Ewe People and the Coming of European Rule", M.A. Thesis, University of London, (unpublished), pp. 182–183.
56. Simpson (CCC) to Kennedy (Freetown), 22 March 1869, CO96/79. Others say that the command was given to Nantwi, Cf. Ramseyer & Kuhne, 1897 *Four Years in Ashantee*, James Nibbet & Co Ltd., London 1897, pp. 57 & 136; Ward, *A History of Ghana*, p.241; Wilks, *Asante*, p.225.
57. Ellis (1893), p.260; Claridge, Vol.I, p.576; Kimble, *A Political History*, p.269.
58. Akwamu Tradition, cited by Ward, *A History of Ghana*, p.230.
59. Rev. Zimmerman (Odumase-Krobo) to Shrenk (Akuropon, Akuapem), 17 May 1869, cited in Shrenk to Russell, Chief Civil Commandant, Eastern Districts, 21 May 1869, CO96/80.
60. Simpson to Kennedy, 2 March 1869, CO96/79.
61. *Ibid*.
62. Simpson (Akwamufie) to Kennedy Freetown), 2 March 1869, CO96/79. It is claimed that the Akwamu would have killed him but for the intervention of Adu Bofuo, Commander of the Asante forces. (Cf. Claridge, Vol.I, p.579 & Ward, *A History of Ghana*, p.242). It must have been Asamoa Nkwanta then who interceded to save him, if indeed Simpson's life was in danger. One is inclined to think that this was a piece of exaggeration by Simpson.
63. Simpson to Kennedy, 2 March 1869, CO96/79.
64. Simpson (Odumase-Krobo) to the Asantehene, 8 March 1869, copy enclosed in Simpson to Kennedy, 22 March 1869, CO96/79.
65. Simpson (Odumase-Krobo) to "Domprey, commanding the Ackim Forces", 8 March 1869, copy, CO96/79.
66. Simpson (Accra) to Kennedy, 22 March 1869, CO96/79; Horton, *Letters*, pp. 36–37 footnote.
67. Simpson (Odumase-Krobo) to "King Attah, Ackim", 8 March 1869, copy, CO96/79; Kromer (Kyebi) to Basel, 28 July 1869, No Akim 15; Lodholtz (Kyebi) to Mader (Akuropon-Akuapem), 9 August 1869, No.Akim 11, BMA-PJA.
68. Simpson to Kennedy, 19 June 1869, CO96/79.
69. Kennedy (Freetown, SL) to Simpson (CCC), 7 April 1869 ; Granville (CO) to Kennedy (Freetown), 17 May 1869, CO96/79.
70. Kennedy to Simpson, 7 April 1869, CO96/79.
71. Granville (CO) to Kennedy (Freetown), 17 May 1869, CO96/79.
72. Rev. Zimmerman (Odumase-Krobo) to E. Shrenk (Akuropon-Akuapem), 17 May 1869, BMA-PJA; Simpson to Kennedy, 20 May; Shrenk to Russell, Chief Civil Commandant, Eastern Districts (Accra), 21 May 1869, CO96/80. Other writers put the size of Adu Bofuo's army at 20,000–30,000. Moreover, it is said that Adu Bofuo's force

formed the eastern most column of a three-pronged impending Asante invasion of the Protectorate. Cf. Ellis (1893), p.260; Claridge, Vol.I, p.276; Ward, *A History of Ghana*, p.241. So far the only pieces of contemporary evidence nearest to this claim are
  (i) the false and alarmist interpretation which the people of Ada put on Adu Bofuo's movements (cf. King Dosu, Ada, to Russell, 30 August 1869, CO96/81) and,
  (ii) a false alarm from Elmina Castle (Cf. Colonel Boers to Simpson, 8 April 1869, as Enclosure in Simpson to Kennedy, 9 April 1869, CO96/79). Wilks (*Asante*, pp. 224–226) touches on these events. His interpretation is completely different from mine.
73. Simpson to Kennedy, 20 May 1869, CO96/79.
74. Oben Darko (Battor) to Russell (Accra), 6 June 1869, CO96/80.
75. Dompre ("Afframay Camp") to Russell (Accra), 23 May 1869, CO96/80.
76. Dompre ("Agoteam" i.e. Agotime) to Mr. Addo, 27 August 1869, CO96/81. Mr. Addo, like several other Accra merchants, had business connections in the Lower Volta area.
77. *Ibid.*
78. *Ibid.*
79. Simpson to Oben Darko ("Bartor"), 16 July 1869, CO96/80, copy.
80. *Ibid.*
81. *Ibid.*
82. Zimmerman (Odumase-Krobo) to Shrenk (Akuropon-Akuapem), 17 May 1869, copy in CO96/80, Lodholtz (Kyebi) to Basel, 4 September 1869, No. Akim 13, BMA-PJA.
83. King Ghartey (Winneba) to Simpson (CCC), 3 July; Simpson to Ghartey, 6 August; Simpson to Kennedy (Freetown, SL), 7 August 1869, CO96/81. King Ghartey was at that time the President of the Mankessim Council which had been formed to oppose the 1867-8, Anglo-Dutch exchange of spheres of influence.
84. Simpson (CCC) to Kennedy (Freetown), 7 August 1869, CO96/81.
85. Lodholtz (Kyebi) to Basel, 5 January 1871, No.Akim 19, BMA-PJA.
86. Simpson to Kennedy, 7 August 1869, CO96/81.
87. *Alias* the Fante Confederation.
88. The "Accra Gentlemen" to Simpson, 31 August 1869, CO96/81. The "Accra Gentlemen" were possibly the educated African elite.
89. "Accra Educated Natives" to Simpson, 14 August; Simpson to Captain Lees (Accra), 21 August 1869, CO96/81. Capt. Lees was the Chief Civil Commandant of the Eastern Districts.
90. Simpson (CCC) to Kennedy (Freetown), 3 October 1869, No.117; also Simpson to Kennedy 18 October 1869 No.124, & Zimmerman (Odumase-Krobo) to Simpson, 22 October 1869, CO96/81.
91. Claridge, Vol.I, p.595; Ward, *A History of Ghana*, p.265.
92. Capt. Lees (Accra) to Ussher (CCC), 16 December 1869, CO96/84.
93. Ussher to Kennedy (Freetown), 17 January 1870, No.33 & 11 February 1870, No.37, CO96/84.
94. Geraldo de Lima ("Vosve") to Mr. Addo, 4 April 1870, as Enclosure in Ussher to Kennedy, 6 April 1870, CO96/84.
95. Ussher's Full Report on the Expedition to Kennedy (Freetown), 8 July 1870, No.90, CO96/85. This source is partially reproduced by Metcalfe, *Documents*, pp. 329–330.
96. Ussher's Report of 8 July 1870.
97. "Convention between His Excellency Herbert Taylor Ussher, Administrator of the Gold Coast Settlements, and Domprey, Commanding the Allied Accra and other Forces Defending the Eastern Districts and the Trans-Volta Districts", dated 31 May 1870 at

"Battoh", CO96/85, 1870, Vol.2.
98. Ussher (H.M.S. Eyo on the Volta) to Kennedy (Freetown) 22 June 1870, CO96/85.
99. Capt. Glover (H.M.S. Eyo on the Volta), 22 June 1870, CO96/85.
100. Earl of Kimberley (CO) to Kennedy (Freetown), 1 August 1870, CO96/85; see Metcalfe, Documents No.272 for reproduction.
101. Reade, Winwoode, *African Sketch-Book*, Vol.II, pp. 129-131. I am grateful to the late Mr. Douglas Jones of the School of Oriental and African Studies, University of London, who drew my attention to it.
102. Ussher (H.M.S. Eyo on the Volta) to Kennedy, 22 June 1870, CO96/83. Claridge (Vol.1, p.607) gives the impression that it was the Ga alone who joined with Hausa Soldiers from Lagos to fight the battle. He is wrong on this subject.
103. The Earl of Kimberley (CO) to Kennedy, 1 August 1870, CO96/85.
104. Ussher to Kennedy, 4 July 1870, CO96/85.
105. Kennedy (Freetown) to the Colonial Office, London, 3 August 1870, CO96/85.
106. *Ibid.*
107. Welman, C. W., 1925, *The Native States of the Gold Coast*, Crown Agents, London, p.14, "Abotia" = Abutia.
108. Claridge, Vol. I, p.613 n.
109. AKT: Adoagyiri (1968/9); see also Claridge, Vol.I, p.607.
110. The *African Times*, 24 October 1870; The *West African Herald*, 31 March 1871.
111. Kennedy (Freetown) to Kimberley (CO, London), 3 August 1870, CO96/85.
112. The plaque is carefully preserved at the palace, Adoagyiri, the town which Dompre's people founded when they were forced to abandon Nsawam in the early 20th century. It was shown to the present author in 1969.
113. Ussher to Kennedy, 8 July 1870, CO96/85. This source is reproduced, in parts, by Metcalfe, *Documents*, No.271, pp. 329-330.
114. AKT: Adoagyiri (1968/9).
115. Amenumey, "Geraldo", *THSG*, Vol.IX, p.71f.
116. Ussher (CCC) to Kennedy (Freetown), 5 September 1870 No.117, CO96/85.
117. Ussher to Kennedy 11 October 1870, No.145; also Ussher to Kennedy, 5 & 12 September; and Kennedy to Kimberley, 19 September 1870, CO96/85. The captive missionaries were Ramseyer, his wife, and baby and Kuhne.
118. *West African Herald*, 31 March 1871.
119. *Ibid.*
120. *Ibid.*
121. *Ibid.*
122. *Ibid.*
123. *Ibid.*
124. "The Humble Petition of Quabinah Fuah, King of "Insawaarmeon" (Nsuaem i.e. Oda), For a full text of the Petition, See Appendix A, pp.237-238.
125. Salmon (CCC) to Kennedy (Freetown), 13 & 15 December 1871, CO96/92.
126. Metcalfe, *Documents*, p.746.

Chapter 10

THE AKYEM, ASANTE AND THE BRITISH 1871–1875

Akyem impact on political events in the Gold Coast did not stop with the disturbances in the Lower Volta basin discussed in the previous chapter. It also helped in shaping the cause, course and consequences of the conflicts which engulfed Asante and the British during the period between 1871 and 1875. Hitherto, events during that period have been looked at only in the light of Anglo-Asante relations. For example the Asante invaded the Protectorate in the last days of 1872 and much of 1873. Since then there has been a general tendency among observers, both contemporary and subsequent, to attribute the cause of the invasion solely to the British acquisition of Elmina Castle and town from the Dutch in 1872.[1] But a close and careful study of all available records shows unmistakably that strained relations between the three Akyem states, particularly Abuakwa and Kotoku, on the one hand, and Asante, on the other, were a contributory factor. Nor has it ever been pointed out, much less emphasized that the Akyem immensely contributed to the success of the counter-British invasion of Asante in 1874; or that the effects of these events on the Akyem were as far-reaching as they were on the Asante and the British.

Strained Relations Between Western Akyem and the Asante

That the Dutch cession of Elmina Castle and town to the British in April 1872 was a cause of the Asante invasion of the Protectorate has been well established.[2] Lately it has also been suggested, quite rightly, that fundamentally Asante desire to regain its pre-1831 control over the Protectorate states was another cause.[3] Available evidence shows that the hostile attitude and activities of the Akyem peoples against Asante constituted yet another major cause of the assault. The evidence shows clearly that even without the cession issue the attack on the Protectorate would have taken place all the same, on account of strained Akyem-Asante relations.

Events in the Lower Volta area as discussed in Chapter 9, did not end the tension between Akyem Kotoku and Asante. Rather relations between the two worsened, as both the Western and Eastern Akyem seized Asante subjects they could lay hands on, obviously regarding such seizures as a legitimate sequel to the Volta War. The Akyem Kotoku were the worst hostage-takers. The danger such terrorist activities carried was underlined by the Asantehene himself in January 1871. In a letter to the Administrator protesting the seizure of his subjects by the Akyem Kotoku in particular, the Asantehene fumed thus:

while the Assins were seizing and molesting my people on the main road to Cape Coast the Akims [i.e. the Kotoku] on the other hand seriously were molesting and killing my people. Are the Akims not under Your Excellency's protection? Why are they suffered to sacrifice Ashantees for their custom . . . May I ask my friend why should the Akims murder my subjects for nothing . . . I will ask Your Excellency that regarding the Akims, they now have in their possession more than one hundred of my people. May it please Your Excellency to send . . . for my people [from them] and if they refuse to deliver them, Your Excellency will do me a favour to withdraw your protection from them and I will know how to get my people from those cruel and obstinate people.[4]

There was great justification in the Asantehene's accusation against the Akyem Kotoku. In mid-1871 when in response to the constant Kumasi importunities C. S. Salmon, the Acting Administrator at Cape Coast Castle, appealed to the Kotokuhene to free all Asante subjects he was holding in detention, at least twenty-nine were released.[5]

Besides, the Kotoku appear to have threatened Asante with war. Kotokuhene Kwabena Fua reportedly asked one freed Asante detainees to tell the Kumasi authorities that Kotoku was prepared to fight Asante, apparently in a new theatre of war. This so angered Asantehene Kofi Karikari that he saw no reason why he should not accept the challenge.[6] The tension between the two remained for the rest of 1871, with the Asantehene repeatedly requesting the British Protectorate Administration to ostracize Akyem Kotoku so that Asante could go to war against it without violating its friendship with the British. King Karikari of Asante was all the more bent on war with Kotoku because Kotokuhene Kwabena Fuah reportedly boasted of his ancestry to Frimpon Manso,[7] suggesting that he Kwabena Fuah had a long tradition of warrior kings behind him.

The Asantehene was also concerned with Kotoku claims, allegedly put forward by Kwabena Fuah, that during the reign of Kotokuhene Kofi Agyeman the Asante seized one hundred Kotoku subjects. Kwabena Fuah reportedly threatened to grab any Asante subjects found in the Protectorate as long as those Kotoku citizens remained in the possession of Asante.[8] There also seem to have been border clashes between Kotoku and Asante confederate states like Kokufu.[9] Kumasi must have regarded such clashes as proof of Kotoku hostility and aggression against Asante.

Kotoku may have been guilty of all the above charges. But Asante too was partly to blame for the tension. The Asantehene, especially the war party in Kumasi, according to Acting Administrator Salmon, was looking for a pretext to go to war with the Kotoku in order to make amends to the poor performance of the Asante army against the Kotoku during the Volta War.[10]

So serious was the Kotoku-Asante tension that in December 1871 Salmon felt that it must be resolved diplomatically, and quickly too, if war between the two was to be averted. The solution to the problem lay in both Oda and Kumasi. Salmon wrote to advise the Asantehene to drop all his complaints against the Kotoku as well as other Protectorate states because even if the alleged excesses of the Kotoku and the others were true, they were a direct reaction to similar excesses Asante had also committed against those he was now accusing, deeds which the Asantehene had not cared to denounce and condemn.[11]

It was not enough to take the Asantehene to task and allow the matter to rest there. Salmon invited the Kotokuhene to Cape Coast to assist the Administration in investigations into the Asante charges against him. King Kwabena Fua declined the invitation, pleading that the attitude of Asante was very hostile, which made it necessary for him to be constantly on the alert; if Asante relaxed in its attitude, it would be possible for him to proceed to Cape Coast.[12] That the tension had become quite explosive in 1872 was reflected early that year when the Kotoku ruler declined a second invitation to go to Cape Coast, giving the same excuse.[13]

Events in Asante itself also underscored the explosive nature of the Kotoku-Asante tension. The captive missionaries, Ramseyer and Kuhne, as well as the French trader, Bonnat, also a captive in Kumasi, noted Asante plans to invade the Akyem country, Kotoku especially, as soon as the army under Adu Bofuo returned from Krepi.[14] The people of Asante–Akyem reportedly divulged the secret to the Akyem states. Old allegiances [15] obviously induced the Asante-Akyem to reveal the plan. But they paid dearly for that action: four of their chiefs were dragged to Kumasi, tried and executed.[16]

Kotoku was not the only Akyem state hostile to Asante. Abuakwa, and most likely Bosome too, were unfriendly. With respect to Bosome, it was just not feasible to sit on the fence while Kotoku, so close a neighbour, was at loggerheads with Asante. On geographical grounds alone, if not on kinship ties also, an Asante attack on Oda was bound to affect Soadru.

Strained Abuakwa-Asante Relations

As for Abuakwa its bitterness against Asante surprisingly compared with the Kotoku venom for Kumasi. By 1869 enmity had replaced the entente cordiale which had characterized Abuakwa-Asante relations during 1860–1863. In 1869 Okyenhene Amoako Atta I was described as the most determined foe of Asante.[17] Excruciating British pressure, as shown in the previous chapter, explained the change. Between 1869 and 1872 there was no relaxation in the tension between Kyebi and Kumasi. In 1870 Amoako Atta banned all Abuakwa sales of salt to Kwawu because the latter allegedly resold to Asante.[18] Besides, the Abuakwa, like the Kotoku, were in the habit of seizing, robbing, detaining and killing Asante subjects who fell into their hands. In 1871 the Asantehene appealed directly to the Okyenhene to release all Asante citizens detained in Abuakwa. Amoako Atta is reported to have insolently refused to comply. But for the intervention of Administrator Salmon who, through a delegation of Fante Chiefs, secured the release of the detainees,[19] perhaps Asante would have gone to war over the issue.

In the third week of October 1871 Salmon proudly reported the normalisation of relations between Akyem Abuakwa and Asante.[20] The improvement was, however, more apparent than real. The Abuakwa continued to harass and hound Asante subjects found in Eastern Akyem. In April 1872 when the British formally took possession of Elmina Castle and town, there was an order from the Okyenhene to round up all Asante in Eastern Akyem; the order covered even Muslim visitors because they were thought to be spies for Asante.[21] By the end of 1872 the Akyem Abuakwa were holding over eighty Asante citizens in detention.[22] If Kumasi did not officially remonstrate again against Kyebi it was because the Asante government had by then quietly decided on war as a much better means to get its grievances redressed.

Two issues, however, were constraining Asante from immediately taking the field against the Akyem states and others like the Assin. Negotiations were still going on between them and the British in connection with the release of the white captives – Ramseyer, his wife, fellow missionary Kuhne, and the French trader Bonnat. There was also the safety of the Resident Asante Commissioner for Elmina, Yaw Akyeampon, to consider. The two issues were resolved in the last months of 1872. Yaw Akyeampon, for example, returned to Kumasi in the second week of December 1872. The Asante government now felt free to take to the field. By the last week of December 1872 the advance guard of the Asante army had had skirmishes with the Akyem states.[23] What then were the objectives of Asante?

Asante Objectives

On 29th December 1872 the Asantehene granted an interview to Mr. Joseph Dawson, an agent of the British who had been sent to Kumasi to assist a Mr. Plange, another agent, in negotiating the release of the captive whites. In the course of the interview the Asantehene told Dawson that he would proceed with his war plans unless Dawson obtained satisfaction for Asante. By satisfaction King Karikari meant the British restoring the Akyem states, Assin, Denkyira and Wassa to Asante allegiance; the British executing Denkyirahene Kwakye Afram; and the British returning Elmina Castle and town to Asante loyalty and jurisdiction.[24]

Regarding the restoration of the Akyem and other states, that was not the first time Asante was making the proposal. Earlier in September the Kotoko Council in Kumasi had told Mr. Plange that if the Cape Coast Castle authorities could not pay the ransom fee of £2,000.00 sterling being demanded in return for the release of the white captives, at least Assin would be acceptable in lieu of the cash ransom.[25] This was a deal the Asante themselves knew too well that the British would not entertain. Hence the determination to use force to achieve the same goal.

In September 1872 Ramseyer and his fellow captives noted that left to himself, the Asantehene was essentially inclined towards peace. But "the Chiefs", by which term they clearly meant the Kotoko Council of Kumasi, were likely to force his hand in order to have the opportunity to recover the Asante military prestige which had been tarnished in the Krepi (i.e. the Volta) War.[26] Of course a full recovery of that image was impossible without inflicting a defeat on those directly responsible for that ignominy, namely the Akyem Kotoku. The captive missionaries and the captive French trader, however, were not too sure who the immediate target of the impending attack would be. In their published memoirs Ramseyer and Kuhne asserted that to measure themselves with the white man for once was the secret desire of every Asante. From this premise they postulated the British acquisition of Elmina, both castle and town, as the cause of the 1872–3 Asante invasion of the Protectorate.[27] Douglas Coombs, writing in 1963 set much store by this evidence to stress the cession issue as the sole cause of the invasion.[28]

It is, however, crystal-clear from the evidence adduced above that strained relations between the Akyem states and to a lesser extent other more interior Protectorate peoples on the one hand, and Asante on the other, constituted another cause. On this score alone the attack would still have taken place without the cession issue. The Asantehene himself made this clear in March 1873 when he said that the British returning "Denkerahs, Akims, and Assins" to their former positions as subjects of Asante, and also the British "restoring Elmina Fort and people back in the same manner as they were before will be the only thing to appease [Asante]".[29] The Asante government knew very well that the British would not do such a deal. Hence their decision to go to war to achieve what could not be obtained through diplomacy.

The Invasion

The first salvos of the war were directed against the Akyem in the last days of 1872.[30] But it was in February 1873 that the Akyem as well as others like the Assin and the Denkyira received the full force of the invaders. The column of the Asante army which attacked the Akyem was commanded by Yaw Nantwi, one of the Kumasi Chiefs.[31] No further details of the Akyem sector of the war exist in the records consulted by the present author. Circumstantial evidence however, shows that the Akyem chapter of the war must have been brief. Judging from the attitude of Kwabena Fua, the Kotokuhene, the Akyem peoples had been constantly on the alert. Consequently, they were able to repulse the Nantwi force. This success made it possible for them later to send a force of between 3,000 and 4,500 strong to assist in the defence of Assin and Denkyira.[32] Ultimately, Asante failed to achieve the object of its aggression.

The Sagrenti War: Akyem Role

Worse still for the Kumasi government the attack led to a counter-invasion of Asante itself by the British and local forces in early 1874. The Akyem Abuakwa refer to the counter-attack as the "Groba War".[33] It is, however, popularly known in Gold Coast history as the "Sagrenti War".[34]

The Sagrenti war is well documented from Anglo-Asante perspectives. What is not so well known is the important role all the three Akyem states, Abuakwa, Kotoku and Bosome, played to make the assault on Asante a success for the British and the Protectorate. Of all the states and peoples of the Protectorate, the Akyem cooperated best with the British. They alone constituted two of the four local columns which took part in the attack on Asante. The British adopted the strategy of converging attack so familiar to and popular with the Asante. Sir Garnet Wolseley, at the head of the main British regular forces of about 15,000 was to march directly on Kumasi, using the Cape Coast-Assin road. Captain Dalrymple had the command of the African force comprising Denkyira and Wassa, and was to attack from the middle reaches of river Ofin to the west of Wolseley's column. Captain Butler was given the control of the Akyem Kotoku-Bosome contingent; his line of march was to cross river Birem in Western Akyem and descend on the lacustrine Asante states of Kokofu, Kuntanase and others. Finally Captain Glover, assisted by Captain Sartorius, had the task of organizing a force from amongst the Eastern Districts and attack Asante from the eastern direction. Kyebi, the Abuakwa capital became the main military camp of Captain Glover,[35] and eventually it was the Akyem Abuakwa who made up Glover's column.

In terms of actual action there was a tendency on the part of the British to despise the conduct of the Akyem and thereby play down the important contribution they made to the success of the counter-invasion. For example, they were accused of cowardice, untrustworthiness and despicable desertion.[36] What occasioned these damaging remarks were ironically, their very efforts to make the counter-invasion succeed. The efforts were geared towards a secret understanding between the Akyem forces and the Juaben section of the Asante army at a very crucial stage in the war. The understanding came about in the following manner. The Akyem Abuakwa, led by Captains Glover and Sartorius, fought part of the Asante army at Juaso in Asante-Akyem on 24th January 1874. This sector of the Asante army consisted of that division of Asante-

Akyem under the direct jurisdiction of Kumasi: Bompata, Agogo, Kurofa, Adomfe, Juansa, Amantena and several others in what is now Asante-Akyem south. There was also the other part of Asante-Akyem which was under the control of Juaben which included Odumasi, Konongo, Nyabo, Nnobewam, Agyadeago, Dwease Bomfa and several others. Captains Glover and Sartorius and their forces fought the latter on 31st January 1874. The battles were indecisive and Glover hoped to launch another attack in the first week of February.

Then all of a sudden he became aware that the Abuakwa were not only abandoning the frontline but were actually returning home. A few days later the Kotoku and the Bosome also started to return home. The conduct of all three Akyem forces so shocked their white officers that they described the departures as despicable flights at a critical stage in the war.

In reality the withdrawals were not desertions as such: they were the outcome of a secret disengagement agreement reached between the Akyem and the Juaben. The whites were not let into the secret. Commenting on the so-called desertion, Captain Butler for example had this to say:

> the statements of a blind Asante prisoner [-of-war] taken at Mansuah coupled with a verbal message sent by King [Amoako] Attah of Eastern Akim the purpose of which I was not made aware, did much to induce the disgraceful flight.[37]

The fact was that while the war was raging in the Asante-Akyem area secret contacts and communication were going on concurrently between the Abuakwa leadership and the Juaben.[38] Glover found the contact odd and mind-boggling.[39] A disengagement agreement between the Akyem and the Juaben was the result of the secret correspondence.[40] As the Akyem left for home the Juaben too abandoned their positions along the river Anuru (Anum) in the old Nnobewam neighbourhood and eventually submitted to Glover.[41]

Old friendship apparently played a part in bringing about the disengagement understanding between the Akyem Abuakwa and the Juaben. Both parties obviously recalled the non-belligerency pact agreed between them some thirty-five years back, in 1840, which enjoined them never to take up arms against each other. Agbodeka has also arrived at this conclusion.[42].

It has been suggested that the conduct of the Juaben did much to bring about the defeat of Asante because by refusing to fight on, the Juaben made it possible for a well-planned Asante strategy of resistance to miscarry.[43] The point is valid: the Juaben decision to stop fighting enabled Captain Glover to march through eastern Asante to Kumasi without encountering the slightest opposition again from any quarter. It is therefore reasonable to conclude that Akyem Abuakwa diplomacy in Juaben immensely contributed to the success of the British assault on Asante in 1874. This conclusion, however, does not lose sight of other contributory factors such as internal quarrels among the

Juaben themselves and the centuries old rivalry between Juaben and Kumasi.[44] The Akyem contribution becomes all the more significant when it is considered in relation to the fact that barely a few months later, in July 1874 to be precise, the British felt easy in their mind to formally declare the Gold Coast a British Protectorate.

Impact of the Sagrenti War on the Akyem

Hitherto the effects of the Sagrenti War have been seen only from Asante and British viewpoints. It must be stated emphatically that the impact of the war on the Akyem people was as far-reaching as it was on the Asante and the British.

The most immediate effect on the Akyem was what at first sight looked like a refugee problem for the district. Just before, during and some twelve months after the assault on Asante, large numbers of "refugees" from Asante poured into Eastern and Western Akyem. In March 1874 the Kumasi government described them as secessionists responding to incitement and prompting from the rulers of Akyem Abuakwa and Kotoku.[45] The charge is not wholly correct. Some of the so-called "secessionists" were full-blooded Akyem citizens who had been resident in Asante for several decades. This category had found themselves in Asante either as prisoners-of-war or as part of the annual tribute which the Akyem states used to pay to Kumasi during the pre-1825 period when they were vassal to Asante. They had become either domestic slaves or manumitted slave members of Asante families. Others had gone to Asante in the 1840s, having been drawn there, as pointed out in Chapter 6, by marital and other social connections with the returnee Juaben. As soon as news and rumours circulated that the British were about to invade Asante, hundreds of these Akyem in Asante decided to return home at any cost, and many of them actually did.[46] This class of 'migrants' from Asante cannot be labelled "secessionists". Probably it was for their sake that Strahan's administration in July 1874 resolved not to interfere, much less compel, any of the 'migrants' already in the Akyem district to go back to Asante.[47] To have forced their return would have meant consigning Akyem citizens unwittingly to an alien rule under which some of them would have remained slaves as long as independent Asante existed.

Another group of people who also experienced 'family' reunion in the wake of the British invasion of Asante was a number of inhabitants from the eastern and south-eastern districts of the Asante Kingdom, that is Asante-Akyem. Large numbers of them fled into Akyem. Their status was not as simple as the charge of defection or secession suggests. Nor could the Abuakwa and the Kotoku rulers be wholly blamed for their flight into Akyem. It will be recalled that until the early years of the 1820s much of the district of Asante-Akyem constituted the Kingdom of Akyem Kotoku. Political and military pressures from Asante, as has been demonstrated in several of the preceding chapters, forced the Kotoku ruling dynasty to migrate into Akyem south of river Birem during 1823–1825. Those of the Asante-Akyem who for one reason or another could not emigrate with the ruling dynasty at that time, had looked forward to the day they would reunite with their emigrated kinsmen.[48] The Sagrenti War gave them that opportunity to flee and join their kinsmen, relations, and Kings.

Maxwell, acting as Administrator, was not averse to seeing Asante go on the rocks.[49] But as far as the so-called "secessionists" from Asante-Akyem were concerned, he did try to persuade them to go back to their country. In May 1874 he appointed Dr. Skipton Gouldsbury as a Special Commissioner for Akyem and instructed him to go and ask the Asante-Akyem refugees to return home; he was also to ask Kings Amoako Atta and Kwabena Fua not to incite any more defections either from Asante-Akyem or any other part of Asante, as alleged by the Asantehene.[50] Gouldsbury met the bulk of these in Akyem Kotoku, especially Oda, the capital. When he informed them of the Governor's request, they admitted that they had indeed

> escaped from Ashantee during the [British] expedition, but they had returned to their families in Akyem, and that their recent escape was the realization of a hope which had been handed down to them from their fathers and which had grown with their growth and strengthened with their strength.[51]

Therefore, they had no intention to go back to 'Asante-Akyem', even if the Cape Coast government forced them.[52]

Given the historical background of Asante-Akyem, the accuracy of Dr. Gouldsbury's report should not be doubted. By fleeing into Akyem, this group of "refugees" was not merely trying to substitute British protection for Asante rule. Many if not all of them, were attempting to reunite with relatives in Akyem from whom they had been separated for upwards of half a century. To them the fact of coming under British authority was only incidental to the realization of this aspiration of 'family' reunion. Whatever adverse effect their emigration to Akyem was to have on Asante was no concern of theirs. They did not regard themselves as secessionists acting at the instigation of the Akyem rulers.

The Asantehene's charge against the Akyem rulers, especially the Okyenhene, was, to a considerable extent, justifiable in the case of Kwawu. Since 1742 the Kwawu had remained very loyal to Asante. They were perhaps the only people in the south who did not make use of the 1824–1831 upheavals to recover their independence from Asante. From 1874 the Kwawu, in the light of the British and local allied victory in the Sagrenti war, were obliged to review their links with Asante. They decided to secede and they actually did after February 1874.

According to their own tradition collected by the Basel missionary W. Perregaux, soon after the British had signed the Treaty of Fomena with Asante in February 1874 the Kwawu unilaterally severed their subjection to Kumasi.[53] To emphasize the secession they killed Antwi Akomea, then the Resident Asante Commissioner for Kwawu, and forty of his staff.[54]

The tradition accuses Okyenhene Amoako Atta I as being accessory to the slaughter in Kwawu because when the property of the unlucky Resident Commissioner were distributed, the Okyenhene received "a sword with a golden handle".[55] Besides, rumour had it in 1875 that on declaring their independence the Kwawu sent some money to the Kyebi monarchy in order that the Okyenhene might lobby the Protectorate government for Kwawu's admission into the Gold Coast.[56] Up to the end of 1875 the Abuakwa had not been able to do this for the Kwawu; the Kyebi people became worried because they feared that the Kwawu might demand the money back.[57] Giving his reason for parting ways with Asante, Akuamoa, the Kwawuhene, in 1875 said: "I and my land have suffered much from Karikari and I have decided to put myself under the protection of the white man".[58] But it is clear from the evidence above that incitement from the Kyebi monarchy was part of the reason. In a way the Kyebi court had an accomplice in the Basel Mission in Abuakwa.

The Basel missionaries based at Kyebi were equally supportive of the secession move in Kwawu. Led by the Rev. David Asante, the Basel missionaries here took advantage of the Kumasi defeat in the Sagrenti War, to move into Kwawu where they established a Mission Station at Abetifi in 1875-1876. From that time onwards the missionaries encouraged the secession move by pleading with the British Protectorate government to annex Kwawu. Their main, if not the sole, reason was that if Kwawu became subject to Asante again, the Asantehene was as unlikely to let missionaries work in Abetifi as in Kumasi.[59] Though the annexation eventually occurred in 1888, since May 1874 Kwawu had always been there for the taking by the British because from 1875 the Abuakwa and the Basel missionaries never stopped urging the Kwawu to persevere in their secession move.

Abuakwa Subversion in Juaben

Abuakwa subversion against Asante was most conspicuous in Juaben. After the withdrawal of the British and their local allied forces from Asante in early 1874, the Akyem rulers, particularly Abuakwa and Kotoku, incited the Juaben to secede from the Asante polity.[60] The secession move may well have been agreed upon between the Juaben and the Akyem Abuakwa leaders during the disengagement negotiations in January and February, though no direct evidence has been found to support this assertion. The British too are said to have encouraged the Juaben to secede.[61] At any rate after the British pullout from Asante, several of the Juaben arrived in Eastern Akyem: these openly spoke of Juaben plans to secede from Asante.[62]

The government in Kumasi got wind of the secession move and resolved to prevent its realization. In late October and early November, 1874 Kumasi forces invaded Juaben. Immediately after the outbreak of the Civil war in Asante, Okyenhene Amoako Atta I, informed the Protectorate government that his kingdom was being threatened with an attack from Asante; the government should therefore supply him with arms and ammunition to enable him to defend his territory. Initially the government sent the war materials but almost immediately discovered that the intention of the Okyenhene was to go and lend military support to the Juaben. Though the Strahan administration was not unaverse to the scenario of an Asante disintegration, it despatched troops to Akyem Abuakwa to prevent Amoako Atta from carrying out his plans.[63] This measure was necessary to take because Kumasi could cite Akyem involvement in the Asante Civil War as aggression from the Protectorate and therefore a violation of the Fomena Treaty of Peace signed on 13 February 1874. The Juaben were defeated in the Civil War.

The outcome of the Asante Civil War had far-reaching consequences for the Akyem country and its peoples. The district was immediately saddled with a refugee problem. Large numbers of the Juaben who managed to escape capture or death, led by their Chief, Asafo Agyei, fled to Eastern Akyem for asylum.[64] Okyenhene Amoako Atta not only welcomed the hard-pressed Asafo Agyei and his subjects but was also prepared to lend them both moral and material support in further armed conflict with Kumasi. Aside from allowing the Juaben to use Abuakwa as a launching pad, the Okyenhene, encouraged by the Okuapemhene and the Ga rulers, assisted the Juaben to build up arms caches in several parts of the Eastern Districts in anticipation of further war with Kumasi.[65] The Protectorate government learned about these preparations and severely reprimanded Amoako Atta and the other Chiefs for supporting and actually participating in the hostile moves of the refugee Juaben.[66]

The strictures symbolized a change in local British policy towards Asante. Until the outcome of the Kumasi-Juaben war, this policy had had the disintegration of Asante as the ultimate goal. For example it had earlier encouraged the secession of Adanse from Asante. But with the success of Kumasi over Juaben, that policy was no longer tenable, because the Kumasi victory was indicative of Asante resilience which, if not handled with care, might lead to a new armed clash with that power. The British apparently did not have the heart for another war with Asante, so soon after Sagrenti.

The Founding of New Juaben

The British government was, however, prepared to allow Asafo Agyei and his subjects to remain in the Gold Coast Protectorate for as long as they wished. To facilitate the residence of the Juaben refugees the government appealed to the Okyenhene to find them a place for settlement. In view of their own support for the refugees, the Akyem Abuakwa were morally bound to cooperate in the matter of settling them. In late 1875, the Abuakwa made a grant of land between Kukurantumi and the Ahabante area of Akuapem to enable the Juaben refugees to settle there.[67]

The grant of land made it possible for the displaced people from Juaben to found, three years later, a new state which they called New Juaben, with its capital at Koforidua. Thus New Juaben State today is a living testimony of the upheavals which engulfed the Gold Coast Protectorate and Asante in the first half of the 1870s, disturbances in which all the three Akyem states played a major role.

Summary

Between the last days of 1872 and 1873 Asante invaded the Protectorate. Opinion then and later was that the Dutch cession of Elmina Castle and town to the British in early 1872 was the sole cause of the assault. Now it is clear that strained relations between the Akyem peoples and Asante dating back immediately to 1871 and remotely to the 1860s constituted another cause: that on that account alone the invasion would have taken place with or without the cession. Perhaps it was on that score only that the Akyem Abuakwa, Kotoku and Bosome, of all the Protectorate peoples, cooperated best with the British in the counter-invasion of Asante itself in 1874. The wars had very far-reaching effects on the Akyem district and its inhabitants, the most enduring being the founding of the New Juaben State in Akyem Abuakwa.

NOTES AND REFERENCES

1. Brackenbury, H. 1874, *The Ashanti War*, Edinburgh, London, Vol.I, Chapter 2; Ramseyer, F. A. & Kuhne, J., *Four Years in Ashantee*, James Nibbet & Co. Ltd., London, Chapter XXV; Ellis, A. B., 1893, *A History of the Gold Coast of West Africa*, Negro University Press, New York, p.283; Claridge, W. W., 1915, *A History of the Gold Coast and Ashanti*, Frank Cass & Co. Ltd., London, Vol.II, pp. 3–4; Casely Hayford, J. E., 1870, (1970 Ed.), *Gold Coast Native Institutions*, Sweet Maxwell, London, pp. 157 & 242; Balmer, Rev. W. T., 1926, *A History of the Akan Peoples of*

the Gold Coast, London & Cape Coast, p.154; Ward, W. E. F., (Ed.), 1969, *A History of Ghana*, George Allen & Unwin Ltd., London, p.269; Kimble, D., 1963., *A Political History of Ghana*, Oxford University Press, Oxford, p.270; Coombs, D., 1963, *The Gold Coast, Britain and the Netherlands*, Oxford University Press, Oxford, pp. 121–127; Hargreaves, J. D., 1963, *Prelude to the Partition of West Africa*, Macmillan, London, p.167; Agbodeka, F., 1971, *African Politics and British Policy in the Gold Coast 1868–1900*, Longman, London, pp. 44–47; Wilks, I., 1975, *Asante in the Nineteenth Century*, Cambridge University Press, Cambridge, pp. 230–235.
2. *Ibid.*
3. Boahen, A. A., 1976, "Politics in Ghana, 1800–1874", in Ajayi, J. F. A. & Crowder, M., *History of West Africa*, Vol.Two, p.200, Longman, London.
4. H. M. Kofi Karikari, Asantehene, to Ussher (CCC), 31 January 1871; Ussher to Kennedy (Freetown), 17 March 1871, Confidential, CO96/87.
5. Salmon (CCC) to Kennedy (Freetown), 3 August 1871, No.94, CO96/89.
6. Asantehene to Ussher, 31 January 1871, CO96/87.
7. Asantehene to Salmon, 1 September; Crawford (Kumasi) to Salmon, captioned "Minute Details of Interview with H. M. King of Ashantee", dated 7 August 1871, CO96/89. Frimpon Manso was a powerful Kotokuhene who reigned from 1717 to 1740.
8. Salmon (citing the Asantehene) to Kennedy, 31 October 1871, No.124, CO96/89.
9. Salmon (CCC) to Kennedy (Freetown), 21 December 1871, printed in British Parliamentary Papers (Br.P.P.) 1873, Vol.XLIX.
10. Salmon to Kennedy, 31 October 1871, No.124, CO96/89.
11. Salmon to the Asantehene, 6 December; Salmon to John Owusu Ansa (Kumasi), 7 December 1871, CO96/89.
12. Report of Mr. Bentsil on a mission to Nsuaem (Oda), cited in Salmon to Kennedy, 7 December 1871, No.140, CO96/92.
13. Kotokuhene to Salmon, dated "Akim Daa", January 1872, CO96/92.
14. Ramseyer & Kuhne, *Four Years*, p.132. The missionaries wrongly called the first name of the Kotokuhene "Kofi" instead of Kwabena.
15. Up to 1825 the Kotokuhene had been the overlord of much, if not all, of Asante-Akyem, Cf. Chapter 5 for details.
16. Ramseyer & Kuhne, *Four Years*, p.183; Ellis (1893), p.280.
17. Administrator Simpson (Accra) to Kennedy (Freetown), 22 March 1869, CO96/79.
18. David Asante (Begoro) to Widman (Akuropon-Akuapem), 7 March 1870, No Africa 9; Shrenk (Accra) to Basel, 26 August 1870, No Christiansborg, 31a, BMA-PJA.
19. Salmon to Kennedy, 3 October 1871, No.108, CO96/89.
20. Salmon to Kennedy, 19 October 1871, No.119, CO96/89.
21. Lodholtz (Kyebi) to Basel, 13 April 1872, No.153, BMA-PJA.
22. Dr. Fox (Accra) to CCC, 16 January 1874; Administrator Harley's minutes to the Fox Report, 24 January; Harley to the Earl of Kimberley, 10 April 1874, all printed in Br.PP: 1874, Vol.XLVI.
23. Harley to the Asantehene, 24 December 1872; Okyenhene Amoako Atta I to Harley, 11 January 1873, Br.PP: Papers Relating to the Ashantee Invasion, pp. 388–389.
24. Dawson (Kumasi) to CCC, 29 December 1872, Br.PP, Vol.49 p.878.
25. Plange (Kumasi) to CCC, 3 September 1872, Br.PP, Vol. LXLIX, p.614.
26. Kuhne & Ramseyer (Kumasi) to Pope Hennessy (CCC), 3 September 1872, Br.PP, Vol.XLIX, p.614.
27. Ramseyer & Kuhne, *Four Years*, p.205.

28. Coombs, *The Gold Coast*, p.124.
29. Asantehene to Harley (CCC), 20 March 1873, Br.PP: Further Correspondence Respecting the Ashantee Invasion, p.804.
30. Harley to Asantehene, 28 December 1872; Okyenhene Amoako Atta I to Harley, 11 January 1873, Br.PP: Papers Relating, pp. 388-389.
31. Report of Dr. Rowe to Harley, 7 February 1873, as sub-Enclosure No.10, in Pope Hennessey to Kimberley, 10 February 1873, No.135; Evidence of Kwadwo Mensah before Foster, as sub-Enclosure No.6 of Enclosure No.3, in Harley to Kimberley, 14 March 1873, Br.PP: Papers Relating.
32. Harley (CCC) to Kimberley, 8 April 1873 No.204, Br.PP: Papers Relating; David Asante (Kyebi) to Basel, 9 July 1873, No. Akim 21, BMA-PJA.
33. "Groba" is the Akan corruption of Glover, the name of the British Captain who commanded the Eastern Akyem forces.
34. "Sagrenti" is the Akan corruption of "Sir Garnet", the title and first name of Wolseley who had the overall command of the assault on Asante.
35. David Asante's Report on the Basel Mission in Akyem for the Year 1874 dd. 11 January 1875, No.218, BMA-PJA.
36. Wolseley (Fomena, in Adanse) to Kimberley, 26 January 1874, Br.PP: Latest Despatches of Sir Garnet Wolseley, No.6 Series; Glover (Obogu in Asante-Akyem) to Wolseley 21 & 28 January and 4 February 1874, Br.PP: Further Correspondence; Butler, *Akimfoo: A History of a Failure*, London, 1874, pp. 281-282.
37. Butler (Trebe, in Kokofu, Asante) to Wolseley, 2 February 1874, Br.PP: Further Correspondence.
38. Brackenbury, *The Ashantee War*, Vol.II, p.275.
39. Stanley, H. M., 1875, *Coomasie and Magdala*, Sampson, Low & Marston, London, p.183; Agbodeka, *African Politics*, p.54.
40. Glover to Wolseley, 4 February 1874, Br.PP; Ellis, *A History of the Gold Coast*, p.345; Agbodeka, *African Politics*, p.54.
41. Glover ("Essiemampon") to Wolseley, 10 February 1874, in Stanley, *Coomasie*, p.251, Brackenbury, *The Ashantee War*, Vol.II, p.264. "Essiemampon" is clearly Asieninpon, a town a few kilometers to south-east of Kumasi.
42. Agbodeka, *African Politics*, p.54.
43. *Ibid*.
44. I am grateful to Professor Adu Boahen, formerly of the History Department, University of Ghana, who drew my attention to these issues.
45. The Asantehene, cited in Governor Maxwell to Kimberley (CO), 19 March 1874, Br.PP: Further Correspondence.
46. Missionary Lodholtz's Report on the Basel Mission Station at Kyebi for the 1st Quarter of 1873, dd.29 April 1873, No. Akim 20, BMA-PJA; AAT: Begoro, Kwaben, Pamen & Ekoso (1925/6).
47. Governor Strahan (CCC) to Carnavon (CO), 3 July 1874, Br.PP: Further Correspondence.
48. Report of Dr. S. Gouldsbury on his mission to Akyem in May–June 1874, dated Elmina Castle, 12 July 1874, CO96/112; As-AkT: Bompata, (1968/9).
49. Maxwell to Kimberley, 19 March 1874, Br.PP: Further Correspondence: Maxwell to Okyenhene Amoako Atta I, 31 March 1874, ADM 1/7/10, cited by Addo-Fening, "The Background to the Deportation of King Asafo Agyei", *THSG*, Vol.XIV, Part 2, 1973, p.216, n.17.
50. Report of Dr. Gouldsbury on his mission to Akyem, 12 July 1876, CO96/112.

51. *Ibid.*
52. *Ibid.*
53. Perregaux, W., "A Few Notes on Kwahu (Quahoe a Territory in the Gold Coast Colony, West Africa)", in Journal of African Society (*JAS*), Vol.II, No.8, 1902-3, pp. 448-9.
54. Perregaux, *Op. cit.*, p.448.
55. *Ibid.*
56. Ramseyer, Werner and Weimer (Kyebi) to Basel, 3 January 1876, No.238, BMA-PJA.
57. *Ibid.*
58. David Asante's 1st Quarterly Report on the Kyebi Mission Station for Year 1875 and his mission to Kwawu, dd.29 April 1875, No.247, BMA-PJA.
59. Ramseyer, Werner & Weiner (Kyebi) to Basel, 3 January 1876, No.238, BMA-PJA.
60. The allegation by the Asantehene, cited in Maxwell to Kimberley, 19 March 1874, Br.PP: Further Correspondence, Cf. also Juaben Tradition, in Rattray, R. S., 1929, *Ashanti Law and Constitution*, Oxford University Press, Oxford, p.175.
61. Agbodeka, *African Politics*, pp.78-105.
62. David Asante (Kyebi) to Basel n.d. No.215, BMA-PJA: also "The History of New Juaben and the relations between the Chiefs" (Enclosure) in ADM IV 1437, cited by Addo-Fening, "The background to the deportation of King Asafo Agyei and the foundation of New Dwaben", in *THSG*, Vol.XIV, No.2 (1973), p.217.
63. Strahan to Carnavon, 6 & 13 November 1875; Colonial Office Minutes on Strahan's 6th November Despatch dd.14 December 1875, CO96/116; Agbodeka, *African Politics*, p.108.
64. Adolf Mohr (Begoro) to Basel, 26 December 1875, No.255, BMA-PJA.
65. Strahan (CCC) to Carnavon, 16 November 1875, CO96/116.
66. Agbodeka, *African Politics*, pp. 88 & 108.
67. Ramseyer, Werner & Weimer (Kyebi) to Basel, 3 January 1876, No.238, BMAPJA.

Chapter 11

CONCLUSION

This study has examined relations between the three Akyem states and their neighbours, intra-Akyem affairs as well as Akyem relations with the European trading presence in the Gold Coast in the eighteenth and nineteenth centuries.

The survey started with a cursory look at the origins and history of the states up to the end of the seventeenth century. From the brief glance certain tentative conclusions can be drawn:

(i) that the nuclei of Abuakwa and Kotoku as centralized states in the Akyem country were founded in the sixteenth century but fortified in the middle years of the seventeenth century;
(ii) that founders and fortifiers were immigrants from Adanse;
(iii) that Bosome was founded in the first decade of the eighteenth century by migrants from Asante.

The evidence also shows that the Akyem country up to the early 1820s included present-day Asante-Akyem and that it was here that Kotoku before the 1820s was located. Abuakwa was in the Birem basin.

During the last quarter of the seventeenth century ambition to achieve hegemony over others and the desire to gain easy and unhindered access to the European trade on the coast plunged both Abuakwa and Kotoku into conflicts with especially their southern neighbours some of whom were pursuing similar objectives.

The conflicts continued with greater intensity and frequency in subsequent centuries. During the first twenty-eight years of the eighteenth century, the two goals eluded Abuakwa and Kotoku largely because of their inability to cooperate in exerting sustained military pressures on the southern neighbours. One reason for the lack of cooperation was Kotoku's preoccupation with Asante, a concern justified by the outbreak of a major war between the two in 1717–1718.

By 1728 Asante pressure on Kotoku had eased substantially. Consequently, Kotoku was able to join Abuakwa in defeating Akwamu in 1729–1730 and Agona in 1738. The impact of the victory over Akwamu was particularly tremendous, even revolutionary. Firstly, the defeated Akwamu ruling lineage abandoned their original home and empire west of the Volta and fled to lower trans-Volta where they founded the Akwamu state as we know it today. Secondly, Abuakwa absorbed into its states complex the pre-1729

Akwamu territory which included such places as Asamankese, Akwatia, Tafo. Kyebi, Adeisu and Adoagyiri. Thirdly, an Abuakwa sub-Chief called Ofori Kuma organized the Akuapem, former subjects of Akwamu, into a centralized state on the Akan model. Fourthly and finally, the Abuakwa and the Kotoku emerged as coastal powers as they took over from the defeated Akwamu an empire which not only included Kamana, Kwawu and Akuapem but also embraced the Ga and the Adangbe.

Success created its own peculiar problems for the two states. Out of jealousy and necessity Asante attacked and defeated Abuakwa and Kotoku in 1742-1744. The defeat led to the collapse of the Akyem empire. It also forced Kotoku to acknowledge Asante supremacy in 1744. In contrast Abuakwa resisted Asante for the next forty years. During that four-decade period, Asante never gained easy access to the European trade on the eastern sector of the Gold Coast. It was not until after 1783 when Abuakwa submitted, that all other states and peoples in eastern Gold Coast west of the Volta finally acknowledged the overlordship of Asante.

Between 1784 and 1807 Abuakwa and Kotoku remained loyally subject to Asante because they lacked daring and dynamic leaders who could kick against Asante power. The situation changed as from 1807 when Atta Owusu became the King of Abuakwa. Between 1810 and 1811, he launched a powerful but a shortlived liberation movement against Asante. Kotokuhene Kwadwo Kuma continued the struggle from 1812. The movement finally collapsed in 1816 when Asante defeated Kuma and his Abuakwa and Akuapem allies, and forced all three to return to their vassal status.

All this time the position of Bosome had been nebulous. Up to 1816 not much had been heard of it. However, after 1818 Bosome, in terms of Gold Coast politics, began to tick. For example in the early 1820s migrants led by Koragye Ampaw fleeing the anger of Kumasi arrived to increase the population of Bosome as well as hurl it into the main-stream of Gold Coast politics which at this stage was aimed at freeing states and peoples south of Asante from the Kumasi yoke. By the early 1820s an Anglo-Danish-led Southern Alliance, of which all three Akyem peoples were members, had formed against Asante. The alliance defeated Asante in 1826. By virtue of the Peace Treaty of 1831 all the Akyem states, like almost all other southern peoples, regained their independence.

The pre-1831 upheavals and violent developments in Asante after that year obliged the Akyem peoples to go through other traumatic experiences. For example the Kotoku in 1825 had emigrated from their ancestral home in what is now Asante-Akyem into Abuakwa. They refused to return thither in spite of the 1831 Peace Treaty. From the 1830s they became glorified refugees in eastern Akyem Abuakwa. The refugee problem increased for Abuakwa in 1832 when the ruling lineage of Juaben with a section of their subjects sought asylum in Abuakwa. The Juaben remained till 1840-1841 when they finally returned to their country.

By contrast the Kotoku stayed put even though their residence in Eastern Akyem was, on the whole, not a happy experience. Tension developed between them and their Abuakwa hosts, exploding into hot war in 1860. To minimise, if not eliminate the tension, the Kotoku leadership emigrated from Eastern to Western Akyem that very year and there founded a new capital, initially called Nsuaem but later changed to Oda. The emigration to Western Akyem brought the Kotoku no immediate peace. For one thing, the Abuakwa monarchy continued to dispute the site on which they settled, claiming in 1863 that it was within its jurisdiction. It was not until 1870 when, by the Akaanten Settlement, peace was restored between Abuakwa and Kotoku. For another, relations between them and the Bosome deteriorated as the years passed by.

But by far the greatest crisis they encountered in Western Akyem was war with Asante in 1863. With allied support from Bosome, Agona and Gomoa the Kotoku weathered the storm, to the discomfiture of the Asante aggressors and the unspoken delight of the British Protectorate Administration of the Gold Coast. So impressed were the British with the Kotoku performance against Asante in 1863 that for the first time in their long contact with the Gold Coast the British thought of invading Asante itself. Had the British Home Government allowed it, the British would have invaded Asante as early as the early 1860s. Faced with the refusal of the British Home Government, the Protectorate Administration had to come to some form of peace accommodation with Asante in 1866. By then the Lower Volta basin had already emerged as the next theatre of war between Kotoku (supported by the other Akyem peoples) and Asante. From 1865 trade interests and traditional as well as ethnic animosities threw the basin into a turmoil which eventually involved not only the various peoples in the area but also the Kotoku, Asante, the Ga and the British. The conflict resulted in the emergence of two hostile alliances, one led by the Kotoku, the other by Asante. Wars were fought between 1866 and 1869 and the Asante-led alliance suffered considerably, even though the Kotoku lost their great warrior chief, Dompre, through what seems to have been an assassination plot.

The Lower Volta violence dovetailed into a breakdown in 1870 of the cordial relations between the Kotoku of Nsawam and the Ga who up to 1869 had been allies and partners in the Volta upheavals. As a result of the hostilities spanning 1860-1870 all three Akyem peoples cultivated a culture of hostage-taking directed solely against Asante, regarding this activity as a legitimate sequel to the wars. Just as hostage-taking of the Akyem had been the immediate cause of the 1863 Asante invasion of the Protectorate, so it

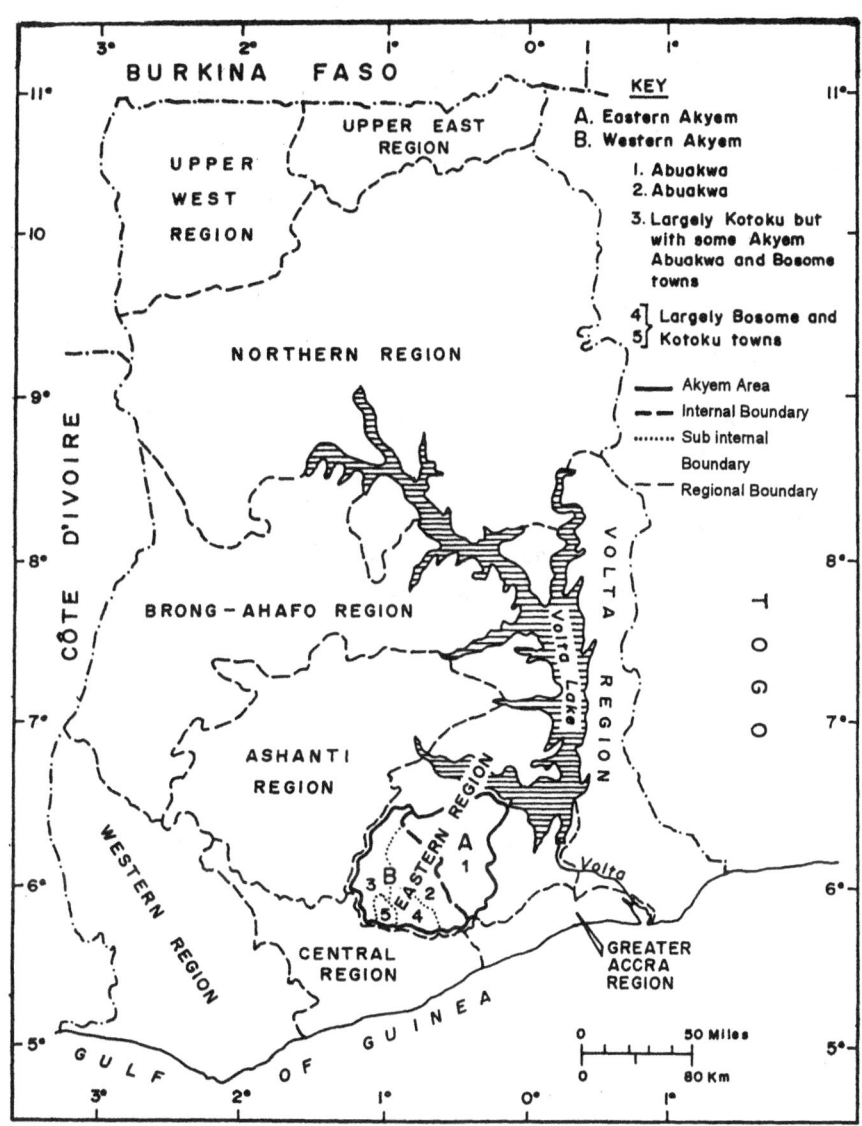

Fig. 7: Modern Ghana showing the Akyem Area

combined with one or two other factors to bring about the 1872–1873 Asante assault on the Protectorate. Unfortunately, for the authorities in Kumasi, that aggression produced the counter-British attack on Asante itself in 1874, the Sagrenti War. The Akyem played a major role to make the attack on Asante a success. First, they alone provided two of the four indigenous columns which assisted the British. Second, their successful diplomacy in Juaben went a long way to weakening Asante's resistance. The impact of Sagrenti on the Akyem was as far-reaching as it was on the British Protecting Power and Asante. Of the several effects the war had on the Akyem perhaps the most enduring was the founding, in and after 1875, of the New Juaben State, with Koforidua as its capital, on the soil of Akyem Abuakwa.

Finally the study reveals graphically that commotion, flux and change characterized much of the Gold Coast during the seventeenth, eighteenth and nineteenth centuries. As a result of the numerous inter-state, inter-ethnic wars, countless individuals, families and sometimes whole communities found themselves not only uprooted but also transplanted from one part of the Gold Coast to another. Herein seems to lie an explanation for the existence today of people of the same ethnic origin living in different parts of the country. How many of the uprooted found their way across the Atlantic Ocean as servile hands in the Americas and the Carribean islands only goodness knows.

APPENDICES

APPENDIX A

Sir,

"THE HUMBLE PETITION OF QUABINA FUAH, KING OF INSWAR-MOON AND ITS DEFENDENCIES SHOWETH: (Unedited)

The ancestors of your humble petitioner were originally subjects of the Kings of Ashantees but through tyranny and oppression of his conduct towards your humble petitioner's ancestors, fought the King of Ashantees in their way to Akim, and declare independence in the year 1816, in the reign of your humble petitioner's ancestor Kojo Coomah, King of Geddam (now Inswar-moon) from Ashantee crown, previous to the arrival of Sir Charles MacArthy.

He was succeeded by Agiman, your humble petitioner's predecessor from the year 1816 to the present time, your humble petitioner's Government, neither your humble petitioner offended Your Excellency since your humble petitioner's ancestors sworn allegiance to the British Government – and they having become protectorate to the British Government.

The Ashantees molested Your humble petitioner's subjects daily. That your humble petitioner in exercise and obedience to Your Excellency's command, humbly does represent to Your Excellency the grief and sorrow your humble petitioner has been undergone for several months since your humble petitioner's five principals of his captains, viz:

Quamin Afultin	
Kojo Aboki	
Quamin Dumprey (Jnr.)	Cape Coast Jail
Obin Dalco	
Quasi Boar	Accra Jail

were sentenced to imprisonment for such lines of misconduct towards your humble petitioner's protectors (the British Government) for crimes having been committed by them of which crimes judgement preferred against them, of misconducts and misdoings, and were sentenced to imprisonment for several years.

Your humble petitioner is aware of the crimes they have sinned against our British Government of which your humble petitioner is a loyal subject – although they deserved punishment greater than the present ones, but Her Majesty's throne is a throne of mercy for the offender and the wicked, and Your Excellency's Government is a seat of mercy and justice, holding the one on Your Excellency's right hand for pardoning offences of the wicked, and the left hand for punishment of the wickedness of the times for disobedience.

Your humble petitioner crave earnestly and entreats Your Excellency to pardon and forgive them (the prisoners) for their first offence, and bind them for future obedience of which your humble petitioner doubt not that they will commit such lines of misconducts and more, as their crimes will be a warning to your petitioner's subjects for the future. Your humble petitioner begs to entreat your Excellency for release. Your humble petitioner and his chiefs humbly bring Your Excellency's observation that the prisoners were imprisoned on account of refusing summons from the Judicial Assessor's Court, but no other guilty beside their disobedience of refusing summons.

Your humble petitioner and his chiefs had given up the Ashantee captives in his district, by your Excellency's command and begs humbly to release your humble petitioner's captains from imprisonment.

And as in duty bounds your humble petitioner and his chiefs ever pray.

(Sd) Qquabina Fuah
King of Inswarmoon

Chiefs Marks:

Quabina X Essimen, Chief of Yinasi
Quamin X Abanqua, Chief of Formasi
Quacoe X Abrooqua, Chief of Insooasoo
Quabina X Domprey, Chief of Imoosasoo
Quamin X Eyimpay, Chief of Abanasi
Quabina X Apia Agey, Chief of Bancamee
Acqusi X Dalco, Chief of Mansu
Amba X Coomah, Queen of Swaidol
Quabina X Ampartah Chum of Asuboah
Kojo X Moley, Chief of Inswarmoon
Yaw X Dumprey, Chief of Inswarmoon
Acquaasi X Manu, Chief of Inswarmoon
Acquaasi X Enchee, Chief of Inswarmoon
Cofee X Amanee, Chief of Inswarmoon
Quacoo X Toodah, Chief of Inswarmoon
Quamin X Accon Ennee, Chief of Inswar-moon
Cofee X Tettey, Chief of Inswar-moon
Cofee X Kessi (interpreter)
Quabina X Saikee, Chief of Inswar-moon
Acquaasi X Effom, Chief of Inswar-moon
Cofee X Asail, Chief of Inswarmoon

Inswar-moon, 17 July, 1871

True copy
(Sd) Salmon
    (Ag. Administrator)

Source: C.O.96/88, 1871 Vol.2, PRO, London

APPENDIX B

ABUAKWA RULERS OF THE EIGHTEENTH AND NINETEENTH CENTURIES

TRADITIONAL

(According to Reindorf & Danquah)

1. Ofori Panin, c.1733
2. Baa Kwante, died 1742
3. Pobi (1743)
4. Twum Ampoforo (deposed and killed)
5. Obirikorane, died 1770
6. Apraku, died 1770
7. Attah Wusu Yiakosan, died 1811
8. Asare Bediako, suicide, 1811
9. Kofi Asante, died 1811
10. Twum II
11. Queen Dokua (reigned from 1817)
12. Atta Panin
13. Atta Obiwon, died 1866
14. Amoako Atta I, 1866–1888
15. Amoako Atta II, 1888–1911

REVISED

(In the light of Euro. sources)

1. Ofori [Panin] i.e. 1704–1727.
2. Baa Kwante, 1727–1742.
3. Pobi, 1742–1765.
4. Obirikoran 1765–1784
5. Ampofo or Ampofro [Twum] 1784–1794
6. Apraku, 1794–1807
7. Atta Owusu, 1807–1811
8. Asare Bediako 1811 (Suicide)
9. Kofi Asante, 1811–1816
10. Dokuwa or Dokuaa, 1817–1842 (abdicated 1842, died 1856)
11. Atta Panin, 1842–1858
12. Atta Obiwom (or Buom) 1858–1867.
13. Amoako Atta I, 1867–1887
14. Amoako Atta II, 1887–

APPENDIX C

KOTOKU KING LIST

(According to Ex-Kotokuhene Frimpon Manso III)

NAME	REMARKS IN THE LIGHT OF REINDORF AND CONTEMPORARY EUROPEAN SOURCES
1. Yarawere	
2. Boadi Nianim	
3. Akrofi Brempon	Left Adanse with some of his subjects and eventually settled in what is Asante-Akyem today.
4. Asiedu Apenten	May have been the Kotokuhene killed in war with Asante in 1701.

5.	Ofosuhene Apenten	Beginning of reign possibly 1701; killed in war with Asante in 1717.
6.	Frimpon Manso	Evidence from Contemporary European sources suggests him to have reigned from 1717 to 1740.
7.	Ampem	
8.	Kwahene Broni	
9.	Gyamarankum	
10.	Karikari Apau or Apaw	Succeeded Frimpon Manso; was killed in war with Asante in 1742, according to contemporary European sources.
11.	Opoku	
12.	Kwakye Adeyefe	
13.	Kwadwo Kuma	Reigned from 1812 to 1816 when he got killed in war with Asante.
14.	Afrifah Akwada	
15.	(Aboatendomhene as Regent)	
16.	Kofi Agyeman	Enstooled 1825; died 1867
17.	Kwaben Fua	Successor to Agyeman; Captain Butler met him in person during the Sagrenti War of 1874.
18	Atta Fua I	

APPENDIX D

BOSOME RULERS TO c.1876: TRADITIONAL LIST[1]

1. Mpim
2. Ntiamoa Panin
3. Boampadu
4. Oware Agyekum
5. Kesse Taa
6. Ntow Kroko
7. Bosompem Ntow
8. Akrasi Panin
9. Koragye Ampaw
10. Kwame Marfo
11. Amma Amoakoaa[2]
12. Kofi Ahenkora[3]

---

1. The virtual absence of contemporary or even near contemporary sources on this state has not made it possible to attempt a close check on the traditional list. But even as it stands, the list cannot be said to be complete, judging from the term 'Panin' attached to Ntiamoa and Akrasi. Since the term means First, clearly there were later Ntiamoas and Akrasis.

2. She was the Bosomehene at least in the early 1860s. Captain des Ruvignes met her at Soadru in 1860 and Captains Brownwell and Williams also met her and Kotokuhene Kofi Agyeman during the Asante invasion of Western Akyem in 1863.

3. He was the Bosomehene in at least 1871. Captain Butler met him during the Sagrenti War.

BIBLIOGRAPHY

CONTEMPORARY SOURCES: ARCHIVAL

A. BRITISH: PUBLIC RECORD OFFICE, LONDON

(i)   T 70/ Series:
T 70/50   Letters from Africa, 1685–1698
    51   Letters from Africa, 1698–1703
    52   Letters from Africa, 1703–1715
    53   Letters from Africa, 1720–1728
    54.   Letters from Africa, 1728–1728
T 70/29   Inward letters from Africa, 1751–1753
    30   Inward letters from Africa, 1753–1762
    31   Inward letters from Africa, 1762–1773
    32.   Inward letters from Africa, 1773–1781
    33   Inward letters from Africa, 1781–1799
    34   Inward letters from Africa, 1799–1806
    35   Inward letters from Africa, 1807–1813
    36   Inward letters from Africa, 1813–1818
    40   Inward letters from Africa, 1816–1818 Mission to Asante
    41   Inward letters from Africa, April–September 1817
T 70/1515–T 70/1586   Miscellaneous Correspondence, 1726–1807
T 70/974   Accra Day-books, 1752–1758
T 70/974^A Accra Day-books, 1756–1758
T 70/   977–8 Accra Day-books, 1762–1765
T 70/   979 Accra Day-books, 1759–1761
T 70/   978–984 Accra Day-books 1768–1818
T 70/1007 – T 70/1107   Cape Coast Castle Day-books, 1754–1815
T 70/1479   Letters to and from Richard Miles, 1750f
T 70/1182   Apam Day-books. 1784

(ii) CO Series:
CO 98/1^A Minutes of the Council of Merchants, CCC, 1829–1844
CO 96/1   Correspondence between Cape Coast Castle and Elmina Castle, 1833–1856
CO 96/2   Correspondence between CCC & the Colonial Office, 1842–1843
CO 96/4–CO 96/16   Correspondence between CCC & CO. 1844–1849
CO 96/18–19   Correspondence between CCC & CO, 1880
CO 96/22–23   Correspondence between CCC & CO, 1831
CO 96/25   Correspondence between CCC & CO, 1832

CO 96/27-28	Correspondence between CCC & Co. 1853
CO 96/30-31	Correspondence between CCC & CO, 1855
CO 96/38-39	Correspondence between CCC & CO, 1856
CO 96/41	Correspondence between CCC & CO, 1857
CO 96/43-44	Correspondence between CCC & CO, 1858
CO 96/45	Correspondence between CCC & CO, 1859
CO 96/47	Correspondence between CCC & CO, 1860 January-June
CO 96/48	Correspondence between CCC & CO, 1860 Freeman & Governor
CO 96/49	Correspondence between CCC & CO, 1880 July-December
CO 96/53-55	Correspondence between CCC & CO, 1881
CO 96/57-58	Correspondence between CCC & CO, 1862
CO 96/80-82	Correspondence between CCC & CO, 1863
CO 96/63-64	Correspondence between CCC & CO, 1864
CO 96/67-68	Correspondence between CCC & CO, 1865
CO 96/70-72	Correspondence between CCC & CO, 1866
CO 96/74	Correspondence between CCC & CO, 1867
CO 96/76-77	Correspondence between CCC & CO, 1868
CO 96/79-81	Correspondence between CCC & CO, 1869
CO 96/84-85	Correspondence between CCC & CO, 1870
CO 96/87-89	Correspondence between CCC & CO, 1871
CO 96/92-94	Correspondence between CCC & CO, 1872
CO 96/96-103	Correspondence between CCC & CO, 1873
CO 96/111-112	Correspondence between CCC & CO, 1874
CO 96/115-116	Correspondence between CCC & CO, 1875
CO 96/73	Individual Despatches 1866
CO 96/98	Individual Despatches 1868
CO 96/108-110	Individual despatches 1873
CO 96/114	Individual despatches 1874
CO 96/356-387	Correspondence between CCC & CO, 1900
CO 96/374	Correspondence between CCC & CO, 1900
CO 402/1	Entry Books, 1847
CO 402/2-3	Entry Books, 1847-1852
CO 402/4	Entry Books, 1852-1857
CO 267/117	Merchant Despatches from the Gold Coast, 1832
CO 267/126	Merchant Despatches from the Gold Coast, 1834
CO 267/131	Merchant Despatches from the Gold Coast, 1835
CO 267/136	Merchant Despatches from the Gold Coast, 1836
CO 267/144	Merchant Despatches from the Gold Coast, 1837
CO 267/150	Merchant Despatches from the Gold Coast, 1838
CO 267/162	Merchant Despatches from the Gold Coast, 1840

CO 267/168   Merchant Despatches from the Gold Coast, 1841
CO 267/170   Dr. Madden– Report on the Gold Coast etc., 1841–1843

(iii) BRITISH PARLIAMENTARY PAPERS (BPP):
Select Committee Report on West Africa, 1842
Select Committee Report on West Africa, 1865
Correspondence Relating to the Ashantee Invasion 1873, Vol.XLVIX
Further Correspondence Relating to the Ash. Invasion 1874 Vol.XLIX
Correspondence Relating to the Fante Confederation, 1873 Vol.XLIX

(iv) OTHER BRITISH DOCUMENTS
Crooks, J. J., 1923, Records Relating to the Gold Coast settlements from 1750 to 1874, Dublin.
Metcalfe, G. E., 1964, Great Britain and Ghana: Documents of Ghana History 1807–1957, Suffolk.

B   DANISH: RIGSARKIVET, Copenhagen:

Documents of the Danish West India and Guinea Company (VgK):
Breve og. Dokumenter inkomme eg udgaade, 1683–4, 1689, & 1698–1705 (1pkt)
Breve og. Dokumenter inkomme eg udgaade, 1705–1722 (pkt)
Breve og. Dokumenter inkomme eg udgaade, 1722–1730
Dag-journaler fort paa Christiansborg Castle, Osu, 1668–1705
Sekretpretokoller paa Christiansborg Castle 1723–1754
Diariehoger paa Christiansborg Castle, 1744–1754
Diverse arkivaller fra Guinea (DAFC), 1805, 1811–1813
Guineiske Journaler (GJ) 1755–1768
Sager til Guineiske Journaler (STGJ), 1806, 1806–1819–1820
Guineiske Journaler Vol. A, 1799–1804
Guineiske Journaler Vol. B. 1804–1820
Guineiske Journaler Vol. C. 1821–1827
Guineiske Journaler Vol. D. 1828–1830
Guineiske Journaler Vol. E. 1831–1834
Guineiske Journaler Vol. F. 1835–1840
Guineiske Journaler Vol. G. 1841–1844
Guineiske Journaler Vol. B. 1845–1846
Guineiske Journaler Vol. I. 1847–1850
Sager till Guineiske Journaler 1776–1849
Sager till Guineiske Journaler 1850
Department for udeurigake anliggender (DFUA), 1804–1847

C. DUTCH: Rijksarchief, the Hague; Balme Library, Legon Ghana:

(i) The Furley Collection, University of Ghana, Legon
Dutch Records, Blue Books 1–7, 1610–1657
Dutch and other European Records, 1658–1664, 1665–1679, 1680–1700
Letters and Papers from Guinea, 1699–1720
Miscellaneous Records, 1699–1811
Dutch Documents, WIC, transl, by E. P. Collins, 1700–1780
Journals & Correspondence, WIC, 124A, 1810–1816
Diaries and Correspondence, 1815–1823
Diaries and Correspondence, 1830–1847

(ii) Governor-General Daendel's Journal & Correspondence, 1815–1817
(iii) A. Van Dantzig's Dutch Documents Relating to the Gold Coast, Part I 1680–1710 & Part II 1719–1740 (Legon 1971). With the exception of Albert Van Dantzig's all the Dutch sources consulted in Ghana were cross-checked with the originals at the Hague. Consequently, the original references are cited, e.g. *WIC* or *NBKG*.

D. GERMAN: BASEL MISSION ARCHIVES:

Basel Mission Gold Coast Correspondence, c.1844–1888
(Abstracts by Paul Jenkins, Legon 1970.)

E. NEWSPAPERS

London Times, 26 October 1861
African Times, 24 October 1870
West African Herald, 31 March 1871.

F. MISCELLANEOUS:

Report on Land Disputes in the Adansi Division of Ashanti (Obuasi District), L.448.
Stool Lands Boundaries Settlement (Akwamu Order, in Gold Coast Gazette Extraordinary, No.6 (1956).
Akyem Abuakwa Stool Lands Declaration, May 1838.
Nsawam Native Affairs, Case No.76/191, Ghana National Archives.
Documents Relating to Akyem Settlements in, and Claims to, Ashanti-Akim, File No. D46, Kumasi Archives.

ORAL TRADITIONS

Akyem Abuakwa Traditions (AAT), gathered under the auspices of Okyenhene Nana Ofori Atta I during the 1925/6 period.
Akyem Abuakwa Traditions (AAT), collected by author in 1868/9.
Akyem Bosome Traditions ABT), compiled for author by Bosomehene Nana Oware Agyekum II in 1968/9.
Akyem Kotoku Traditions (AKT), collected by author in 1968/9.
Asante-Akyem Traditions (As–AkT), gathered by author in 1968/9.
Ameyaw, K., 1966, Akim Oda Traditions, IAS acc. No.KAG/7.
Ameyaw, K., 1963, Asamankese Traditions, IAS acc. No.KAG/4.
Ameyaw, K., 1963, Akwatia Traditions, IAS acc. No.KAG/2.
Daaku, K. Y., 1969, Oral Traditions of Adanse, Legon.
Daaku, K. Y., 1969, Oral Traditions of Assin-Twifo, Legon.
Daaku, K. Y., 1970, Oral Traditions of Denkyera, Legon.

CONTEMPORARY BOOKS

Astley, T., 1745, *A New General Collection of Voyages and Travels*, Frank Cass & Co. Ltd., (1968 edn.), London, Vols. I & II.
Barbot, J., 1732 "A Description of the Coast of North and South Guinea", in Churchhill, *Collection of Voyages and Travels*, London.
Beecham, J., 1841, Ashantee and the Gold Coast, Dawson of Pall Mall, London.
Biorn, A. R., 1788, Beretning, Om de Danske Forter og. Negerier paa Guineakysten, Copenhagen.
Bosman, J., 1705, *A New and Accurate Description of the Coast of Guinea*, Frank Cass & Co. Ltd., (1967 edn.), London.
Bowdich, T. E., 1819, A Mission from Cape Coast Castle to Ashantee, Frank Cass & Co. Ltd., (1966 edn.), London.
Brackenbury, H., 1874, *The Ashantee War*, 2 Vols., Frank Cass & Co. Ltd. London.
Burton, R. F., & Cameron, V. L., 1883, *To the Gold Coast for Gold*, Chatto & Windus, London,.
Butler, W. F., 1875, *Akim-foo, A Narrative of a Failure*, London,.
Christaller, J. G., 1881, *A Dictionary of Asante and Fante Language called Tshi*, Basel Mission Book Depot, (1933 edn.), Basel.
Cruickshank, B., 1853, *Eighteen Years on the Gold Coast*, Frank Cass & Co. Ltd., (1966 edn.), London.
Dapper, O., 1668, *Naukeurige Beschrivinge der Afrikaensche* (Amsterdam), adapted in Ogilby, J., 1690, *Africa*, London.

Duncan, J., 1846, *Travels in West Africa, 1845-1846*, Frank Cass & Co. Ltd., (1968 edn.), London.
Dupuis, J., 1824, *Journal of a Residence in Ashantee*, Frank Cass & Co. Ltd., London.
Ellis, A. B., 1883, *The Land of Fetish*, Negro University Press, New York.
Ellis, A. B., 1887, *The Tshi Speaking People of the Gold Coast*, Negro University Press, New York.
Ellis, A. B., 1893, *A History of the Gold Coast of West Africa*, Negro University Press, New York.
Freeman, T. B., 1843, *Journal of Two Visits to the Kingdom of Ashanti*, Frank Cass & Co. Ltd., (1968 edn.), London.
Isert, P. E., 1783, *Voyage en Guinea*, Paris.
Horton, J. A. B., 1868, *West African Countries and Peoples*, Frank Cass & Co. Ltd., London.
Horton, J. A. B., 1870, *Letters on the Political Conditions of the Gold Coast*, Frank Cass & Co. Ltd., (1970 edn.), London.
Hutton, W., 1821, *A Voyage to Africa*, Longman, Hurst, Rees Orme & Brown, London.
Meredith, H., 1812, *An Account of the Gold Coast of Africa*, Frank Cass & Co. Ltd., London.
Ramseyer, F. A. & Kuhne, J., 1897, *Four Years in Ashantee*, James Nibbet & Co. Ltd., London.
Reade, W. W., 1873, *The African Sketch-Book*, 2 Vols., London.
Reindorf, C. C., 1895, *The History of the Gold Coast and Asante*, Basel Mission Book Depot, Basel.
Roemer, L. F., 1760, *Tilforladelig Efferretning om Kysten Guinea*, Copenhagen, transl. (parts) by K. Bertelsen, 1985, IAS, Legon.
Samson, E., 1908, *A Short History of Akuapem and Akuropon, an Autobiography*, Accra.
Thonning, F., 1802, *Kort de Danske Residdelser*, Guinea.
Villault, S., 1968, "Abstract of a Voyage to the Coast of Africa and Guinea in 1868", in Astley, *A New General Collection of Voyages and Travels*, Frank Cass & Co. Ltd., (1968 edn.), London.

LATER WORKS
Books

Affrifah, K., "Christianity and the Akyem of Ghana 1766-1887" (forthcoming).
Agbodeka, F., 1971 *African Politics and British Policy in the Gold Coast 1868-1900*, Northwestern University Press, Longman Group Ltd., London.

Ajayi, J. F. A. & Crowder, M. (Eds), 1971, *History of West Africa*, 2 Vols., Longman, London.

Ajayi, J. F. A. & Espie, I., (Eds), 1968, *A Thousand Years of West African History*, Ibadan University Press, Ibadan..

Akinjogbin, I., 1967, *A. Dahomey and Its Neighbours, 1708–1818*, Cambridge University Press, Cambridge.

Akuffo, B. S., 1950, *Ahemfie Adesua*, Exeter.

Anonymous, 1913, *Native Reports in Tshi (Twi Kasa mu Akuapem ne Eho Nsem anase Abasem)*, Akuropon.

Balmer, Rev. W. T., 1926, *A History of the Akan Peoples of the Gold Coast*, London & Cape Coast.

Blake, W. J., 1937, *European Beginnings in West Africa*, Greenwood Press, Westport, Connecticut.

Boahen, A. A., 1966, *Topics in West African History*, Longman, London.

Boateng, E. A., 1959, *A Geography of Ghana*, Cambridge University Press, Cambridge.

Bourret, F. M., 1954, *The Gold Coast*, Cambridge University Press, Cambridge.

Busia, K. A., 1951, *The Position of the Chief in the Modern Political System of Ashanti*, Oxford University Press, London.

Casely-Hayford, J. E., 1903, *Gold Coast Native Institutions*, Sweet & Maxwell, (1970 edn.), London.

Christensen, J. B., 1954, *Double Descent Among the Fante*, New Haven.

Claridge, W. W., 1915, *A History of the Gold Coast and Ashanti*, Frank Cass & Co. Ltd., (1964 edn.), London, 2 Vols.

Coombs, D., 1963 *The Gold Coast, Britain and the Netherlands*, Oxford University Press, Oxford.

Daaku, K. Y., 1970, *Trade and Politics on the Gold Coast, 1600–1720*, Oxford University Press, Oxford.

Danquah, J. B., 1928, *Akim Abuakwa Handbook*, Foster Groom & Co., London.

Danquah, J. B., 1929, *Gold Coast; Akan Laws and Customs and the Akim Abuakwa Constitution*, London.

Danquah, J. B., 1938, *An Objectified History of Akim Abuakwa*, London.

Danquah, J. B., 1941, *The Akan Doctrine of God*, Frank Cass & Co. Ltd., (1969 edn.), London.

Davies, K. G., 1957, *The Royal African Company*, London.

Debrunner, H. W., 1967, *A History of Christianity in Ghana*, Waterville, Accra.

Dickson, K. B., 1969, *A Historical Geography of Ghana*, Cambridge University Press, Cambridge.

Dike, O., 1956, *Trade and Politics in the Niger Delta, 1830–1885*, Oxford University Press, Oxford .

Fage, J. D., (Ed.), 1969, *A History of West Africa,* Cambridge University Press, Cambridge.
Field, M. J., 1948 Akim-Kotoku: *An Oman of the Gold Coast,* Cambridge University Press, Cambridge.
Forde, D. & Kaberry, P. M., (Eds), 1967, *West African Kingdoms in the Nineteenth Century,* Cambridge University Press, Cambridge.
Fuller, F., 1921, *A Vanished Dynasty: Ashanti,* Cambridge University Press, Cambridge.
Fynn, J. K., 1971, *Asante and its Neighbours, 1700–1807,* Northwestern University Press, Longman Group Ltd., London.
Hargreaves, J. D., 1967, *Prelude to the Partition of West Africa,* London.
Hill, P., 1938, *The Gold Coast Farmer,* Cambridge University Press, Cambridge.
Hill, P., 1963, *The Migrant Cocoa Farmer of Southern Ghana,* Cambridge University Press, Cambridge.
Kani, T. Y., 1931, *Akanfoo Amammere,* Accra.
Kimble, D., 1963, *A Political History of Ghana, 1850–1928,* Cambridge University Press, Cambridge.
Kyerematen, A. A., 1964, *Panoply of Ghana,* London.
Kwamena-Poh, M. A., 1973, *Government and Politics in the Akuapem State, 1730–1850,* Northwestern University Press, Longman Group Ltd., London.
Larsen, K., 1919, *De Danske Guinea,* Copenhagen.
Macdonald, G., 1898, *The Gold Coast Past and Present,* Longman, London.
McEwan, P. J. N., 1968, *Nineteenth Century Africa,* London.
Mensah Sarbah, J., 1897, *Fanti Customary Law,* Frank Cass & Co. Ltd., London.
Mensah Sarbah, J., 1906, *Fanti National Constitution,* Frank Cass & Co. Ltd., (1968 edn.), London.
Metcalfe, G. E., 1962, *Maclean of the Gold Coast,* Oxford University Press, Oxford.
Meyerowitz, E. L. R., 1952, *Akan Traditions of Origin,* Faber &Faber, London.
Meyerowitz, E. L. R., 1951, *The Sacred State of the Akan,* Faber & Faber, London.
Nketia, J. H., 1963, *Drumming in the Akan Communities of Ghana,* London.
Norregaard, G., 1968, *Danish Settlements in West Africa, 1658–1850,* Boston University Press, Boston.
Ofori Atta II (Okyenhene Nana), 1949, *Odwira Festival,* Kyebi.
Priestely, M., 1969, *West African Trade and Gold Coast Politics,* Oxford University Press, Oxford.

Rattray, R. S., 1923, *Ashanti*, Oxford University Press, Oxford.
Rattray, R. S., 1929 *Ashanti Law and Constitution*, Oxford University Press, Oxford.
Reynolds, E., 1974, *Trade and Economic Change in the Gold Coast, 1807–1874*, Longman, London.
Smith, N., 1966, *The Presbyterian Church of Ghana, 1835–1960*, Waterville, London.
Sutherland, D. Afua, 1934, *State Emblems of the Gold Coast*, Accra.
Vansina, I., R. Mauny, R and L. V. Thomas (Eds), 1964, *The Historian in Tropical Africa*, Cambridge University Press, Cambridge.
Ward, W. E. F.,(Ed.), 1969, *A History of Ghana*, George Allen & Unwin Ltd., London.
Welman, C. W., 1925, *The Native States of the Gold Coast*, Crown Agents, London.
Wilks, I., 1975, *Asante in the Nineteenth Century*, Cambridge University Press, Cambridge.

ARTICLES

Adams, C. D., 1957, "Activities of Danish Botanists in Guinea, *THSG*, Vol.III, Pt.I.
Addo-Fening, R., 1973, "The Background to the Deportation of King Asafo Agyei and the Foundation of New Dwaben", *THSG*, Vol.XIV, No.2.
Addo-Fening, R., 1974, "The Pax Britannica and Akyem Abuakwa, C., 1874–1904", *Universitas* (Legon), Vol.3, No.3, June.
Addo-Fening, R., 1985, "The 'Akim' or 'Achim' in 17th Century and 18th Century Historical Context: Who were they?" in *Institute of African Studies Research Review*, New Series Vol.4, No.2, Legon.
Affrifah, K., 1975, "The Impact of Christianity on Akyem Society 1852–1887", *THSG*, Vol.XVI(i).
Agbodeka, F., 1964, "The Fanti Confederacy, 1865–1869", *THSG*, Vol.VIII.
Agyeman-Dua, 1960, "Mampong Ashanti: A Traditional History", *THSG*, Vol.IV, Part 2.
Amenumey, D. E. K., 1968, "Geraldo de Lima: A Reappraisal", *THSG*, Vol.IX.
Ameyaw, K., Kwawu, 1966, "An Early Forest State", *GNQ*, No.9.
Boahen, A. A., 1966, The Origins of the Akan, *GNQ*, No.9.
Boahen, A. A., 1973, "Arcany or Accany or Arcania and the Accanists of the Sixteenth and Seventeenth Centuries European Records", *THSG*, Vol.XIV, Part I.
Collins, E., 1962, "The Panic Element in Nineteenth Century British Rela-

tions with Ashanti", *THSG*, Vol.V Pt.II.

Coombs, D., 1958, "The Place of the Certificate of Apology in Ghanaian History", *THSG*, Vol.III, Part III.

Daaku, K. Y., 1965, "The European Traders and the Gold Coast States, 1630–1720", *THSG*, Vol.VIII.

Daaku, K. Y., 1966, "Pre-Ashanti States", *GNQ*, No.9.

Debrunner, H. W., 1956, "Notable Danish Chaplains on the Gold Coast", *TGCTHS* Vol.II, Part I.

Dickson, K. B., 1961, "The Development of Road Transport in Southern Ghana and Ashanti since 1850", *THSG*, Vol.V, Part I

Fage, J. D., "The Administration of George Maclean on the Gold Coast", *TGCTHS*, Vol.I, Part IV.

Fynn, J. K., 1966, "The Rise of Ashanti", *GNQ*, No.9.

Fynn, J. K., (not dated), "Akim Abuakwa Kings of the Eighteenth Century"; a Chronology, Seminar Paper, Department of History, Legon.

Fynn, J. K., 1965, "The Reign and Times of Kusi Obodum", *THSG*, Vol.VIII.

Fynn, J. K., 1973, "Asante and Akyem Relations 1700–1831", *Institute of African Studies Research Review*, Vol.9, No.1, Legon.

Grey, R., 1971, "Portuguese Musketeers on the Zambesi", *JAH*, Vol.XII, No.4.

Gordon, J., 1953, "Some Oral Traditions of Denkyera", *TGCTHS*, Vol.I, Pt.III.

Jenkins, P., 1971, "Twentieth Century Abuakwa Politics in the light of Nineteenth Century Basel Mission Records – Questions about the Role of the Youngmen", Seminar Paper, Legon 1971.

Jenkins, P., 1972, "A Conflict of Faiths at Kukurantumi", *THSG*, Vol.XIII, Pt.II.

Johnson, Marion, 1965, "Ashanti East of the Volta", *THSG*, Vol.VIII.

Johnson, Marion, 1964, "Migrants' Progress", *BGGA*, Vol.9, No.2, 1964.

Jones D. H., 1970, "Problems of African Chronology", *JAH*, Vol.XI, No.2.

Kea, R., 1969, "Akwamu-Anlo Relations, 1750–1913", *THSG*, Vol.X.

Kea, R., 1971, "Firearms and Warfare in the Gold and Slave Coasts from the Sixteenth to the Nineteenth Centuries", *JAH*, Vol.XII, No.2.

Kumah, J. K., 1968, "The Rise and Fall of the Kingdom of Denkyera", *GNQ*, No.9.

Kwamena-Poh, M. A., 1970, "The Emergence of Akuapem State: 1730–50", *GNQ*, No.II.

Metcalfe, G. E., 1955, "Some Aspects of British Gold Coast Policy in Mid-Nineteenth Century", *TGCTHS*, Vol.I, Part V.

Ozanne, P., in Shinnae, P. (Ed.), 1971, *The African Iron Age*, Oxford.

Perregaux, W., 1902, "A Few Notes on Kwawu (Quahoe), a Territory in the Gold Coast of West Africa", *Journal of African Society*, Vol.II, No.8.

Priestley, M. & Wilks, I.G., 1960, "Ashanti Kings in the Eighteenth Century,

a Revised Chronology", *JAH*, Vol.I, No.1.
Priestley, M., & Richard Brew, 1968, "Eighteenth Century Trader at Anomabo", *THSG*, Vol.X.
Priestley, M., 1961,"The Ashanti Question and the British; Eighteenth Century Origins, *JAH*, Vol.2.
Rodney, W., 1969, "Gold and Slaves on the Gold Coast", *THSG*, Vol.X.
Swanzy, H., 1956, "A Trading Family in Nineteenth Century Gold Coast", *THSG*, Vol.II Part.II.
Tenkorang, S., 1968, "The Importance of Firearms in the Struggle between Ashante and the Coastal States", *THSG*, Vol.IX.
Wallis, J. R., 1952–3, "The Kwahus – Their Connection with the Afram Plains", *TGCTHS*, Vol.I.
Wilks, I. G., 1957, "The Rise of the Akwamu Empire, 1850–1710", *THSG*, Vol.III, Part II.
Wilks, I. G., 1958, "A Note on Twifo and Akwamu", *THSG*, Vol.III, Pt.III.
Wilks, I. G., 1968, "Danish Settlements in West Africa, A Review", *JAH*, Vol.IX.
Wolfson, F., 1953, "A Price Agreement on the Gold Coast – the Krobo Oil Boycott, 1858–1866", *Economic History Review* (*EHR*), Vol.VI, No.I.

UNPUBLISHED THESES

Amenumey, D. E. K., 1964, "The Ewe People and the Coming of European Rule", MA (University of London).
Tenkorang, S., 1964, "British Slave Trading Activities on the Gold and Slave Coasts in the Eighteenth Century and Their Effects on African Society", M.A., (University of London).
Wolfson, F., 1950, "British Relations with the Gold Coast, 1843–1880", Ph.D., London.
Kea, R., 1974, "Trade, State Formation and Warfare in the Gold Coast, 1800–1826", Ph.D., London.

INDEX

Adanse, 1, 6, 7
Addo-Fening, R., 2
Afro-European Alliance, 1
Akaanten Settlement, 164–165
Akuapem, 2, 13, 25, 51, 110, 134, 199
    see also, Akuapim
Akwamu, 15, 26, 46, 51, 58, 63, 66, 83, 103, 238–239
Akyem Abuakwa, 1, 6, 7, 14, 103, 134
Akyem Economy, 14, 18, 139, 200
    Forest to Forts trade, 3
    Gold industry, 55, 60, 140
    Trade with Akwamu, 27
    Trade with Ga-Adangbe, 27, 51, 59
Akyem Kotoku, 1–3, 7, 14–15, 52, 56, 112, 118–119, 122, 128–129, 173–175, 178, 199, 208, 223, 238
Akyem peoples, 1–2, 46, 122, 128, 134, 174, 230
Akyem states, 2
Anglo-Danish Competition, 137, 141
Asante Akyem, 7, 11, 13
Asona, 1, 11, 14
Attah Owusu, 87, 105–110, 122
Begoro, 1, 14
Blankson, G., 192
Boahin, A. A., 2
Bond of 1844, 141
Bosman, W., 1, 14, 26
Bosome, 2, 23–24, 119–120, 122, 128, 132, 137, 146, 173–175, 185, 239
    see also Akyem Bosome
Butler, W. F., (Major), 2
Christian Missionary Activities
    Basel Evangelical Mission Society, 2, 151, 171
    Protestants, 16, 171
Christiansborg Castle, 15, 133–137
Danquah, J. B., 2
Denkyira, 1, 9, 11, 23
Dompreh (Chief), 199, 215
Dutch diplomacy, 59–62
Eastern Sector Alliance, 78–79
Firearms, 16–17
    Abuakwa and Kotoku, 17–18, 25
    Dutch traders, 16, 25
    English traders, 16
    Portuguese traders, 16
    Royal Africa Company of England, 16

Foreign Relations
    Abuakwa and Agona, 30, 66
    Abuakwa and Akwamu, 26, 102–105
    Abuakwa and Asante, 66–68, 108–109, 225–227
    Abuakwa and Assin, 28
    Abuakwa and Fante, 28, 66
    Abuakwa and Kotoku, 24–26, 32, 58, 66, 69, 104, 121, 129, 147–148
    Akwamu and Asante, 37
    Akyem and Akwamu, 64
    Akyem and Asante, 115, 117, 135, 223–224
    Akyem and Dutch, 60
    Kotoku and Akuapem, 155–156
    Kotoku and Asante, 35, 41, 149–150, 192–193, 224
    Pax Akyema, 54
    Swedru Pact, 31
    Territorial integrity, 25
Freeman, T. B., 147, 152–155, 165, 203–204
Frimpong-Manso, 41, 46, 56, 66
Fynn, J., 2
Ga-Adangbe, 2, 27, 47–48, 52, 60–61, 103, 108–111, 121, 146, 201–203, 215, 238
    see also Ga
Guan, 13, 51
Intra-Akyem relations, 3, 17
Kotobiante, 12, 14
Kotoku, see Akyem Kotoku
Kukurantumi, 12, 14, 171, 175
Kuma, Kwadwo, 111–115, 122
MacCarthy, C., 112, 116–117, 121
Maclean, G., 1, 133, 138
Migration, 7
    Abuakwa and Kotoku, 7, 11, 63, 103–105, 141, 185, 237–240
    Adanse and Akyem, 9, 11, 120
    Adanse migrants, 13–14
    Asona migrants, 8, 11
    Atoam migrants, 9, 12–13
    Bosome migrants, 120, 129, 132
    Juaben refugees, 131–132, 134–135
    Kokobiante migrants, 11
    Kotoku migrants, 173–176

Obirikoran, 88–96
Ofori Attah, I., 3, 40
Ofori Panin, 3, 12
Ofori Kumaa, 51–52
Opoku Ware I, 75–79, 87, 89
Oral history, 1, 3, 12
   see also Oral tradition
Osei Kwadwo, 88–96
Osei Tutu, 23, 35–38
Owusu Ansah, 187–189
Oyoko clan, 14, 17
Peace Treaty, 128–129, 133–134
Pine, C. C., 152, 165
Pine, R., 176, 186–190
Pobi, Asomani, 76–87
Poll Tax, 146, 151
Sasraku, Ansa, 14, 15, 26
Simpson (Gov.), 205–207
Southern Sector Alliance, 39, 84–85
Taxes, 54–55, 109
   see also Poll Tax
Volta expedition, 210
Wars
   Abuakwa and Agona, 33
   Abuakwa and Asante, 85, 90, 108
   Abuakwa Civil War, 115–117
   Akantamasu war, 121, 131
   Akyem and Agona, 27–28
   Akyem and Akwamu, 18, 26, 28, 47–48
   Akyem and Asante, 18, 36, 68–70, 75–78, 90–95, 115, 227
   Asante and Denkyira, 18, 35
   Asante and Kotoku, 17, 35, 37, 176–183, 190
   Battle of Bobikuma, 183
   Benna War, 86
   Bosome and Kotoku, 174–175
   Gyadam War, 172
   Inter-state war, 17, 241
   Intra-state war, 17, 241
   Kotoku and Abuakwa, 38, 48, 103–107, 121, 142, 150, 157–161, 199, 208–210
   Kotoku and Ga, 216–218
   Nyanoase War, 50–51
   Sagrenti War, 228–232, 241
Western Sector Alliance, 79–81
Zimmerman (Rev), 204

www.ingramcontent.com/pod-product-compliance
Lightning Source LLC
Chambersburg PA
CBHW071348290426
44108CB00014B/1478